SUZUKA

5

Kouji Seo

TRANSLATED AND ADAPTED BY
David Ury

LETTERED BY
North Market Street Graphics

BALLANTINE BOOKS · NEW YORK

Suzuka volume 5 is a work of fiction. Names, characters, places, and incidents are the products of the author's imagination or are used fictitiously. Any resemblance to actual events, locales, or persons, living or dead, is entirely coincidental.

A Del Rey Trade Paperback Original

Published in the United States by Del Rey Books, an imprint of The Random House Publishing Group, a division of Random House, Inc., New York.

DEL REY is a registered trademark and the Del Rey colophon is a trademark of Random House, Inc.

Publication rights arranged through Kodansha Ltd.

First published in Japan in 2005 by Kodansha Ltd., Tokyo.

ISBN 978-0-345-49828-1

Printed in the United States of America

www.delreymanga.com

9 8 7 6 5 4 3 2 1

Translator/adapter: David Ury
Lettering: North Market Street Graphics

Contents

A Note from the Author

*IT LOOKS LIKE **SUZUKA** IS GOING TO
MAKE IT TO ITS ONE-YEAR ANNIVERSARY,
AND IT'S ALL THANKS TO YOU LOYAL READERS.
TO CELEBRATE THE OCCASION, I BOUGHT A
CAKE AND PUT A SINGLE CANDLE IN IT. I HOPE
NEXT YEAR I'LL BE ABLE TO CELEBRATE
WITH TWO CANDLES.*

Honorifics Explained

Throughout the Del Rey Manga books, you will find Japanese honorifics left intact in the translations. For those not familiar with how the Japanese use honorifics and, more important, how they differ from American honorifics, we present this brief overview.

Politeness has always been a critical facet of Japanese culture. Ever since the feudal era, when Japan was a highly stratified society, use of honorifics—which can be defined as polite speech that indicates relationship or status—has played an essential role in the Japanese language. When addressing someone in Japanese, an honorific usually takes the form of a suffix attached to one's name (example: "Asuna-san"), is used as a title at the end of one's name, or appears in place of the name itself (example: "Negi-sensei," or simply "Sensei!").

Honorifics can be expressions of respect or endearment. In the context of manga and anime, honorifics give insight into the nature of the relationship between characters. Many English translations leave out these important honorifics and therefore distort the feel of the original Japanese. Because Japanese honorifics contain nuances that English honorifics lack, it is our policy at Del Rey not to translate them. Here, instead, is a guide to some of the honorifics you may encounter in Del Rey Manga.

-san: This is the most common honorific and is equivalent to Mr., Miss, Ms., or Mrs. It is the all-purpose honorific and can be used in any situation where politeness is required.

-sama: This is one level higher than "-san." It is used to confer great respect.

-dono: This comes from the word "tono," which means "lord." It is an even higher level than "-sama" and confers utmost respect.

-kun: This suffix is used at the end of boys' names to express familiarity or endearment. It is also sometimes used by men among friends, or when addressing someone younger or of a lower station.

-chan: This is used to express endearment, mostly toward girls. It is also used for little boys, pets, and even among lovers. It gives a sense of childish cuteness.

Bozu: This is an informal way to refer to a boy, similar to the English terms "kid" and "squirt."

Sempai/
Senpai: This title suggests that the addressee is one's senior in a group or organization. It is most often used in a school setting, where underclassmen refer to their upperclassmen as "sempai." It can also be used in the workplace, such as when a newer employee addresses an employee who has seniority in the company.

Kohai: This is the opposite of "sempai" and is used toward underclassmen in school or newcomers in the workplace. It connotes that the addressee is of a lower station.

Sensei: Literally meaning "one who has come before," this title is used for teachers, doctors, or masters of any profession or art.

[blank]: This is usually forgotten in these lists, but it is perhaps the most significant difference between Japanese and English. The lack of honorific means that the speaker has permission to address the person in a very intimate way. Usually, only family, spouses, or very close friends have this kind of permission. Known as *yobisute,* it can be gratifying when someone who has earned the intimacy starts to call one by one's name without an honorific. But when that intimacy hasn't been earned, it can be very insulting.

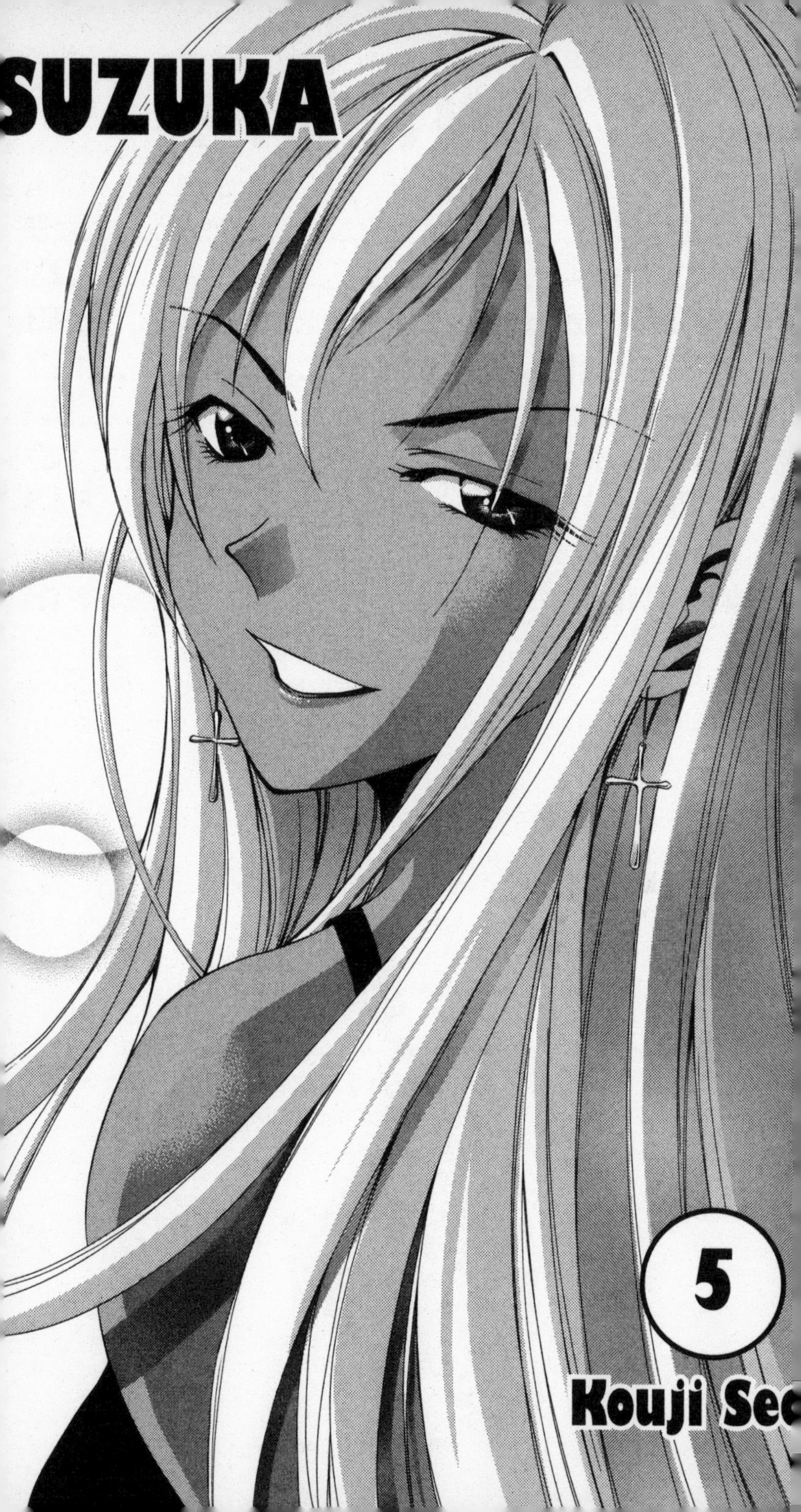
SUZUKA
5
Kouji Se

CONTENTS

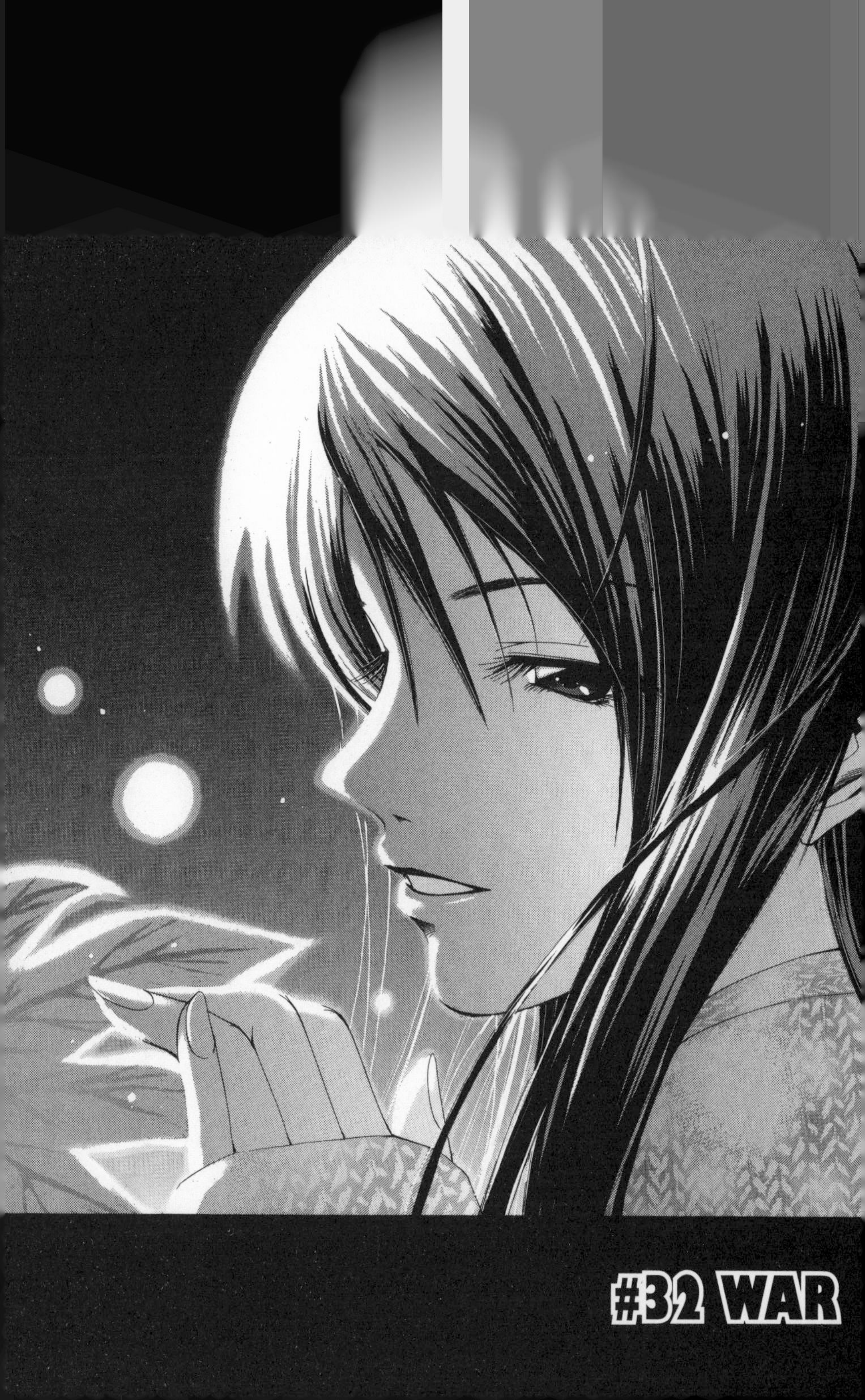

#32 WAR

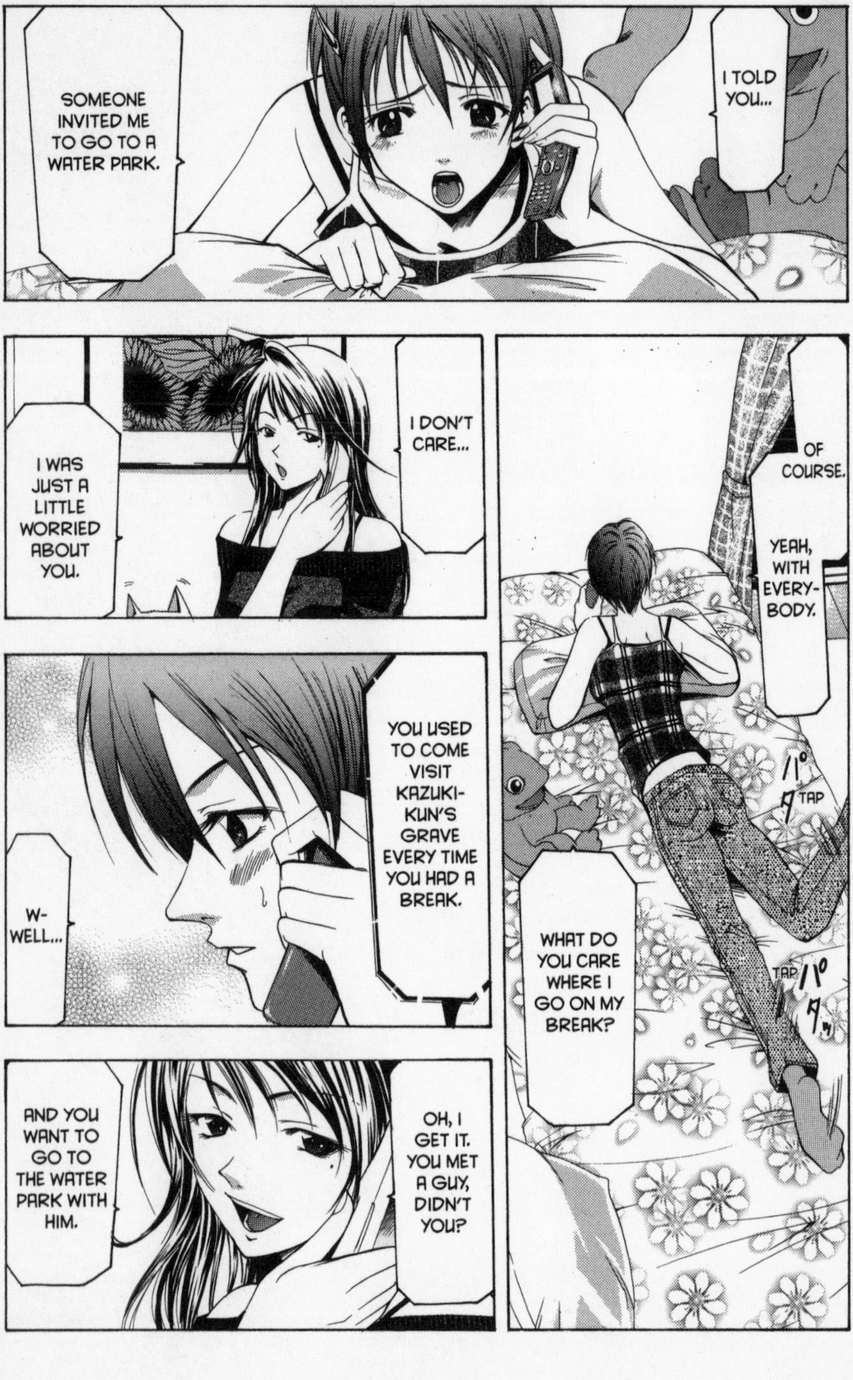
I TOLD YOU...
SOMEONE INVITED ME TO GO TO A WATER PARK.
OF COURSE.
YEAH, WITH EVERY-BODY.
パタ TAP
WHAT DO YOU CARE WHERE I GO ON MY BREAK?
TAP パタ
I DON'T CARE...
I WAS JUST A LITTLE WORRIED ABOUT YOU.
YOU USED TO COME VISIT KAZUKI-KUN'S GRAVE EVERY TIME YOU HAD A BREAK.
W-WELL...
OH, I GET IT. YOU MET A GUY, DIDN'T YOU?
AND YOU WANT TO GO TO THE WATER PARK WITH HIM.

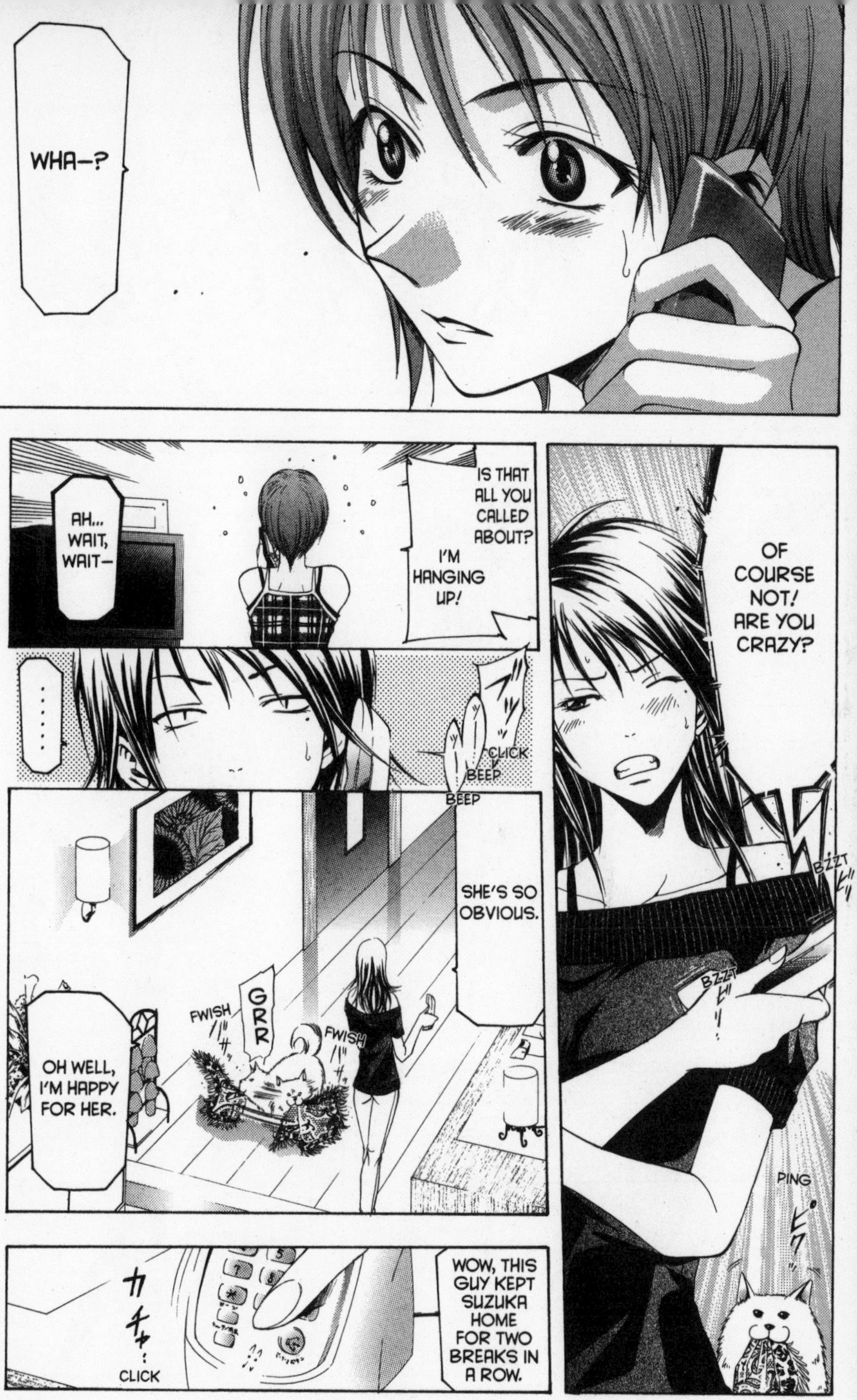
WHA–?
OF COURSE NOT! ARE YOU CRAZY?
BZZT
BZZT
PING
IS THAT ALL YOU CALLED ABOUT?
I'M HANGING UP!
AH... WAIT, WAIT—
......
CLICK
BEEP
BEEP
SHE'S SO OBVIOUS.
GRR
FWISH
FWISH
OH WELL, I'M HAPPY FOR HER.
WOW, THIS GUY KEPT SUZUKA HOME FOR TWO BREAKS IN A ROW.
CLICK

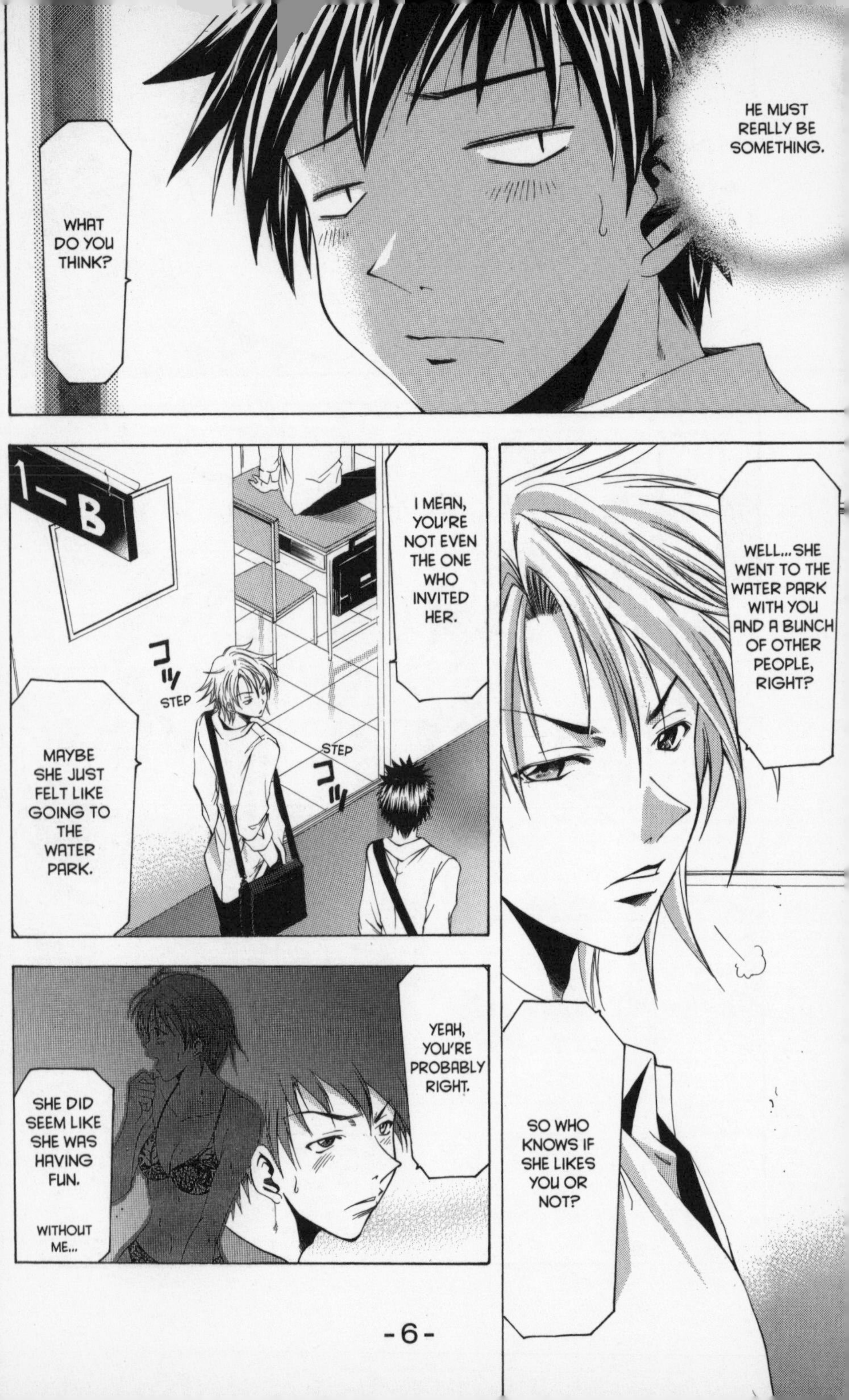
HE MUST REALLY BE SOMETHING.
WHAT DO YOU THINK?
WELL...SHE WENT TO THE WATER PARK WITH YOU AND A BUNCH OF OTHER PEOPLE, RIGHT?
SO WHO KNOWS IF SHE LIKES YOU OR NOT?
I MEAN, YOU'RE NOT EVEN THE ONE WHO INVITED HER.
1-B
コツ STEP
コツ STEP
MAYBE SHE JUST FELT LIKE GOING TO THE WATER PARK.
YEAH, YOU'RE PROBABLY RIGHT.
SHE DID SEEM LIKE SHE WAS HAVING FUN.
WITHOUT ME...

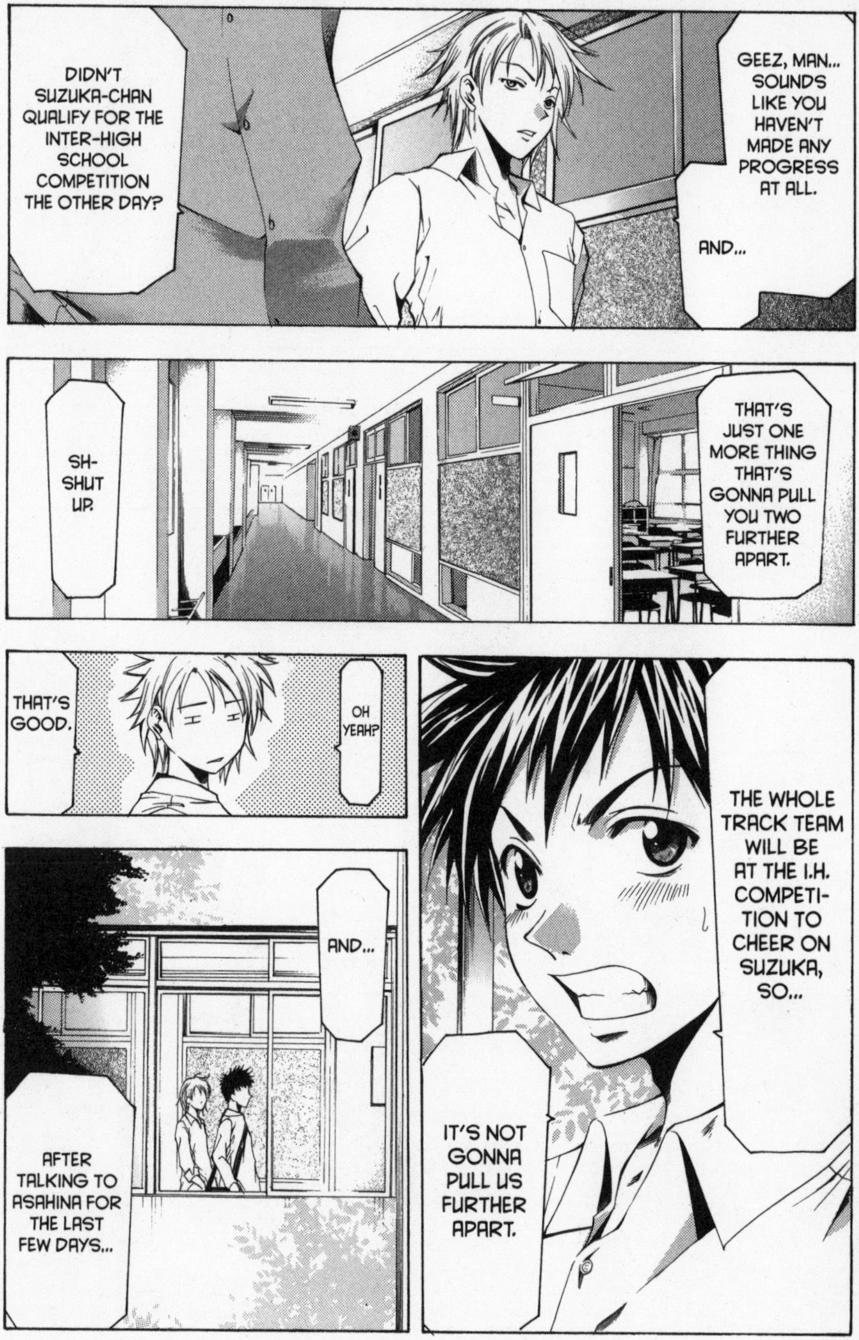
GEEZ, MAN... SOUNDS LIKE YOU HAVEN'T MADE ANY PROGRESS AT ALL.
AND...
DIDN'T SUZUKA-CHAN QUALIFY FOR THE INTER-HIGH SCHOOL COMPETITION THE OTHER DAY?
THAT'S JUST ONE MORE THING THAT'S GONNA PULL YOU TWO FURTHER APART.
SH-SHUT UP.
THE WHOLE TRACK TEAM WILL BE AT THE I.H. COMPETITION TO CHEER ON SUZUKA, SO...
IT'S NOT GONNA PULL US FURTHER APART.
OH YEAH?
THAT'S GOOD.
AND...
AFTER TALKING TO ASAHINA FOR THE LAST FEW DAYS...

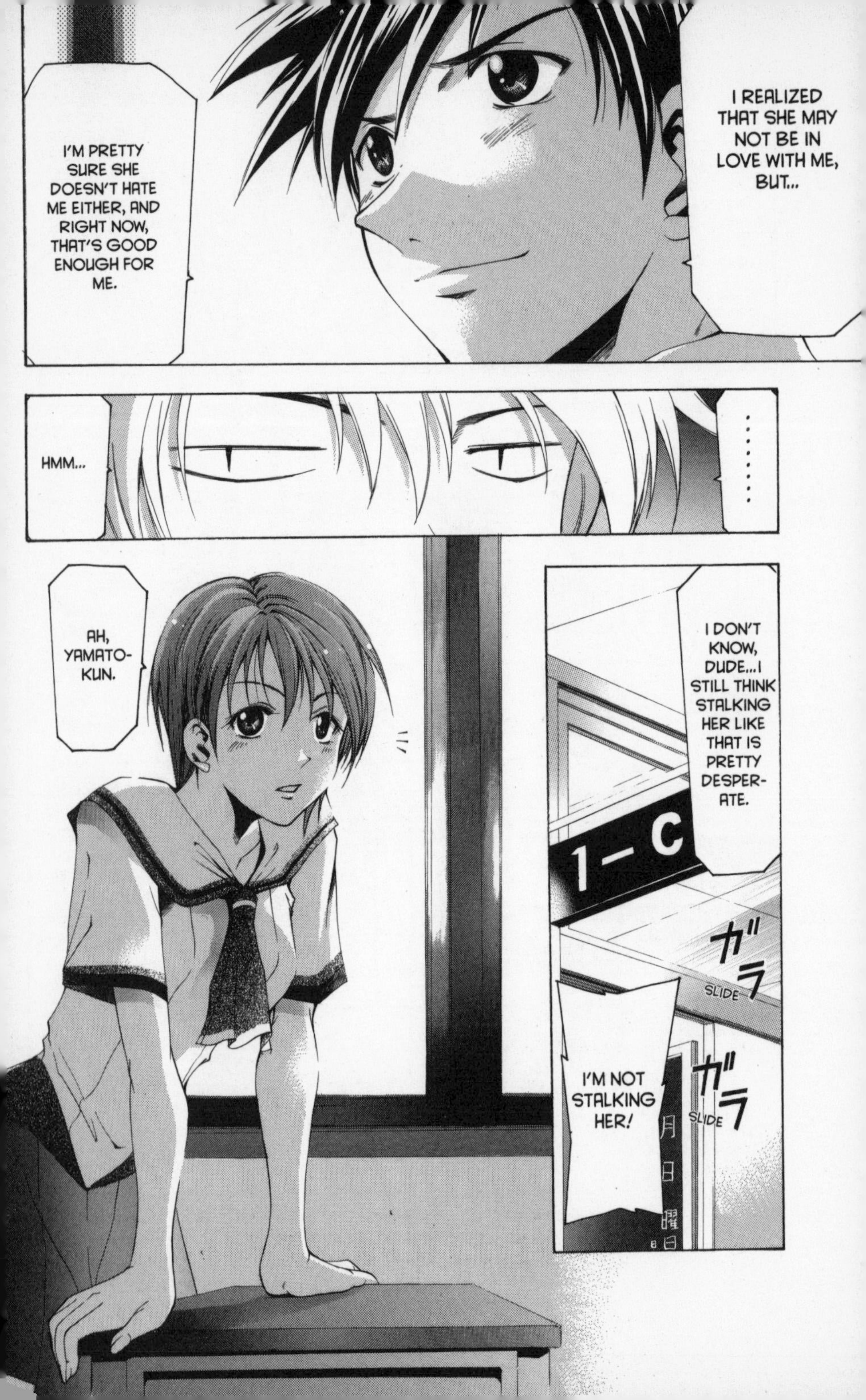
I REALIZED THAT SHE MAY NOT BE IN LOVE WITH ME, BUT...
I'M PRETTY SURE SHE DOESN'T HATE ME EITHER, AND RIGHT NOW, THAT'S GOOD ENOUGH FOR ME.
......
HMM...
I DON'T KNOW, DUDE...I STILL THINK STALKING HER LIKE THAT IS PRETTY DESPER-ATE.
1—C
ガラ
SLIDE
ガラ
SLIDE
I'M NOT STALKING HER!
AH, YAMATO-KUN.

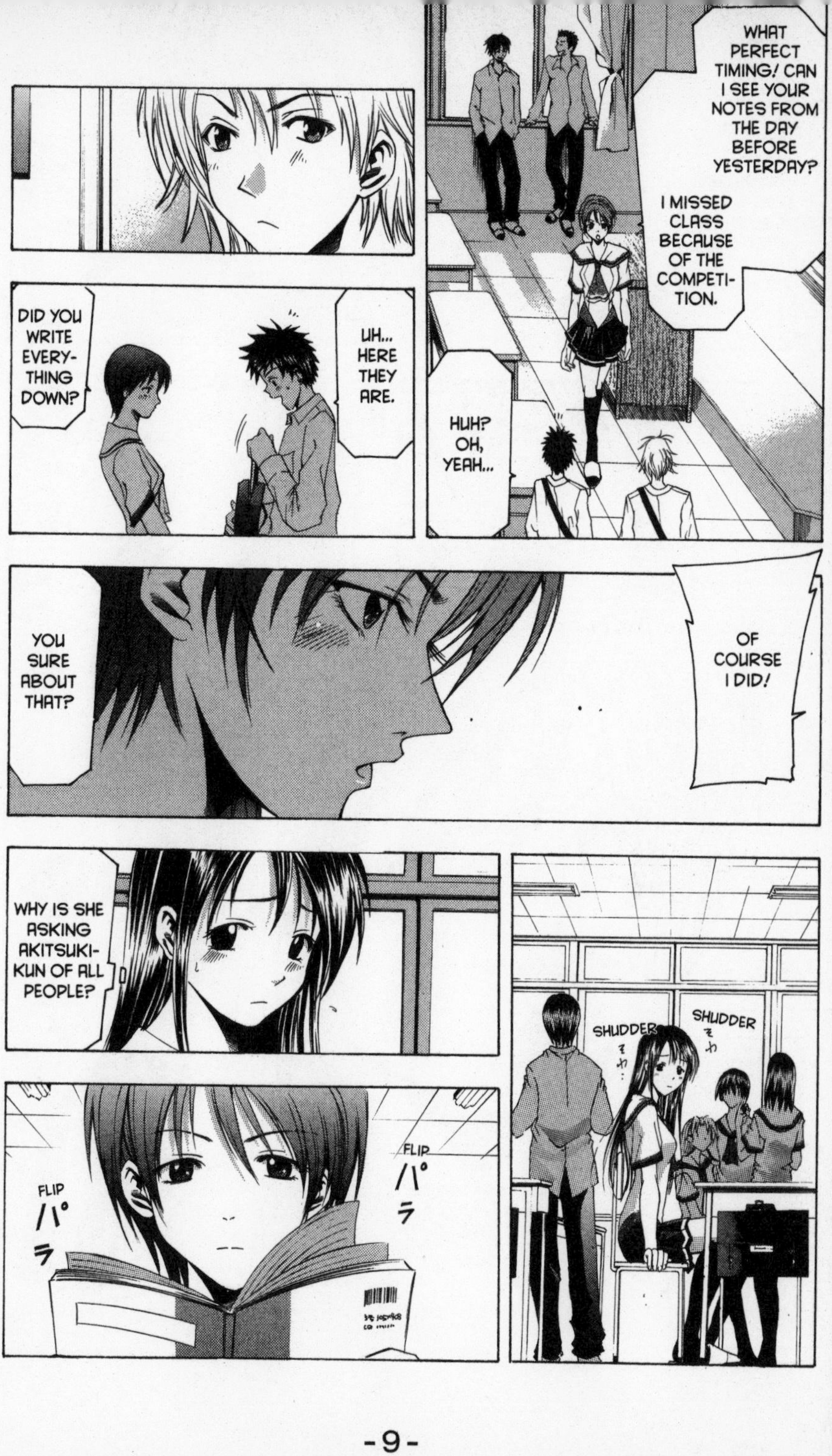
WHAT PERFECT TIMING! CAN I SEE YOUR NOTES FROM THE DAY BEFORE YESTERDAY?
I MISSED CLASS BECAUSE OF THE COMPETITION.
HUH? OH, YEAH...
UH... HERE THEY ARE.
DID YOU WRITE EVERYTHING DOWN?
OF COURSE I DID!
...
YOU SURE ABOUT THAT?
SHUDDER
ざわ
SHUDDER
ざわ
WHY IS SHE ASKING AKITSUKI-KUN OF ALL PEOPLE?
FLIP
パラ
FLIP
パラ

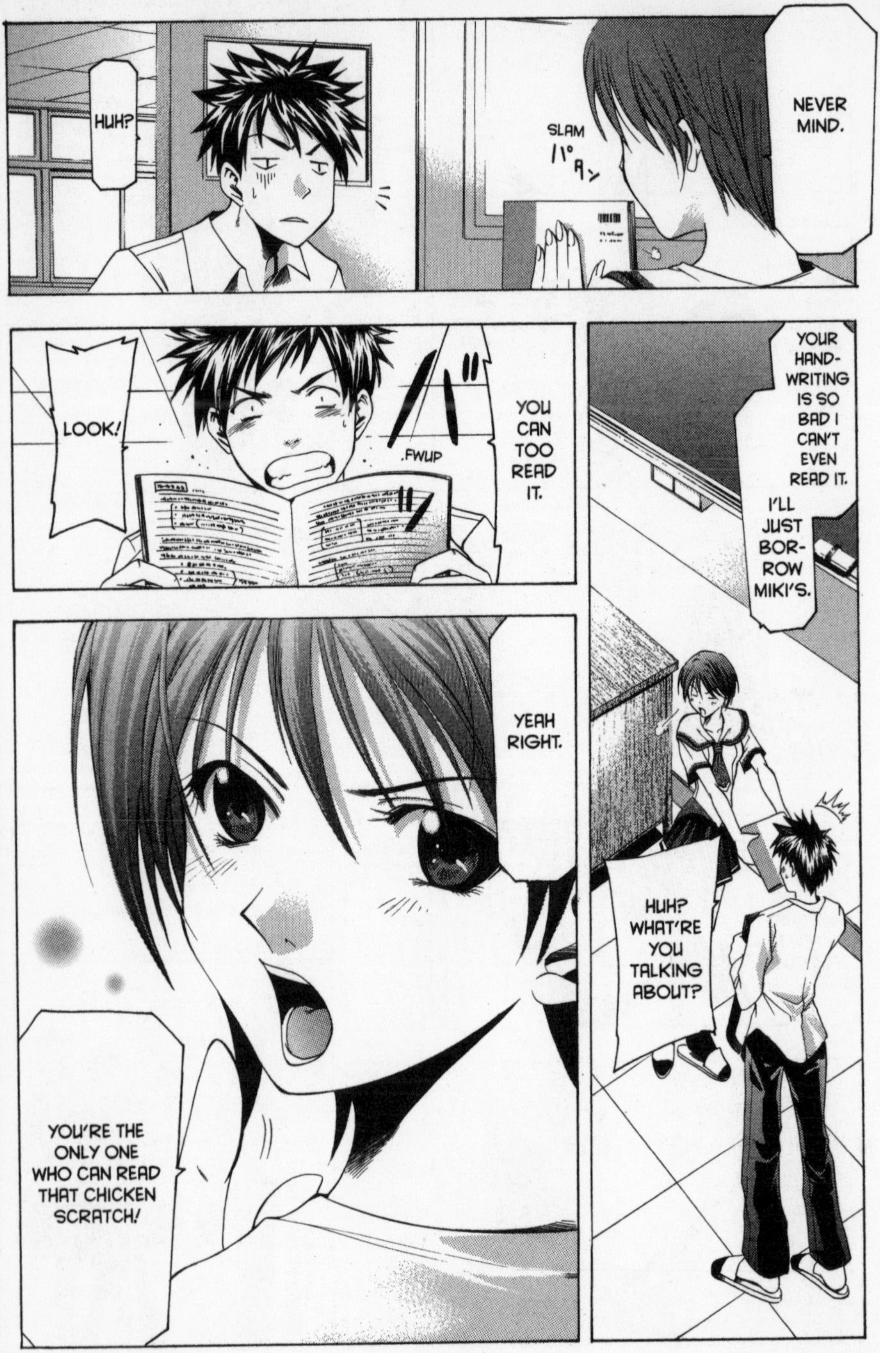
NEVER MIND.
SLAM
パタン
HUH?
YOUR HAND-WRITING IS SO BAD I CAN'T EVEN READ IT.
I'LL JUST BOR-ROW MIKI'S.
HUH? WHAT'RE YOU TALKING ABOUT?
YOU CAN TOO READ IT.
FWUP
LOOK!
YEAH RIGHT.
YOU'RE THE ONLY ONE WHO CAN READ THAT CHICKEN SCRATCH!

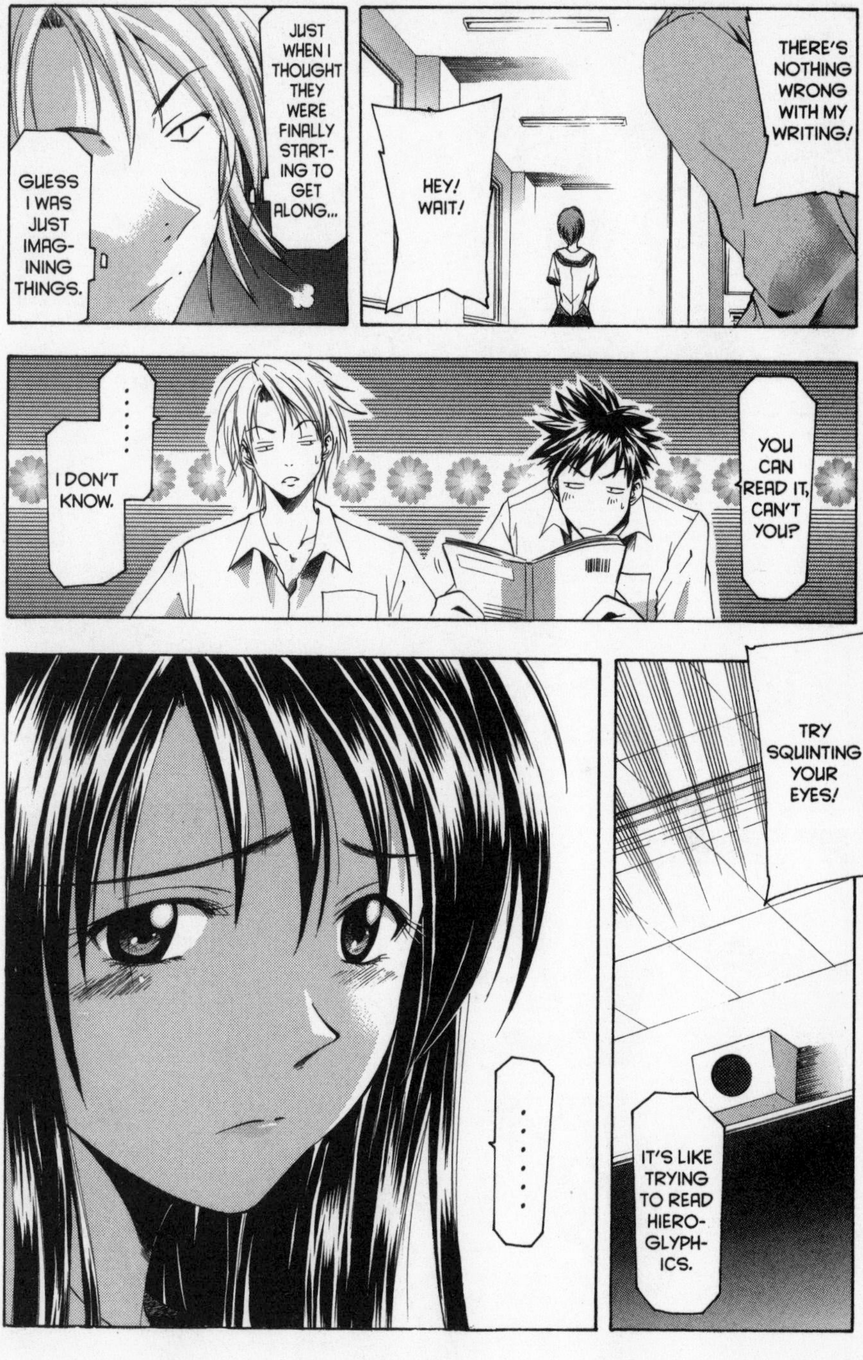
THERE'S NOTHING WRONG WITH MY WRITING!
HEY! WAIT!
JUST WHEN I THOUGHT THEY WERE FINALLY STARTING TO GET ALONG...
GUESS I WAS JUST IMAGINING THINGS.
YOU CAN READ IT, CAN'T YOU?
......
I DON'T KNOW.
TRY SQUINTING YOUR EYES!
IT'S LIKE TRYING TO READ HIEROGLYPHICS.
......

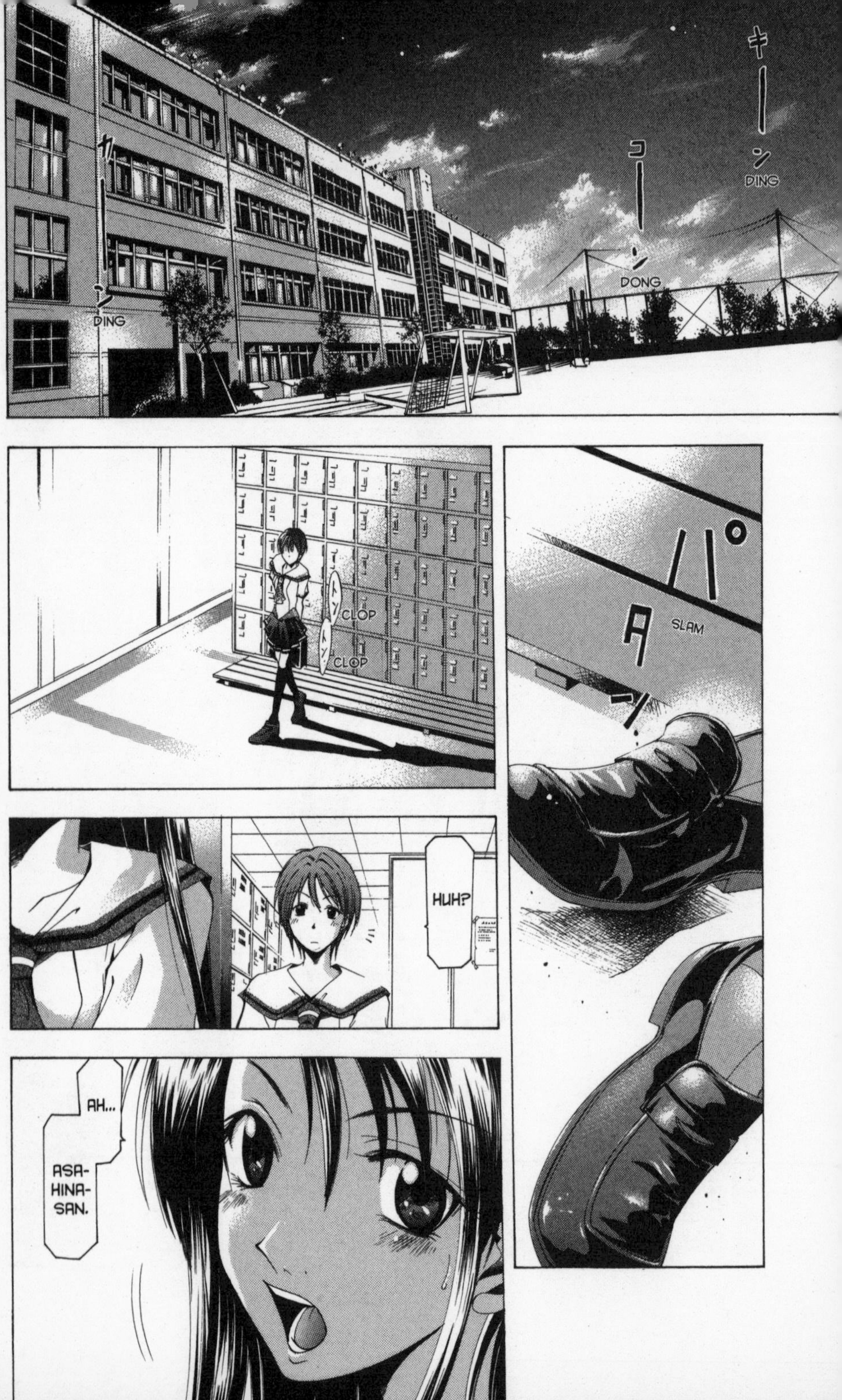
キーン
DING
コーン
DONG
DING
パタ
SLAM
トン
CLOP
トン
CLOP
HUH?
AH...
ASA-HINA-SAN.

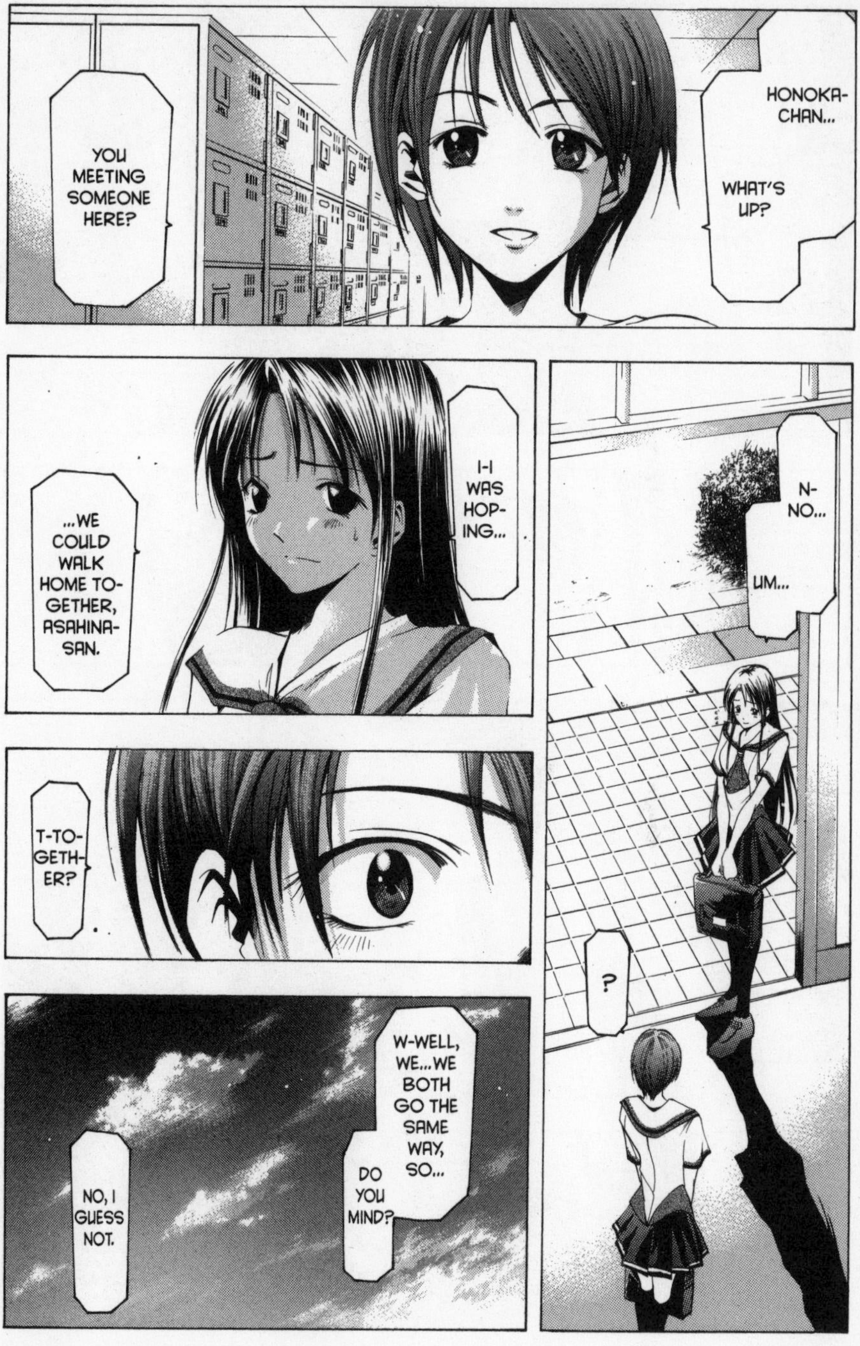
HONOKA-CHAN...
WHAT'S UP?
YOU MEETING SOMEONE HERE?
N-NO...
UM...
?
I-I WAS HOP-ING...
...WE COULD WALK HOME TO-GETHER, ASAHINA-SAN.
T-TO-GETH-ER?
W-WELL, WE...WE BOTH GO THE SAME WAY, SO...
DO YOU MIND?
NO, I GUESS NOT.

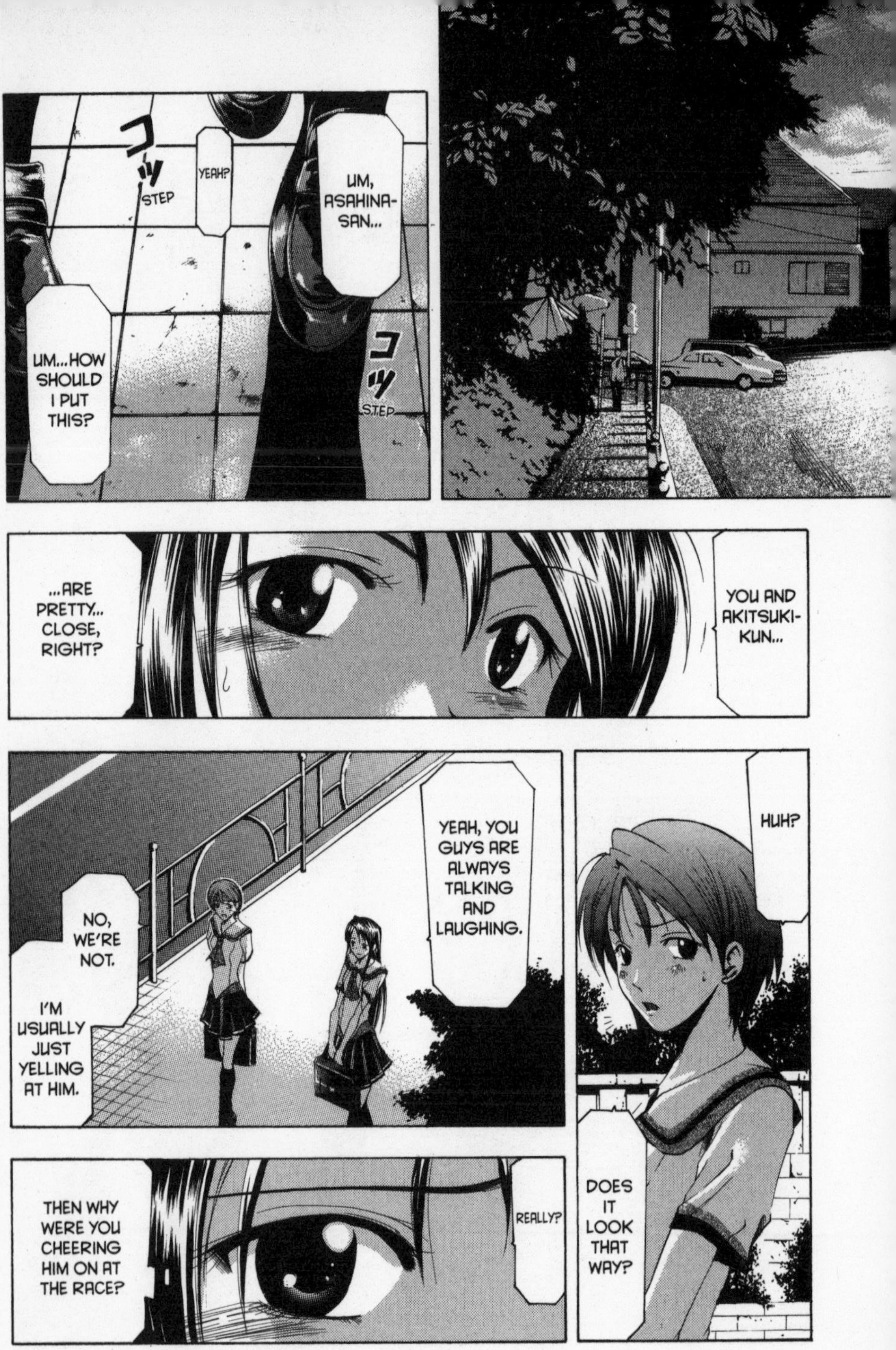
UM, ASAHINA-SAN...
YEAH?
コッ STEP
コッ STEP
UM...HOW SHOULD I PUT THIS?
YOU AND AKITSUKI-KUN...
...ARE PRETTY... CLOSE, RIGHT?
HUH?
DOES IT LOOK THAT WAY?
YEAH, YOU GUYS ARE ALWAYS TALKING AND LAUGHING.
NO, WE'RE NOT.
I'M USUALLY JUST YELLING AT HIM.
REALLY?
THEN WHY WERE YOU CHEERING HIM ON AT THE RACE?

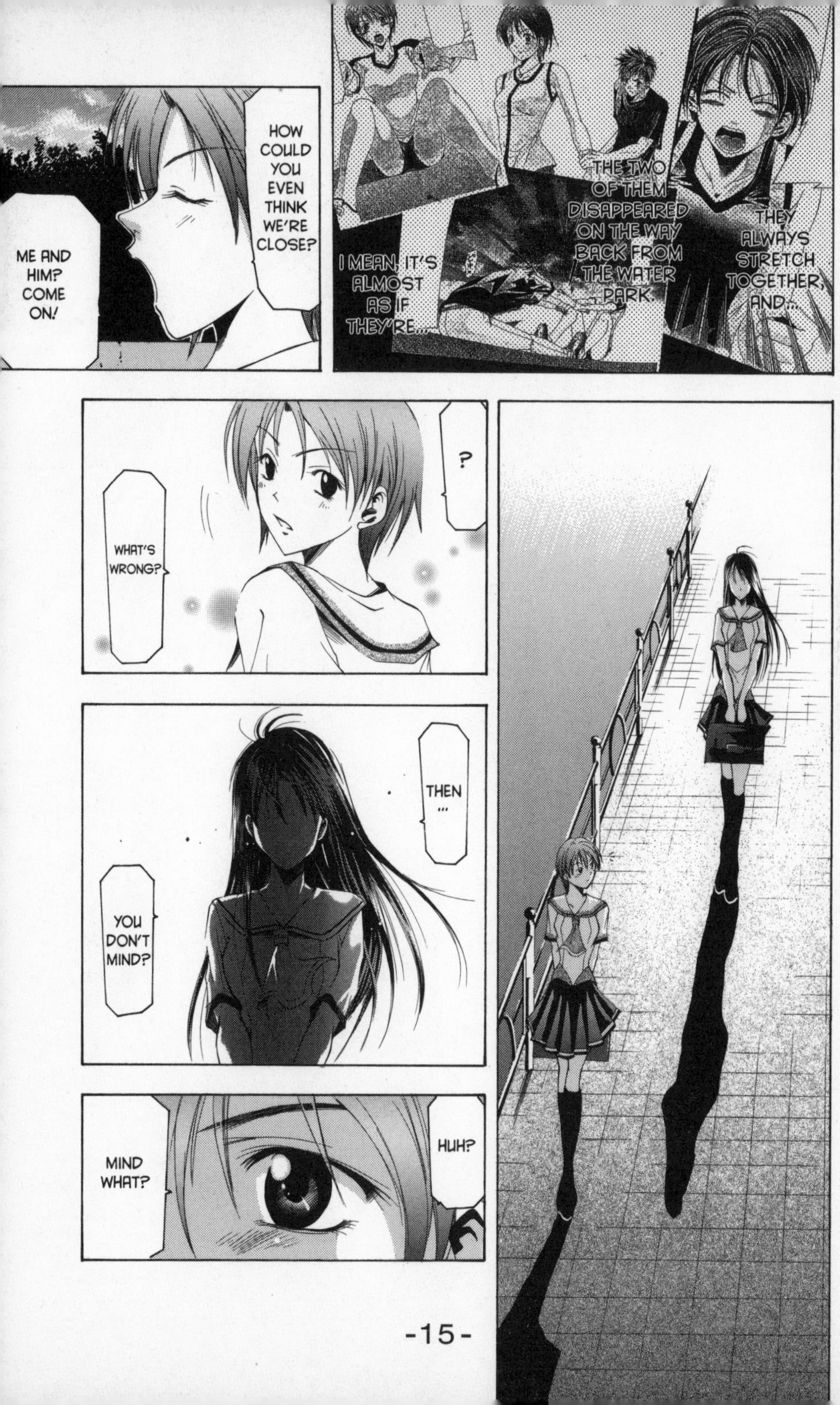
THEY ALWAYS STRETCH TOGETHER, AND...
THE TWO OF THEM DISAPPEARED ON THE WAY BACK FROM THE WATER PARK.
I MEAN, IT'S ALMOST AS IF THEY'RE...
HOW COULD YOU EVEN THINK WE'RE CLOSE?
ME AND HIM? COME ON!
?
WHAT'S WRONG?
THEN...
YOU DON'T MIND?
HUH?
MIND WHAT?

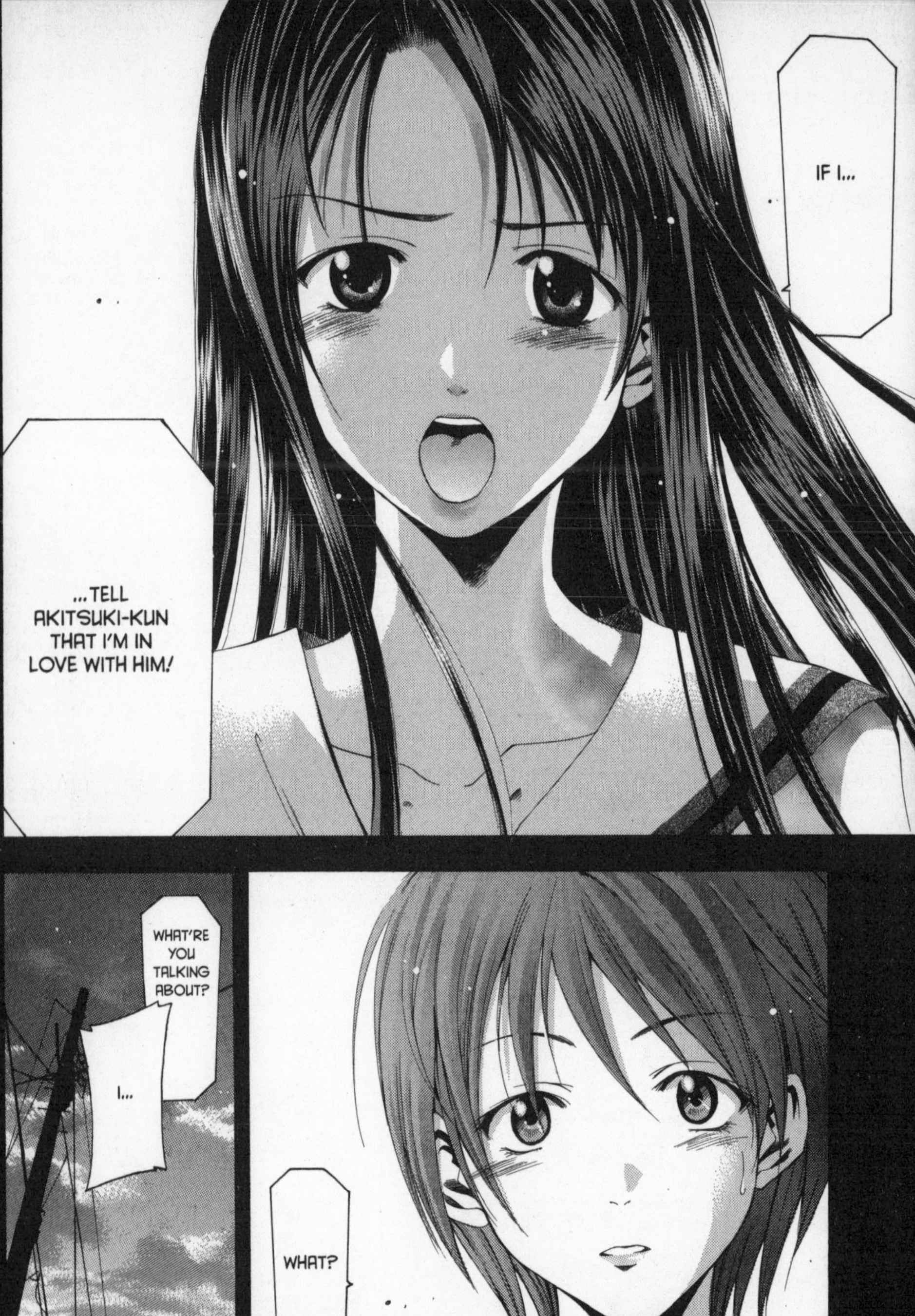
IF I...
...TELL AKITSUKI-KUN THAT I'M IN LOVE WITH HIM!
WHAT?
WHAT'RE YOU TALKING ABOUT?
I...

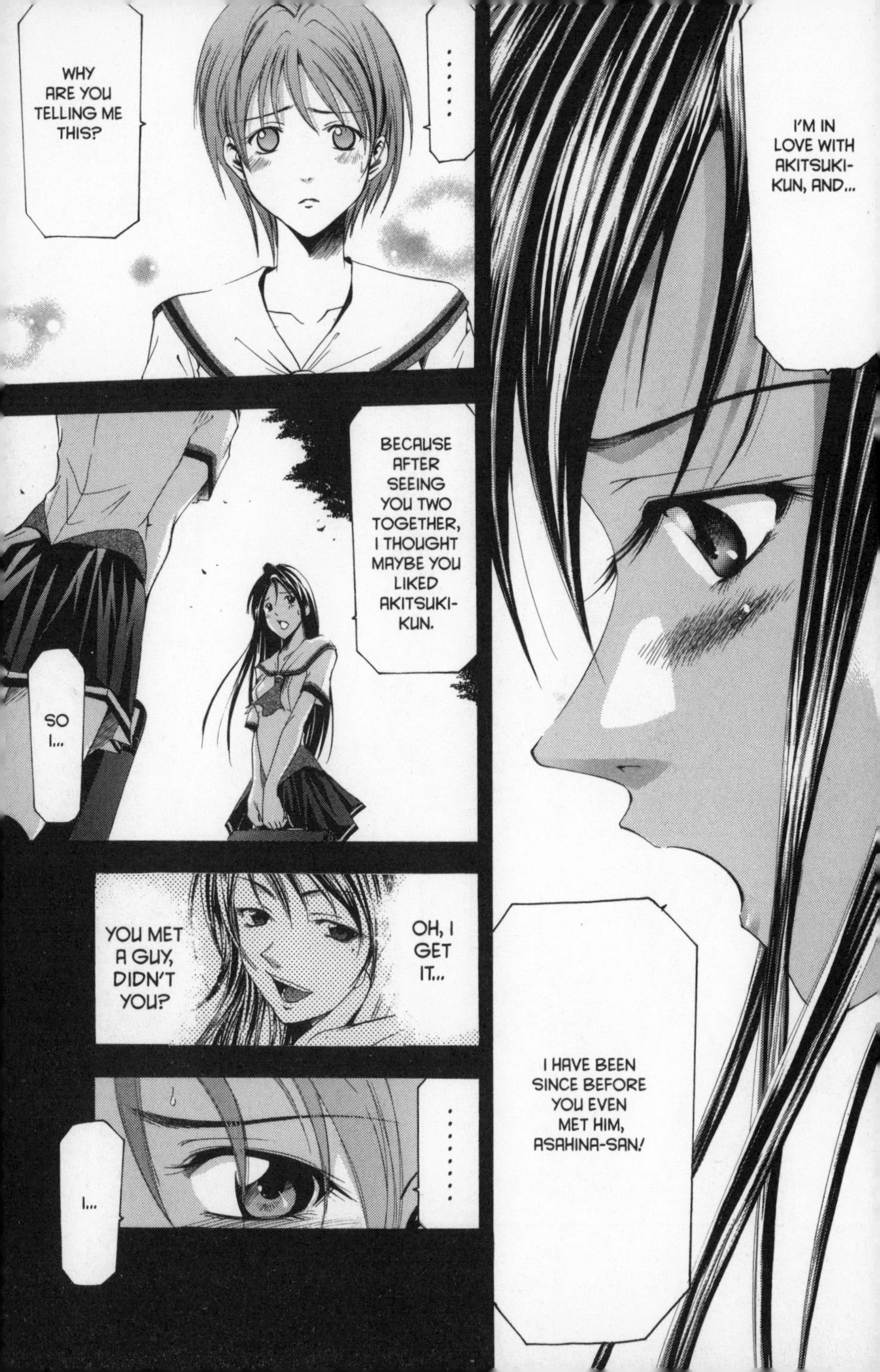
I'M IN LOVE WITH AKITSUKI-KUN, AND...
I HAVE BEEN SINCE BEFORE YOU EVEN MET HIM, ASAHINA-SAN!
......
WHY ARE YOU TELLING ME THIS?
BECAUSE AFTER SEEING YOU TWO TOGETHER, I THOUGHT MAYBE YOU LIKED AKITSUKI-KUN.
SO I...
OH, I GET IT...
YOU MET A GUY, DIDN'T YOU?
......
I...

I CAN'T BELIEVE YOU ACTUALLY THOUGHT I LIKED YAMATO-KUN!

......!

!

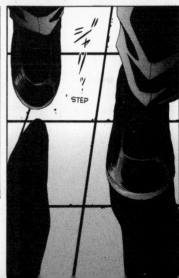

シャッ!!
STEP

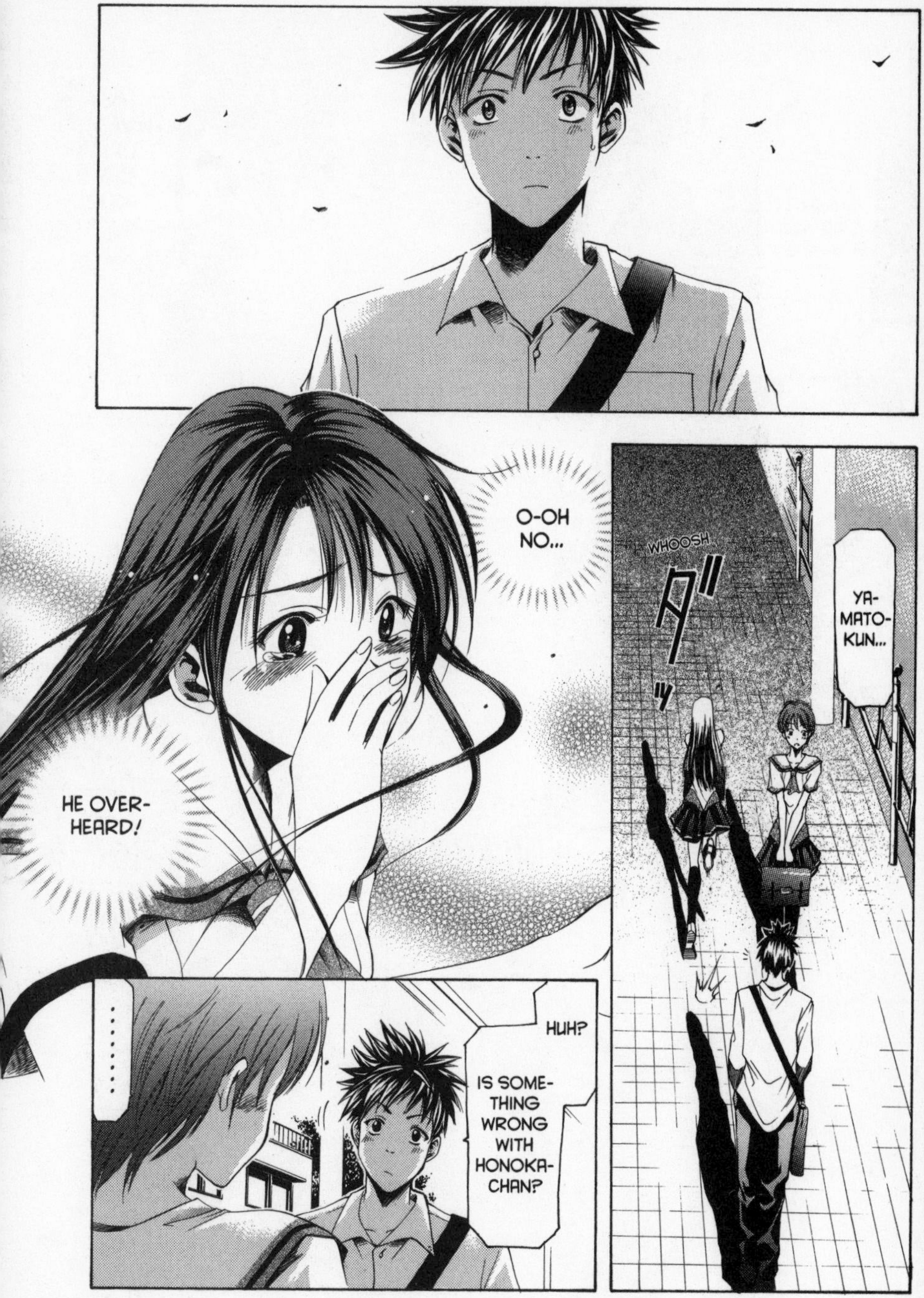
YA-MATO-KUN...
WHOOSH
O-OH NO...
HE OVER-HEARD!
......
HUH?
IS SOME-THING WRONG WITH HONOKA-CHAN?

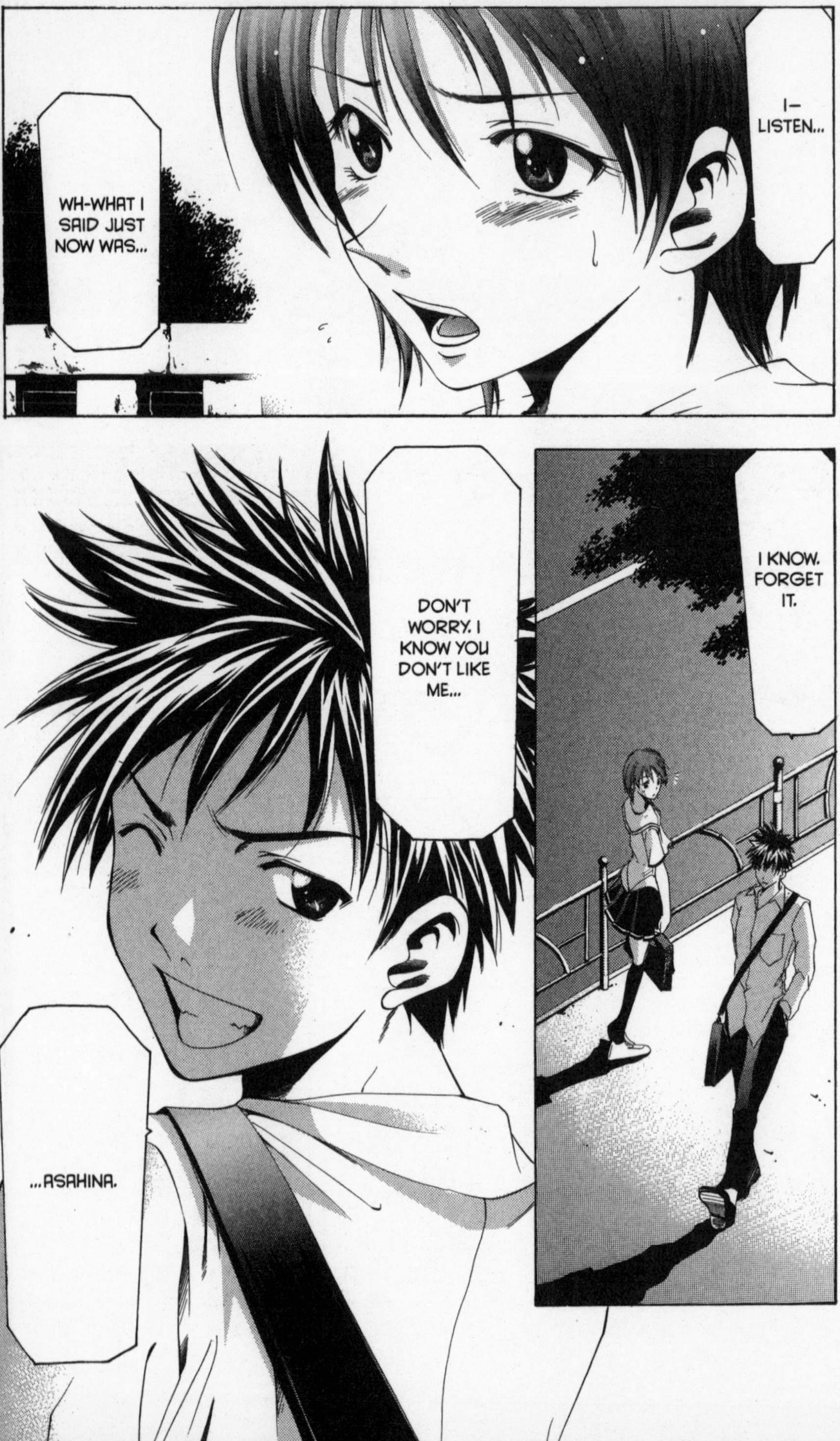
I— LISTEN...
WH-WHAT I SAID JUST NOW WAS...
I KNOW. FORGET IT.
DON'T WORRY. I KNOW YOU DON'T LIKE ME...
...ASAHINA.

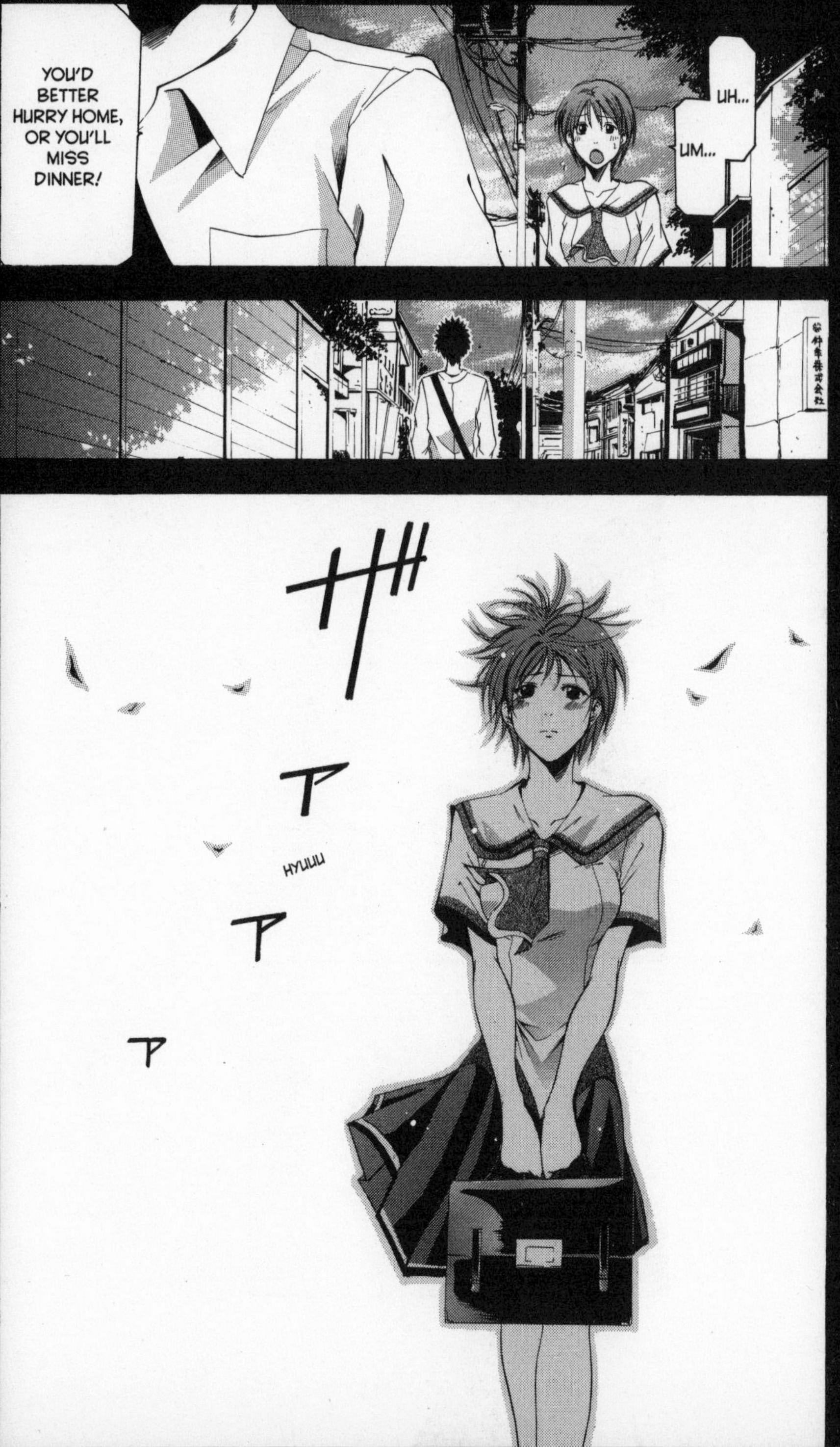
UH...
UM...
YOU'D BETTER HURRY HOME, OR YOU'LL MISS DINNER!
ザァァァ
HYUUU

SUZUKA FOUR-PANEL THEATER NUMBER SEVENTEEN

[I DON'T REALLY MIND, BUT...]

MY EDITORS WERE EXPLAINING THE DETAILS OF THE UPCOMING THAI VERSION OF "SUZUKA."
IN THE THAI VERSION, THE PAGES WILL BE REVERSED. IS THAT OKAY WITH YOU?
MR. ATHLETE—MTA-SAN (35)
OF COURSE, EVEN IF YOU SAY NO, IT'S STILL GONNA BE PRINTED THAT WAY, BUT....
PUFF
... OKAY.
AND THERE'LL BE BLACK LINES OVER ALL THE NIPPLES. ARE YOU OKAY WITH THAT?
IF YOU'RE NOT, THAT MEANS WE JUST WON'T SELL IT.
....
IS THERE ANYTHING ABOUT THIS THAT BOTHERS YOU?
PUFF
YOUR ATTITUDE MAYBE?

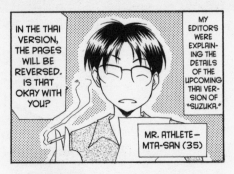

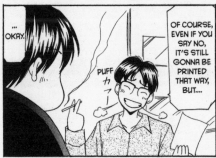

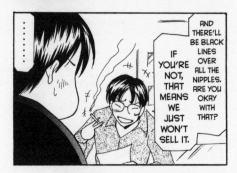

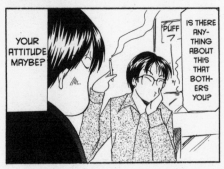

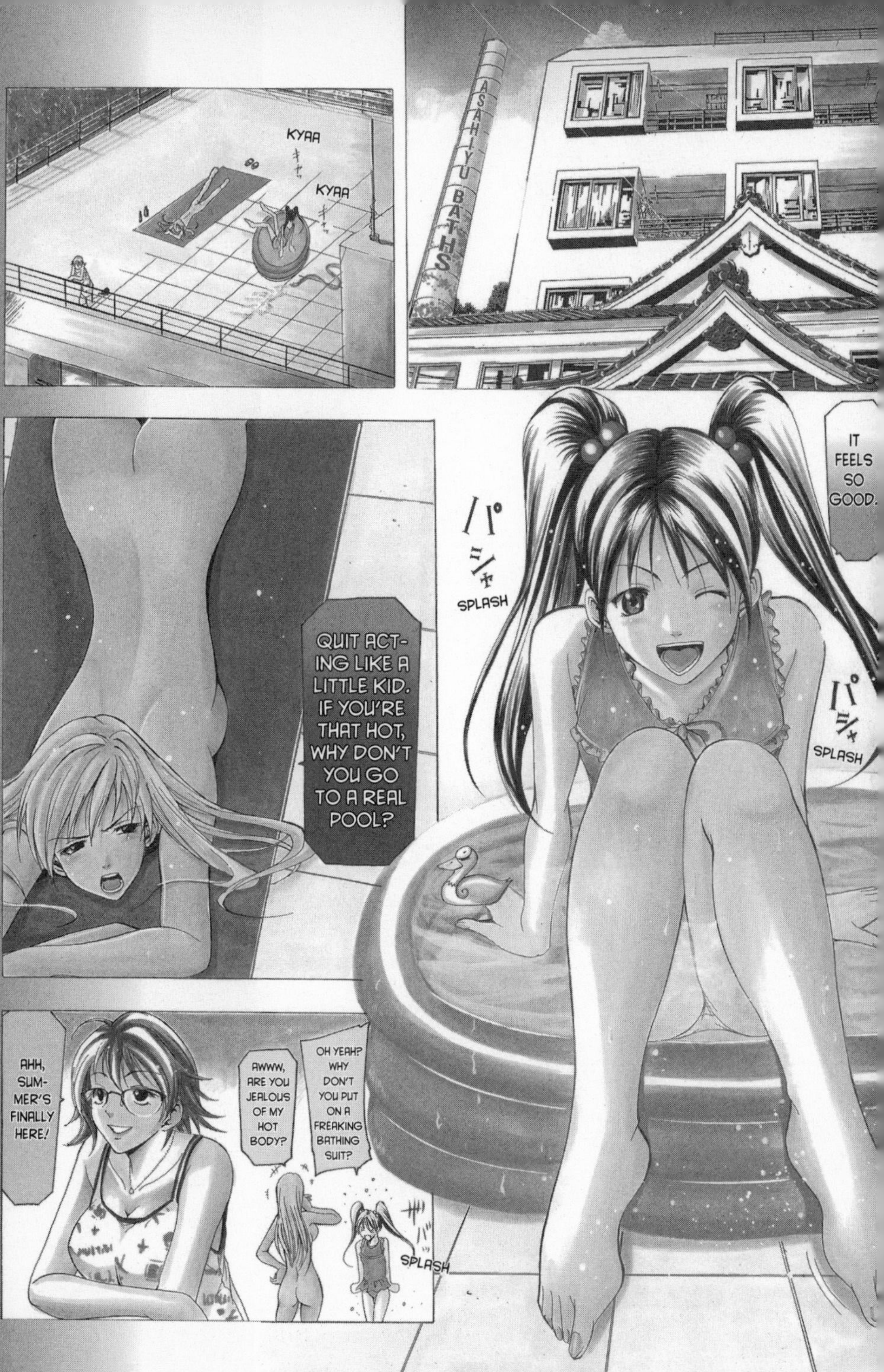
ASAHIYU BATHS
KYAA
KYAA
IT FEELS SO GOOD.
SPLASH
SPLASH
QUIT ACTING LIKE A LITTLE KID. IF YOU'RE THAT HOT, WHY DON'T YOU GO TO A REAL POOL?
OH YEAH? WHY DON'T YOU PUT ON A FREAKING BATHING SUIT?
AWWW, ARE YOU JEALOUS OF MY HOT BODY?
AHH, SUMMER'S FINALLY HERE!
SPLASH

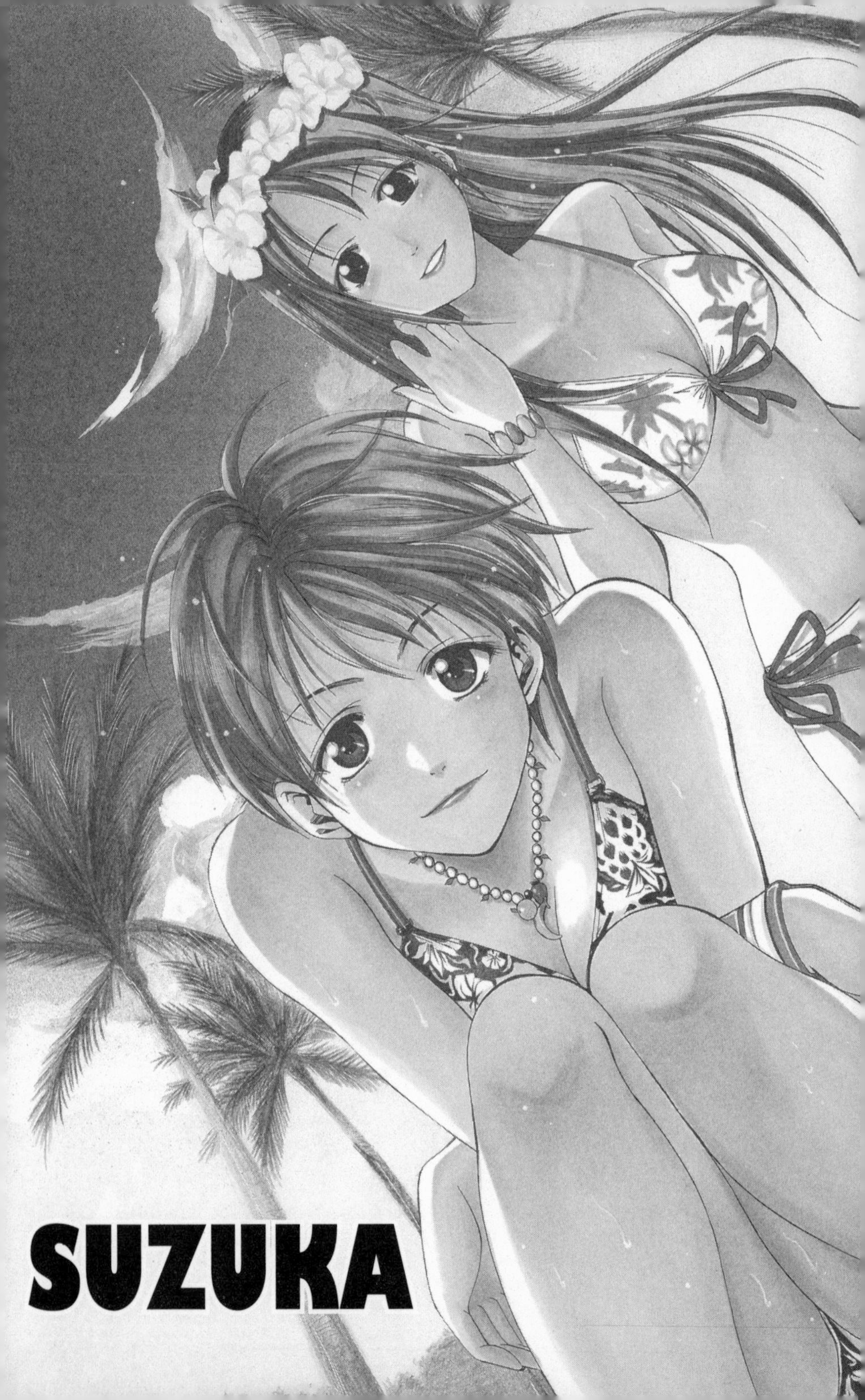
SUZUKA

#33 LIPS

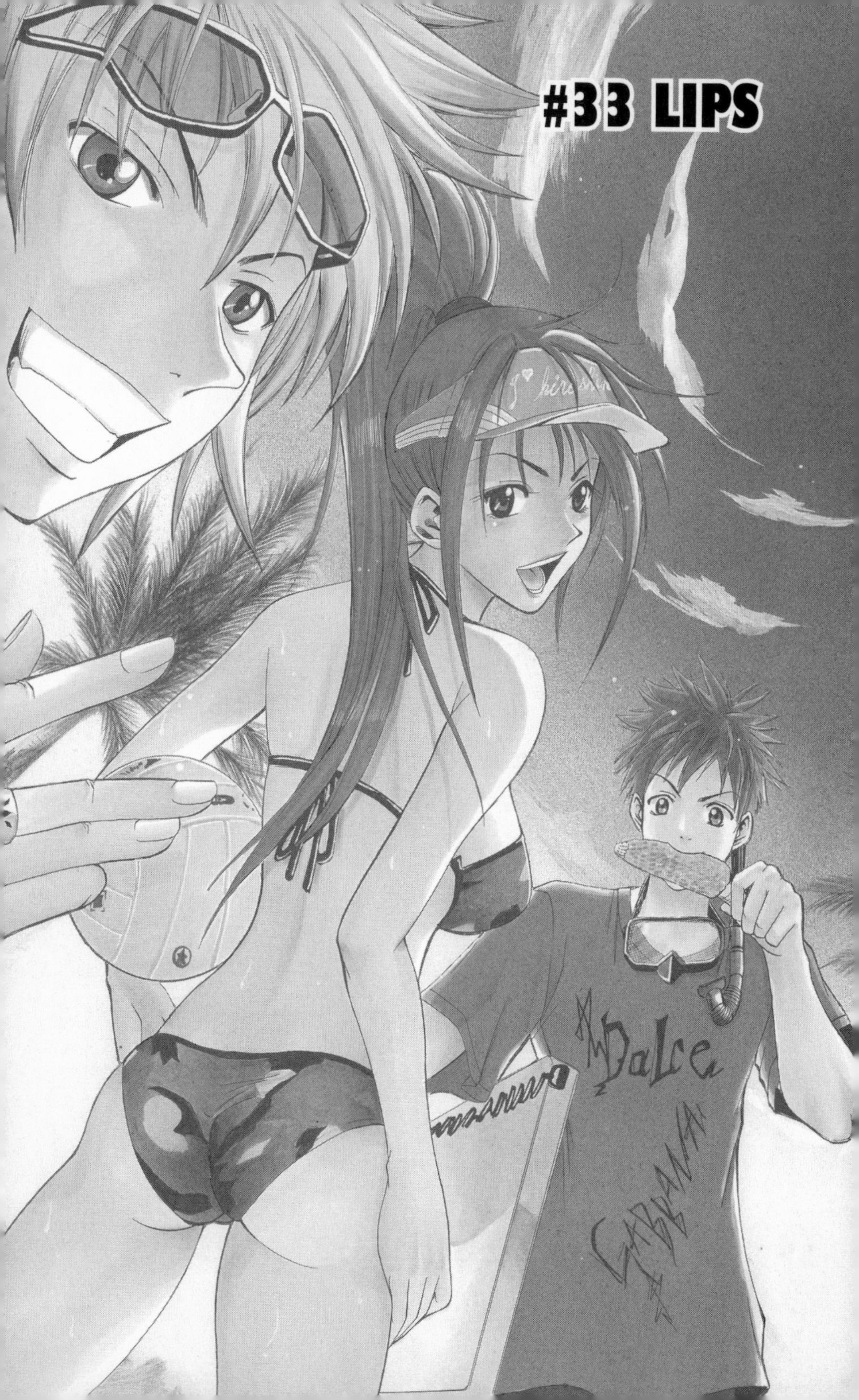

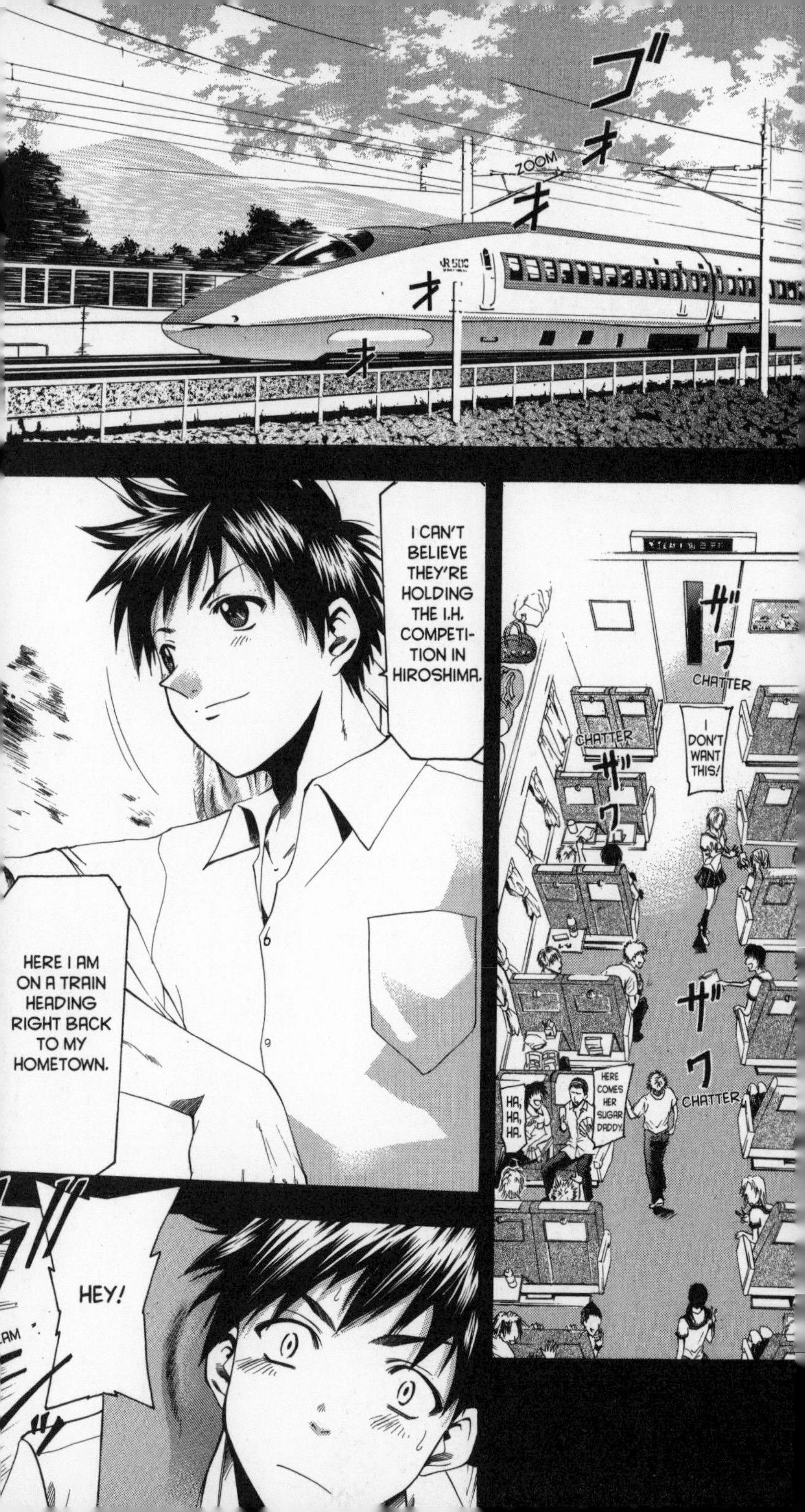
ゴオオオオ
ZOOM
ザワ
CHATTER
I DON'T WANT THIS!
CHATTER
ザワ
ザワ
CHATTER
HERE COMES HER SUGAR DADDY
HA, HA, HA.
I CAN'T BELIEVE THEY'RE HOLDING THE I.H. COMPETITION IN HIROSHIMA.
HERE I AM ON A TRAIN HEADING RIGHT BACK TO MY HOMETOWN.
HEY!

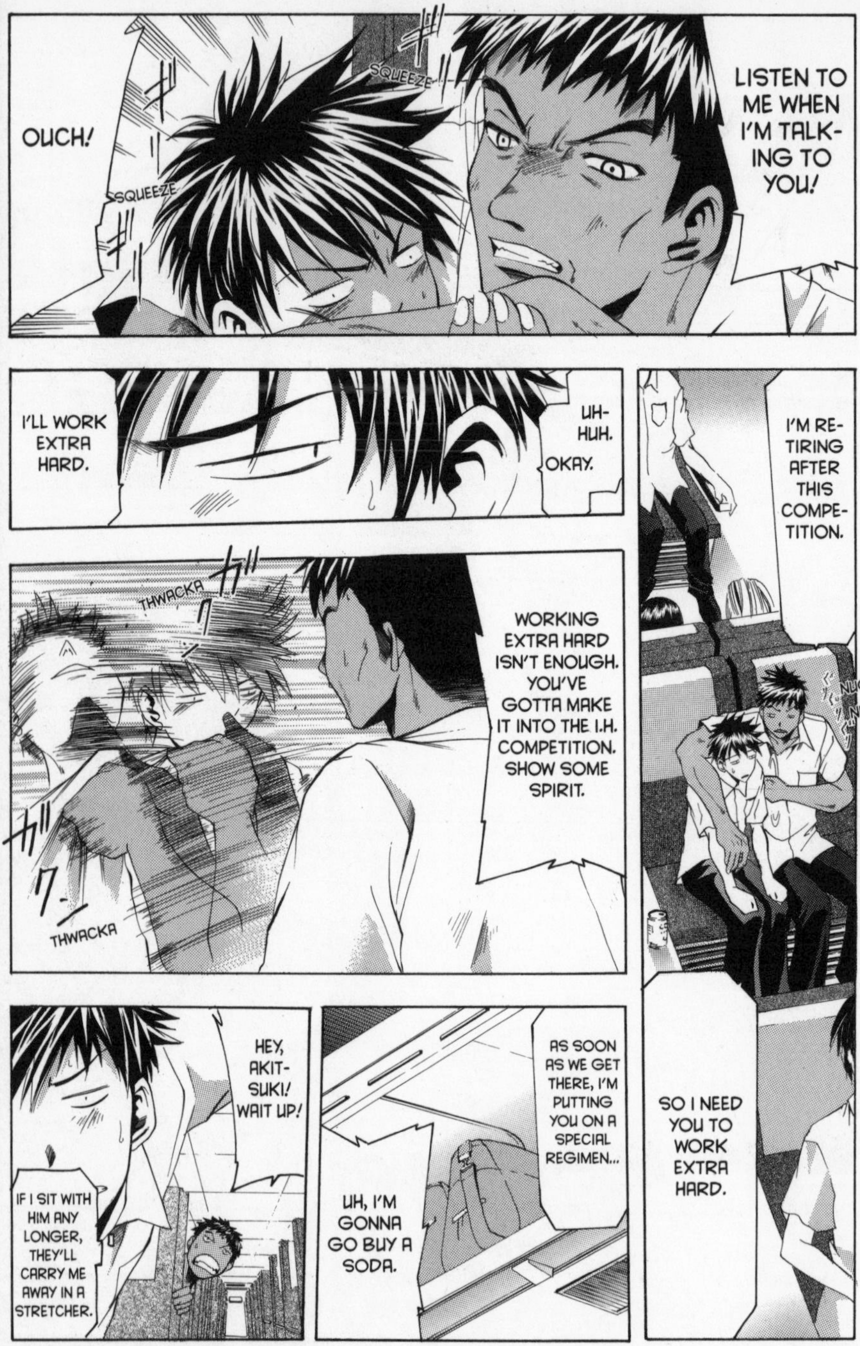
LISTEN TO ME WHEN I'M TALK-ING TO YOU!
SQUEEZE
OUCH!
SQUEEZE
I'M RE-TIRING AFTER THIS COMPE-TITION.
NUGGIE
NUGGIE
SO I NEED YOU TO WORK EXTRA HARD.
UH-HUH.
OKAY.
I'LL WORK EXTRA HARD.
WORKING EXTRA HARD ISN'T ENOUGH. YOU'VE GOTTA MAKE IT INTO THE I.H. COMPETITION. SHOW SOME SPIRIT.
THWACKA
THWACKA
AS SOON AS WE GET THERE, I'M PUTTING YOU ON A SPECIAL REGIMEN...
UH, I'M GONNA GO BUY A SODA.
HEY, AKIT-SUKI! WAIT UP!
IF I SIT WITH HIM ANY LONGER, THEY'LL CARRY ME AWAY IN A STRETCHER.

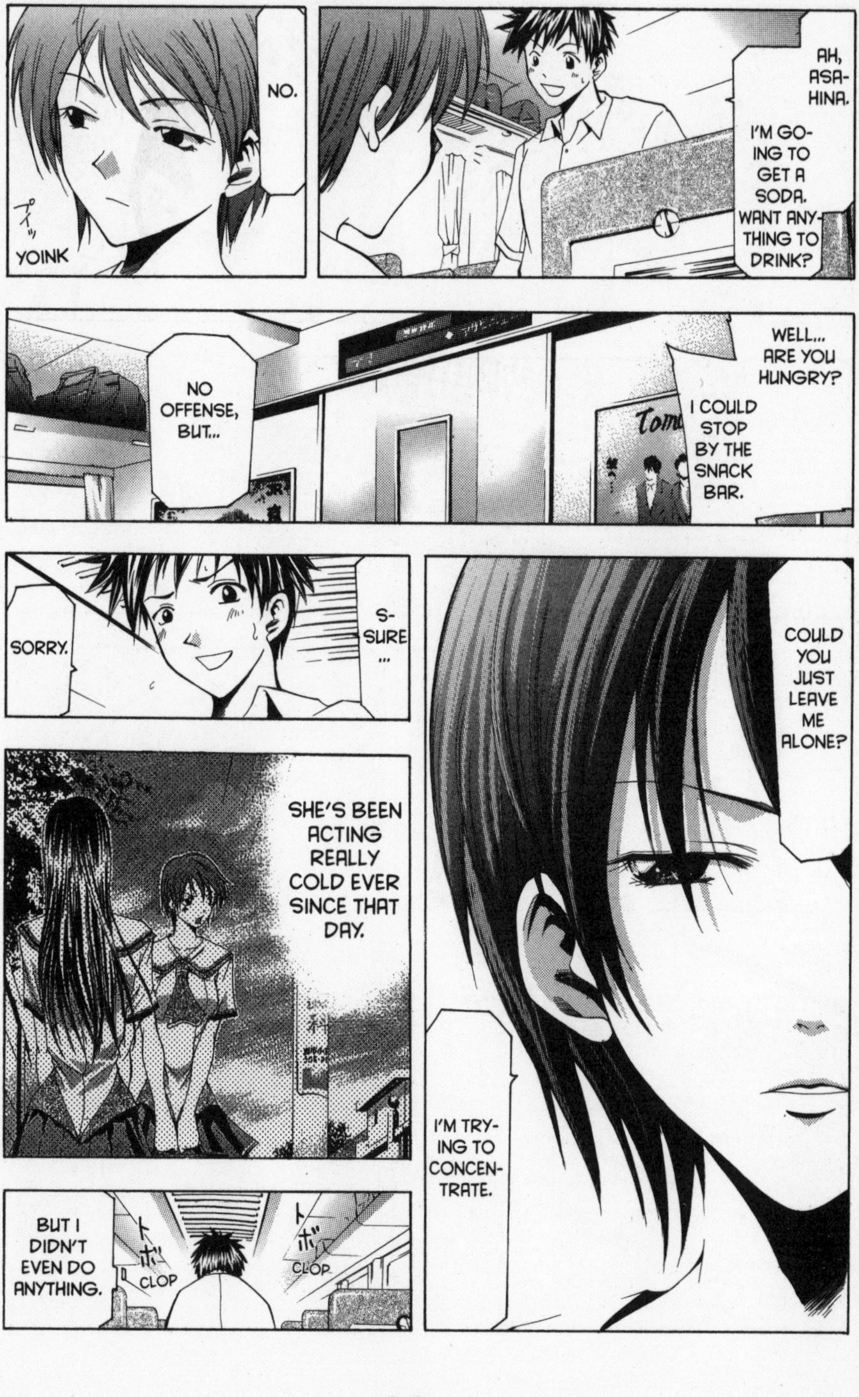
AH, ASA-HINA.
I'M GO-ING TO GET A SODA. WANT ANY-THING TO DRINK?
NO.
プイッ
YOINK
WELL... ARE YOU HUNGRY?
I COULD STOP BY THE SNACK BAR.
NO OFFENSE, BUT...
COULD YOU JUST LEAVE ME ALONE?
I'M TRY-ING TO CONCEN-TRATE.
S-SURE ...
SORRY.
SHE'S BEEN ACTING REALLY COLD EVER SINCE THAT DAY.
トボ
CLOP
トボ
CLOP
BUT I DIDN'T EVEN DO ANYTHING.

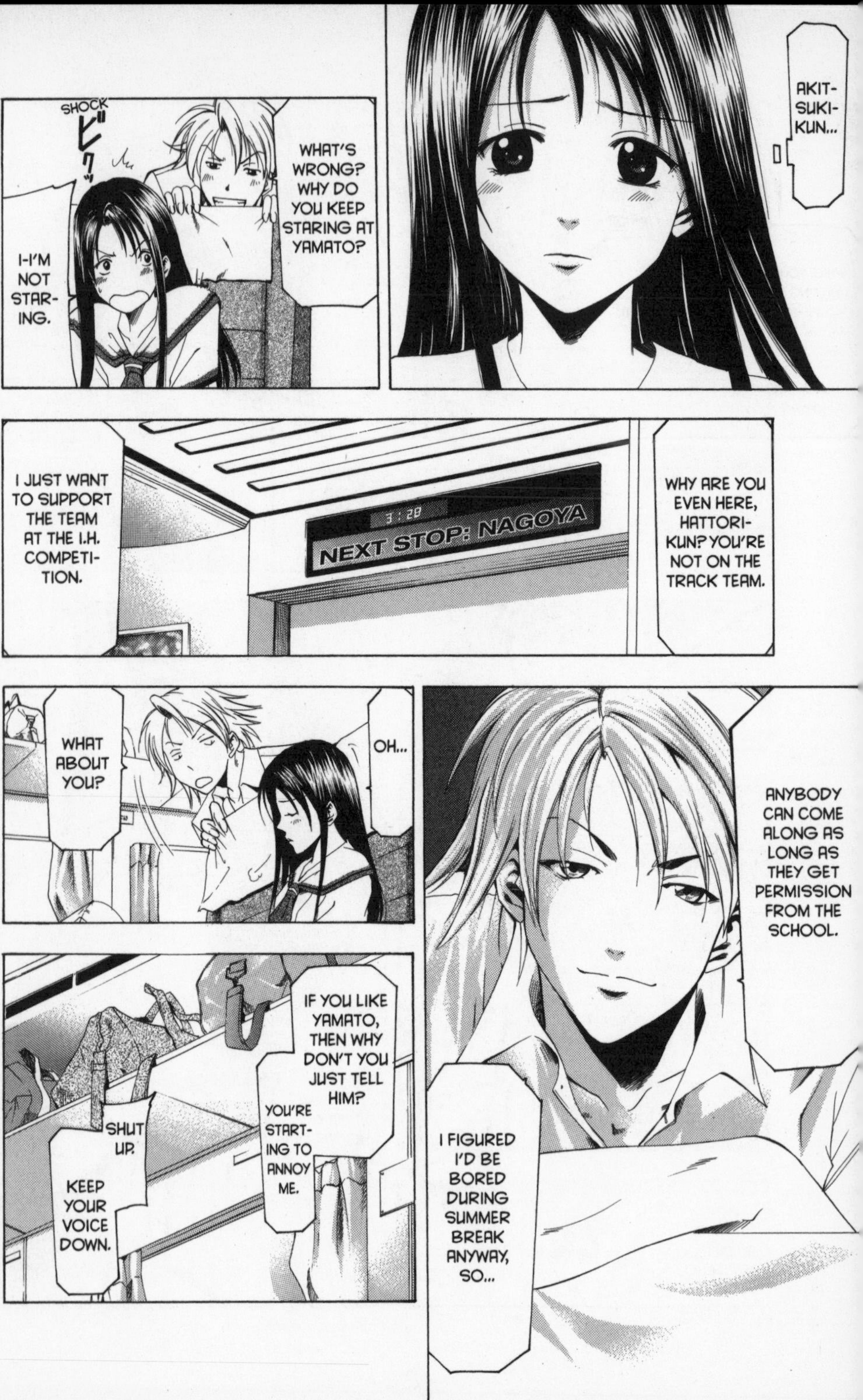
AKIT-SUKI-KUN...
SHOCK
WHAT'S WRONG? WHY DO YOU KEEP STARING AT YAMATO?
I-I'M NOT STAR-ING.
WHY ARE YOU EVEN HERE, HATTORI-KUN? YOU'RE NOT ON THE TRACK TEAM.
3:28
NEXT STOP: NAGOYA
I JUST WANT TO SUPPORT THE TEAM AT THE I.H. COMPETI-TION.
ANYBODY CAN COME ALONG AS LONG AS THEY GET PERMISSION FROM THE SCHOOL.
I FIGURED I'D BE BORED DURING SUMMER BREAK ANYWAY, SO...
OH...
WHAT ABOUT YOU?
IF YOU LIKE YAMATO, THEN WHY DON'T YOU JUST TELL HIM?
YOU'RE START-ING TO ANNOY ME.
SHUT UP.
KEEP YOUR VOICE DOWN.

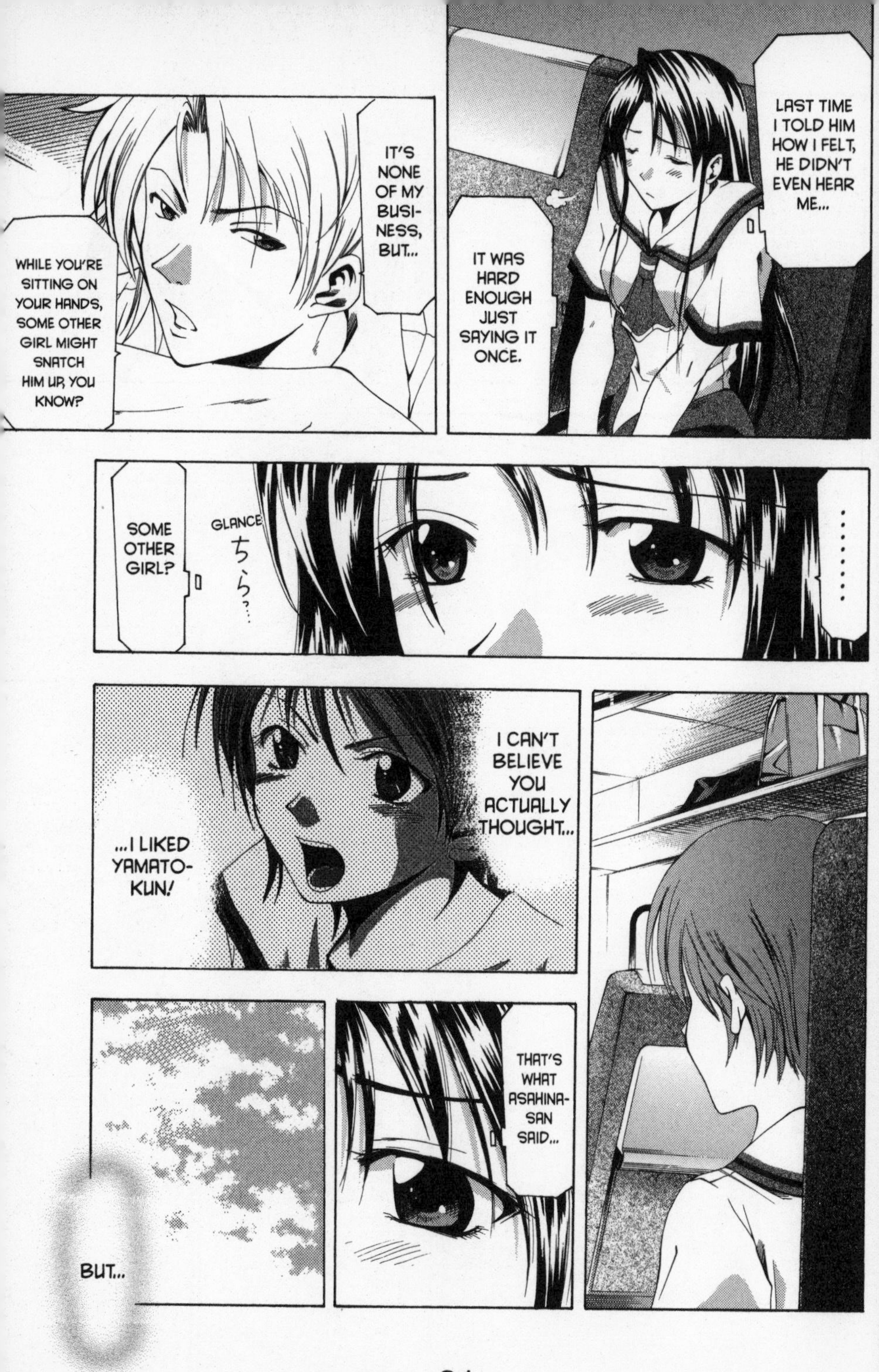
LAST TIME I TOLD HIM HOW I FELT, HE DIDN'T EVEN HEAR ME...
IT WAS HARD ENOUGH JUST SAYING IT ONCE.
IT'S NONE OF MY BUSINESS, BUT...
WHILE YOU'RE SITTING ON YOUR HANDS, SOME OTHER GIRL MIGHT SNATCH HIM UP, YOU KNOW?
......
SOME OTHER GIRL?
GLANCE
ちらっ…
I CAN'T BELIEVE YOU ACTUALLY THOUGHT...
...I LIKED YAMATO-KUN!
THAT'S WHAT ASAHINA-SAN SAID...
BUT...

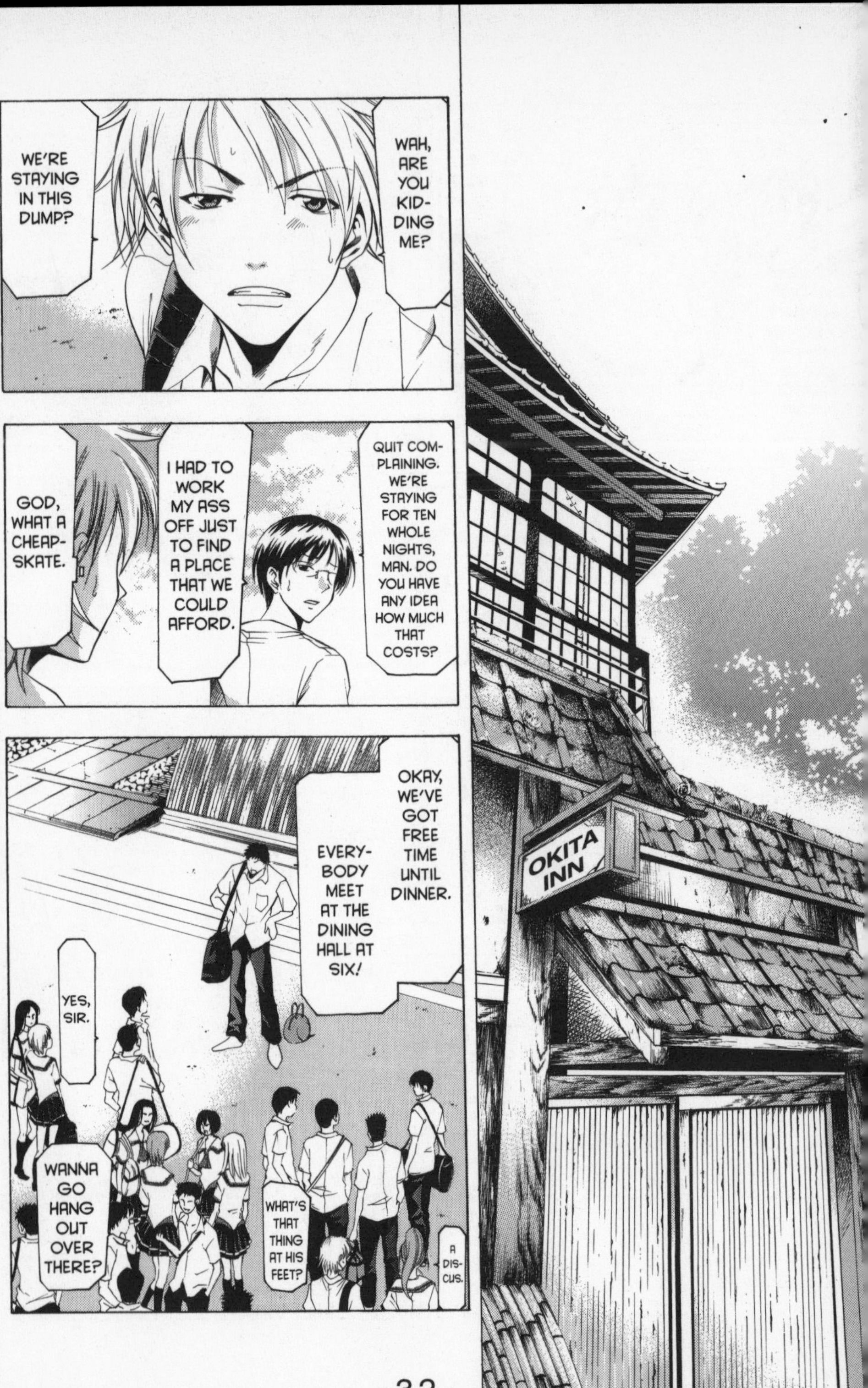
OKITA INN
WAH, ARE YOU KID-DING ME?
WE'RE STAYING IN THIS DUMP?
QUIT COM-PLAINING. WE'RE STAYING FOR TEN WHOLE NIGHTS, MAN. DO YOU HAVE ANY IDEA HOW MUCH THAT COSTS?
I HAD TO WORK MY ASS OFF JUST TO FIND A PLACE THAT WE COULD AFFORD.
GOD, WHAT A CHEAP-SKATE.
OKAY, WE'VE GOT FREE TIME UNTIL DINNER.
EVERY-BODY MEET AT THE DINING HALL AT SIX!
YES, SIR.
WHAT'S THAT THING AT HIS FEET?
A DIS-CUS.
WANNA GO HANG OUT OVER THERE?

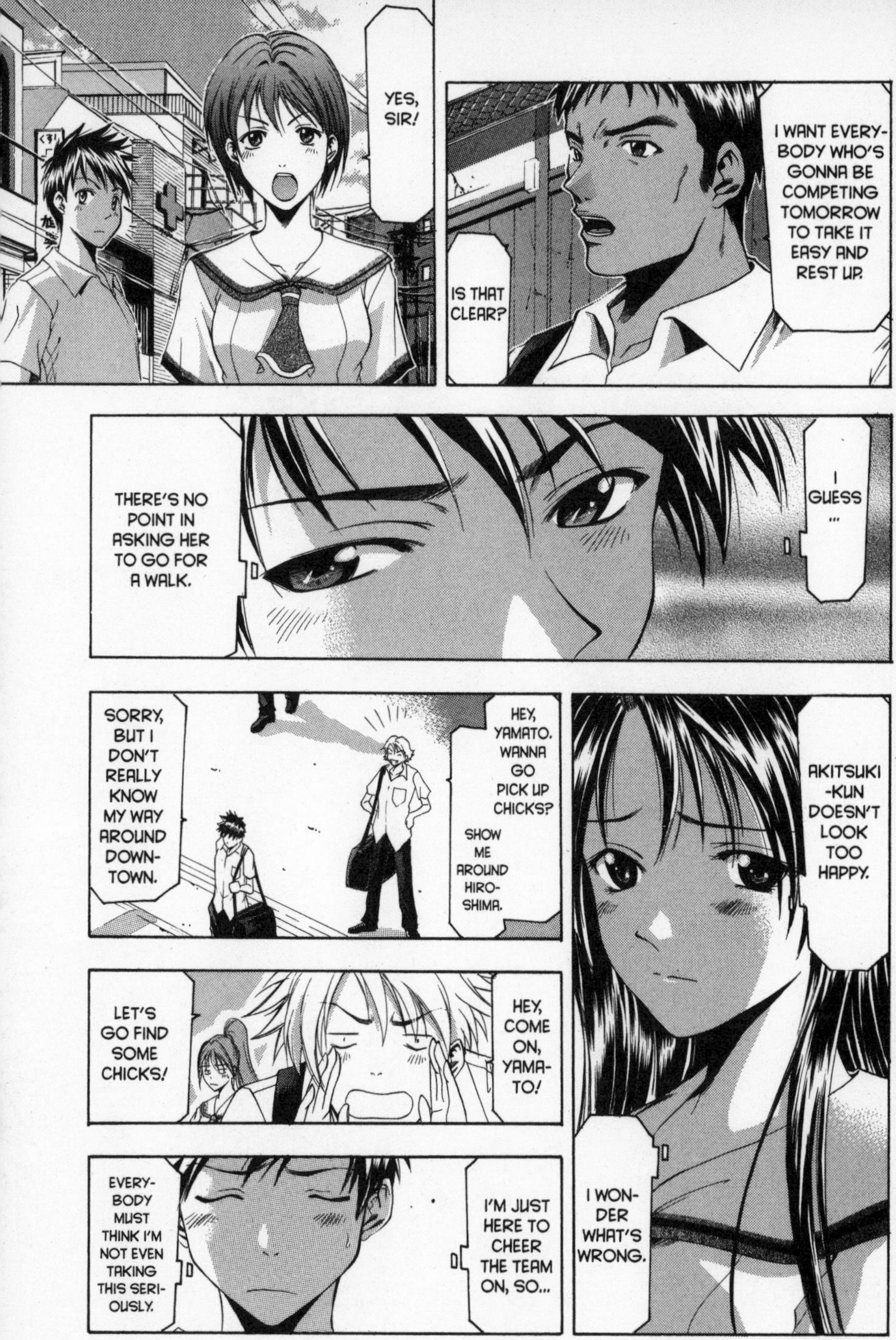
I WANT EVERYBODY WHO'S GONNA BE COMPETING TOMORROW TO TAKE IT EASY AND REST UP.
IS THAT CLEAR?
YES, SIR!
I GUESS ...
THERE'S NO POINT IN ASKING HER TO GO FOR A WALK.
AKITSUKI-KUN DOESN'T LOOK TOO HAPPY.
I WONDER WHAT'S WRONG.
HEY, YAMATO. WANNA GO PICK UP CHICKS?
SHOW ME AROUND HIROSHIMA.
SORRY, BUT I DON'T REALLY KNOW MY WAY AROUND DOWNTOWN.
HEY, COME ON, YAMATO!
LET'S GO FIND SOME CHICKS!
I'M JUST HERE TO CHEER THE TEAM ON, SO...
EVERYBODY MUST THINK I'M NOT EVEN TAKING THIS SERIOUSLY.

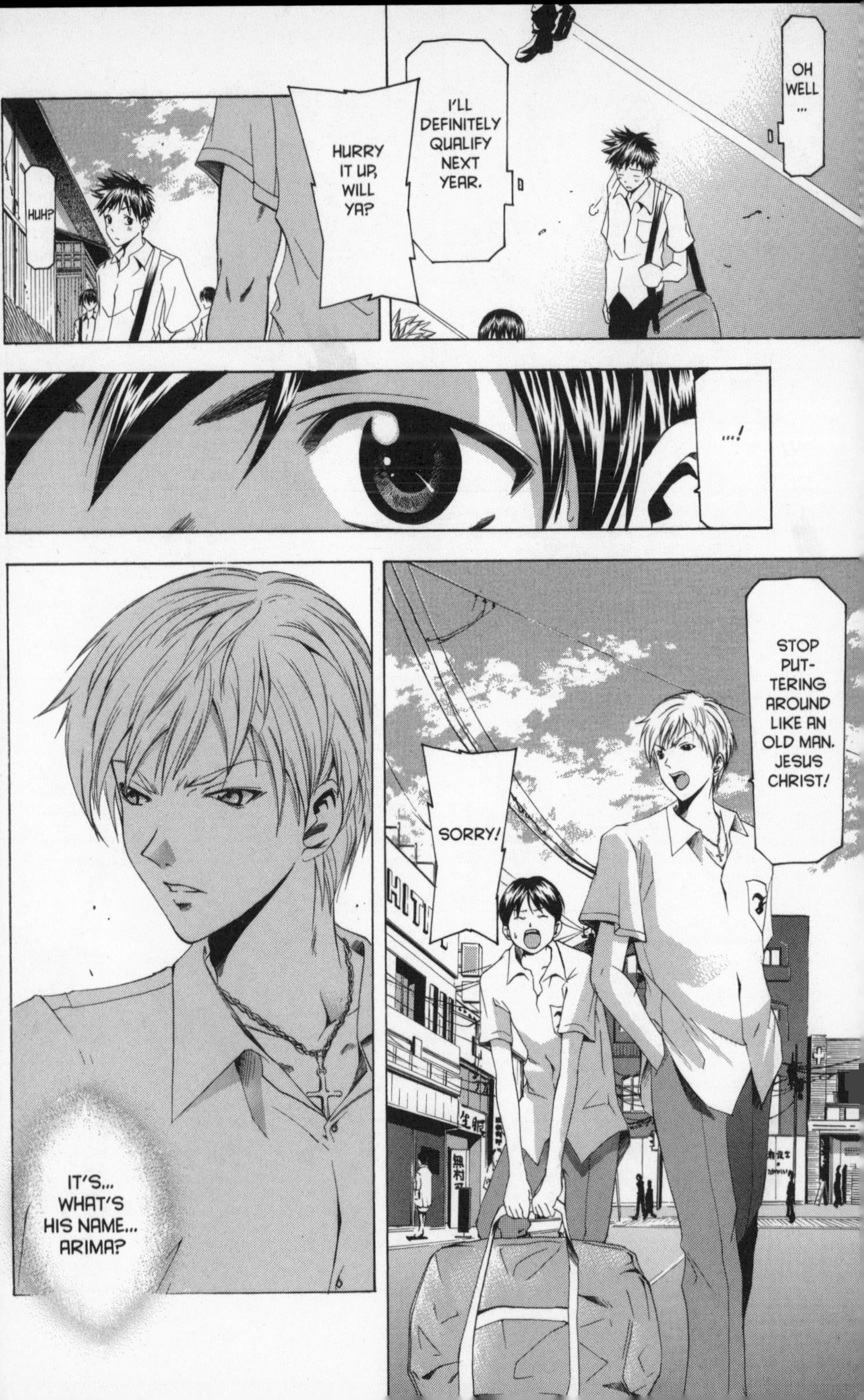
OH WELL ...
I'LL DEFINITELY QUALIFY NEXT YEAR.
HURRY IT UP, WILL YA?
HUH?
...!
STOP PUT-TERING AROUND LIKE AN OLD MAN. JESUS CHRIST!
SORRY!
IT'S... WHAT'S HIS NAME... ARIMA?

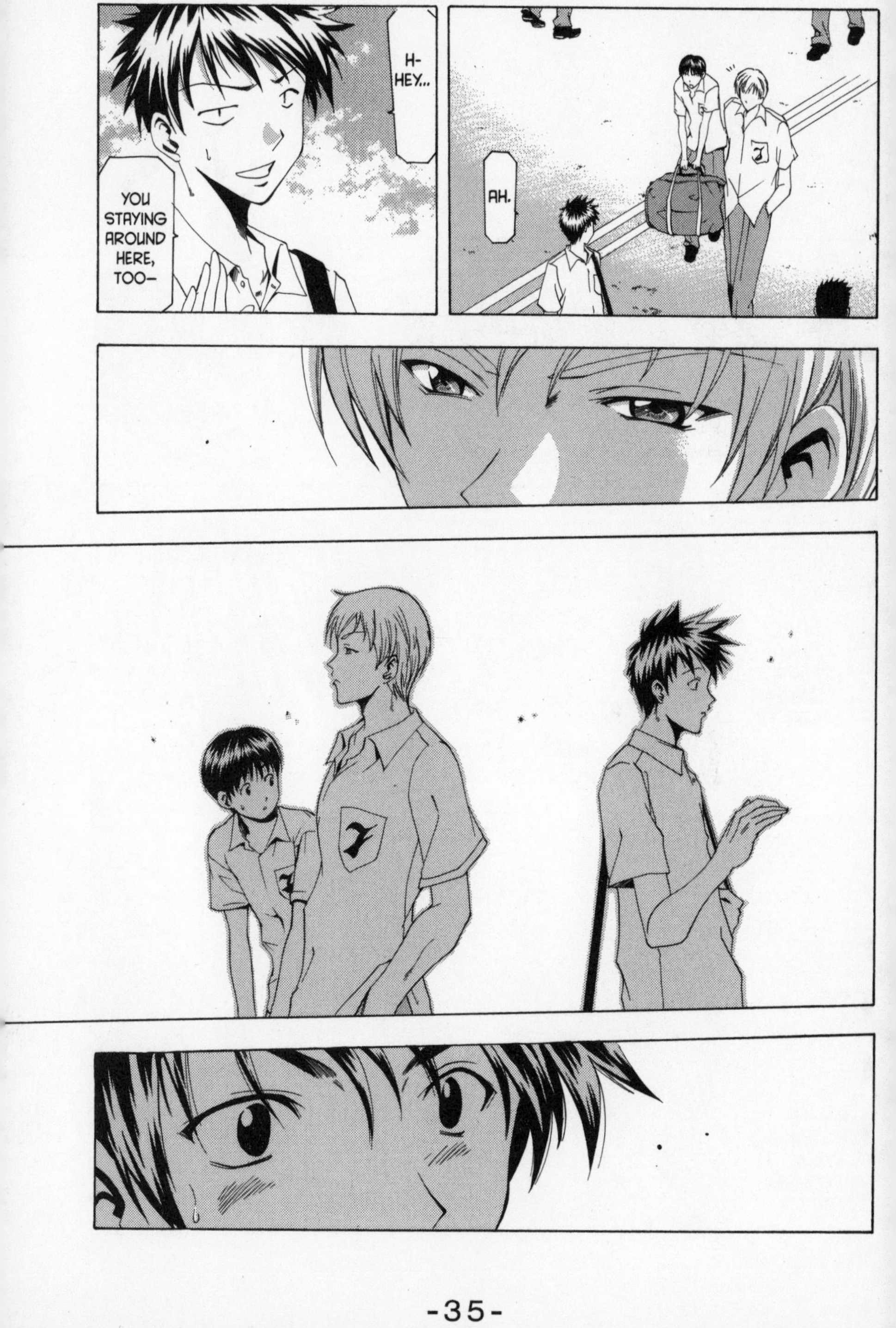
AH.
H- HEY...
YOU STAYING AROUND HERE, TOO—

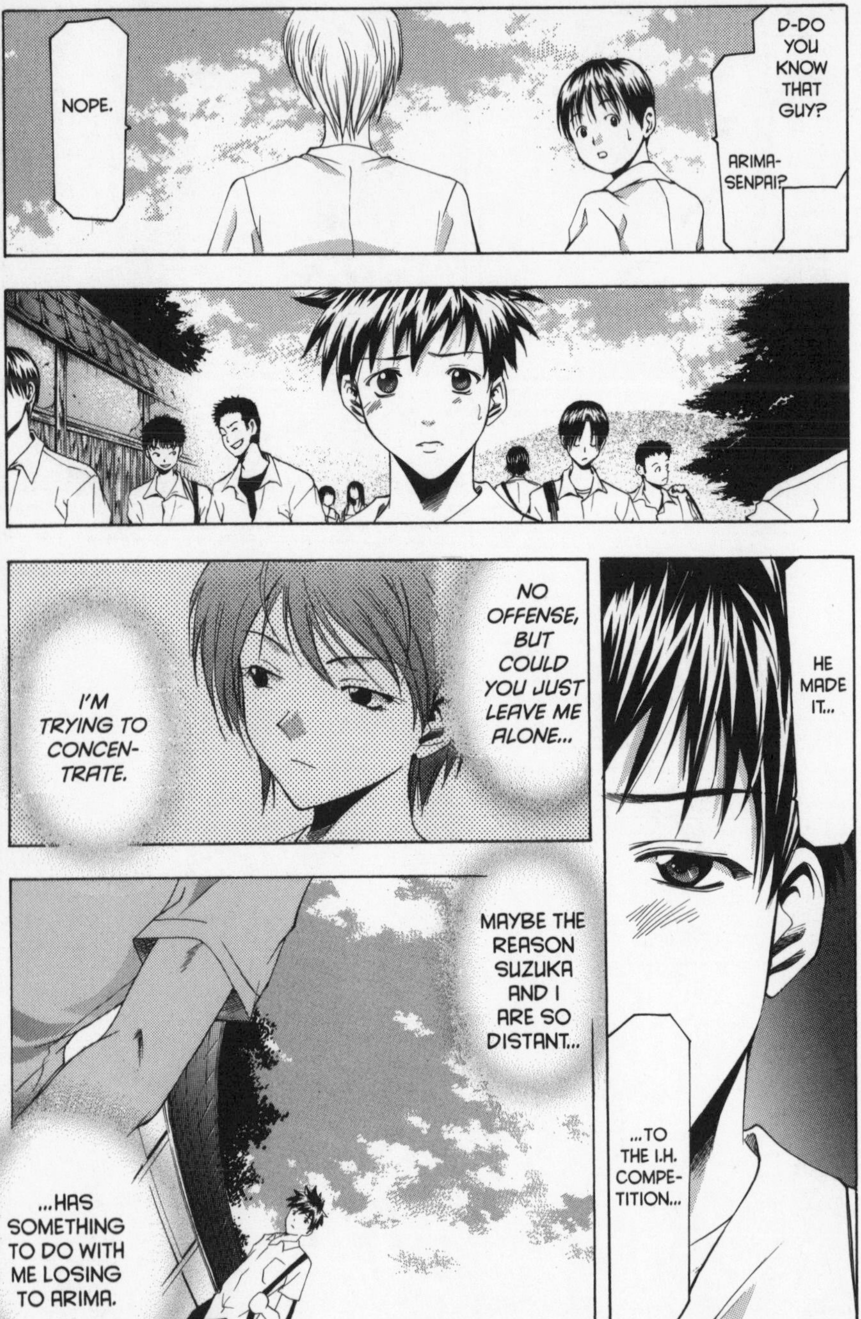
D-DO YOU KNOW THAT GUY?
ARIMA-SENPAI?
NOPE.
HE MADE IT...
...TO THE I.H. COMPETITION...
NO OFFENSE, BUT COULD YOU JUST LEAVE ME ALONE...
I'M TRYING TO CONCENTRATE.
MAYBE THE REASON SUZUKA AND I ARE SO DISTANT...
...HAS SOMETHING TO DO WITH ME LOSING TO ARIMA.

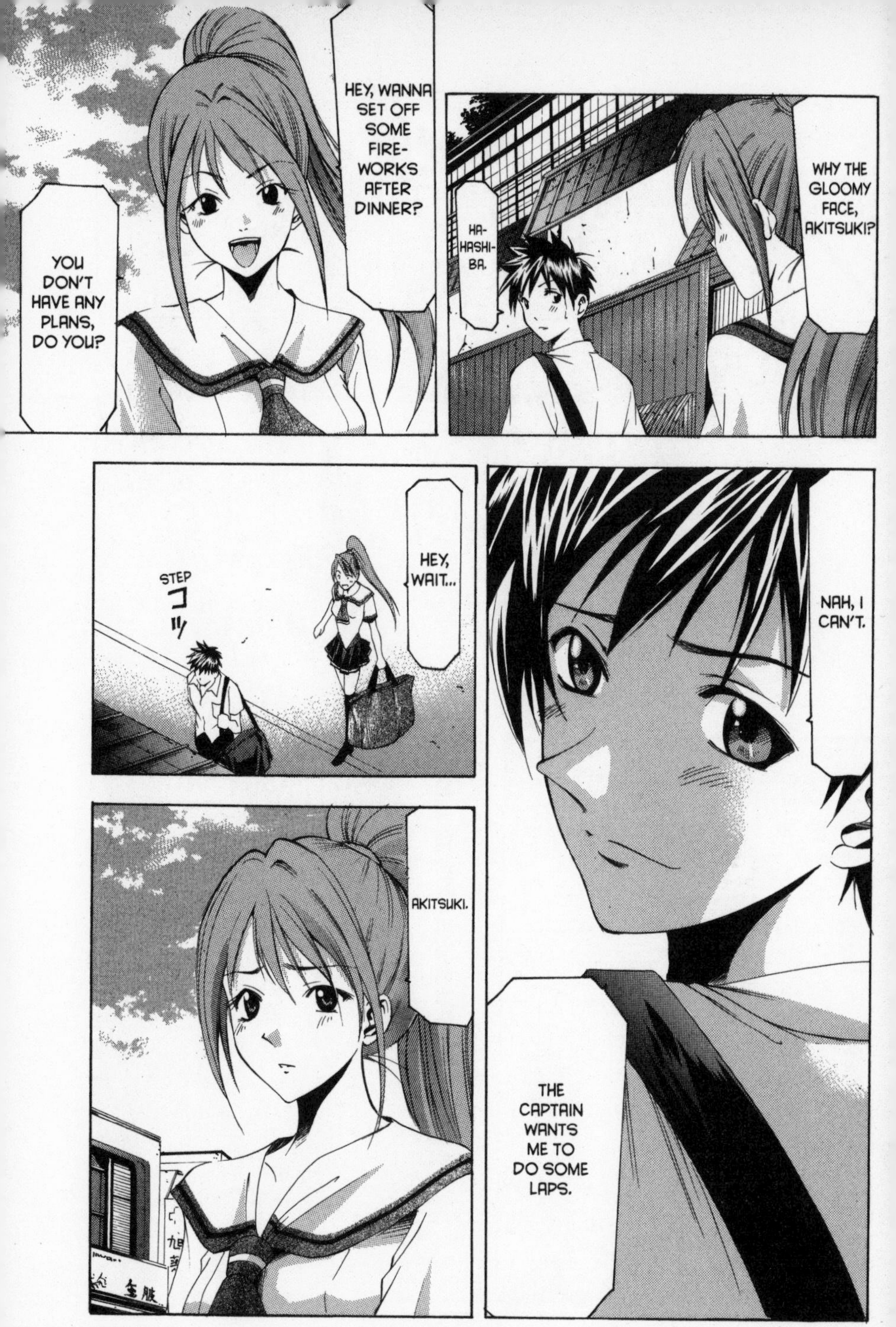
WHY THE GLOOMY FACE, AKITSUKI!?
HA-HASHIBA.
HEY, WANNA SET OFF SOME FIRE-WORKS AFTER DINNER?
YOU DON'T HAVE ANY PLANS, DO YOU?
NAH, I CAN'T.
THE CAPTAIN WANTS ME TO DO SOME LAPS.
HEY, WAIT...
STEP
コツ
AKITSUKI.

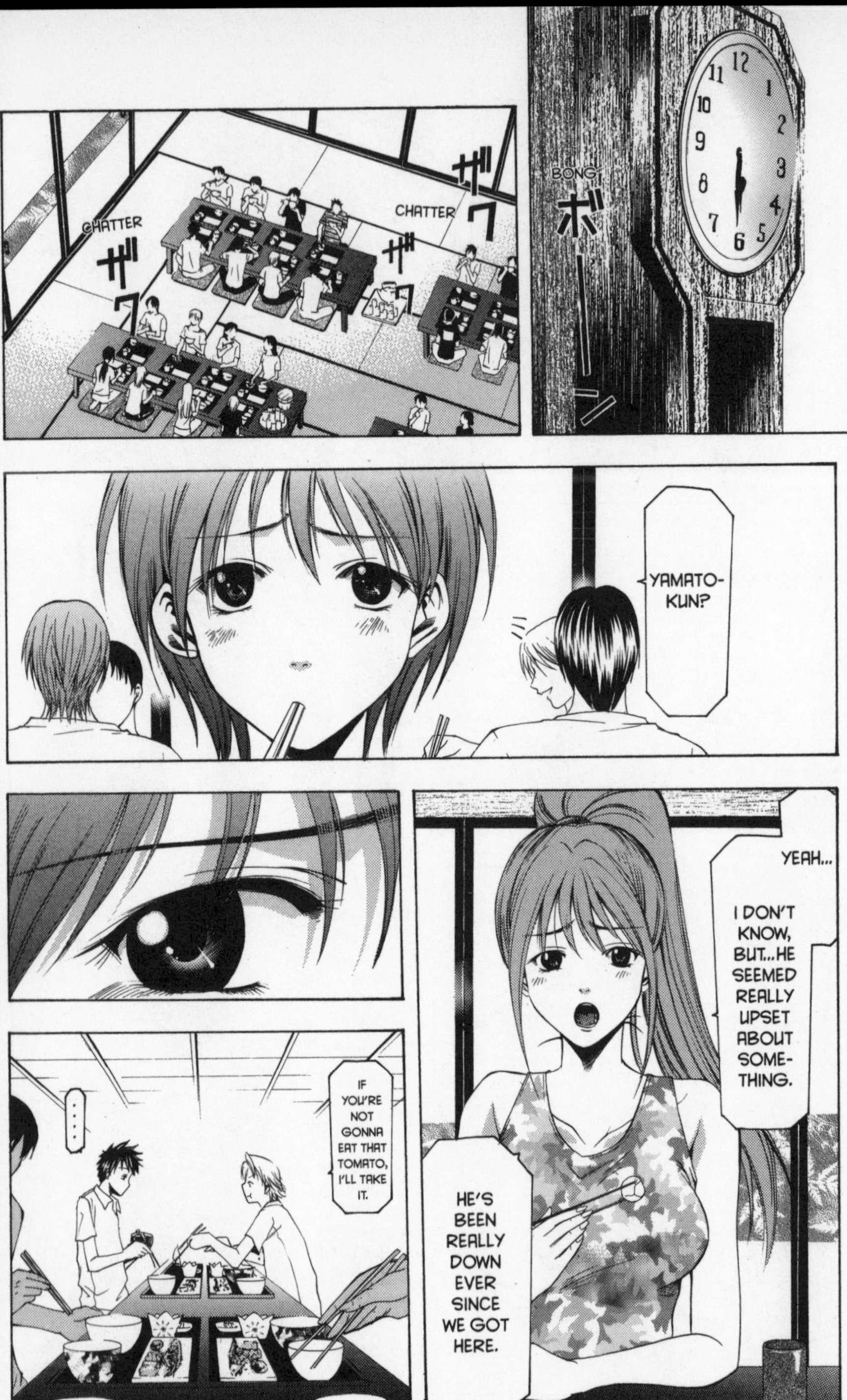
BONG
ボー
CHATTER
ザワ
ザワ
CHATTER
ザワ
YAMATO-KUN?
YEAH...
I DON'T KNOW, BUT...HE SEEMED REALLY UPSET ABOUT SOMETHING.
HE'S BEEN REALLY DOWN EVER SINCE WE GOT HERE.
IF YOU'RE NOT GONNA EAT THAT TOMATO, I'LL TAKE IT.
....

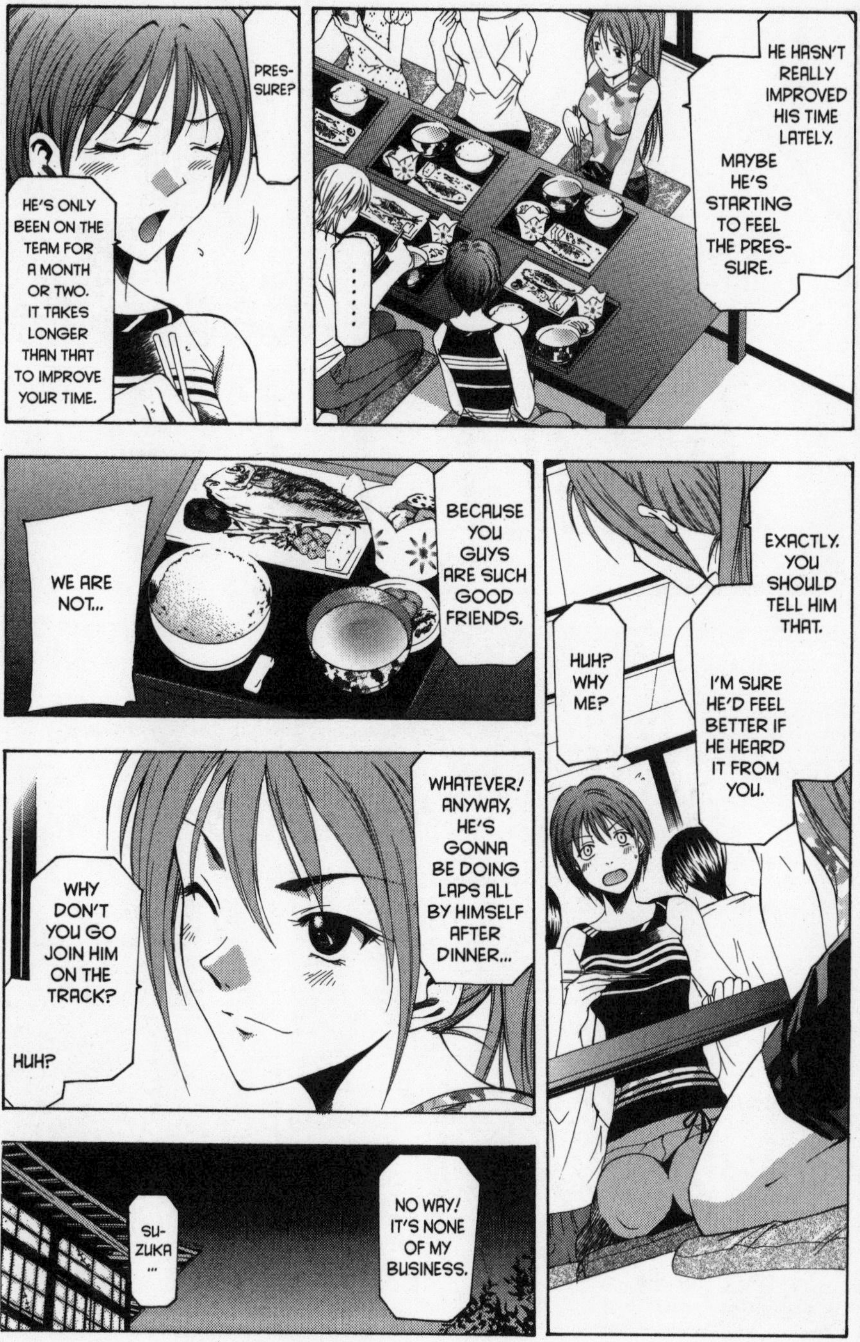
HE HASN'T REALLY IMPROVED HIS TIME LATELY.
MAYBE HE'S STARTING TO FEEL THE PRES-SURE.
......
PRES-SURE?
HE'S ONLY BEEN ON THE TEAM FOR A MONTH OR TWO. IT TAKES LONGER THAN THAT TO IMPROVE YOUR TIME.
EXACTLY. YOU SHOULD TELL HIM THAT.
HUH? WHY ME?
I'M SURE HE'D FEEL BETTER IF HE HEARD IT FROM YOU.
BECAUSE YOU GUYS ARE SUCH GOOD FRIENDS.
WE ARE NOT...
WHATEVER! ANYWAY, HE'S GONNA BE DOING LAPS ALL BY HIMSELF AFTER DINNER...
WHY DON'T YOU GO JOIN HIM ON THE TRACK?
HUH?
NO WAY! IT'S NONE OF MY BUSINESS.
SU-ZUKA ...

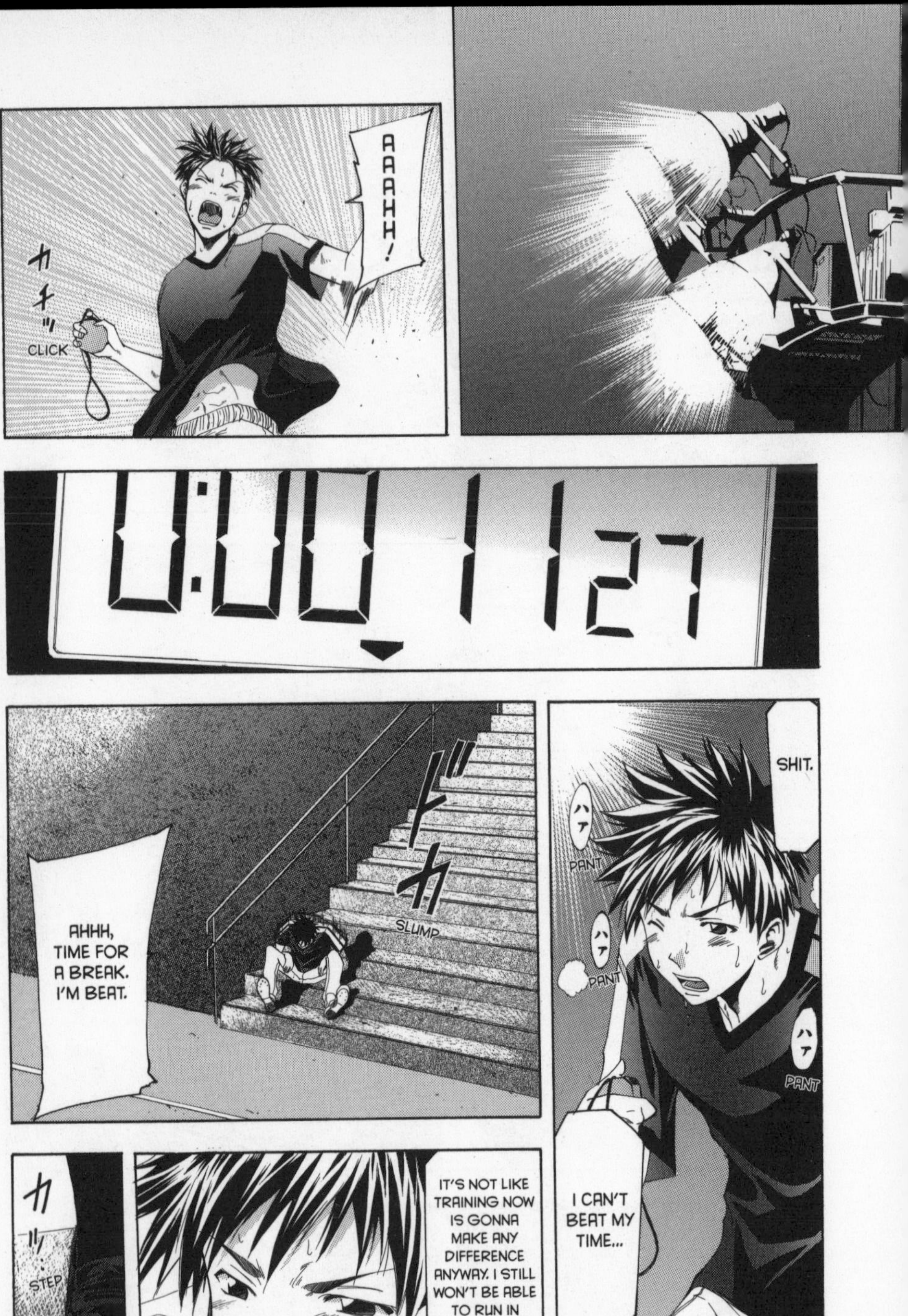
AAAAHH!
カチッ
CLICK
0:00 11 27
SHIT.
ハァ
PANT
ハァ
PANT
ハァ
PANT
I CAN'T BEAT MY TIME...
ドカ
SLUMP
AHHH, TIME FOR A BREAK. I'M BEAT.
IT'S NOT LIKE TRAINING NOW IS GONNA MAKE ANY DIFFERENCE ANYWAY. I STILL WON'T BE ABLE TO RUN IN TOMORROW'S RACE.
カッ
STEP

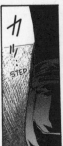

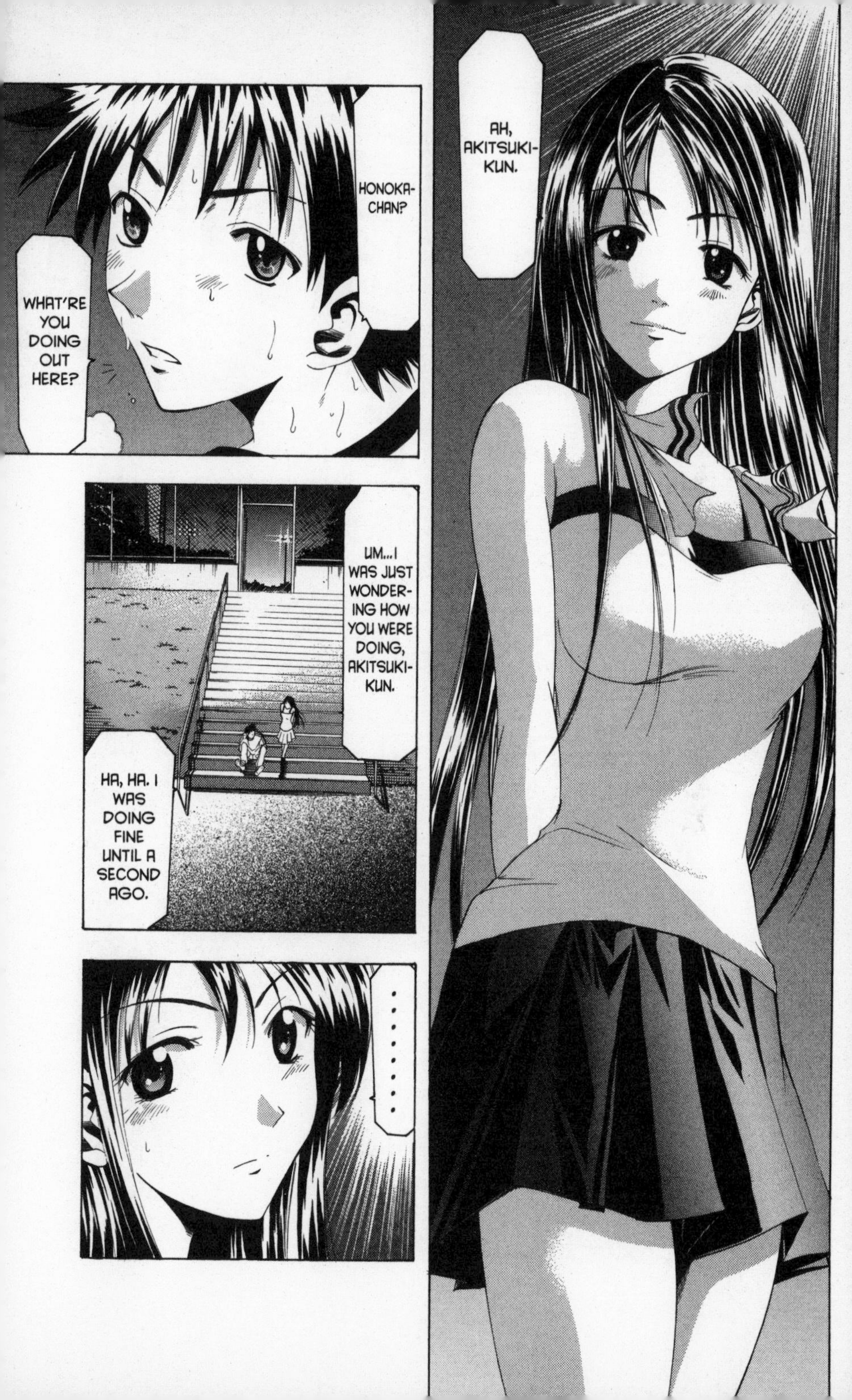
AH, AKITSUKI-KUN.
HONOKA-CHAN?
WHAT'RE YOU DOING OUT HERE?
UM...I WAS JUST WONDERING HOW YOU WERE DOING, AKITSUKI-KUN.
HA, HA. I WAS DOING FINE UNTIL A SECOND AGO.
....

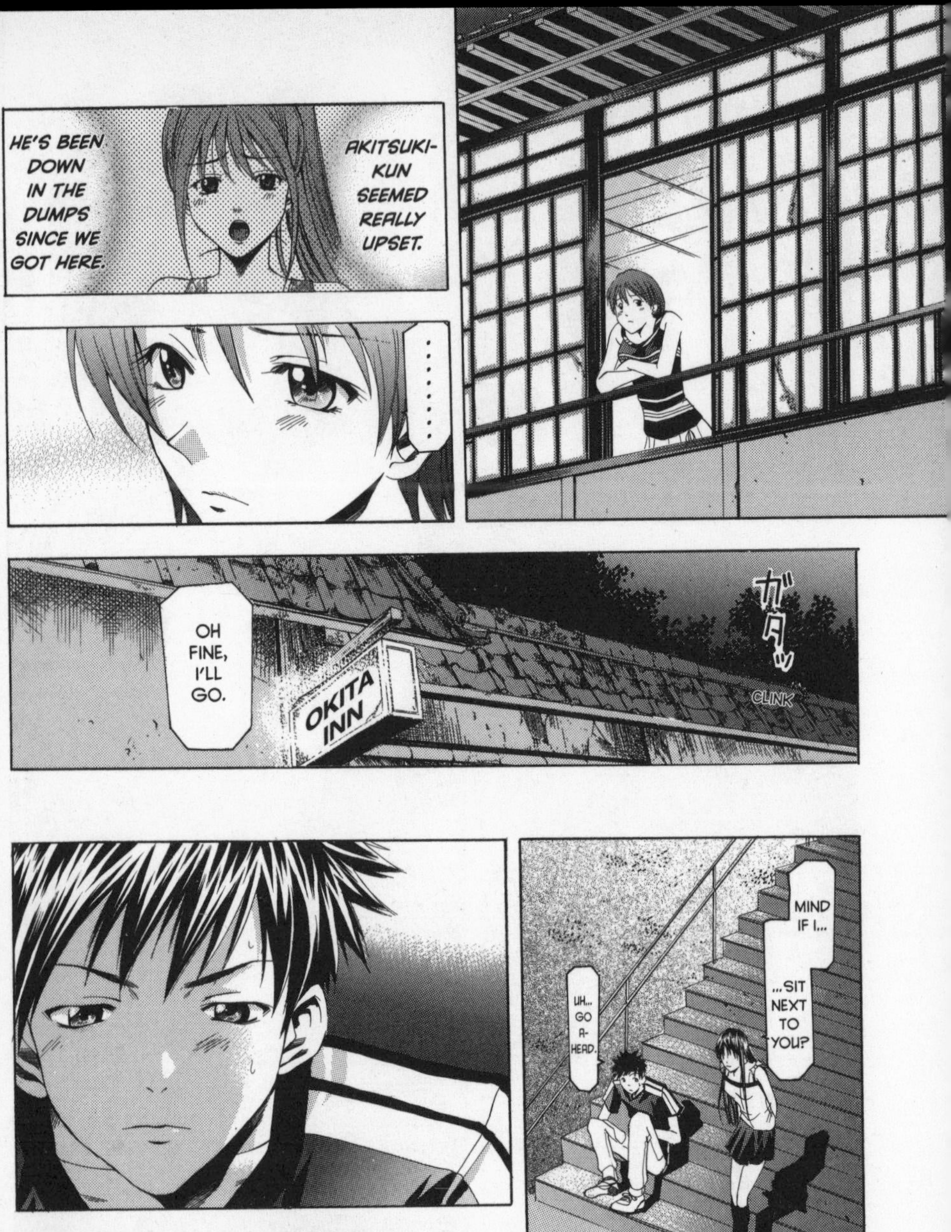
AKITSUKI-KUN SEEMED REALLY UPSET.
HE'S BEEN DOWN IN THE DUMPS SINCE WE GOT HERE.
......
ガタッ
CLINK
OKITA INN
OH FINE, I'LL GO.
MIND IF I...
...SIT NEXT TO YOU?
UH... GO A-HEAD.
HE'S DEFI-NITELY...
...UPSET ABOUT SOME-THING.

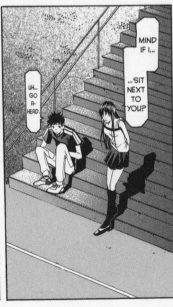

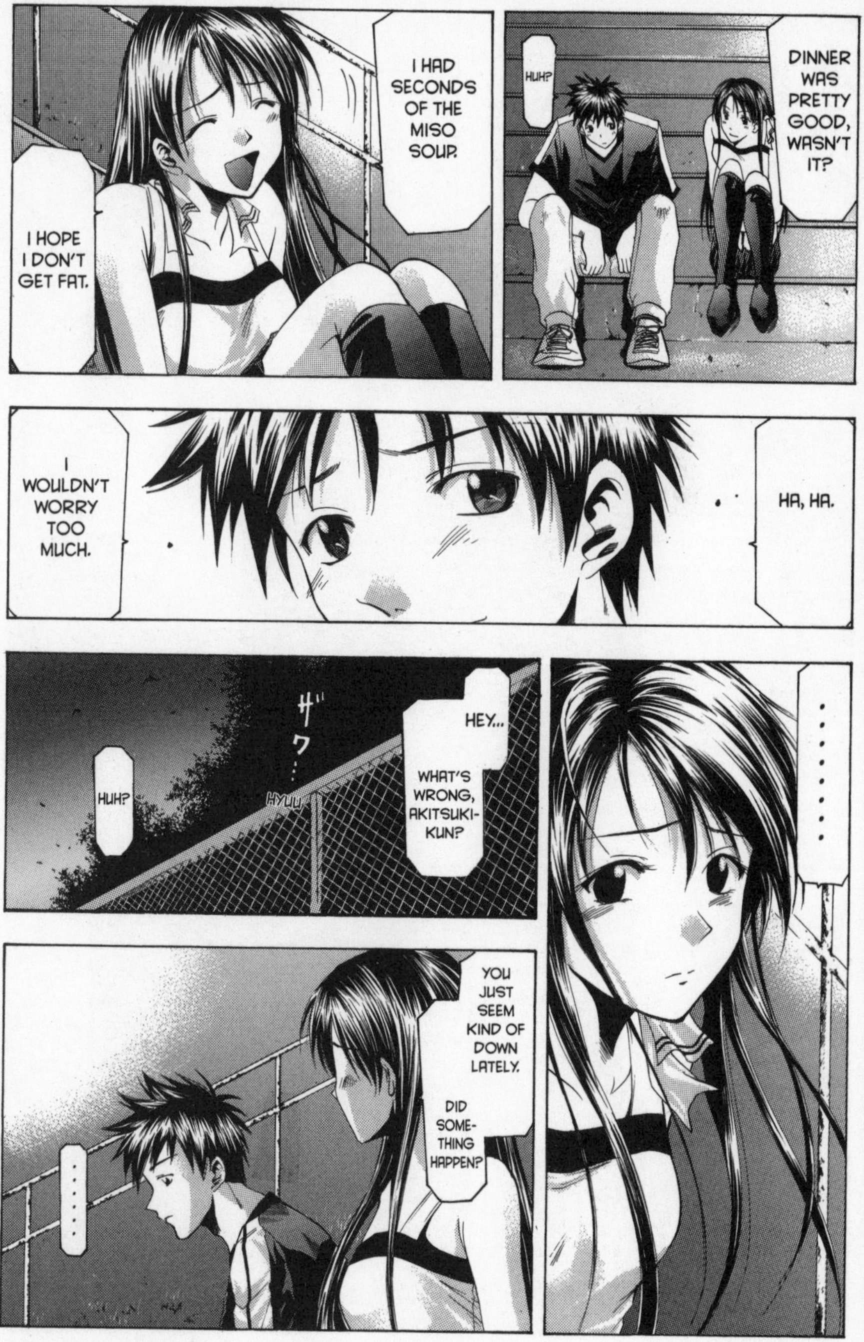
DINNER WAS PRETTY GOOD, WASN'T IT?
HUH?
I HAD SECONDS OF THE MISO SOUP.
I HOPE I DON'T GET FAT.
HA, HA.
I WOULDN'T WORRY TOO MUCH.
......
HEY...
WHAT'S WRONG, AKITSUKI-KUN?
ザワ...
HYUU
HUH?
YOU JUST SEEM KIND OF DOWN LATELY.
DID SOME-THING HAPPEN?
......

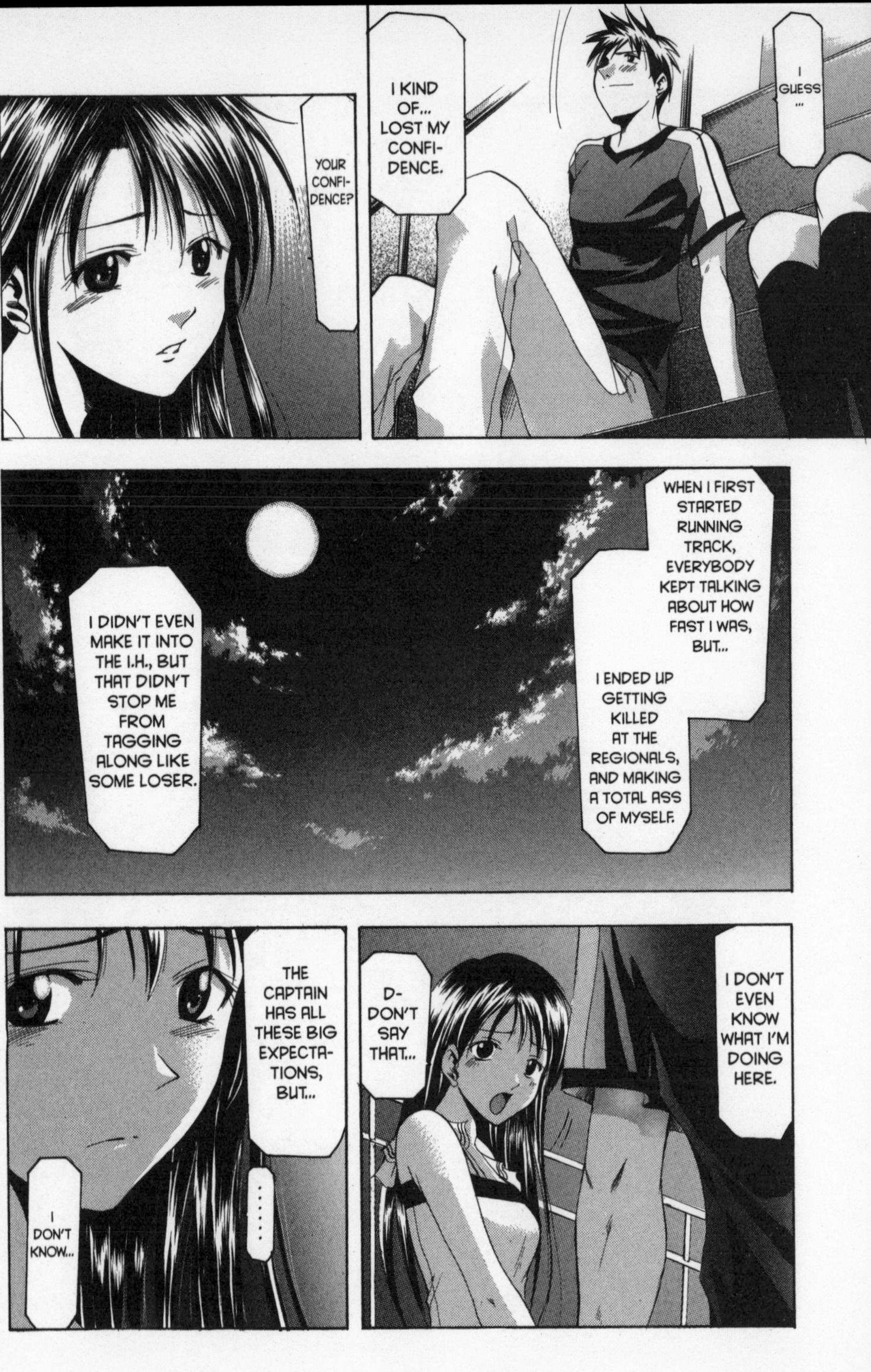
I GUESS...
I KIND OF... LOST MY CONFI-DENCE.
YOUR CONFI-DENCE?
WHEN I FIRST STARTED RUNNING TRACK, EVERYBODY KEPT TALKING ABOUT HOW FAST I WAS, BUT...
I ENDED UP GETTING KILLED AT THE REGIONALS, AND MAKING A TOTAL ASS OF MYSELF.
I DIDN'T EVEN MAKE IT INTO THE I.H., BUT THAT DIDN'T STOP ME FROM TAGGING ALONG LIKE SOME LOSER.
I DON'T EVEN KNOW WHAT I'M DOING HERE.
D-DON'T SAY THAT...
THE CAPTAIN HAS ALL THESE BIG EXPECTA-TIONS, BUT...
......
I DON'T KNOW...

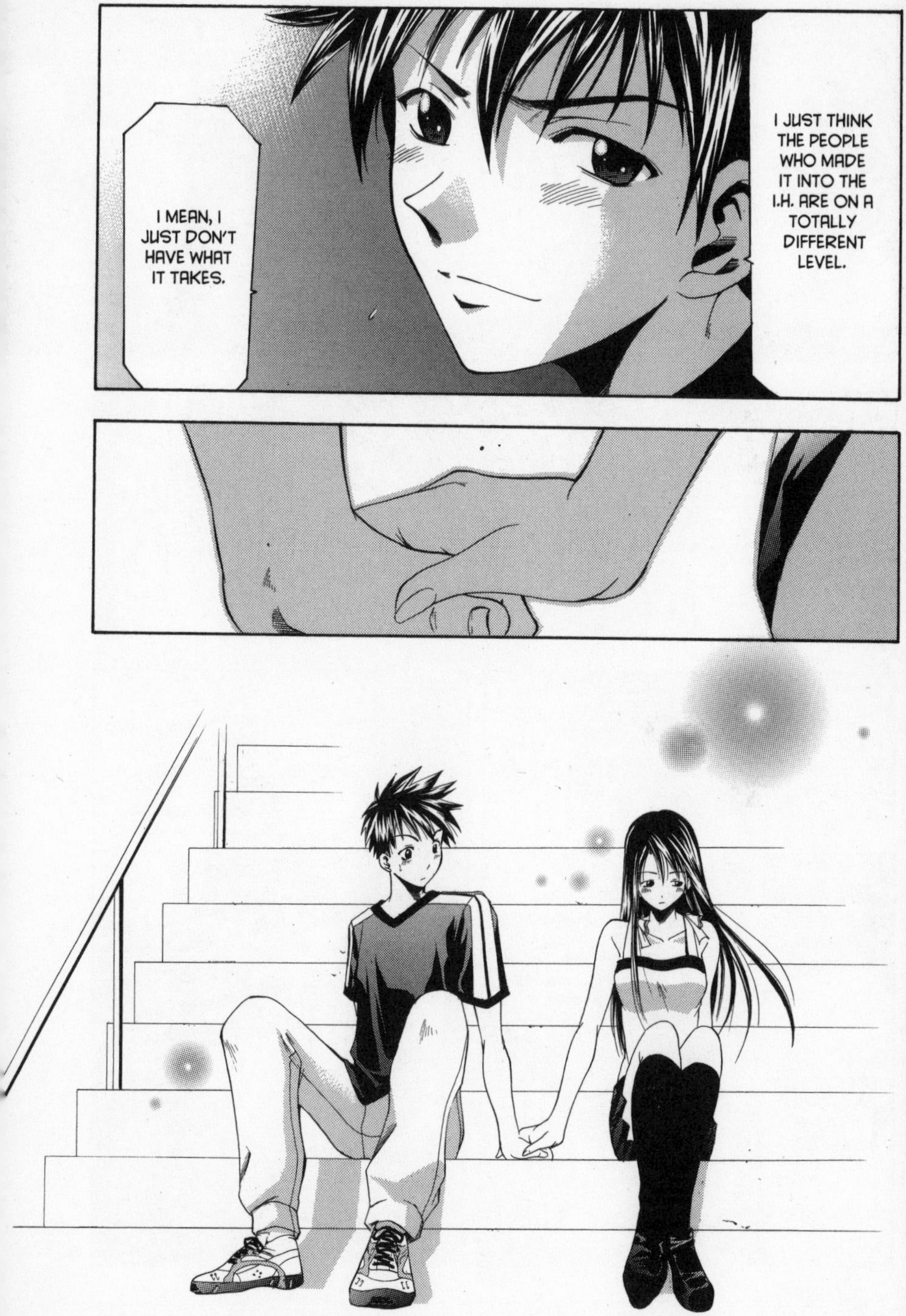
I JUST THINK THE PEOPLE WHO MADE IT INTO THE I.H. ARE ON A TOTALLY DIFFERENT LEVEL.
I MEAN, I JUST DON'T HAVE WHAT IT TAKES.

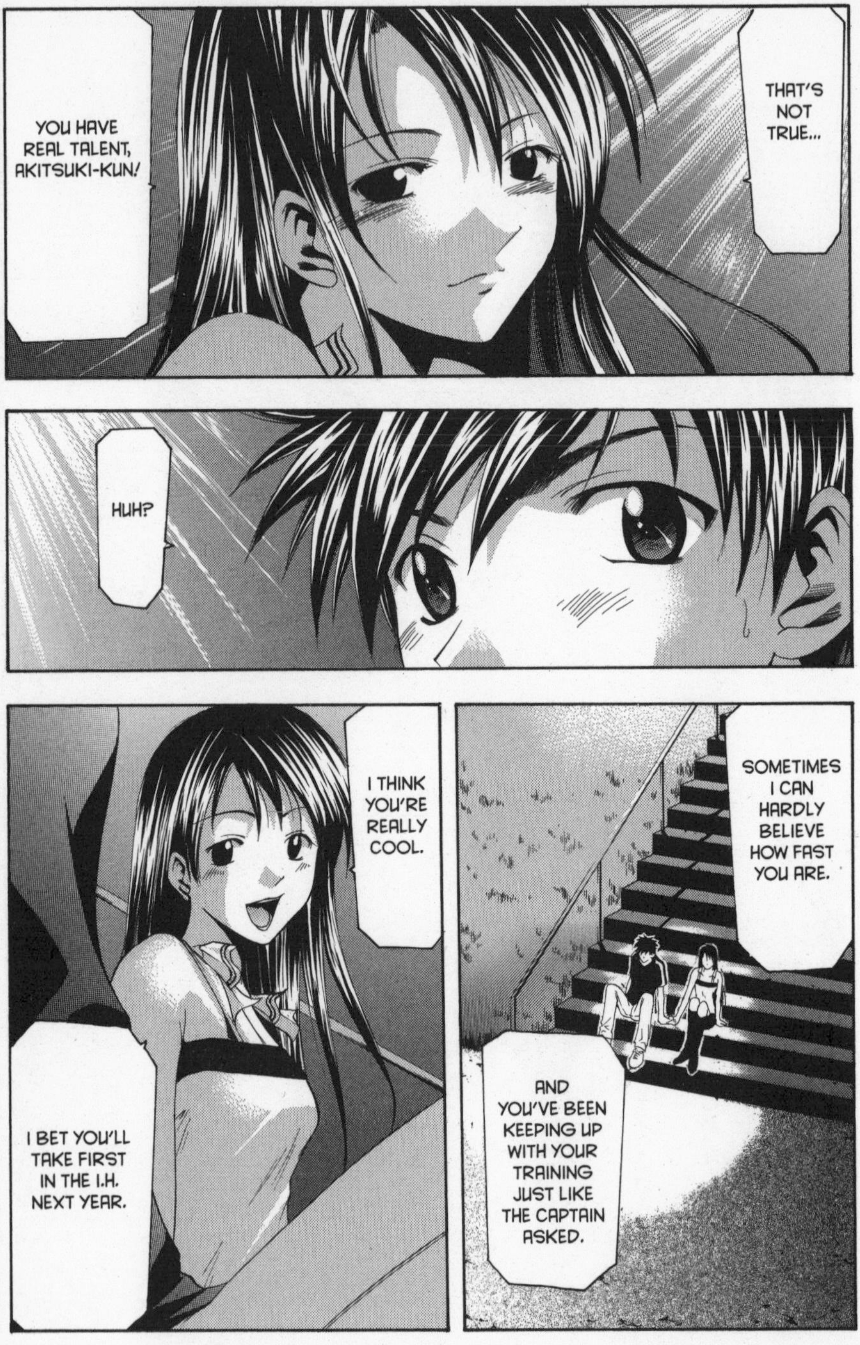
THAT'S NOT TRUE...
YOU HAVE REAL TALENT, AKITSUKI-KUN!
HUH?
SOMETIMES I CAN HARDLY BELIEVE HOW FAST YOU ARE.
AND YOU'VE BEEN KEEPING UP WITH YOUR TRAINING JUST LIKE THE CAPTAIN ASKED.
I THINK YOU'RE REALLY COOL.
I BET YOU'LL TAKE FIRST IN THE I.H. NEXT YEAR.

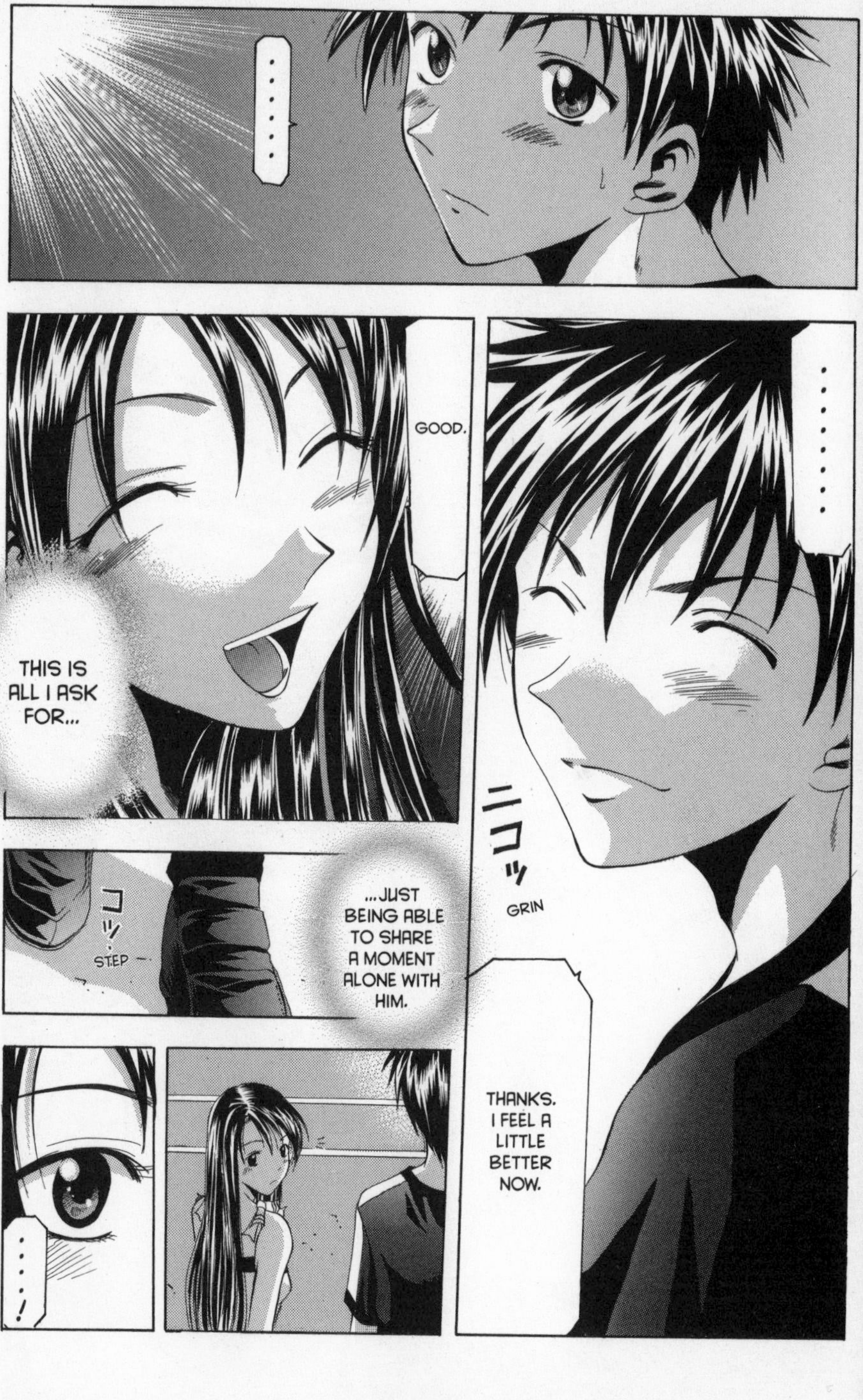
......
....
ニコッ
GRIN
THANKS. I FEEL A LITTLE BETTER NOW.
GOOD.
THIS IS ALL I ASK FOR...
コツ
STEP
...JUST BEING ABLE TO SHARE A MOMENT ALONE WITH HIM.
....!

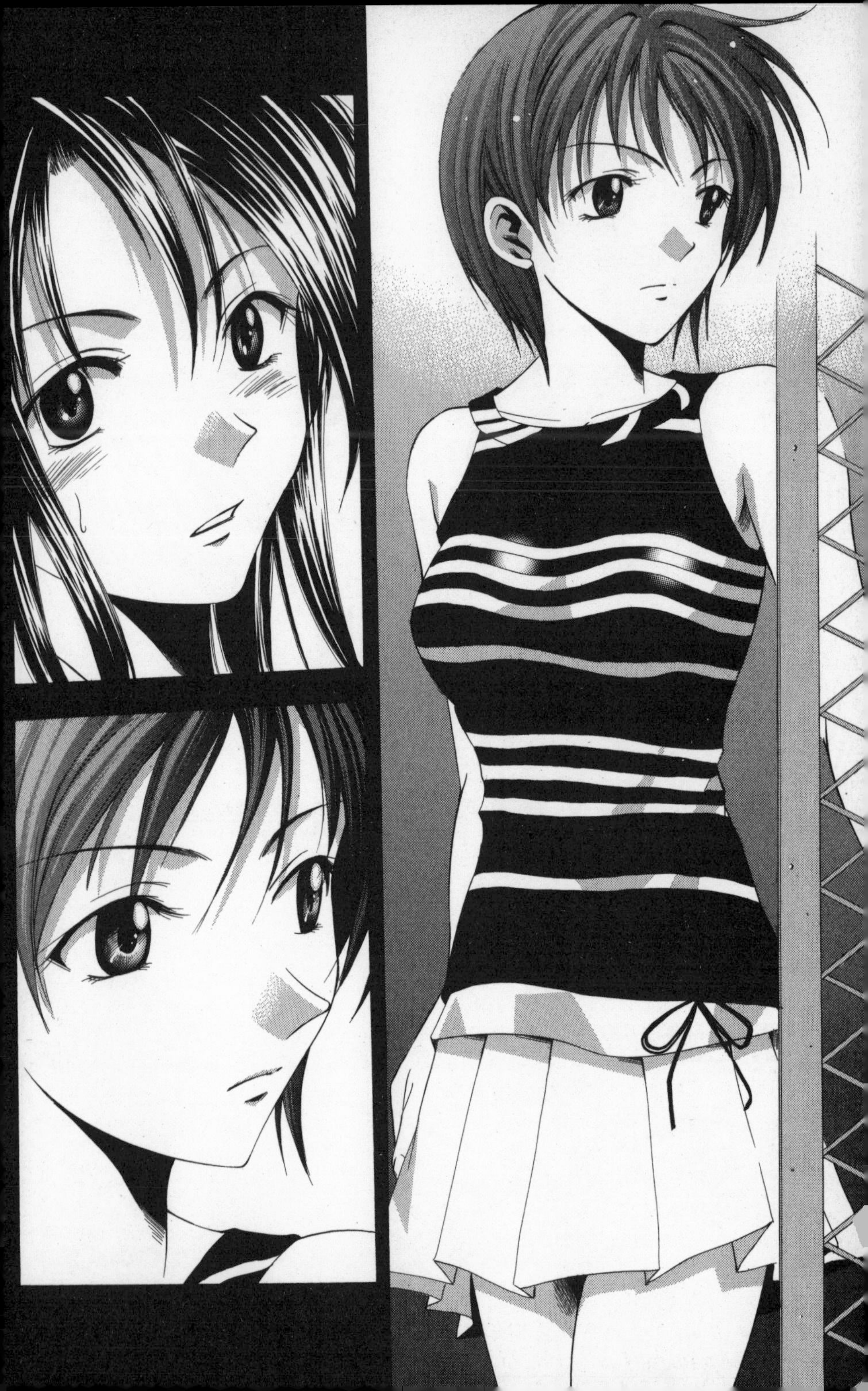

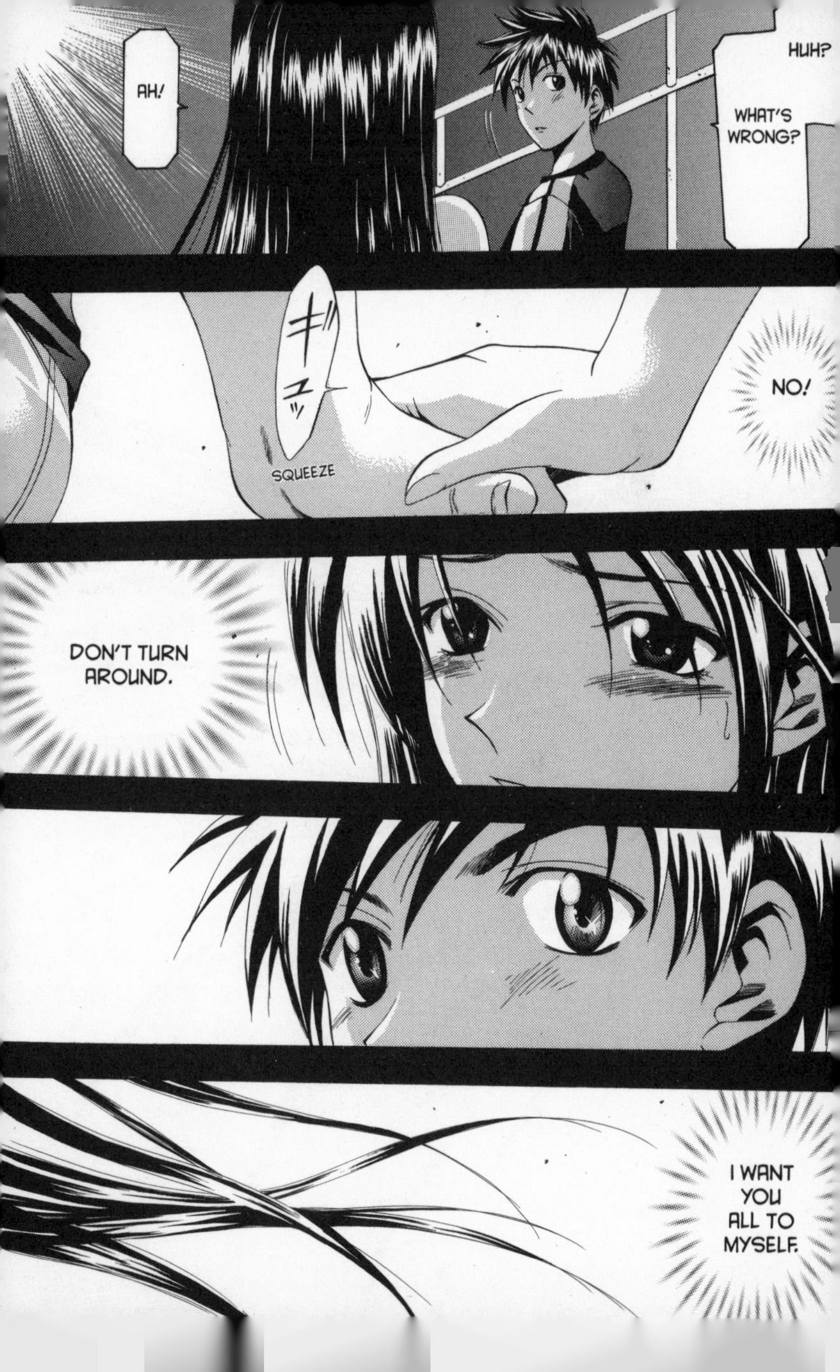
HUH?
WHAT'S WRONG?
AH!
NO!
ギュッ
SQUEEZE
DON'T TURN AROUND.
I WANT YOU ALL TO MYSELF.

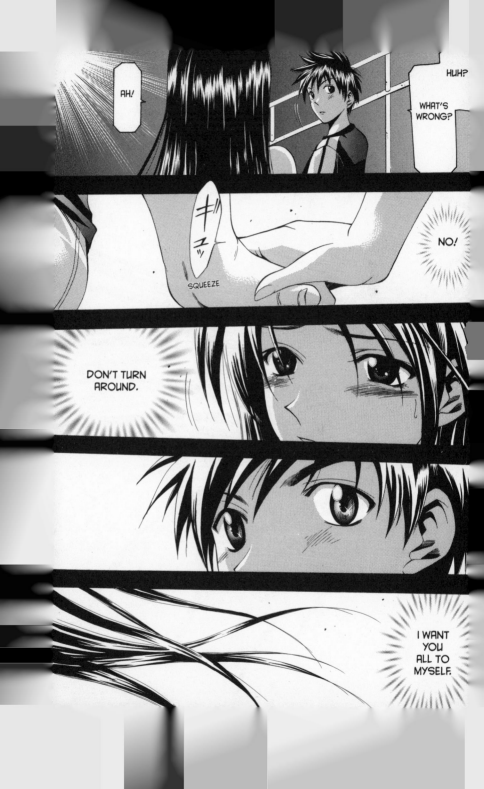

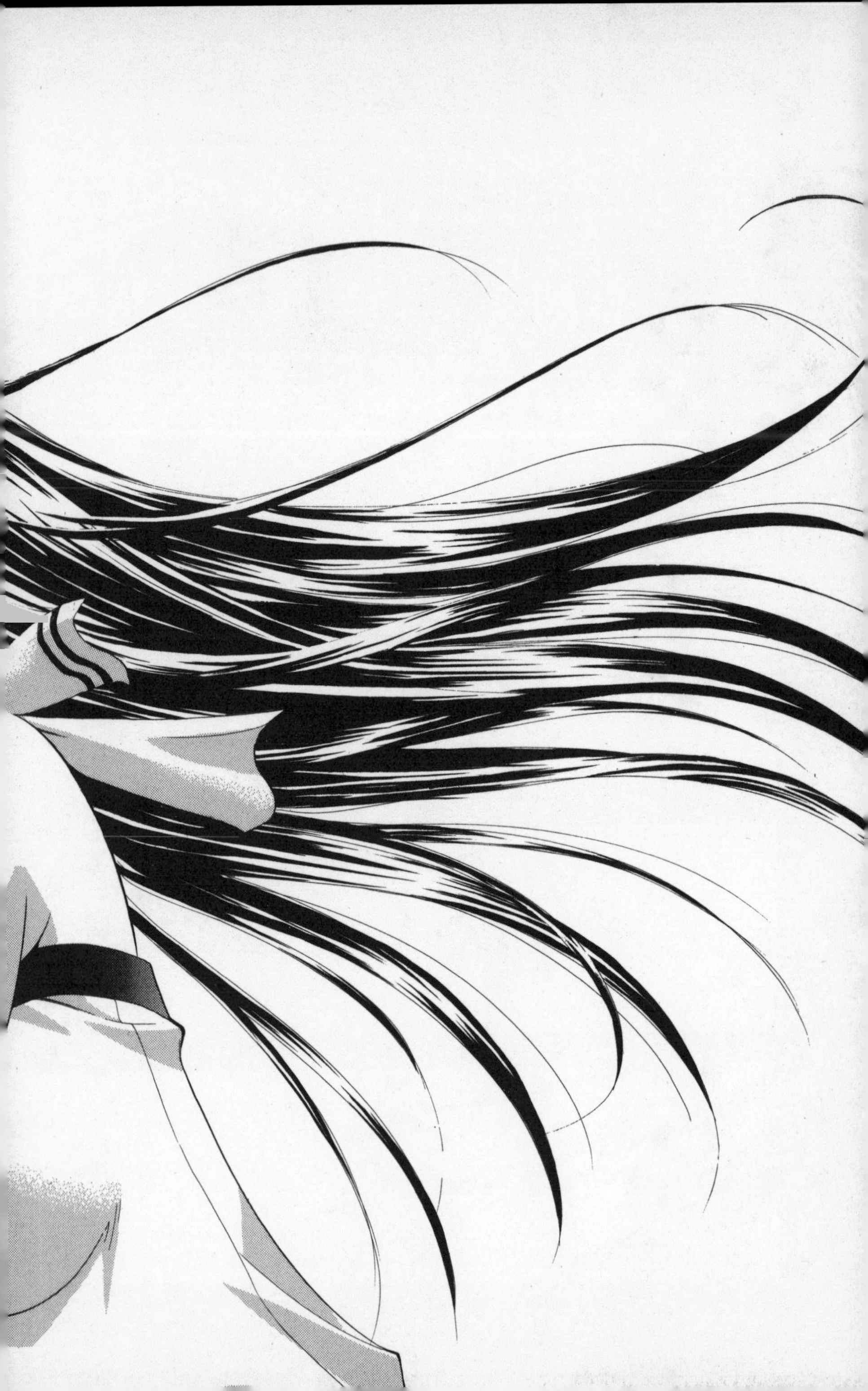

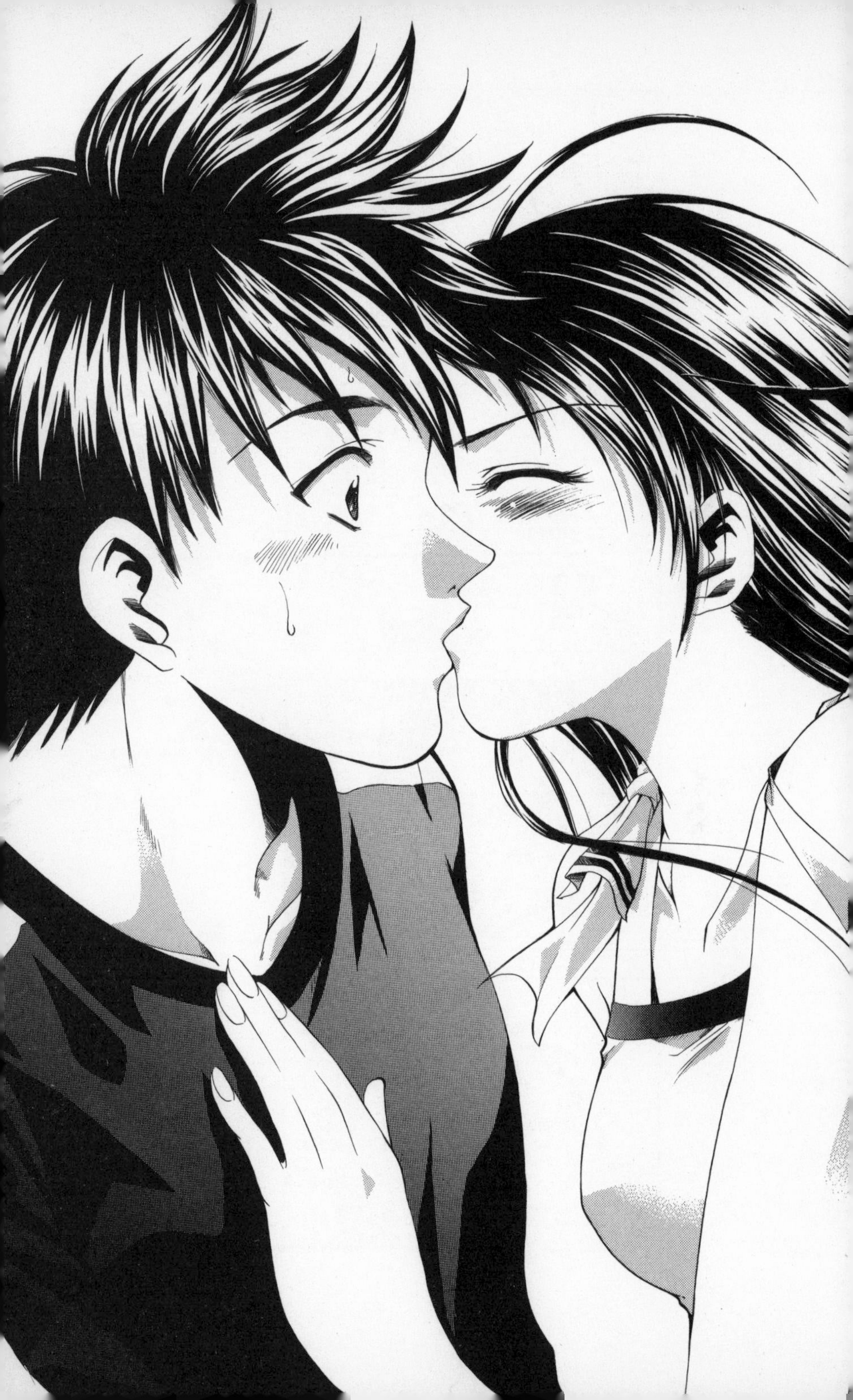

SUZUKA FOUR-PANEL THEATER NUMBER EIGHTEEN

MANGA CRIT

A JOURNALIST CAME TO INTERVIEW ME FOR AN ARTICLE HE WAS DOING CALLED "THE WAY OF MANGA."
SO...
SO...I DEFINITELY DO KEEP THAT IN MIND.
WOW, SEO-SAN REALLY THINKS ABOUT WHAT HE DRAWS.
EDITOR S-KI-SAN (29)
THE FOLLOWING DAY...
THE ENDING IS WAY DIFFERENT...
...FROM WHAT WE TALKED ABOUT IN THE MEETING.
YEAH. AND IT'S BORING, TOO.
BUT THERE'S GOTTA BE SOME DEEP HIDDEN MEANING TO THIS!
SEO-SAN THINKS REALLY HARD ABOUT HIS STORIES.
HE MUST BE SETTING SOMETHING UP.
OH YEAH, I FORGOT ALL ABOUT THE ENDING WE CAME UP WITH IN THAT MEETING.
WHAT?
SHOCK
OOPS.

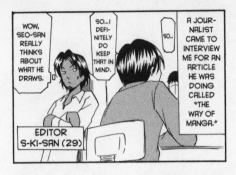

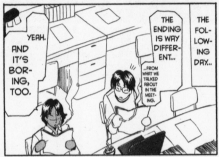

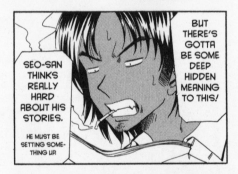

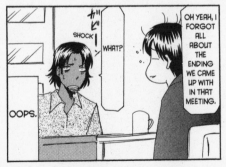

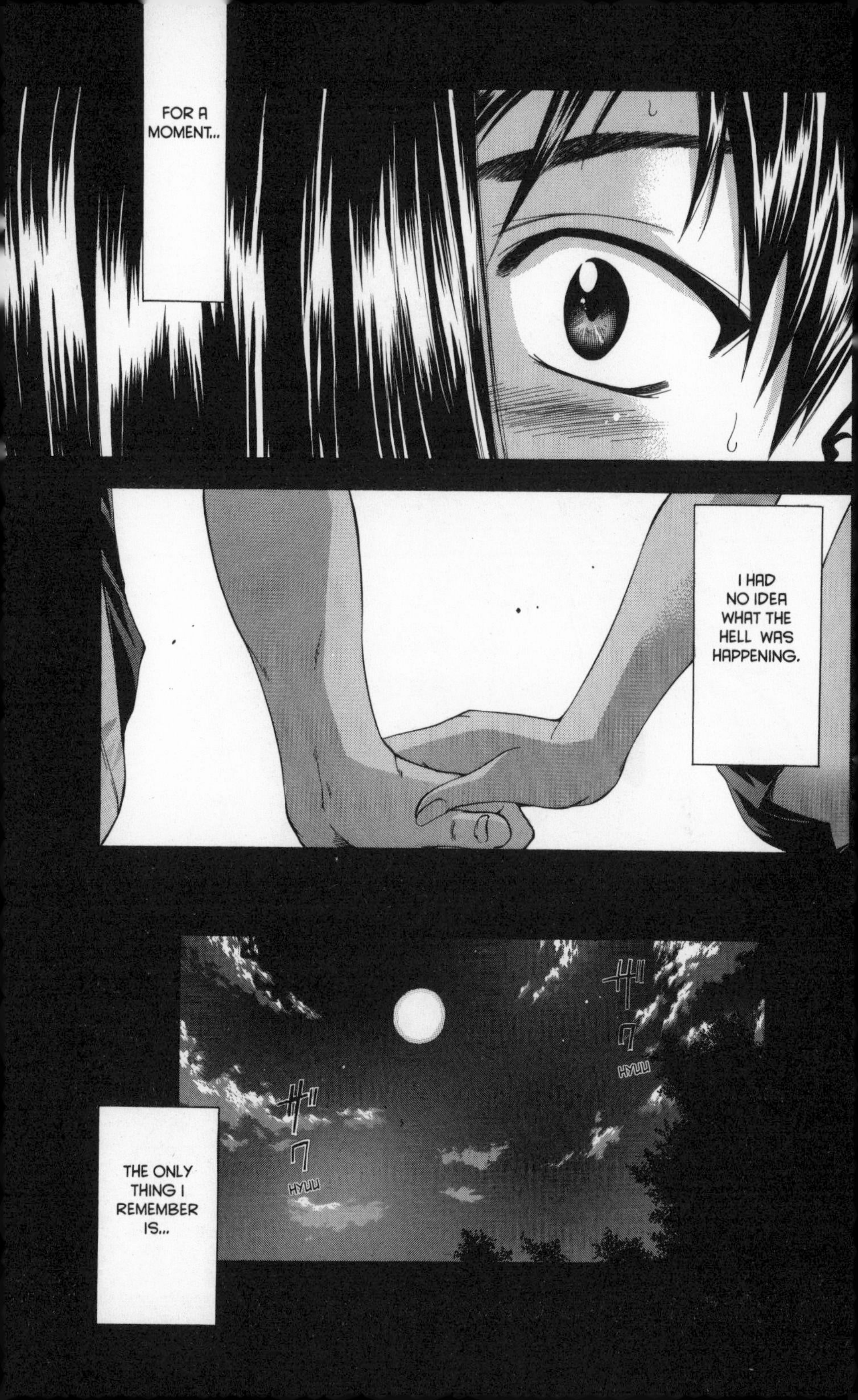

FOR A MOMENT...
I HAD NO IDEA WHAT THE HELL WAS HAPPENING.
HYUU
HYUU
THE ONLY THING I REMEMBER IS...

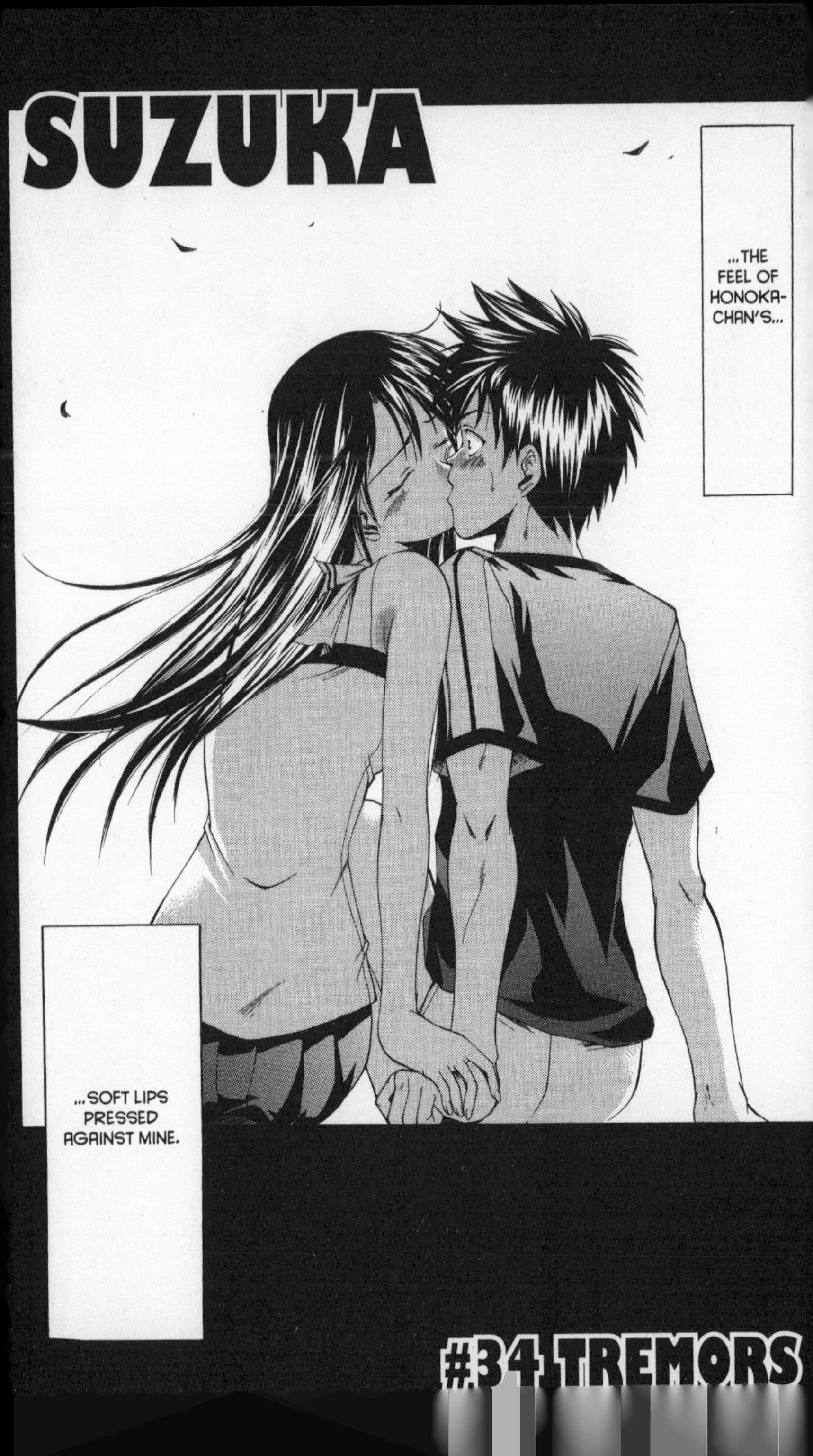
SUZUKA
...THE FEEL OF HONOKA-CHAN'S...
...SOFT LIPS PRESSED AGAINST MINE.
#34 TREMORS

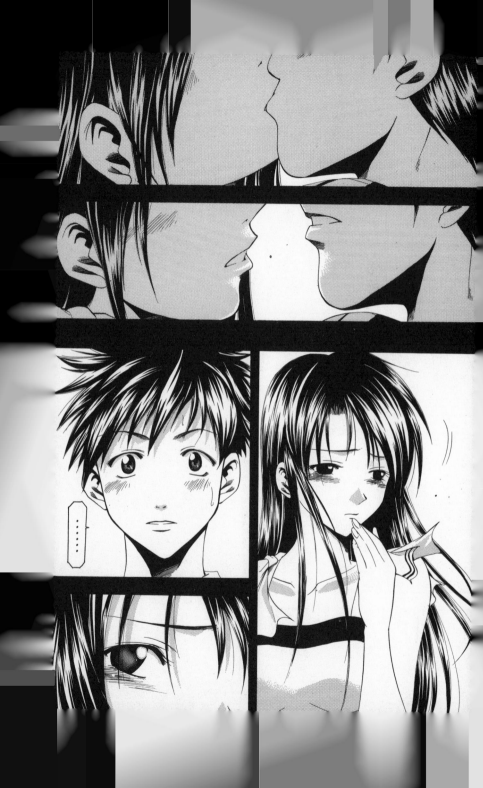

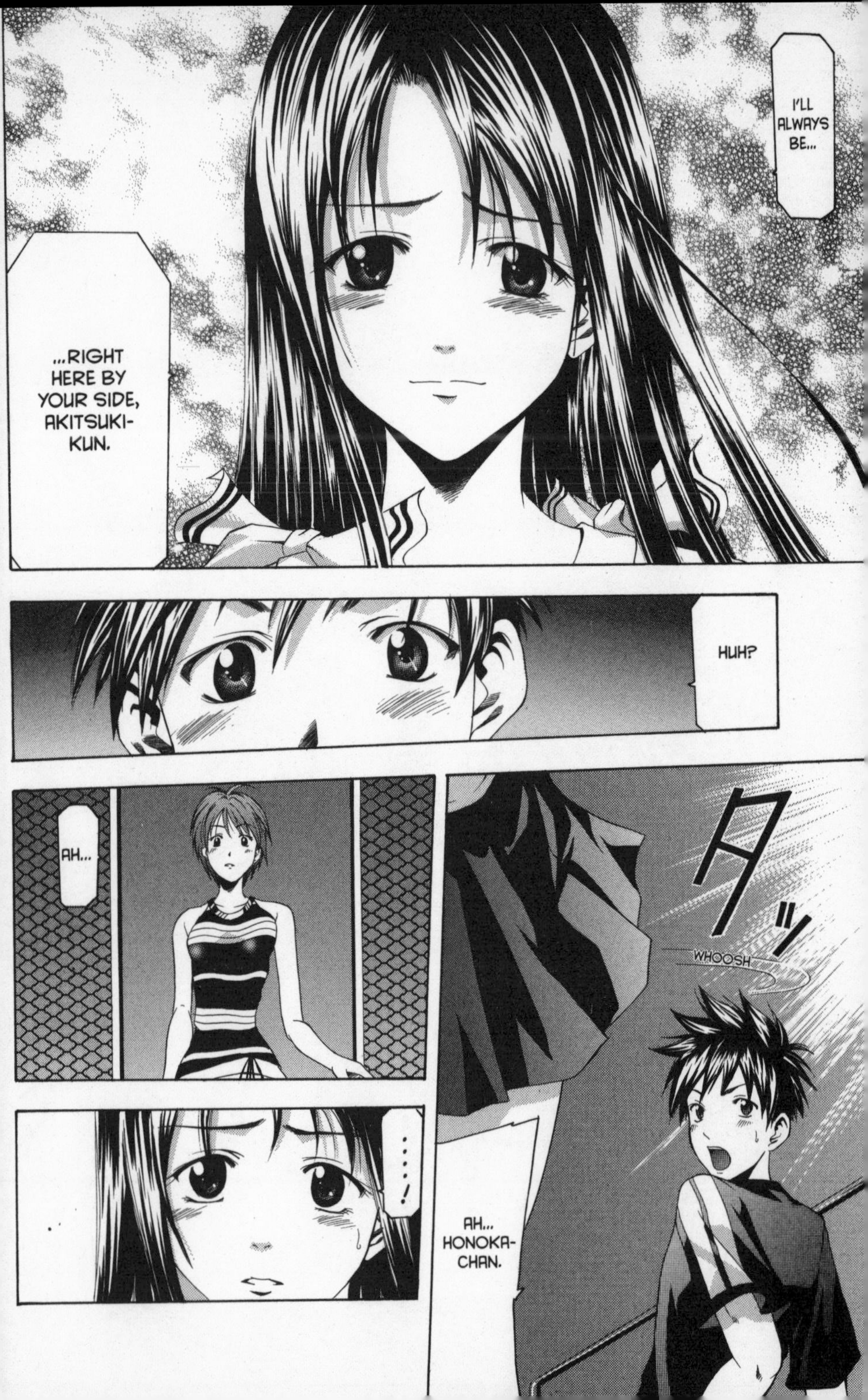
I'LL ALWAYS BE...
...RIGHT HERE BY YOUR SIDE, AKITSUKI-KUN.
HUH?
WHOOSH
AH... HONOKA-CHAN.
AH...
....!

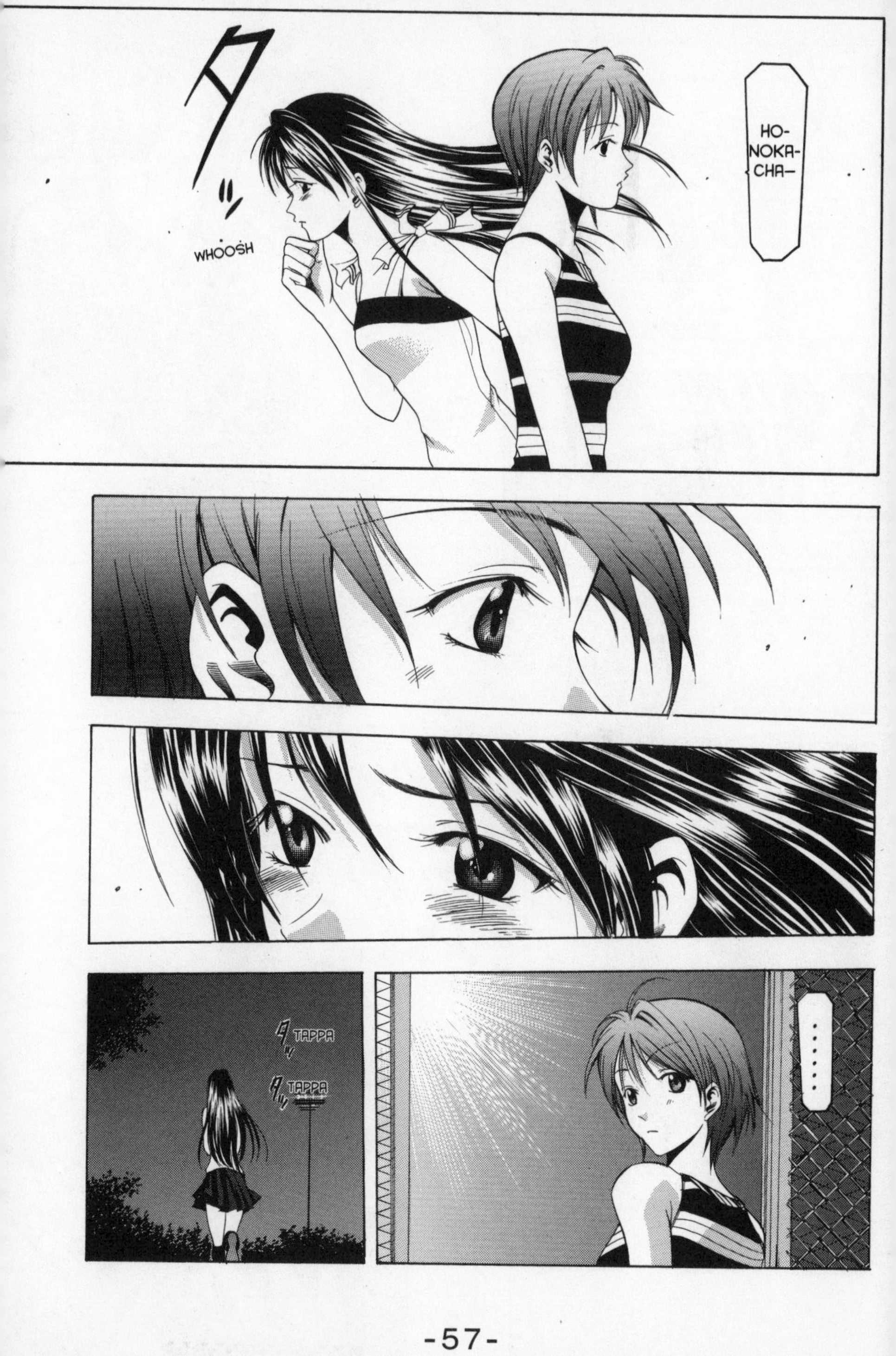
HO-NOKA-CHA—
WHOOSH
......
TAPPA
TAPPA

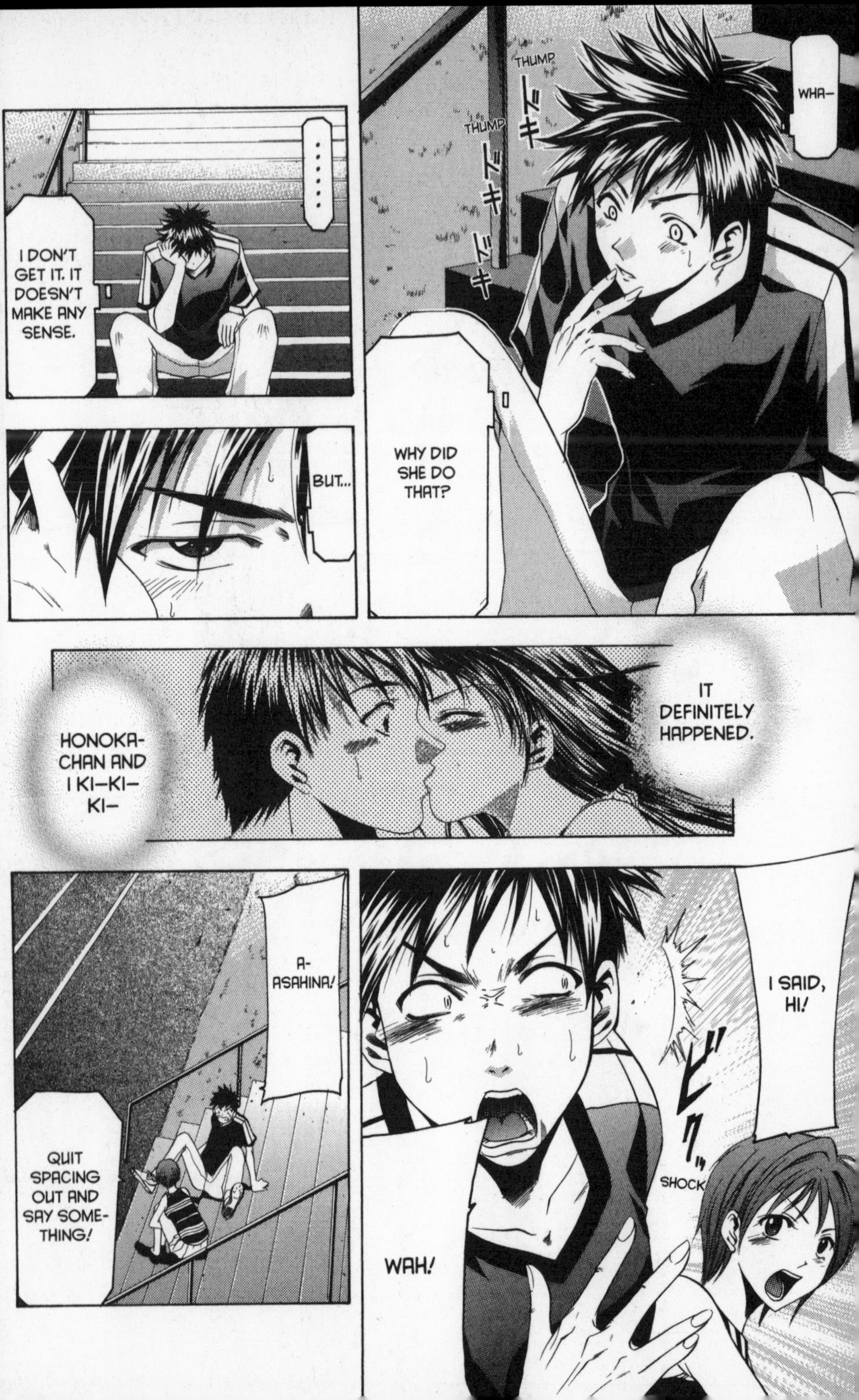
WHA-
THUMP
THUMP
WHY DID SHE DO THAT?
......
I DON'T GET IT. IT DOESN'T MAKE ANY SENSE.
BUT...
IT DEFINITELY HAPPENED.
HONOKA-CHAN AND I KI-KI-KI-
I SAID, HI!
SHOCK
WAH!
A-ASAHINA!
QUIT SPACING OUT AND SAY SOME-THING!

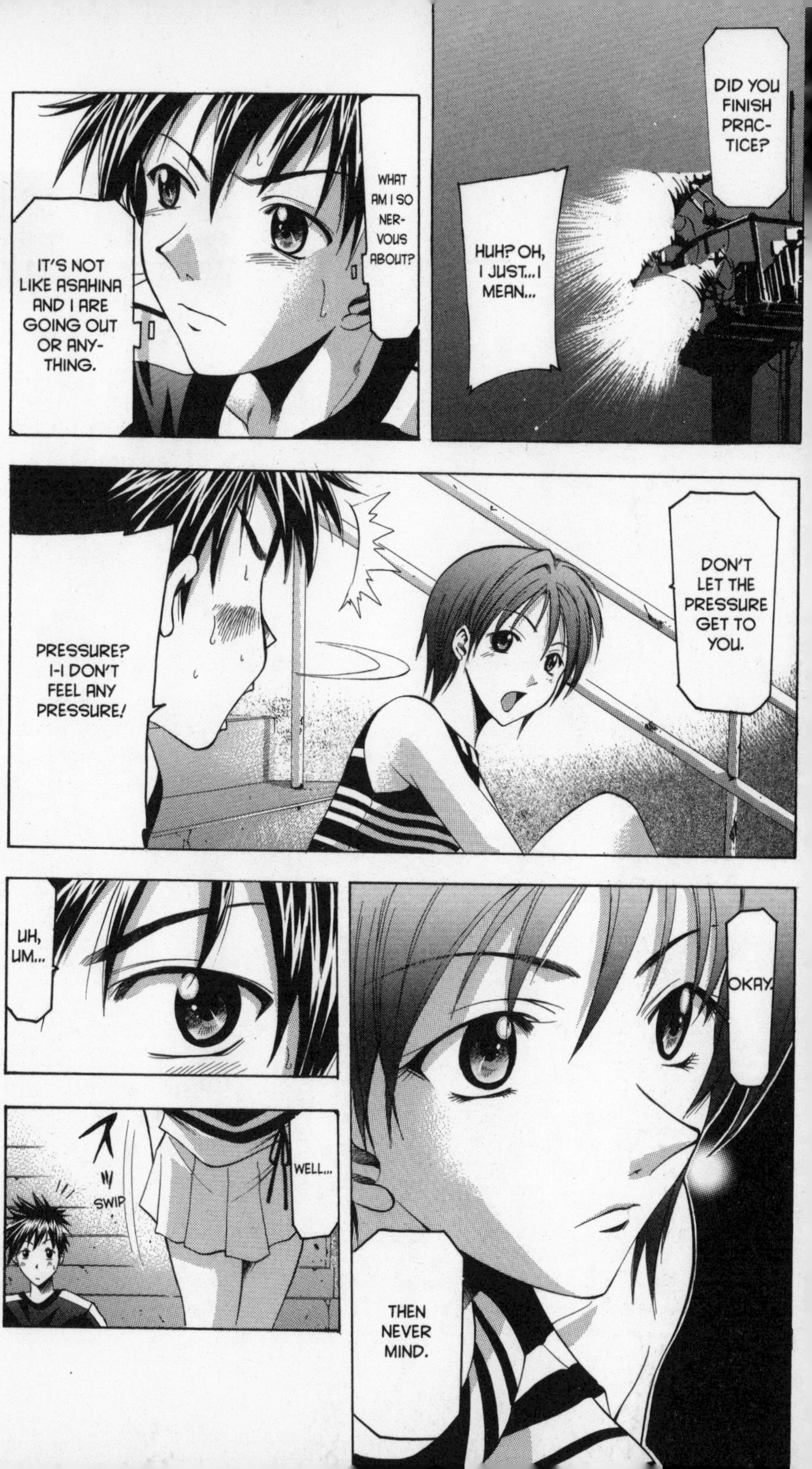
DID YOU FINISH PRAC-TICE?
HUH? OH, I JUST...I MEAN...
WHAT AM I SO NER-VOUS ABOUT?
IT'S NOT LIKE ASAHINA AND I ARE GOING OUT OR ANY-THING.
DON'T LET THE PRESSURE GET TO YOU.
PRESSURE? I-I DON'T FEEL ANY PRESSURE!
OKAY.
UH, UM...
WELL...
SWIP
THEN NEVER MIND.

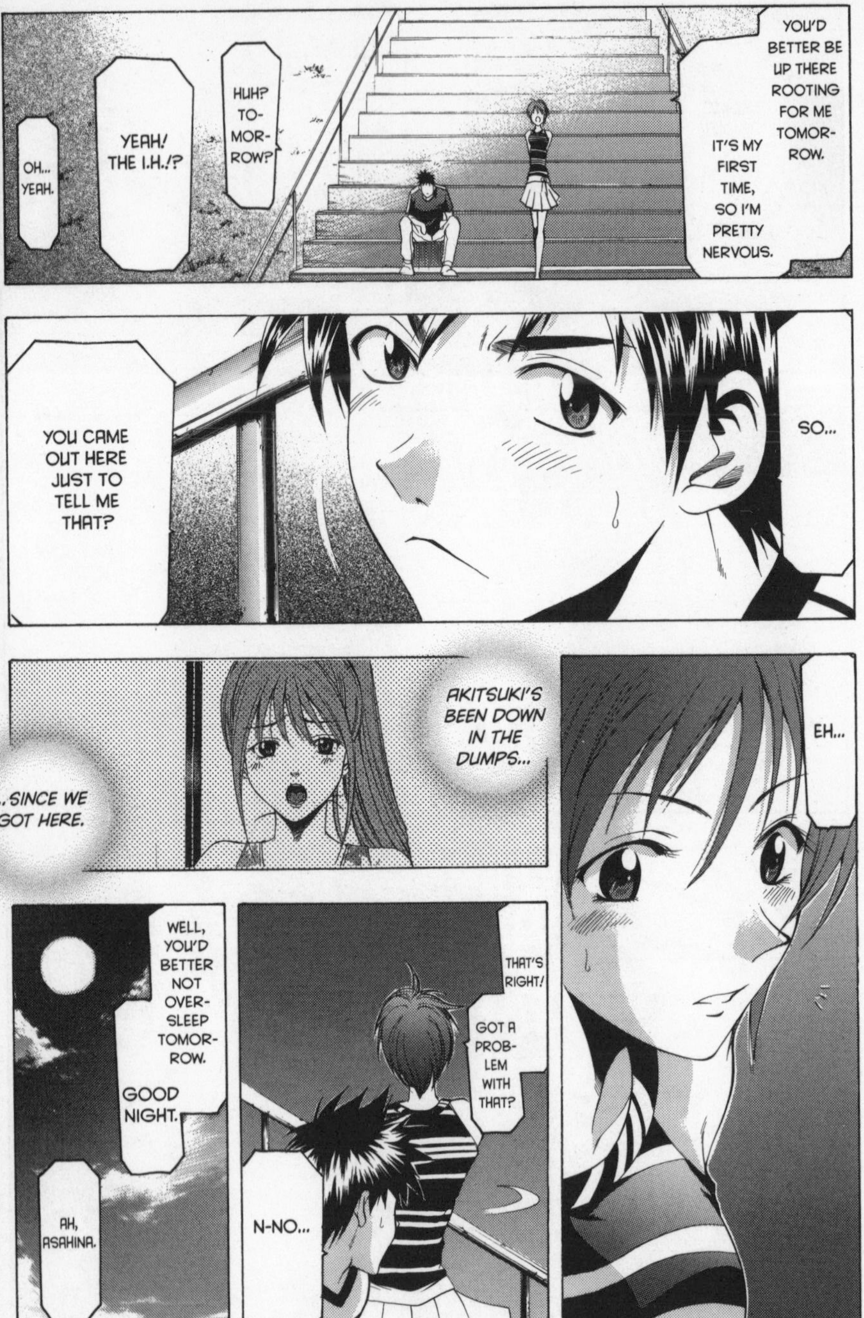
YOU'D BETTER BE UP THERE ROOTING FOR ME TOMORROW.
IT'S MY FIRST TIME, SO I'M PRETTY NERVOUS.
HUH? TOMORROW?
YEAH! THE I.H.!?
OH... YEAH.
SO...
YOU CAME OUT HERE JUST TO TELL ME THAT?
EH...
AKITSUKI'S BEEN DOWN IN THE DUMPS...
...SINCE WE GOT HERE.
THAT'S RIGHT!
GOT A PROBLEM WITH THAT?
N-NO...
WELL, YOU'D BETTER NOT OVERSLEEP TOMORROW.
GOOD NIGHT.
AH, ASAHINA.

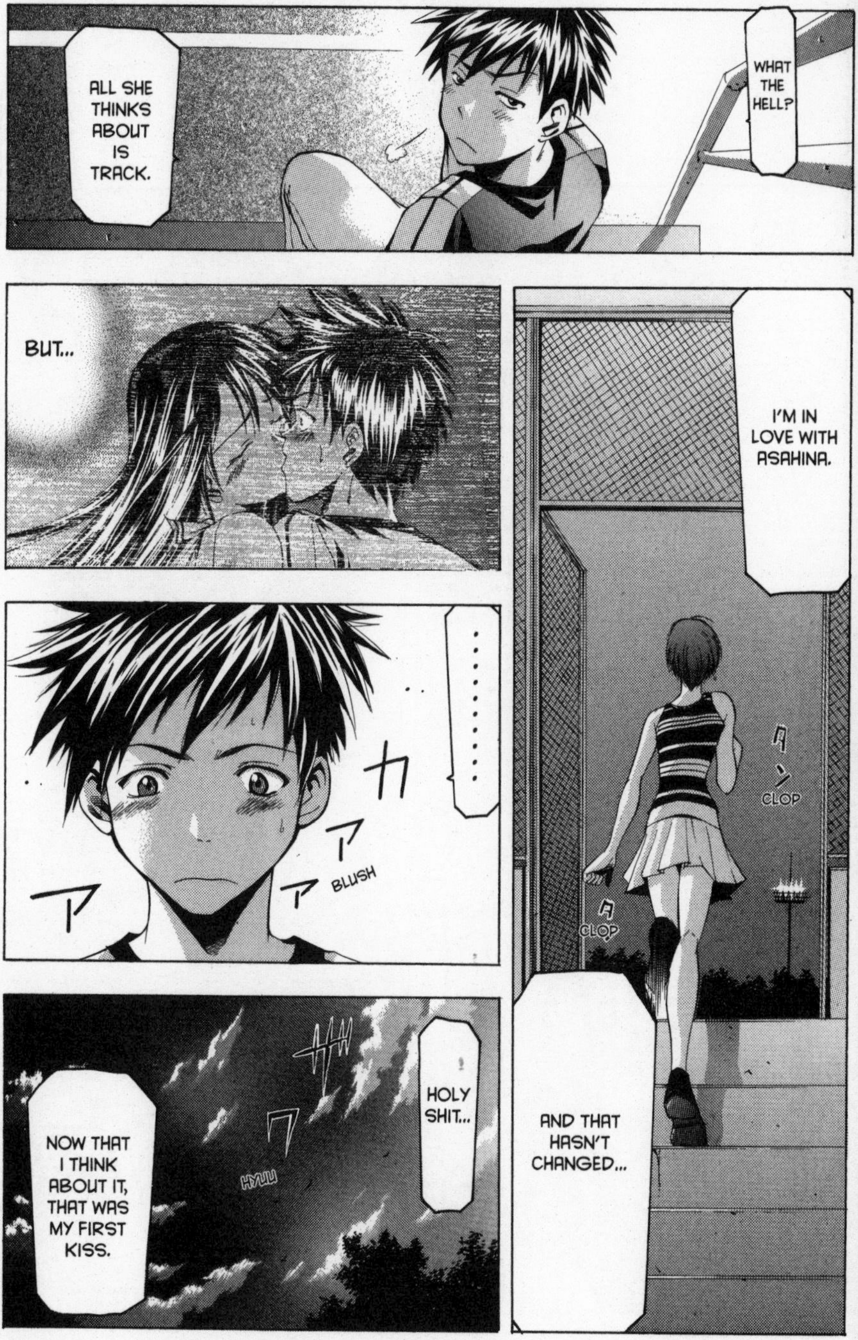
WHAT THE HELL?
ALL SHE THINKS ABOUT IS TRACK.
I'M IN LOVE WITH ASAHINA.
CLOP
CLOP
AND THAT HASN'T CHANGED...
BUT...
......
BLUSH
HOLY SHIT...
HYUU
NOW THAT I THINK ABOUT IT, THAT WAS MY FIRST KISS.

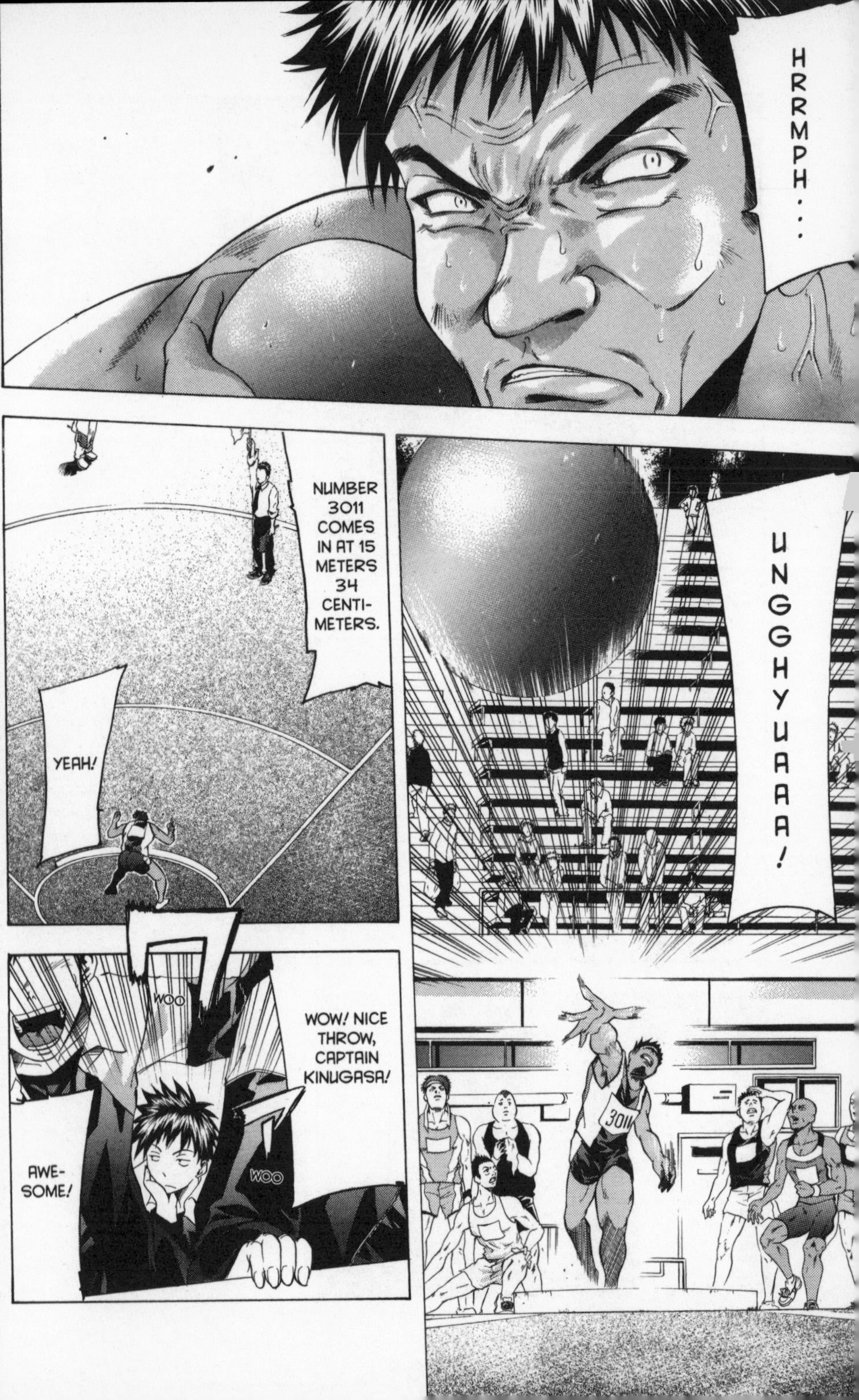
HRRMPH...
UNGGHYUAAAA!
NUMBER 3011 COMES IN AT 15 METERS 34 CENTI-METERS.
YEAH!
WOW! NICE THROW, CAPTAIN KINUGASA!
WOO
WOO
AWE-SOME!

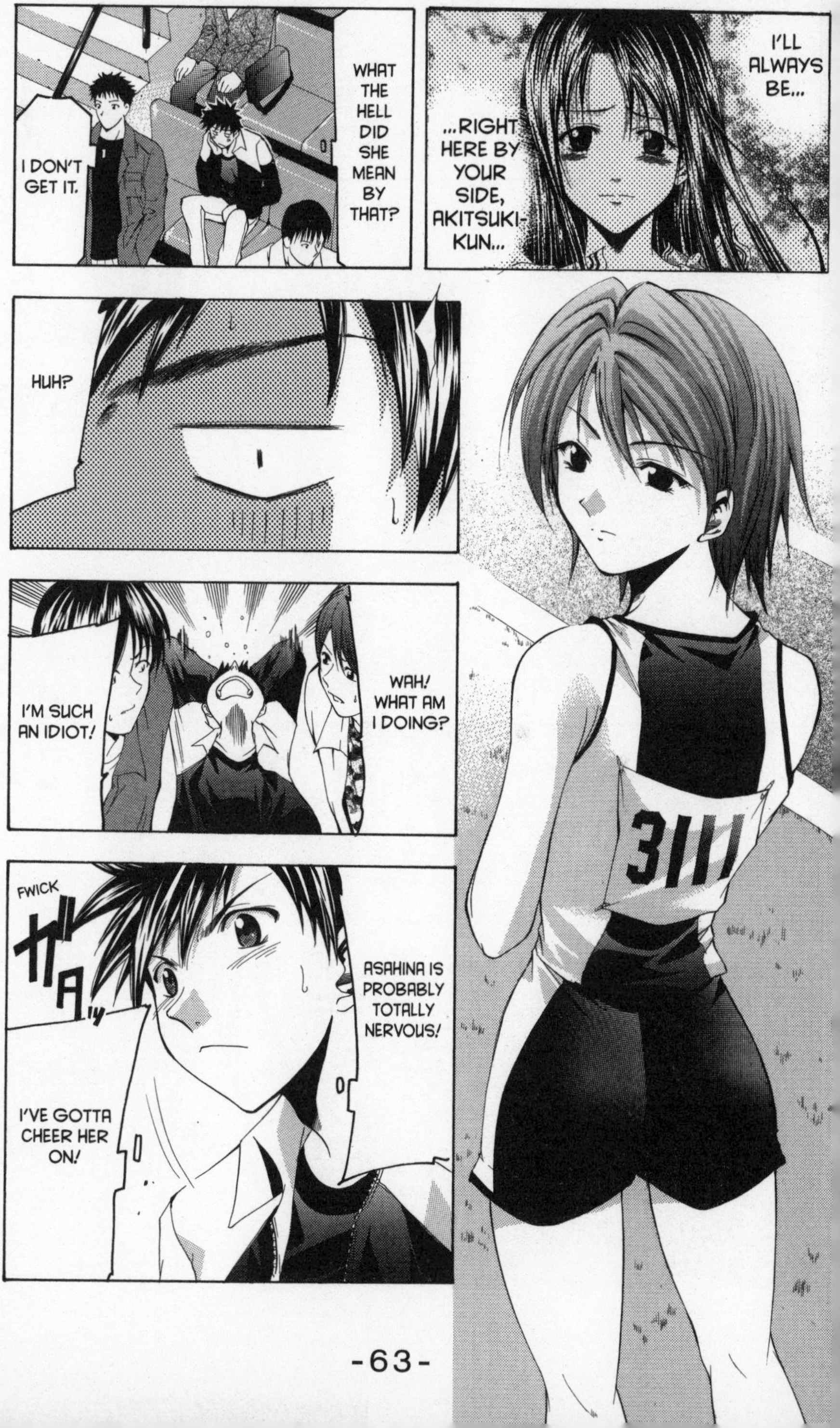
I'LL ALWAYS BE...
...RIGHT HERE BY YOUR SIDE, AKITSUKI-KUN...
WHAT THE HELL DID SHE MEAN BY THAT?
I DON'T GET IT.
3111
HUH?
WAH! WHAT AM I DOING?
I'M SUCH AN IDIOT!
ASAHINA IS PROBABLY TOTALLY NERVOUS!
FWICK
I'VE GOTTA CHEER HER ON!

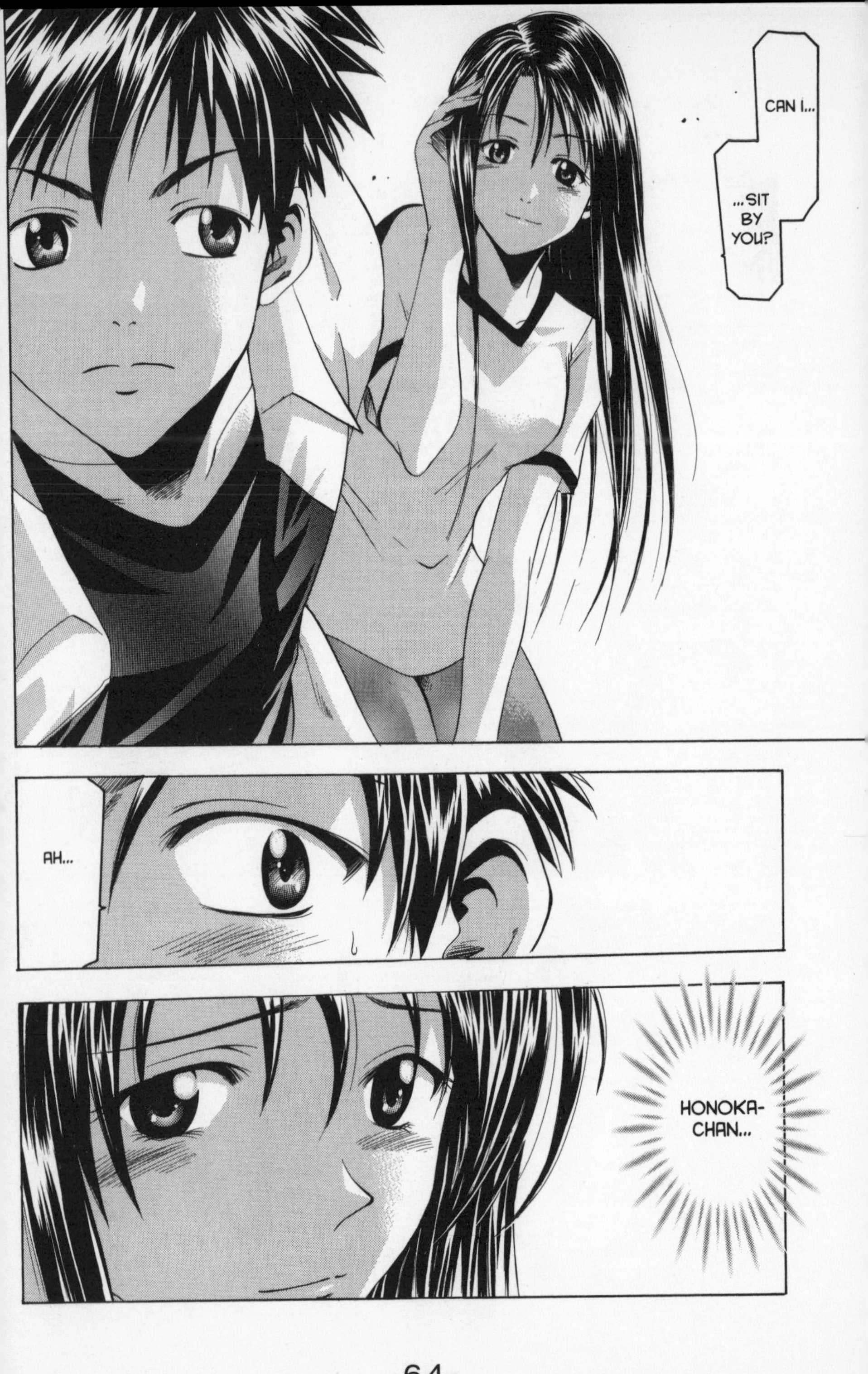
CAN I...
...SIT BY YOU?
AH...
HONOKA-CHAN...

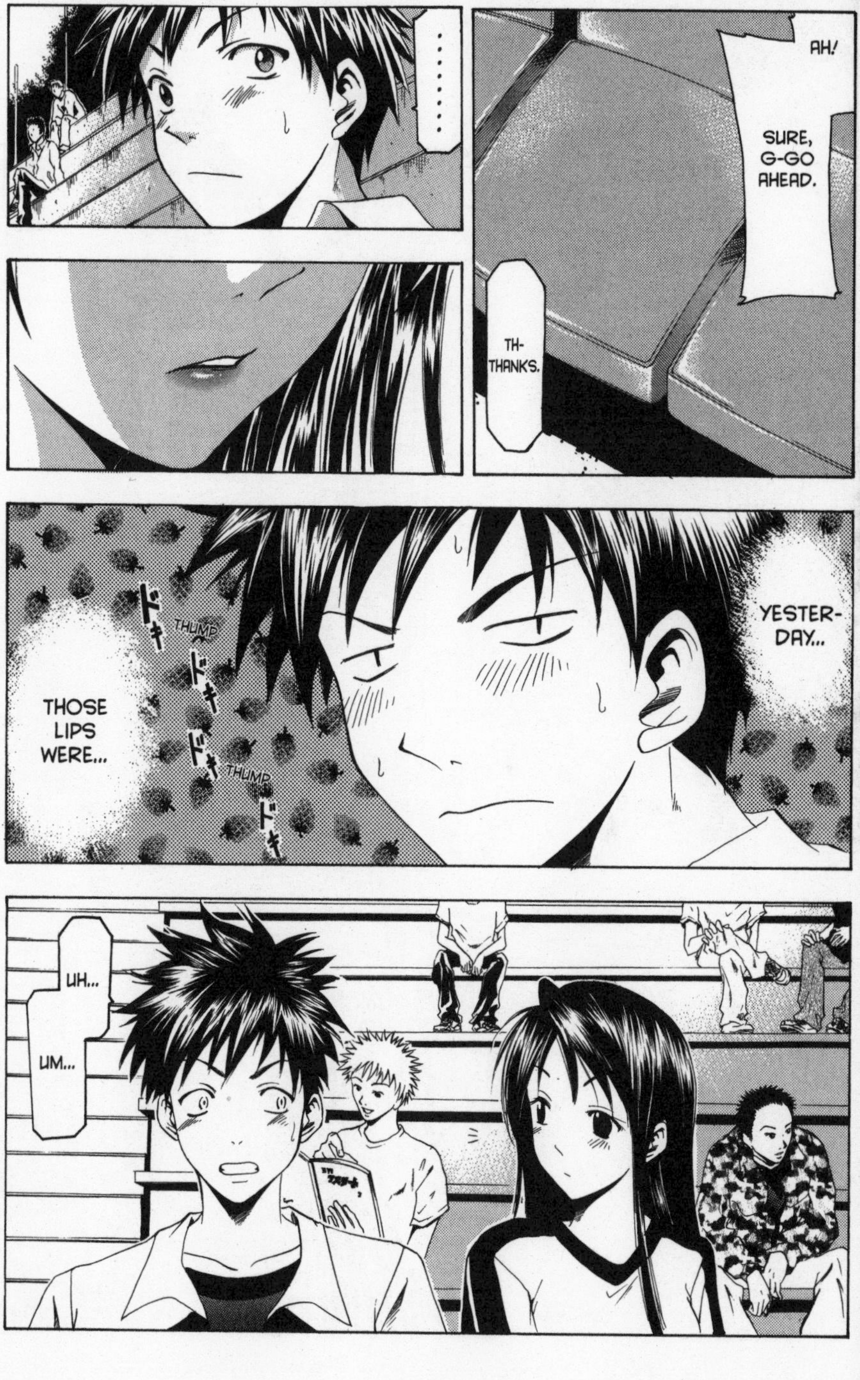
AH!
SURE, G-GO AHEAD.
TH- THANKS.
......
YESTER- DAY...
ドキ
THUMP
ドキ
ドキ
THUMP
ドキ
THOSE LIPS WERE...
UH...
UM...

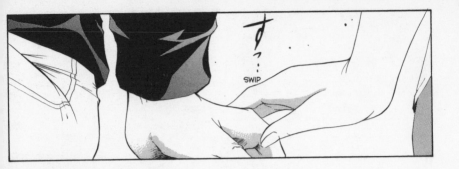

SWIP

I'M SORRY ABOUT YES-TER-DAY.

I KNOW IT WAS A LITTLE SUD-DEN.

...!

THUMP

THUMP

UH... NO...

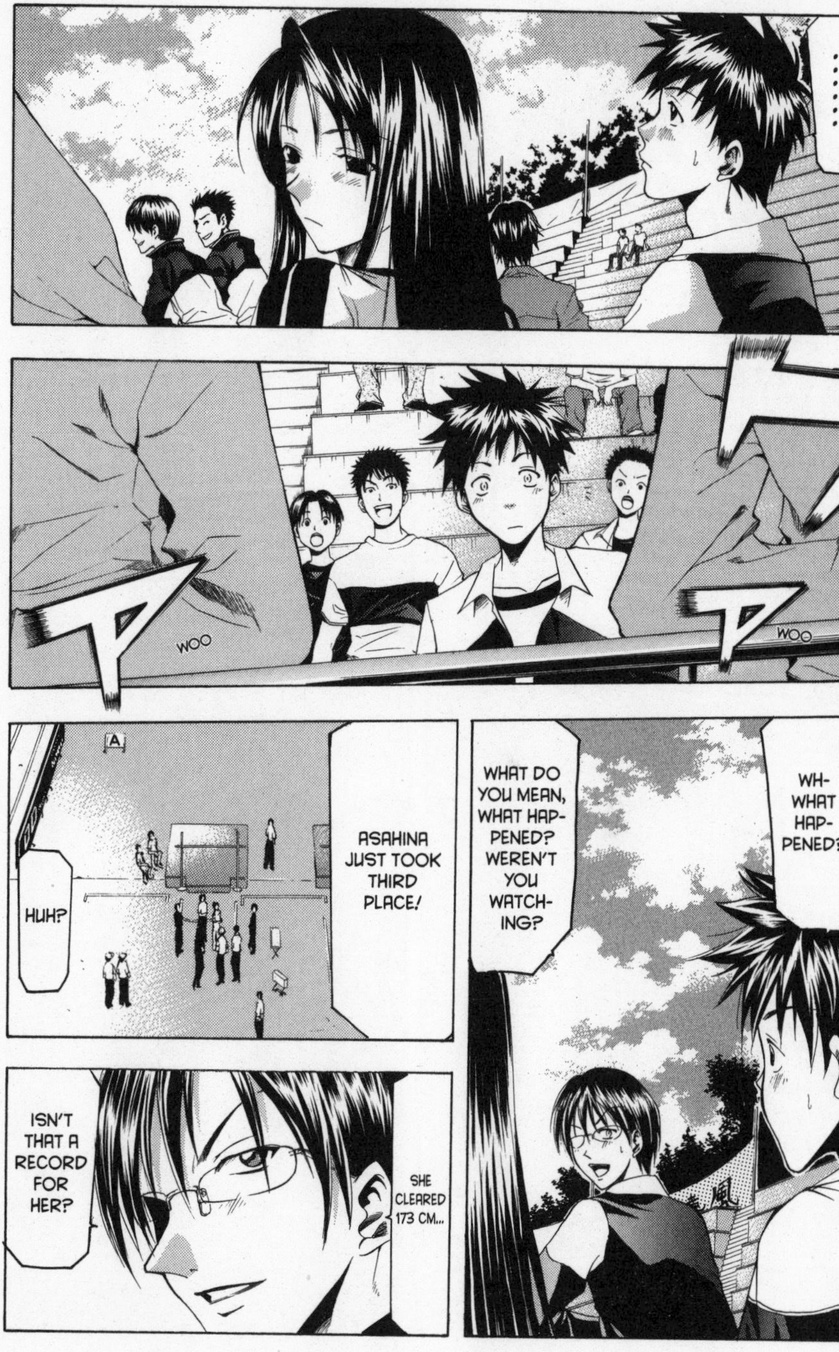
......
WOO
WOO
WH-WHAT HAPPENED?
WHAT DO YOU MEAN, WHAT HAPPENED? WEREN'T YOU WATCHING?
A
ASAHINA JUST TOOK THIRD PLACE!
HUH?
SHE CLEARED 173 CM...
ISN'T THAT A RECORD FOR HER?

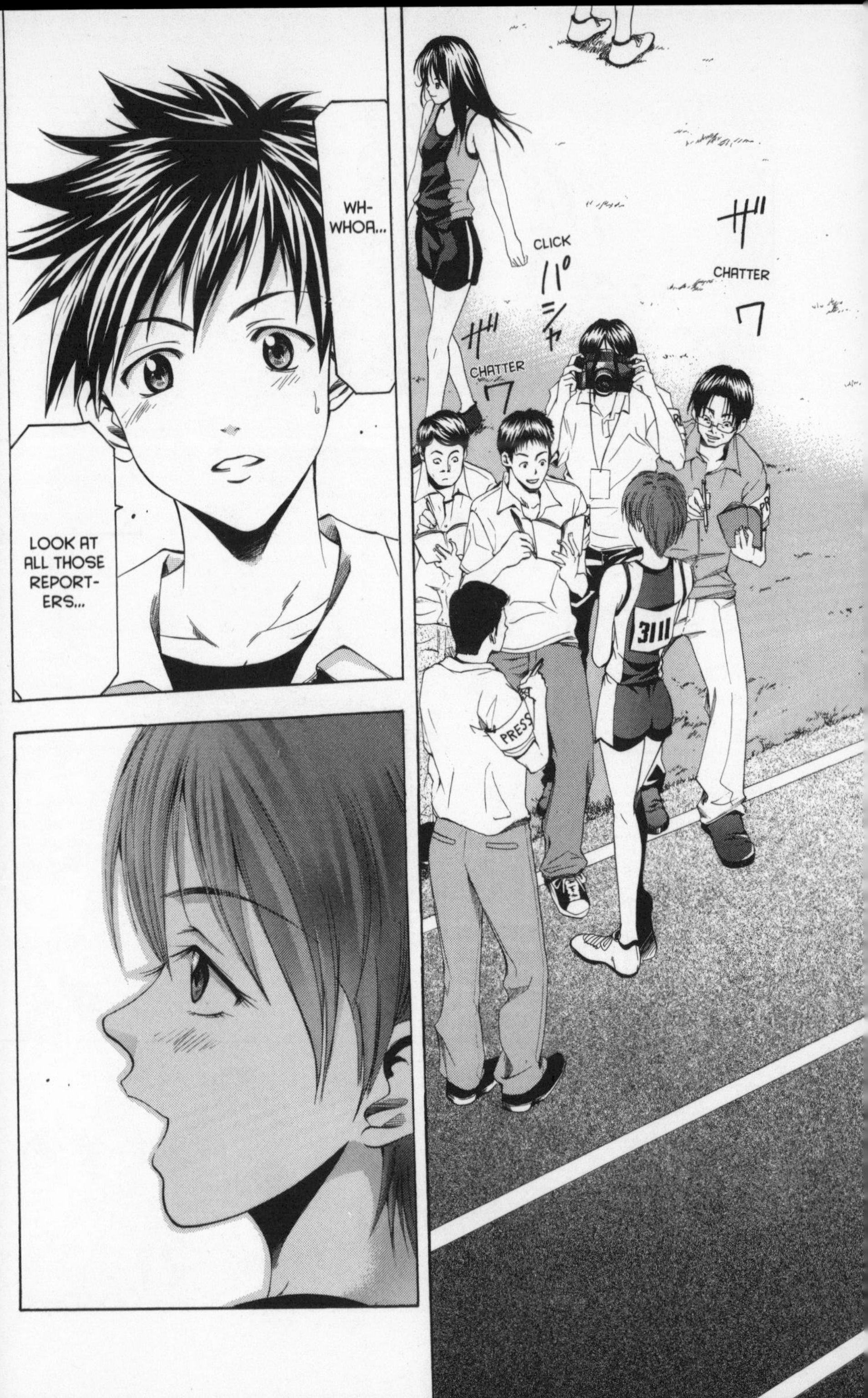
ザ
CHATTER
ワ
CLICK
パシャ
ザ
CHATTER
ワ
WH-WHOA...
LOOK AT ALL THOSE REPORTERS...
PRESS
3111

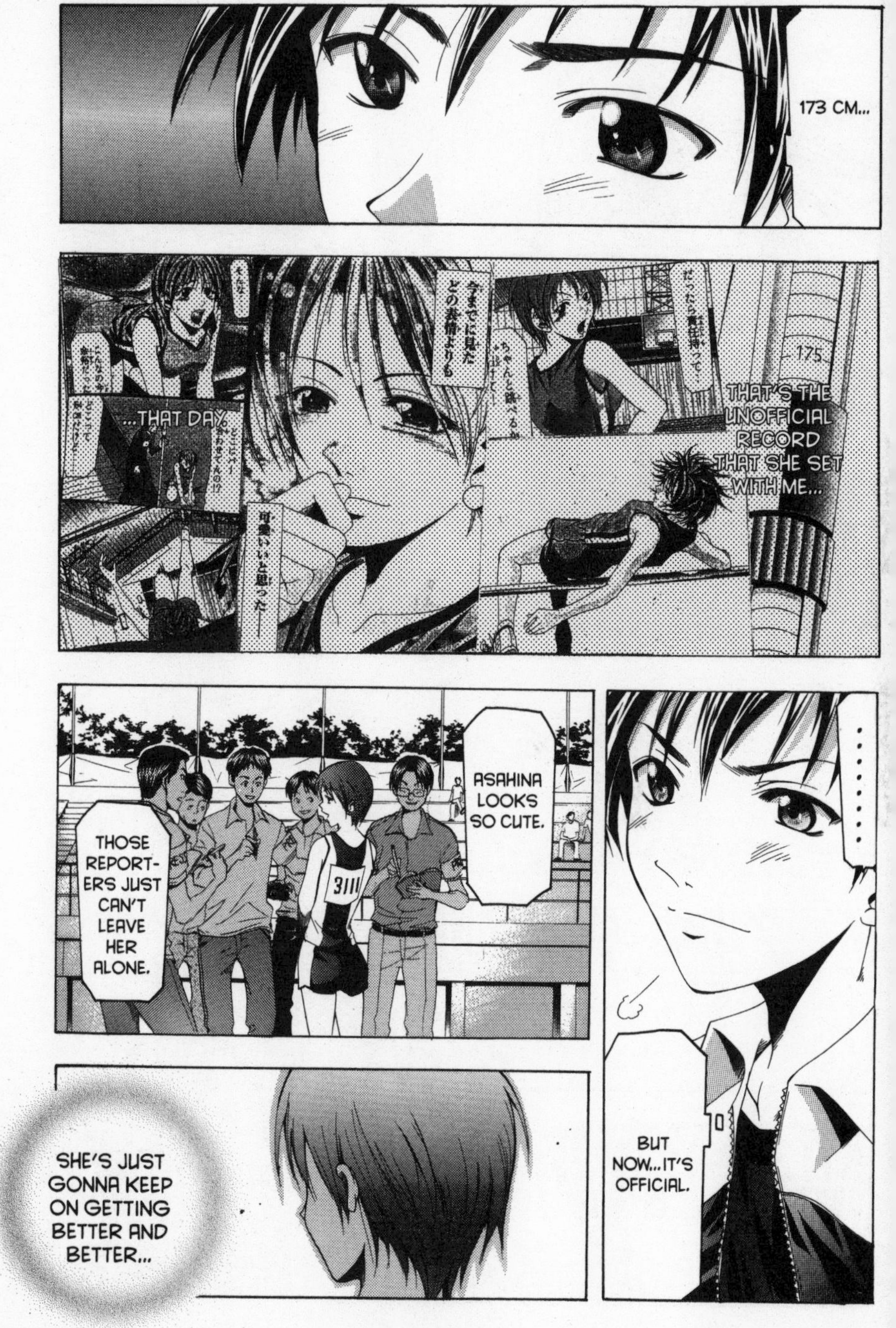
173 CM...
175
THAT'S THE UNOFFICIAL RECORD THAT SHE SET WITH ME...
だったら責任持って…
ちゃんと跳べるか
今までに見たどの表情よりも
可愛いいと思った——
そんな…
...THAT DAY.
......
BUT NOW...IT'S OFFICIAL.
ASAHINA LOOKS SO CUTE.
THOSE REPORTERS JUST CAN'T LEAVE HER ALONE.
SHE'S JUST GONNA KEEP ON GETTING BETTER AND BETTER...

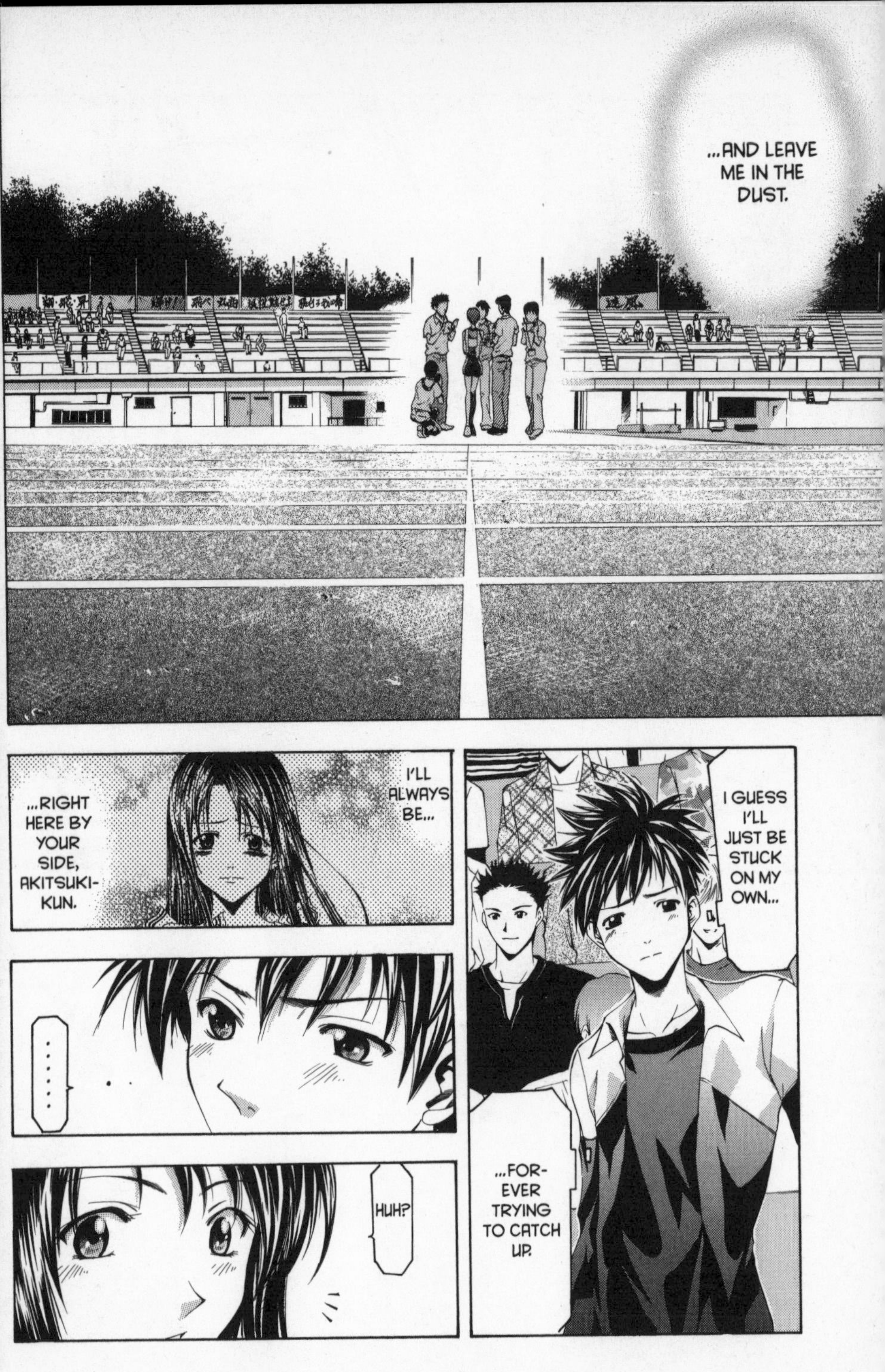
...AND LEAVE ME IN THE DUST.
I GUESS I'LL JUST BE STUCK ON MY OWN...
...FOR-EVER TRYING TO CATCH UP.
I'LL ALWAYS BE...
...RIGHT HERE BY YOUR SIDE, AKITSUKI-KUN.
......
HUH?

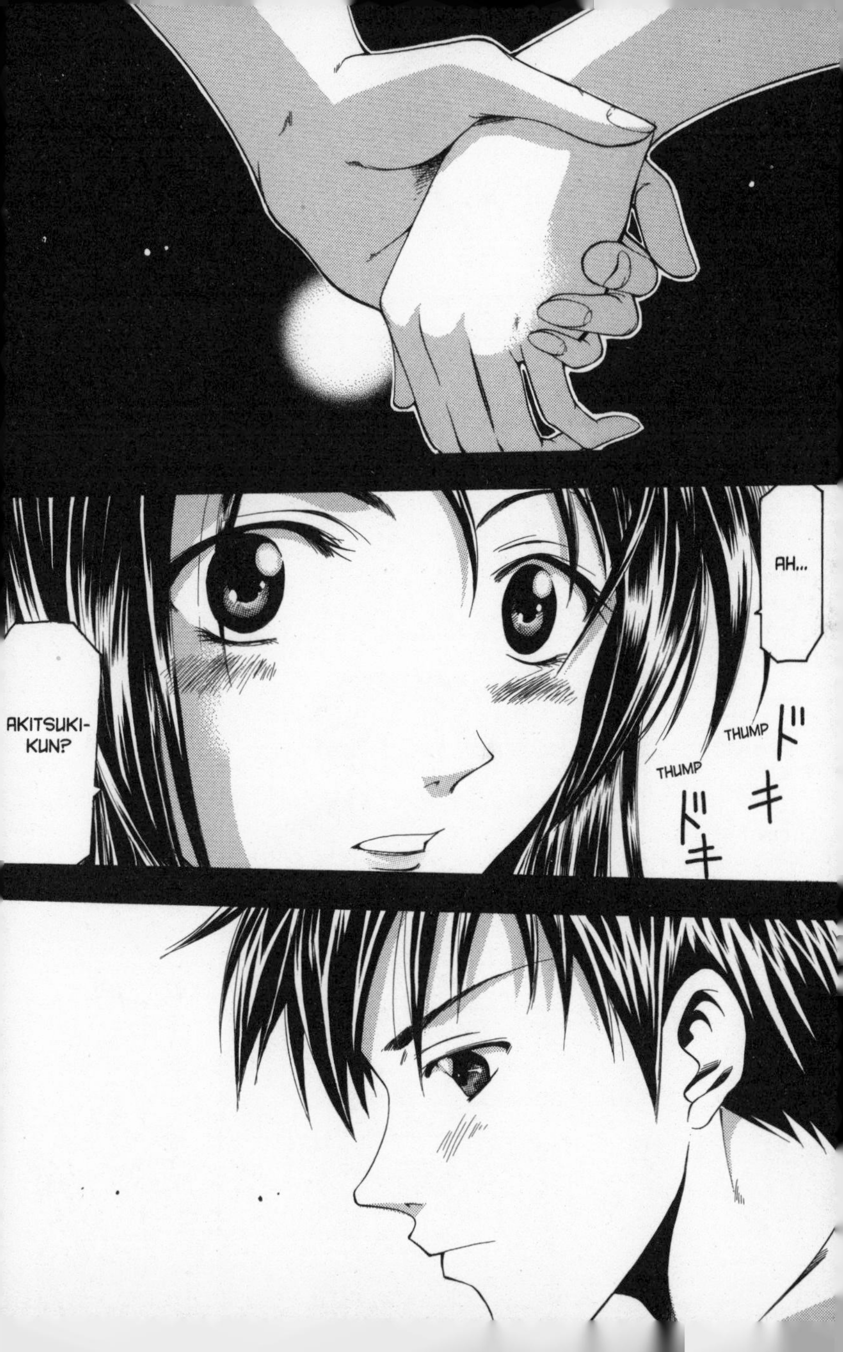
AH...
THUMP
ドキ
THUMP
ドキ
AKITSUKI-KUN?

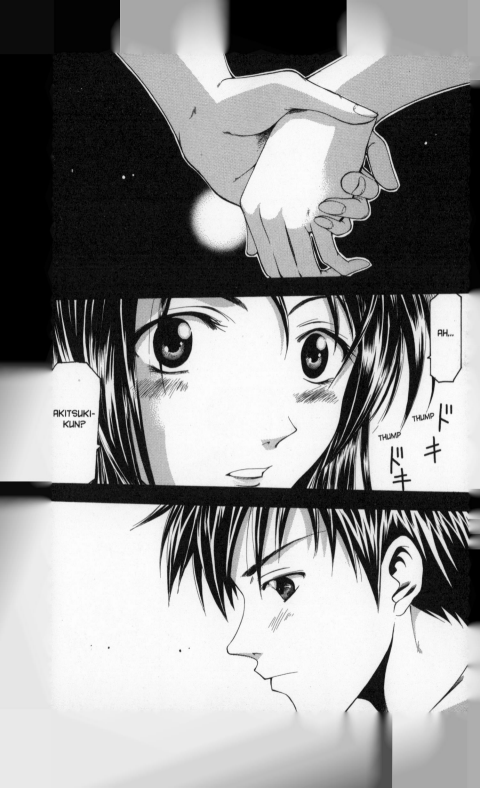

SUZUKA FOUR-PANEL THEATER NUMBER NINETEEN

IS THAT ALL?

YASUNOBU-KUN CALLED ME FROM AUSTRALIA.
HEY, WHAT'S UP?
SO? HOW'S AUSTRALIA?
I CAN'T BELIEVE YOU'RE IN ANOTHER COUNTRY!
HEY, WILL YOU RECORD THAT SOCCER GAME FOR ME? THE ONE NAKATA IS PLAYING IN.
HUH?
THIS CALL'S EXPENSIVE, SO GOTTA GO.
CLICK
BEEP
BEEP
WELL, AT LEAST I KNOW HE'S ALIVE.

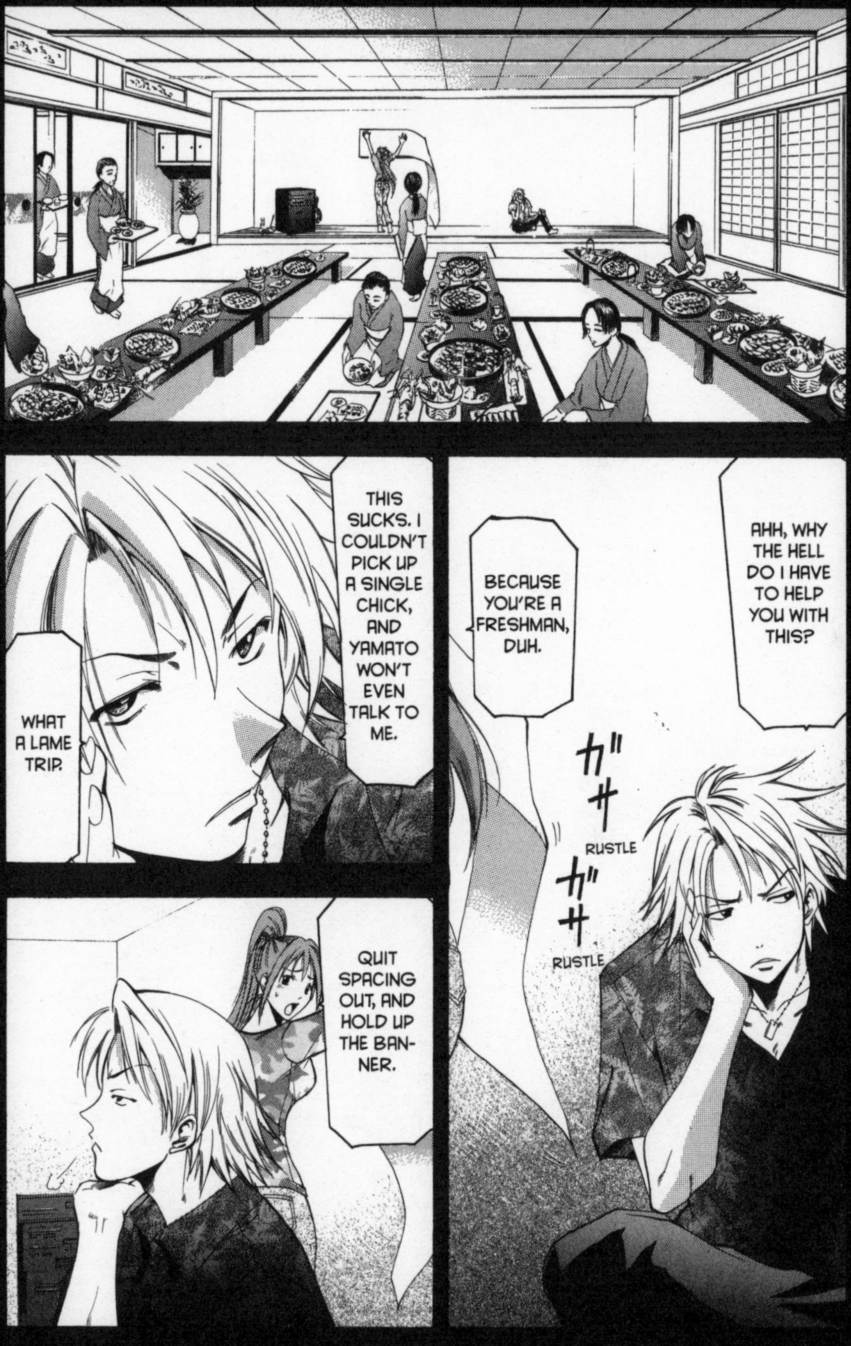
AHH, WHY THE HELL DO I HAVE TO HELP YOU WITH THIS?
BECAUSE YOU'RE A FRESHMAN, DUH.
ガサ
RUSTLE
ガサ
RUSTLE
THIS SUCKS. I COULDN'T PICK UP A SINGLE CHICK, AND YAMATO WON'T EVEN TALK TO ME.
WHAT A LAME TRIP.
QUIT SPACING OUT, AND HOLD UP THE BAN-NER.

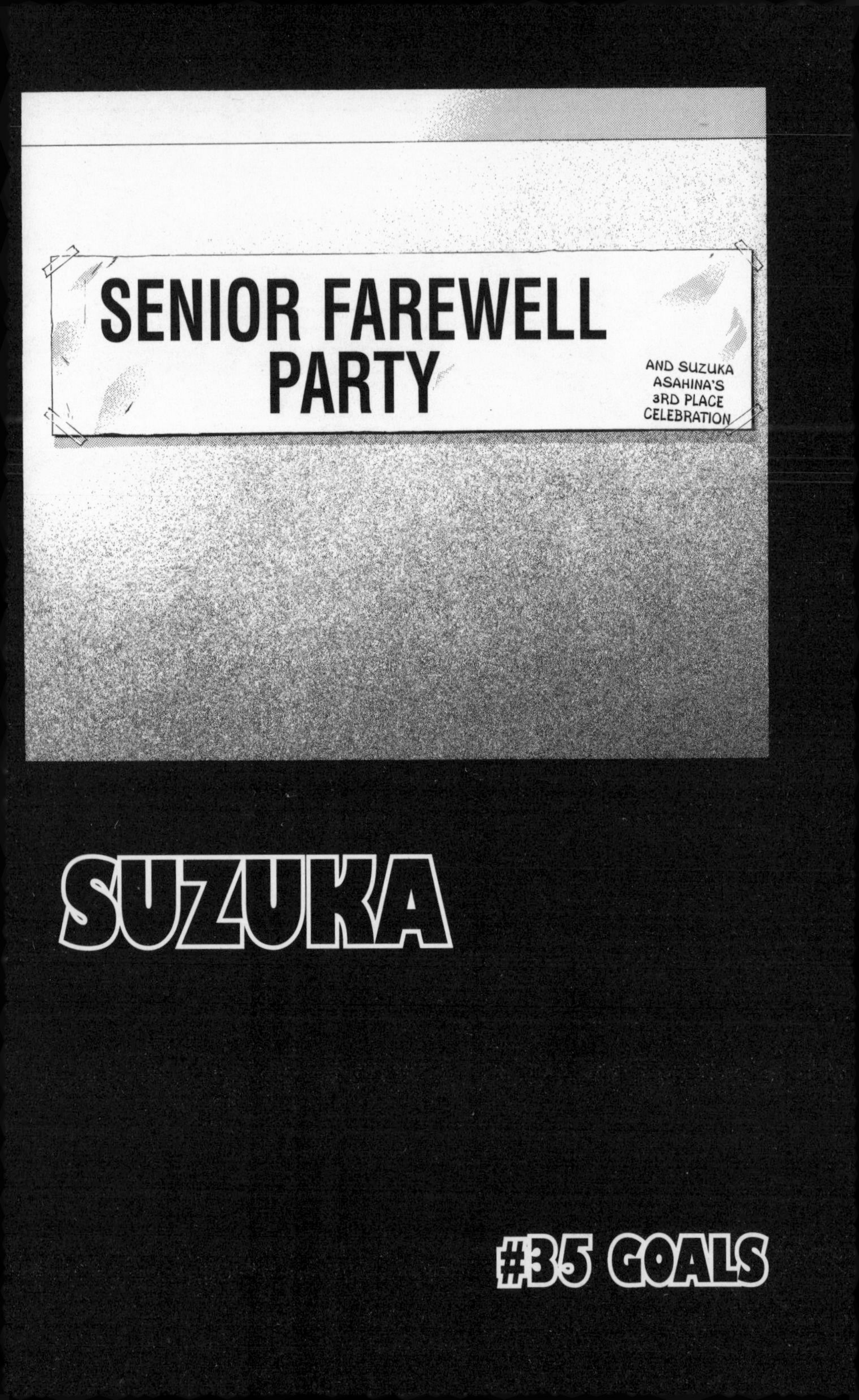
SENIOR FAREWELL PARTY
AND SUZUKA ASAHINA'S 3RD PLACE CELEBRATION

SUZUKA

#35 GOALS

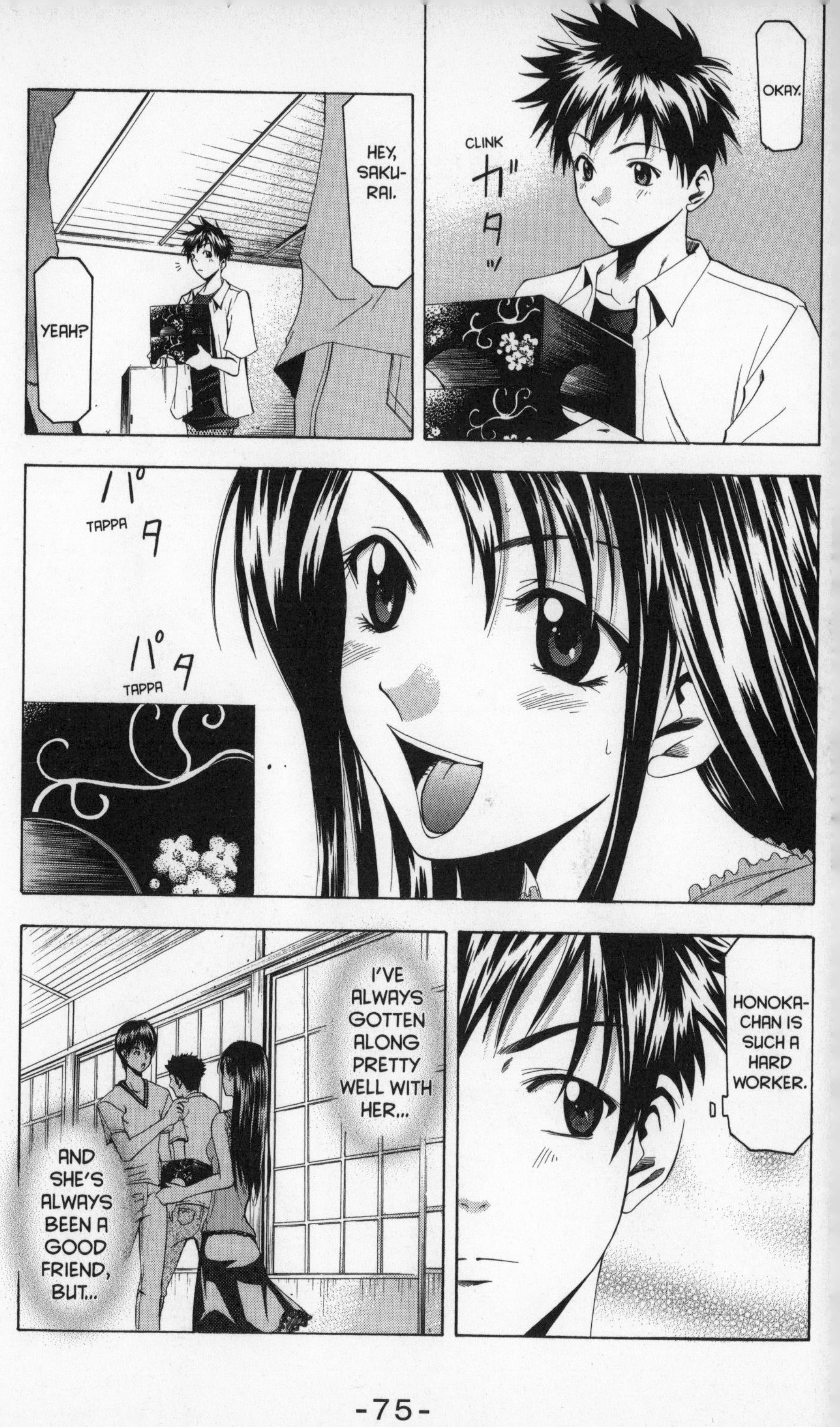
OKAY.
CLINK
ガタッ
HEY, SAKU-RAI.
YEAH?
パタ
TAPPA
パタ
TAPPA
HONOKA-CHAN IS SUCH A HARD WORKER.
I'VE ALWAYS GOTTEN ALONG PRETTY WELL WITH HER...
AND SHE'S ALWAYS BEEN A GOOD FRIEND, BUT...

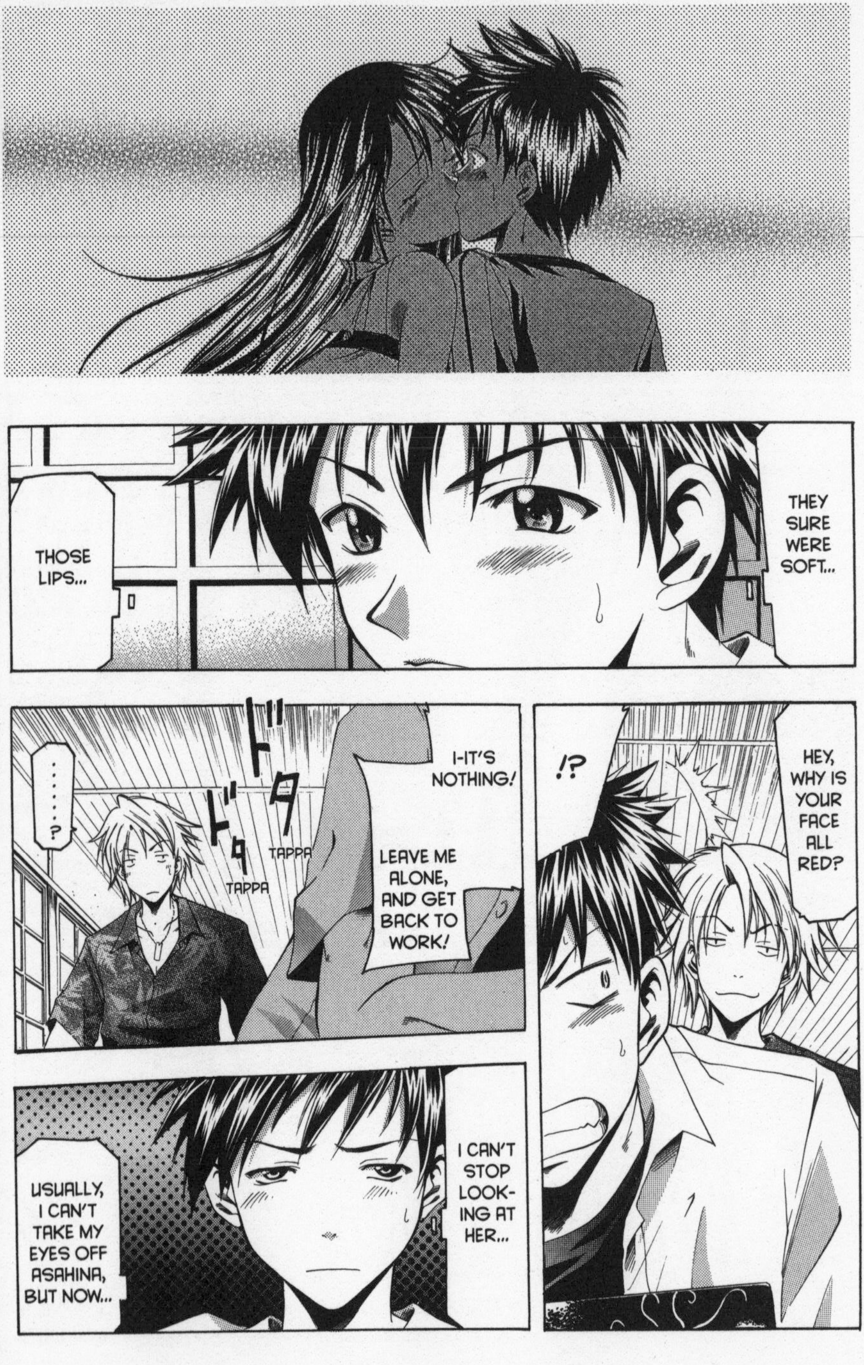
THEY SURE WERE SOFT...
THOSE LIPS...
HEY, WHY IS YOUR FACE ALL RED?
!?
I-IT'S NOTHING!
LEAVE ME ALONE, AND GET BACK TO WORK!
ドタ
TAPPA
ドタ
TAPPA
......?
I CAN'T STOP LOOKING AT HER...
USUALLY, I CAN'T TAKE MY EYES OFF ASAHINA, BUT NOW...

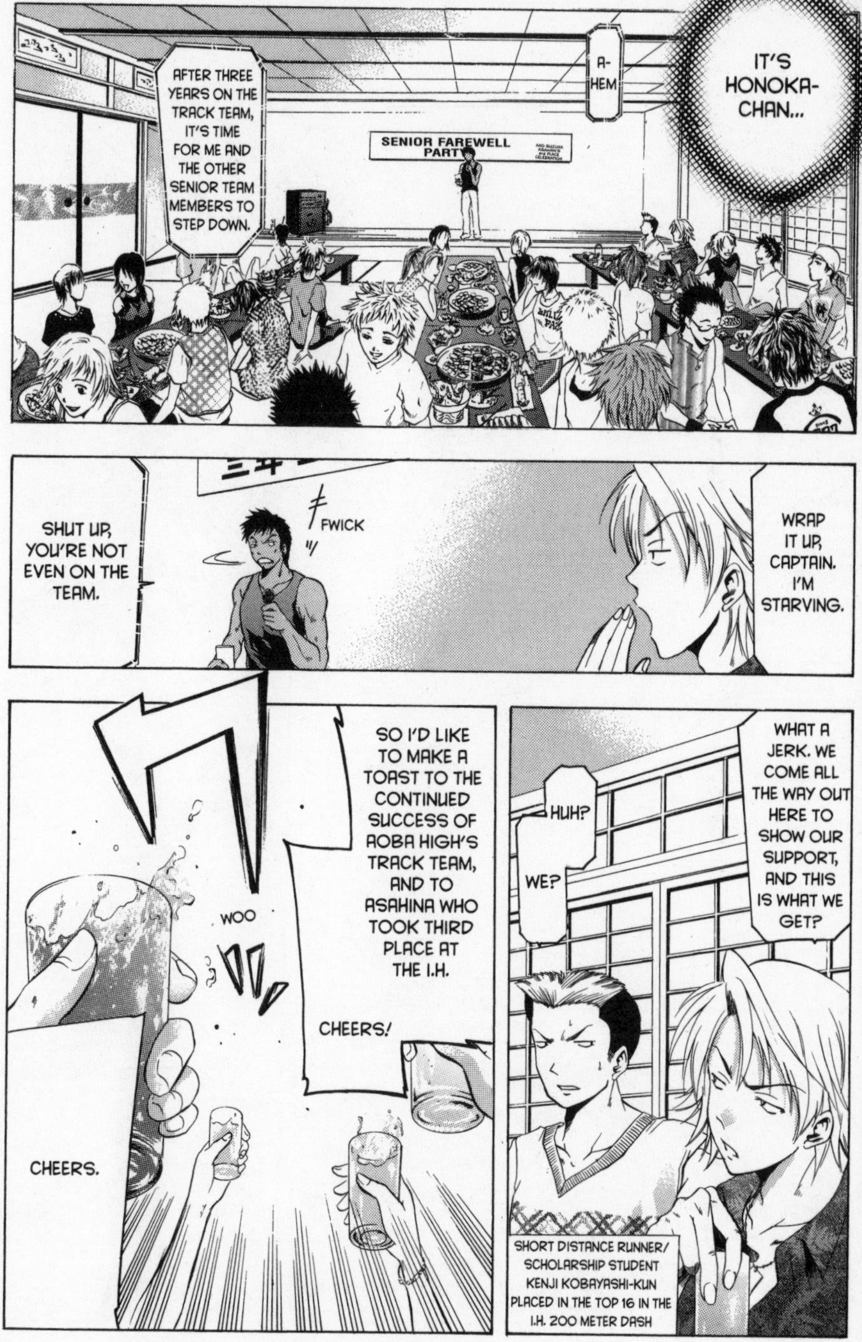
IT'S HONOKA-CHAN...
A-HEM
AFTER THREE YEARS ON THE TRACK TEAM, IT'S TIME FOR ME AND THE OTHER SENIOR TEAM MEMBERS TO STEP DOWN.
SENIOR FAREWELL PARTY
WRAP IT UP, CAPTAIN. I'M STARVING.
FWICK
SHUT UP, YOU'RE NOT EVEN ON THE TEAM.
WHAT A JERK. WE COME ALL THE WAY OUT HERE TO SHOW OUR SUPPORT, AND THIS IS WHAT WE GET?
HUH?
WE?
SHORT DISTANCE RUNNER/ SCHOLARSHIP STUDENT KENJI KOBAYASHI-KUN PLACED IN THE TOP 16 IN THE I.H. 200 METER DASH
SO I'D LIKE TO MAKE A TOAST TO THE CONTINUED SUCCESS OF AOBA HIGH'S TRACK TEAM, AND TO ASAHINA WHO TOOK THIRD PLACE AT THE I.H.
WOO
CHEERS!
CHEERS.

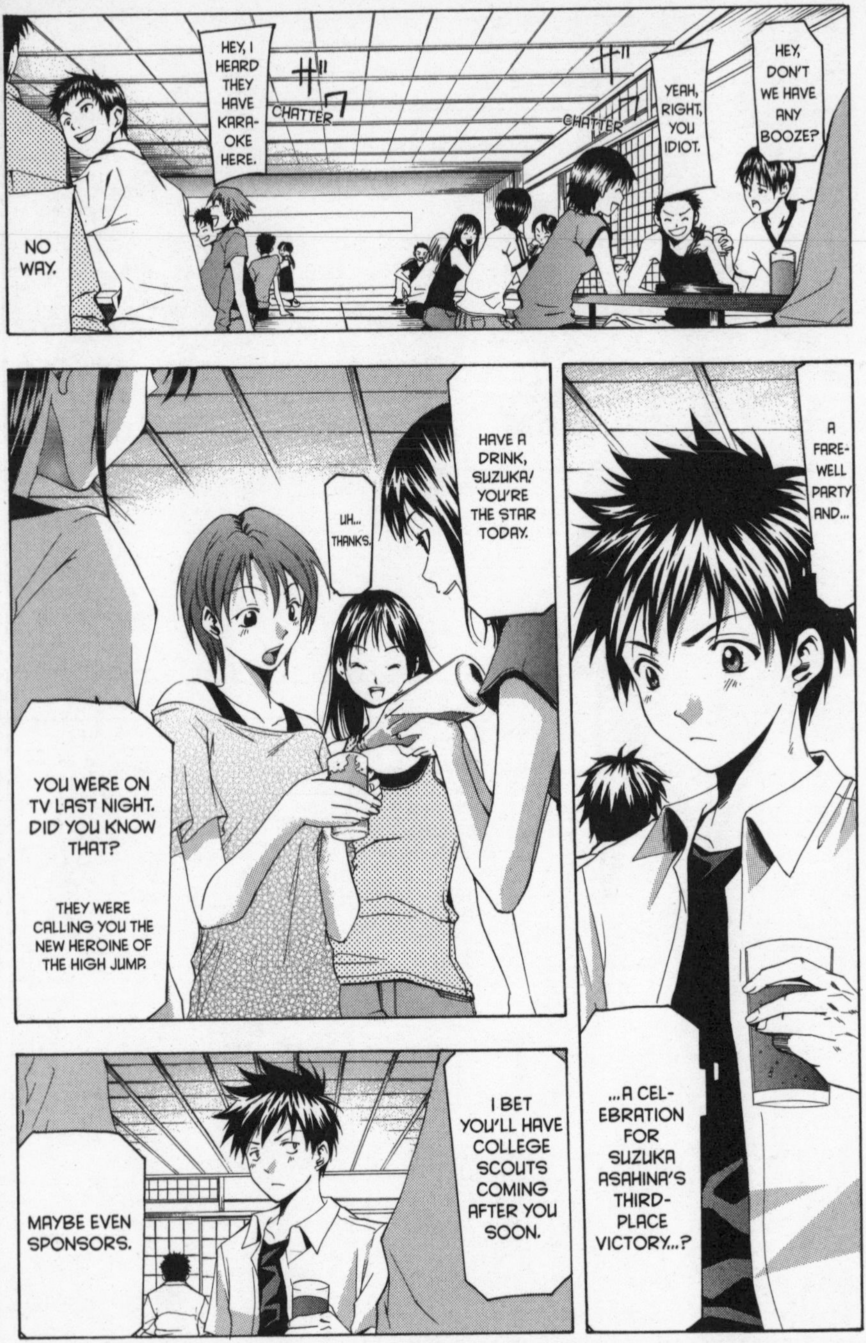
HEY, DON'T WE HAVE ANY BOOZE?
YEAH, RIGHT, YOU IDIOT.
CHATTER
HEY, I HEARD THEY HAVE KARA-OKE HERE.
CHATTER
NO WAY.
A FARE-WELL PARTY AND...
...A CEL-EBRATION FOR SUZUKA ASAHINA'S THIRD-PLACE VICTORY...?
HAVE A DRINK, SUZUKA! YOU'RE THE STAR TODAY.
UH... THANKS.
YOU WERE ON TV LAST NIGHT. DID YOU KNOW THAT?
THEY WERE CALLING YOU THE NEW HEROINE OF THE HIGH JUMP.
I BET YOU'LL HAVE COLLEGE SCOUTS COMING AFTER YOU SOON.
MAYBE EVEN SPONSORS.

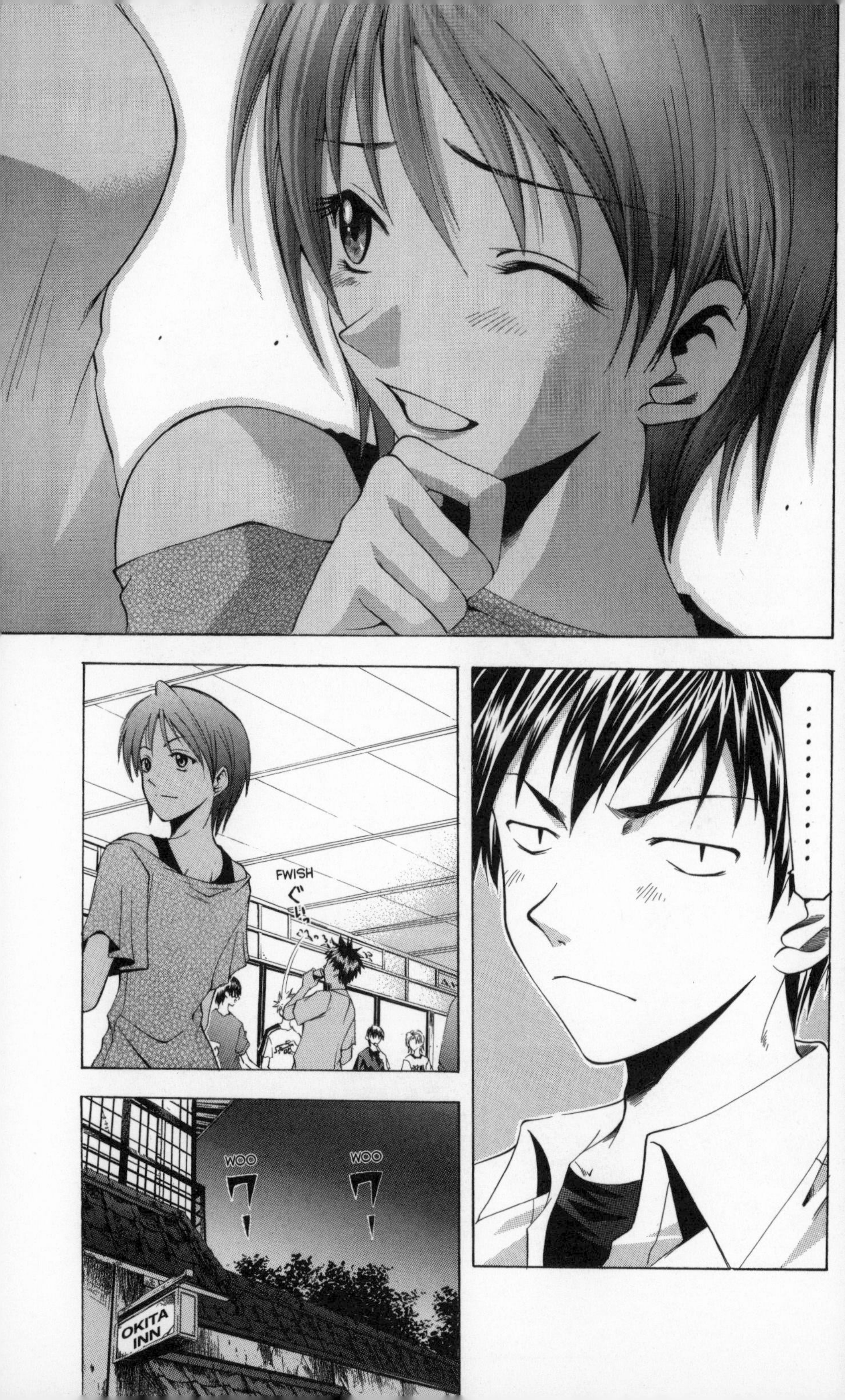
FWISH
WOO
WOO
OKITA
INN

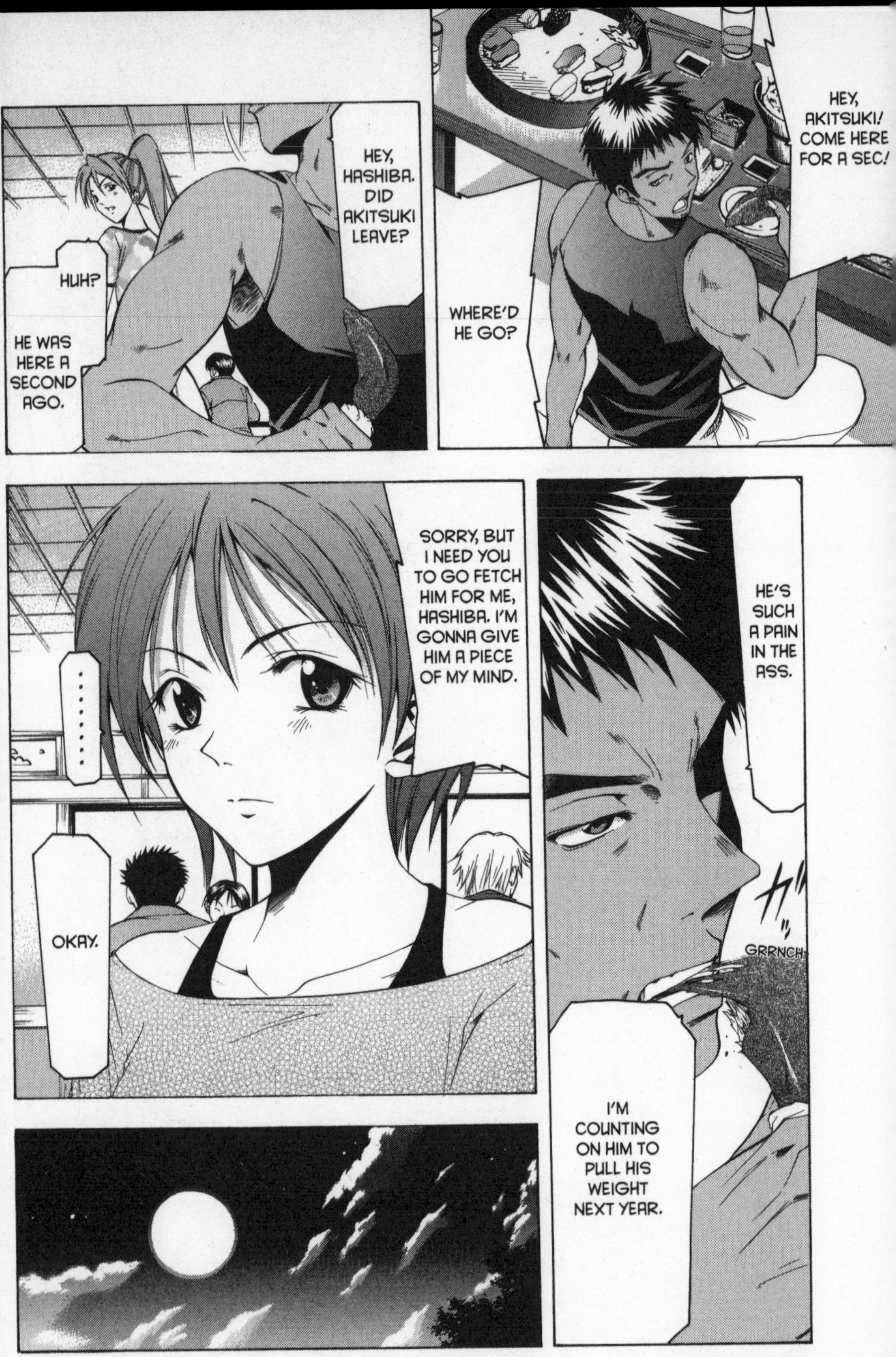
HEY, AKITSUKI! COME HERE FOR A SEC!
WHERE'D HE GO?
HEY, HASHIBA. DID AKITSUKI LEAVE?
HUH?
HE WAS HERE A SECOND AGO.
HE'S SUCH A PAIN IN THE ASS.
GRRNCH
I'M COUNTING ON HIM TO PULL HIS WEIGHT NEXT YEAR.
SORRY, BUT I NEED YOU TO GO FETCH HIM FOR ME, HASHIBA. I'M GONNA GIVE HIM A PIECE OF MY MIND.
....
OKAY.

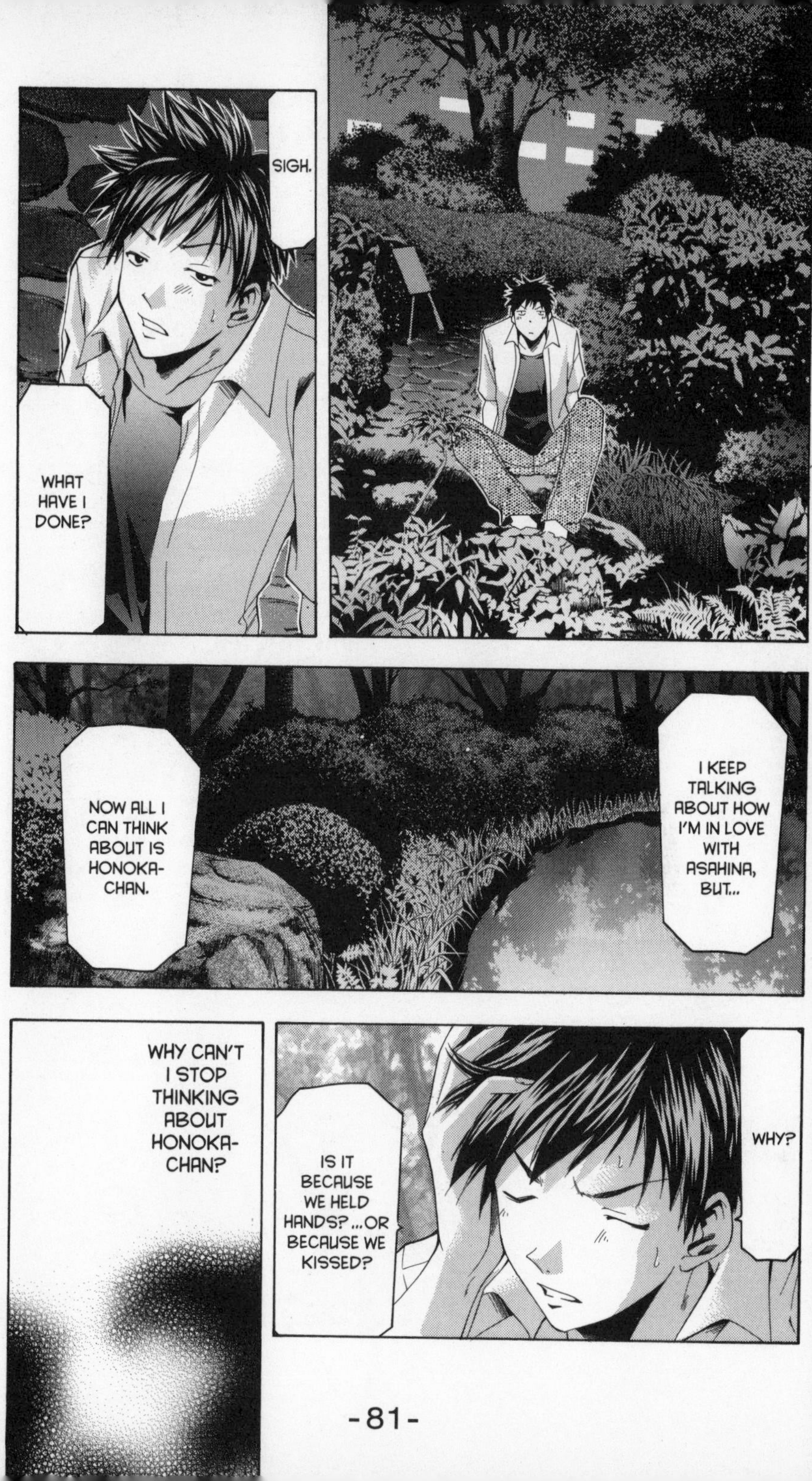
SIGH.
WHAT HAVE I DONE?
I KEEP TALKING ABOUT HOW I'M IN LOVE WITH ASAHINA, BUT...
NOW ALL I CAN THINK ABOUT IS HONOKA-CHAN.
WHY?
IS IT BECAUSE WE HELD HANDS? ...OR BECAUSE WE KISSED?
WHY CAN'T I STOP THINKING ABOUT HONOKA-CHAN?

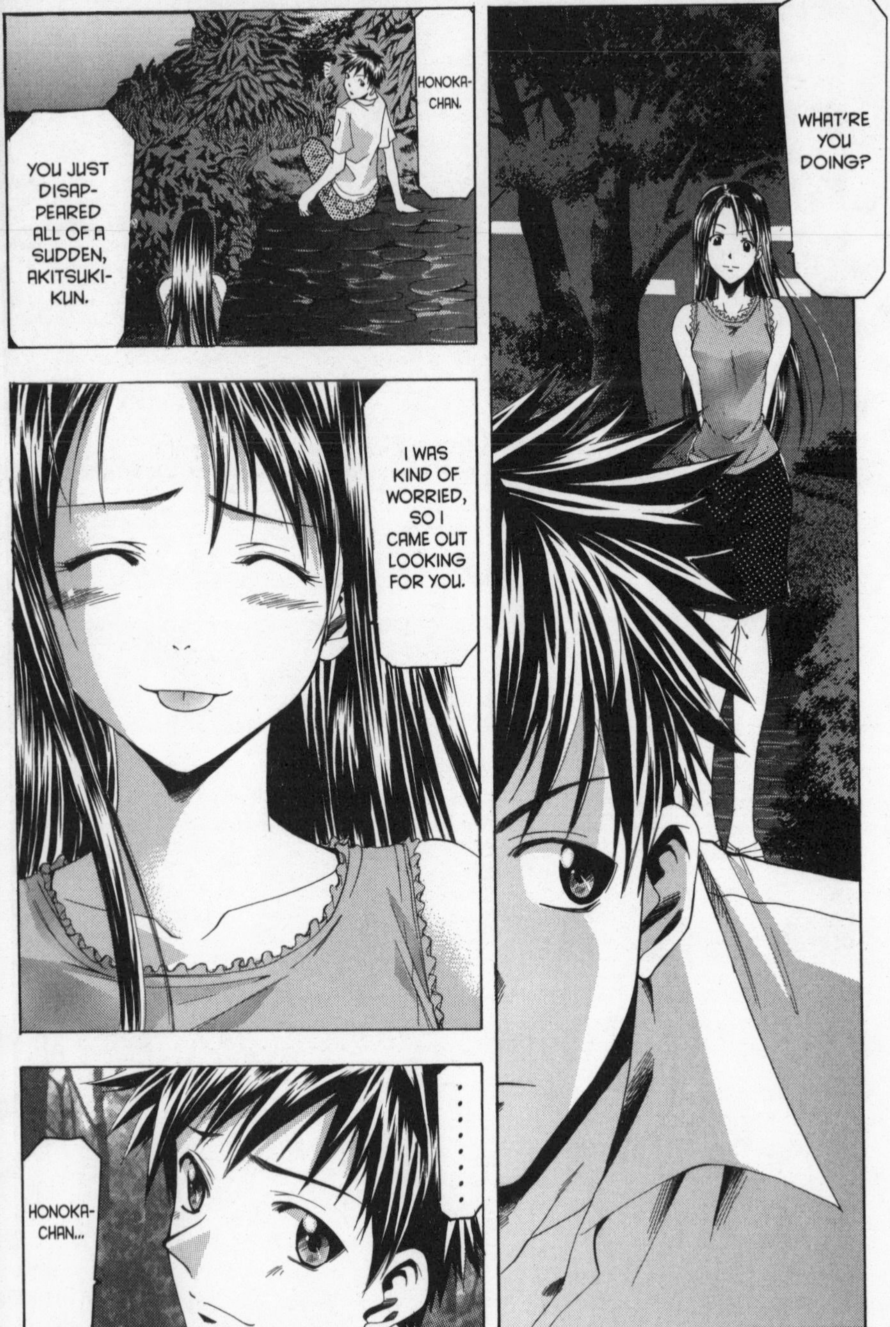
WHAT'RE YOU DOING?
HONOKA-CHAN.
YOU JUST DISAP-PEARED ALL OF A SUDDEN, AKITSUKI-KUN.
I WAS KIND OF WORRIED, SO I CAME OUT LOOKING FOR YOU.
......
HONOKA-CHAN...

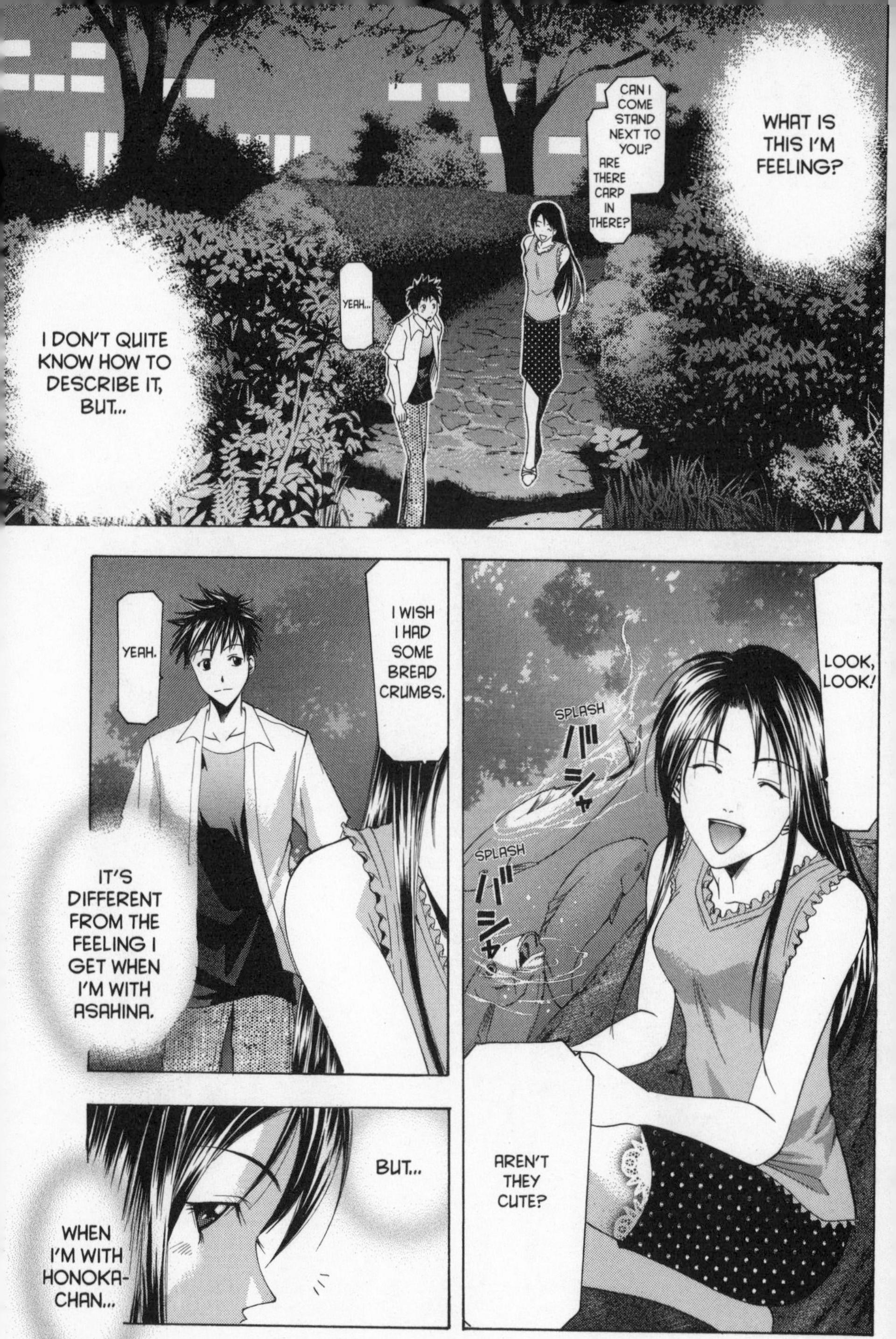
WHAT IS THIS I'M FEELING?
CAN I COME STAND NEXT TO YOU?
ARE THERE CARP IN THERE?
YEAH...
I DON'T QUITE KNOW HOW TO DESCRIBE IT, BUT...
LOOK, LOOK!
SPLASH
バシャ
SPLASH
バシャ
AREN'T THEY CUTE?
I WISH I HAD SOME BREAD CRUMBS.
YEAH.
IT'S DIFFERENT FROM THE FEELING I GET WHEN I'M WITH ASAHINA.
BUT...
WHEN I'M WITH HONOKA-CHAN...

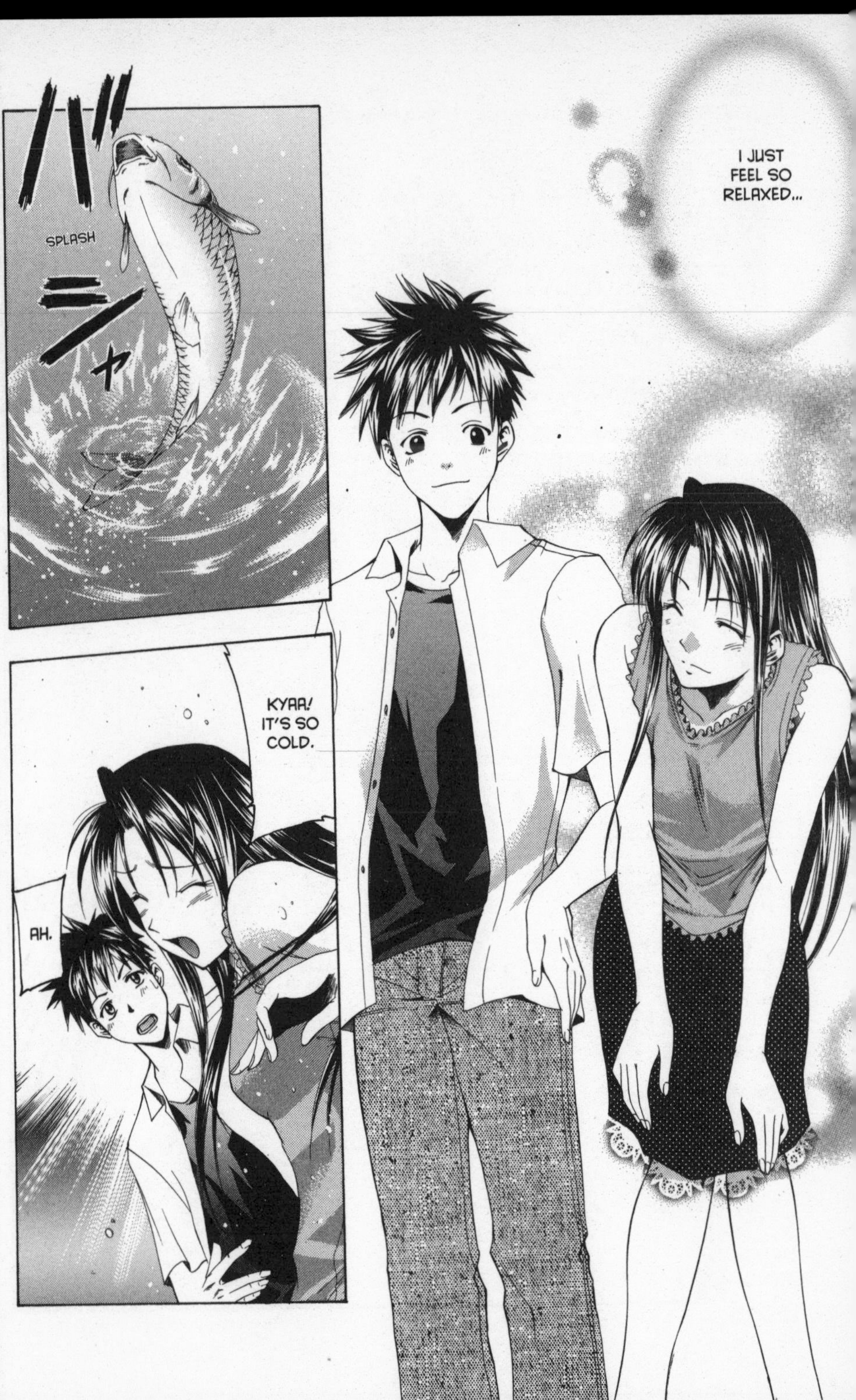
I JUST FEEL SO RELAXED...
バシャ
SPLASH
KYAA! IT'S SO COLD.
AH.

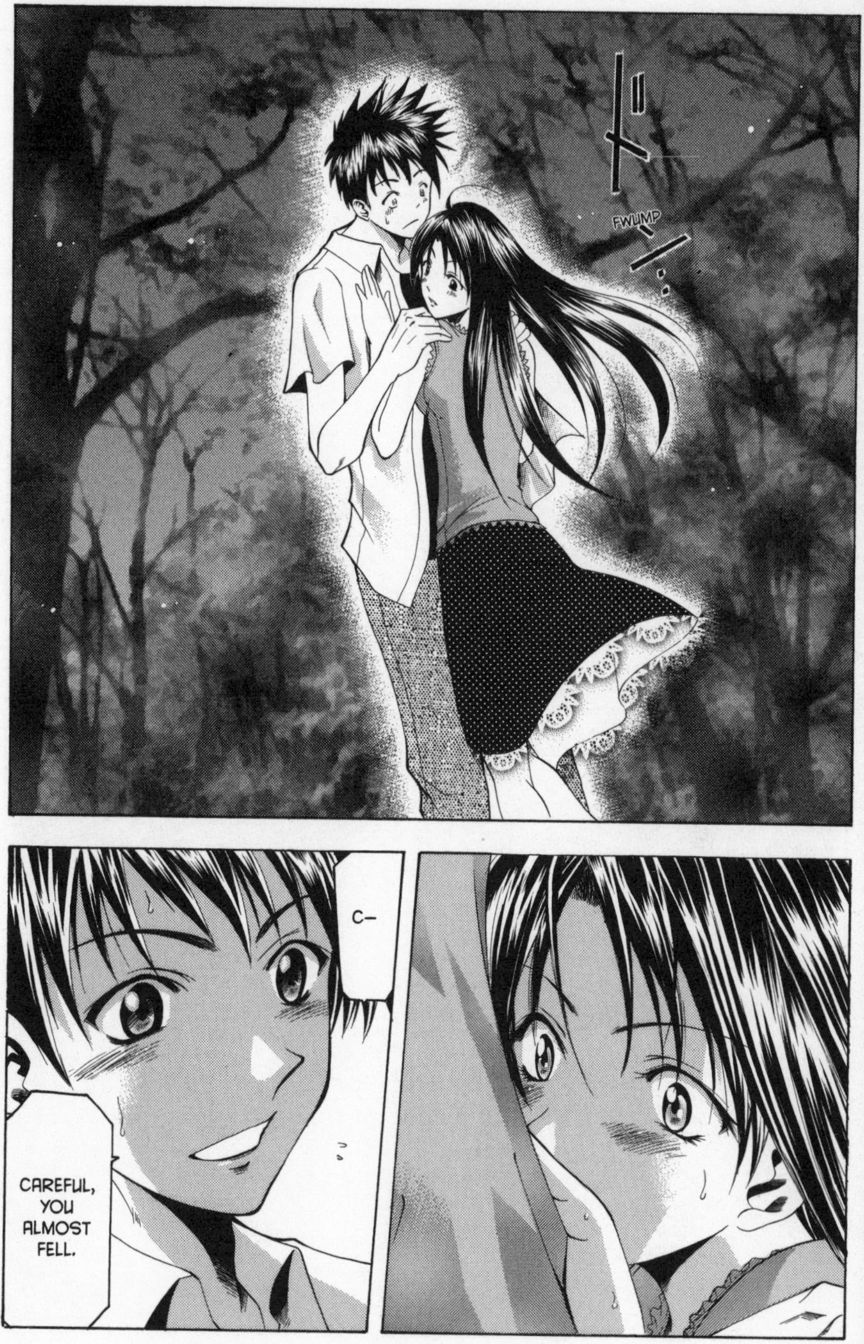
FWUMP
C–
CAREFUL, YOU ALMOST FELL.

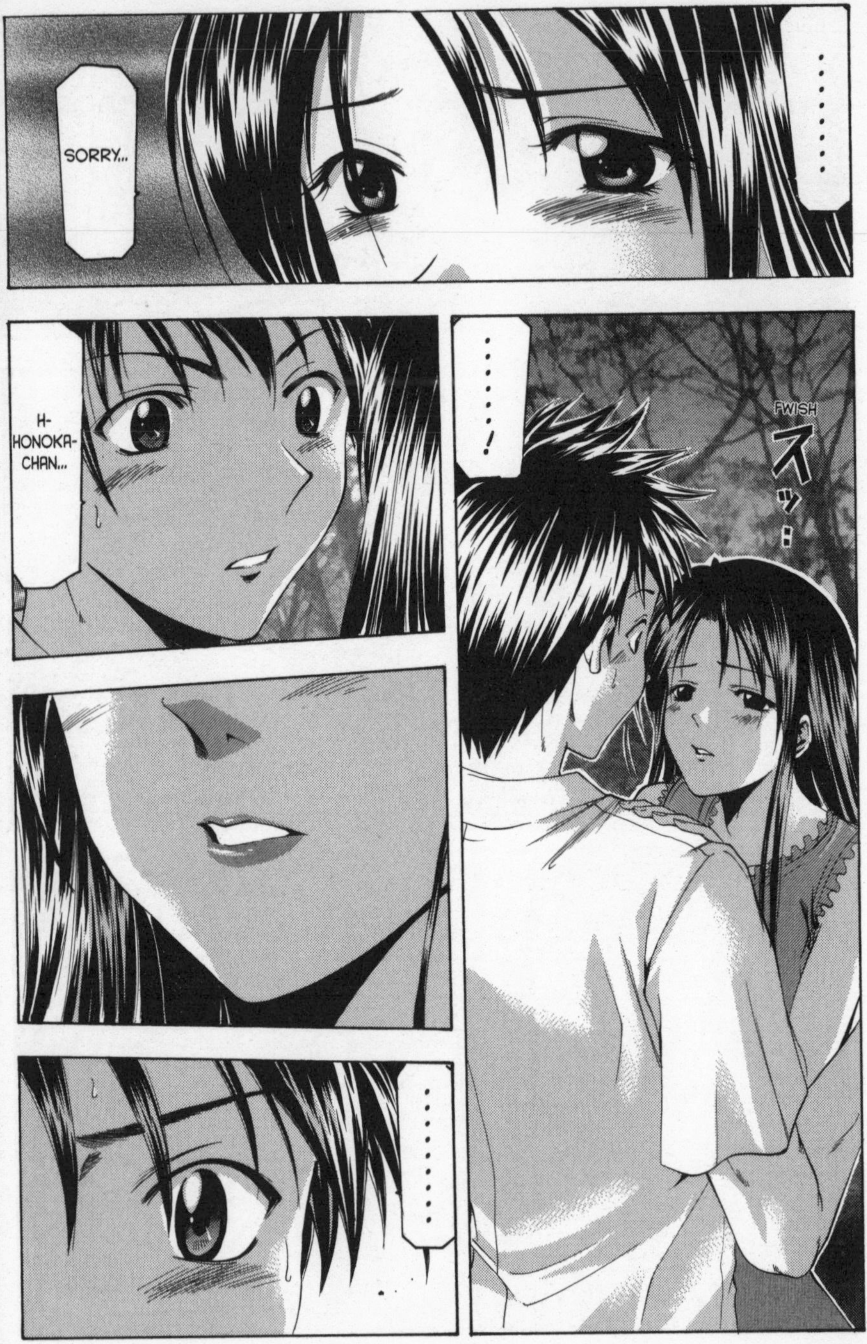
....
SORRY...
......!
FWISH
スッ!
H-HONOKA-CHAN...
....

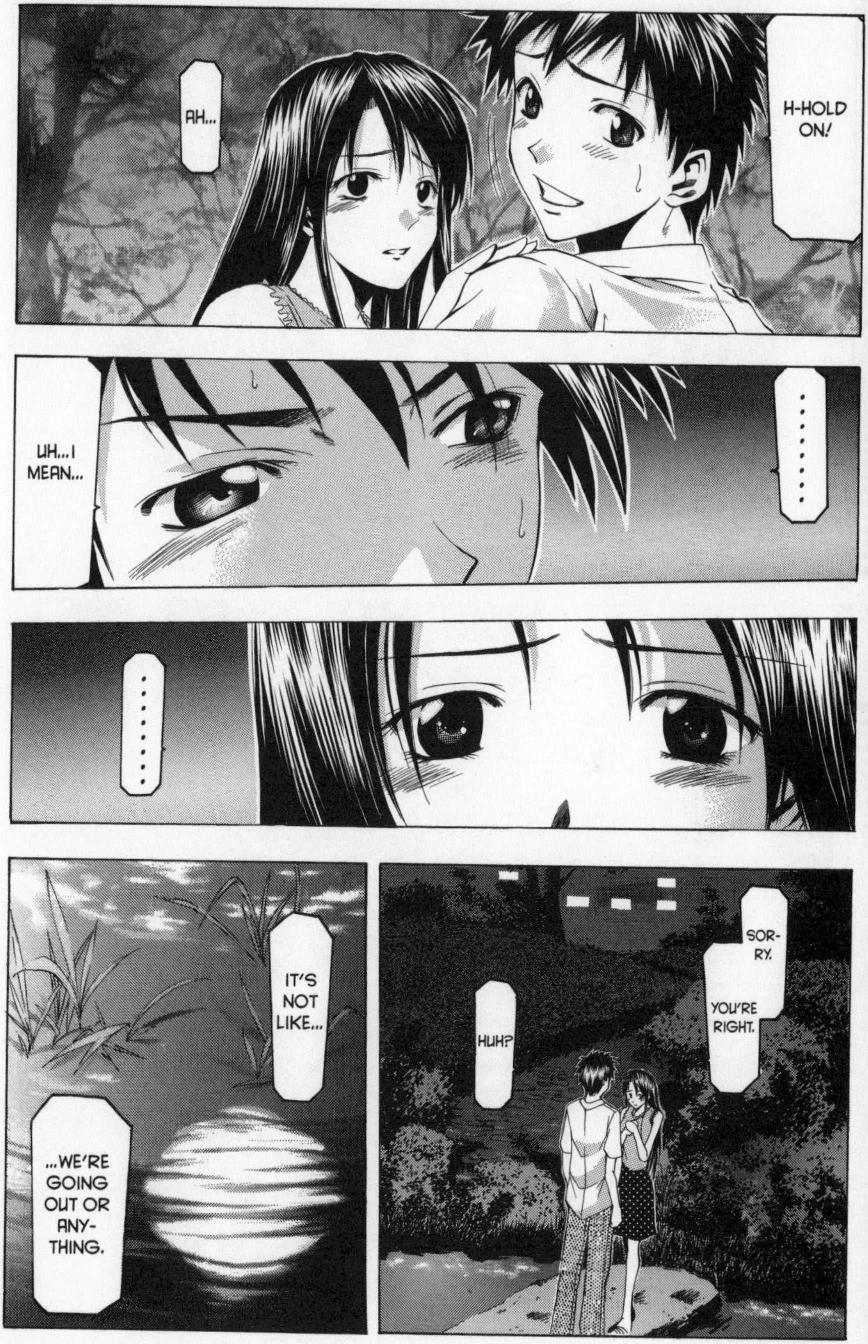
H-HOLD ON!
AH...
......
UH...I MEAN...
....
SOR-RY.
YOU'RE RIGHT.
HUH?
IT'S NOT LIKE...
...WE'RE GOING OUT OR ANY-THING.

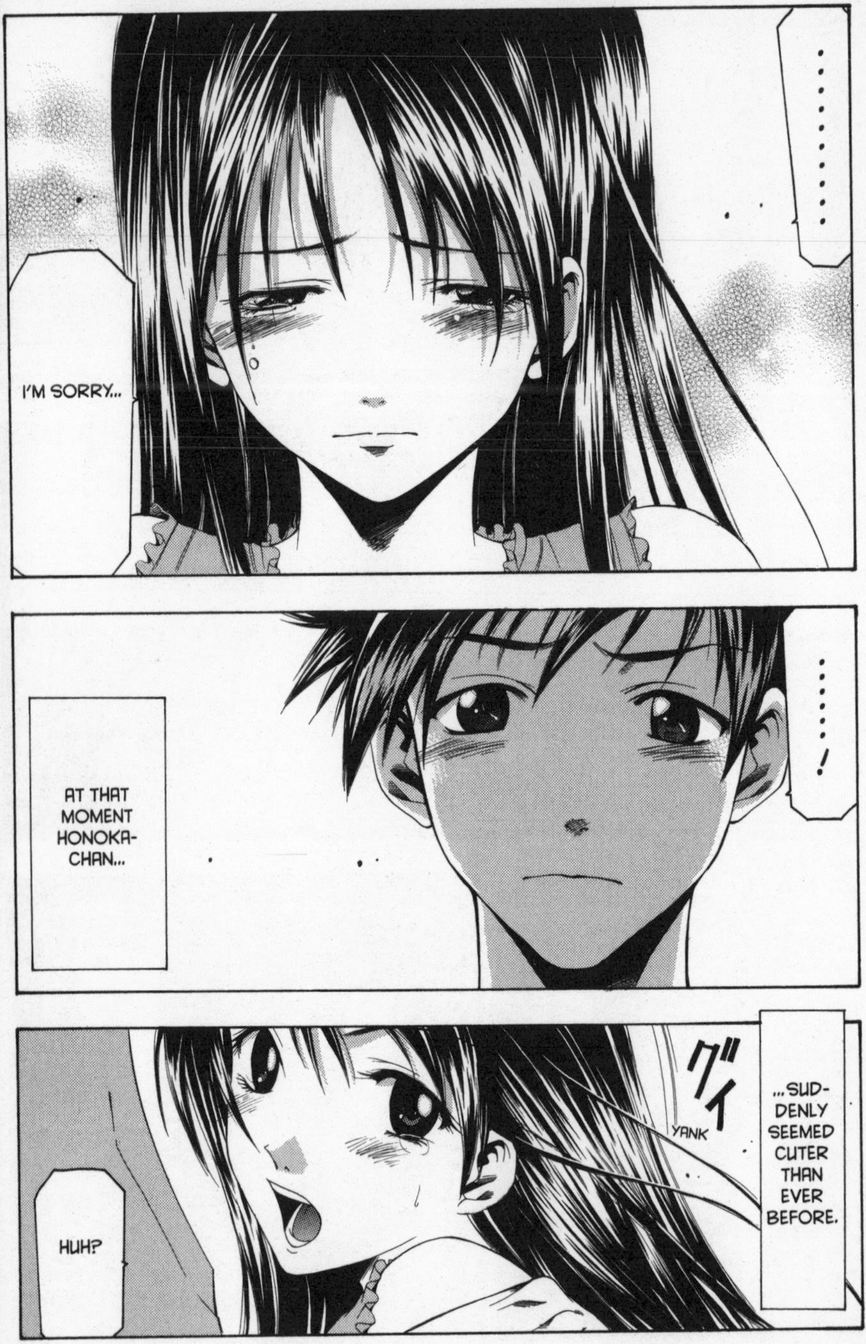
....
I'M SORRY...
......!
AT THAT MOMENT HONOKA-CHAN...
...SUD-DENLY SEEMED CUTER THAN EVER BEFORE.
グイ
YANK
HUH?

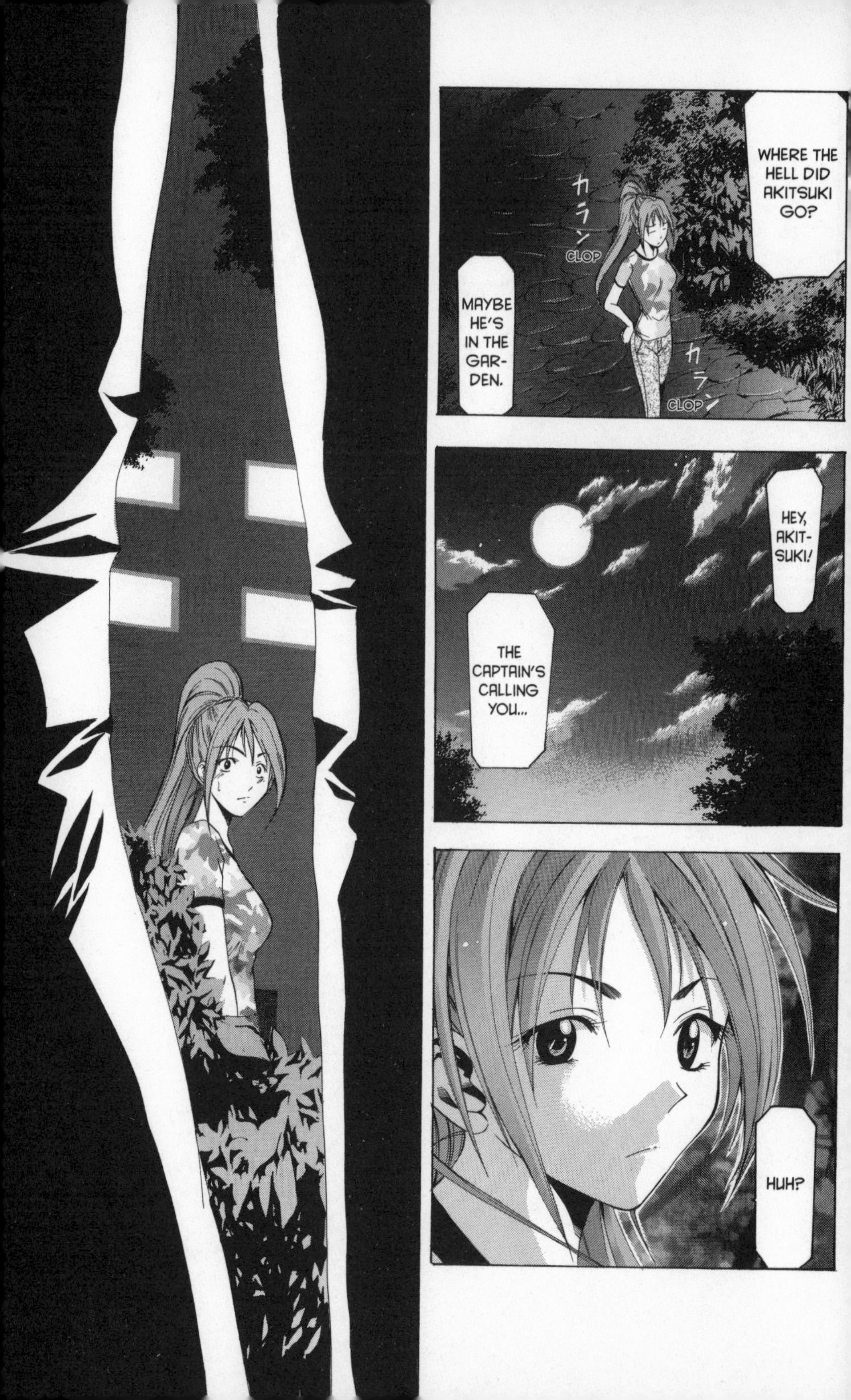
WHERE THE HELL DID AKITSUKI GO?
カラン
CLOP
MAYBE HE'S IN THE GAR-DEN.
カラン
CLOP
HEY, AKIT-SUKI!
THE CAPTAIN'S CALLING YOU...
HUH?

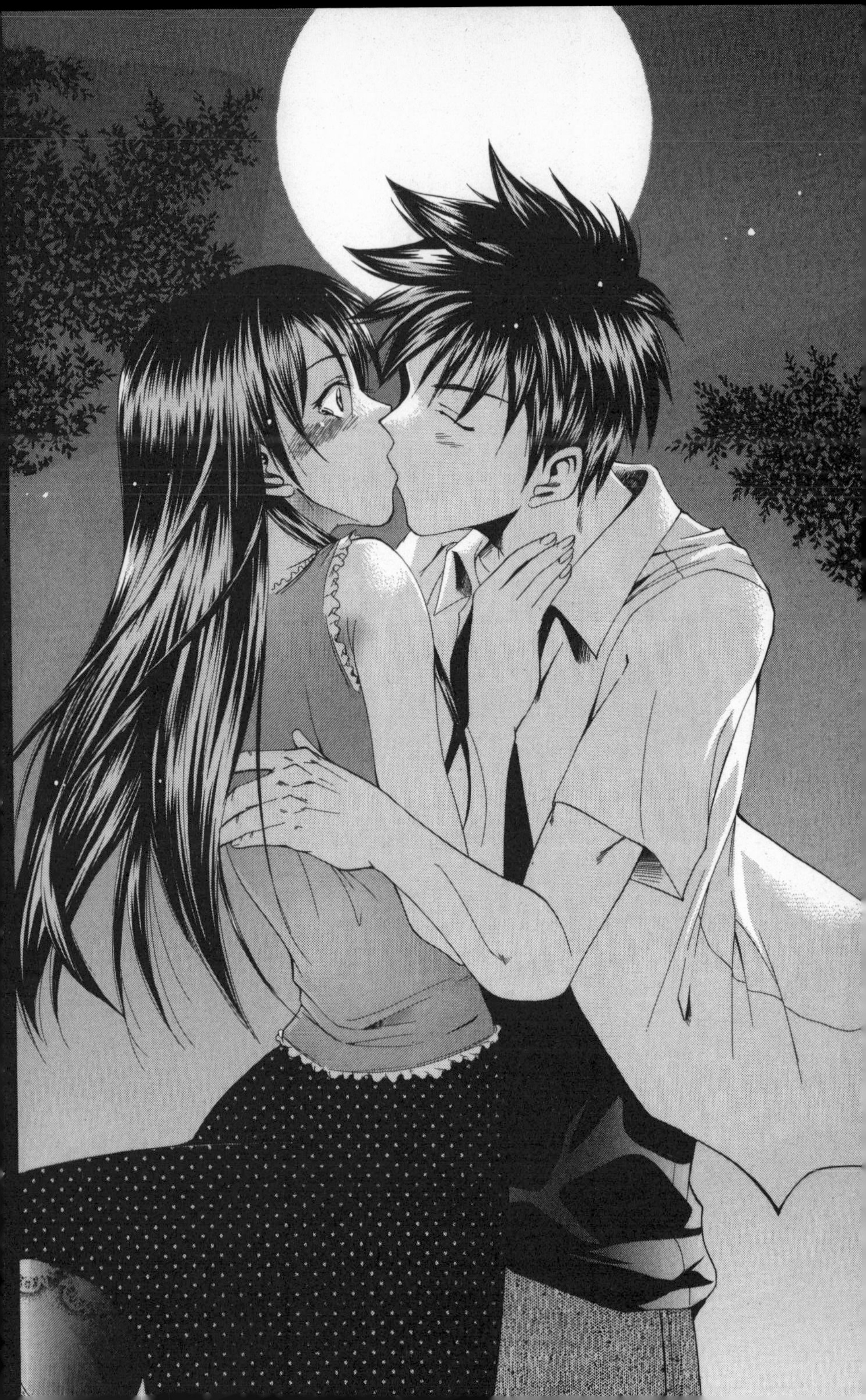

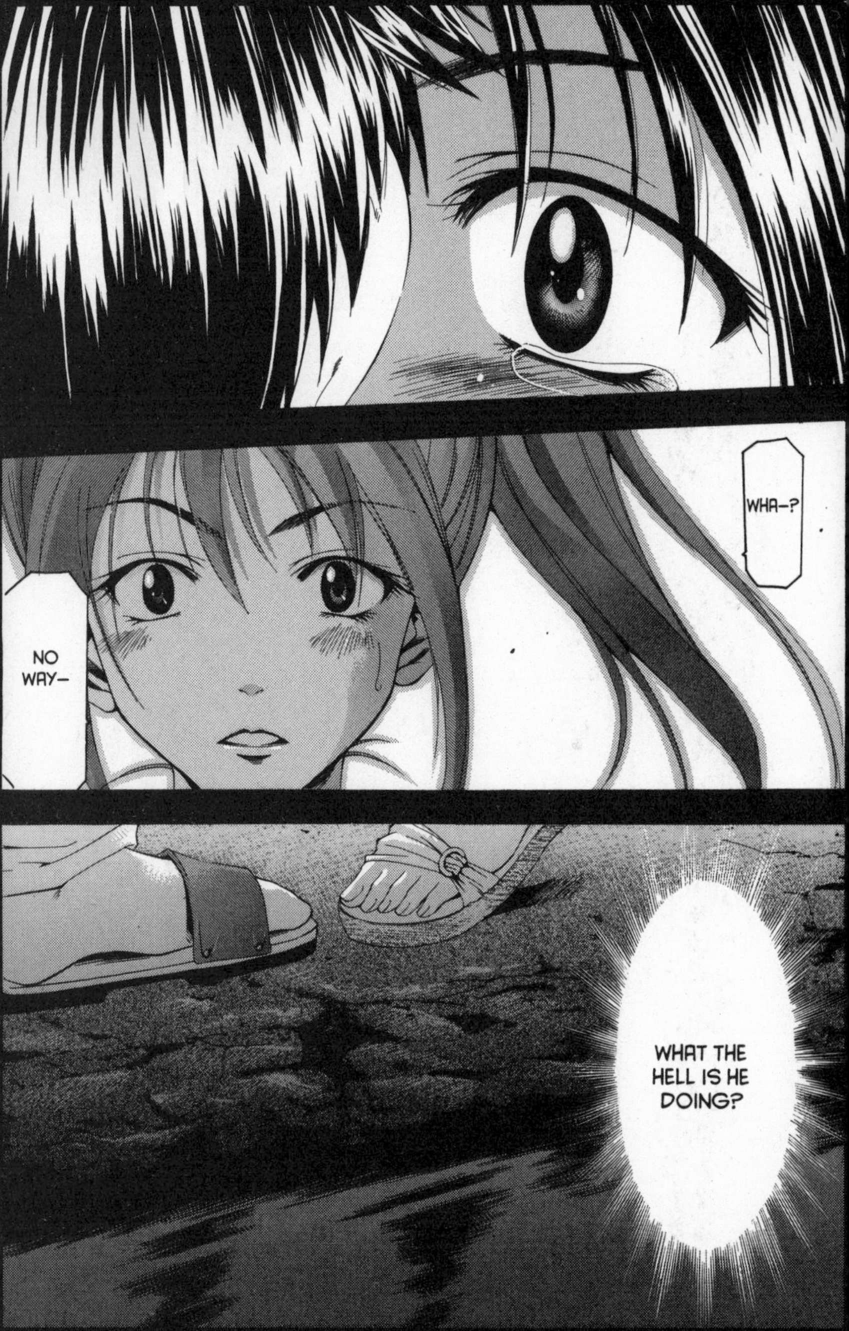
WHA–?
NO WAY–
WHAT THE HELL IS HE DOING?

SUZUKA FOUR-PANEL THEATER NUMBER TWENTY
CHOICES

ON THE WAY HOME FROM A RE-SEARCH TRIP.
WHAT DO YOU WANNA EAT, SEO-KUN? CRAB? STEAK?
YOU CAN HAVE ANY-THING YOU WANT.
REALLY?
WELL, CRAB SOUNDS GOOD, BUT I THINK I'M IN MORE OF A MEAT-EATING MOOD.
I'D LIKE TO GO SOME-WHERE I COULDN'T GO ON MY OWN.
ALL RIGHT, MEAT IT IS.
WE TOOK AN HOUR-LONG TAXI RIDE.
AH, IT'S CLOSED.
STEAK HOUSE
WHA-?
Closed
WELL, AS LONG AS WE'RE IN THE NEIGHBOR-HOOD, I GUESS WE COULD GO TO THAT OTHER PLACE.
A RAMEN SHOP
THEIR STIR-FRIED MEAT AND VEGGIES ARE REALLY GOOD.
ズルズル
THE MISO STIR-FRY IS GOOD, TOO.
SO MUCH FOR GOING SOME-WHERE I COULDN'T USUALLY AFFORD.

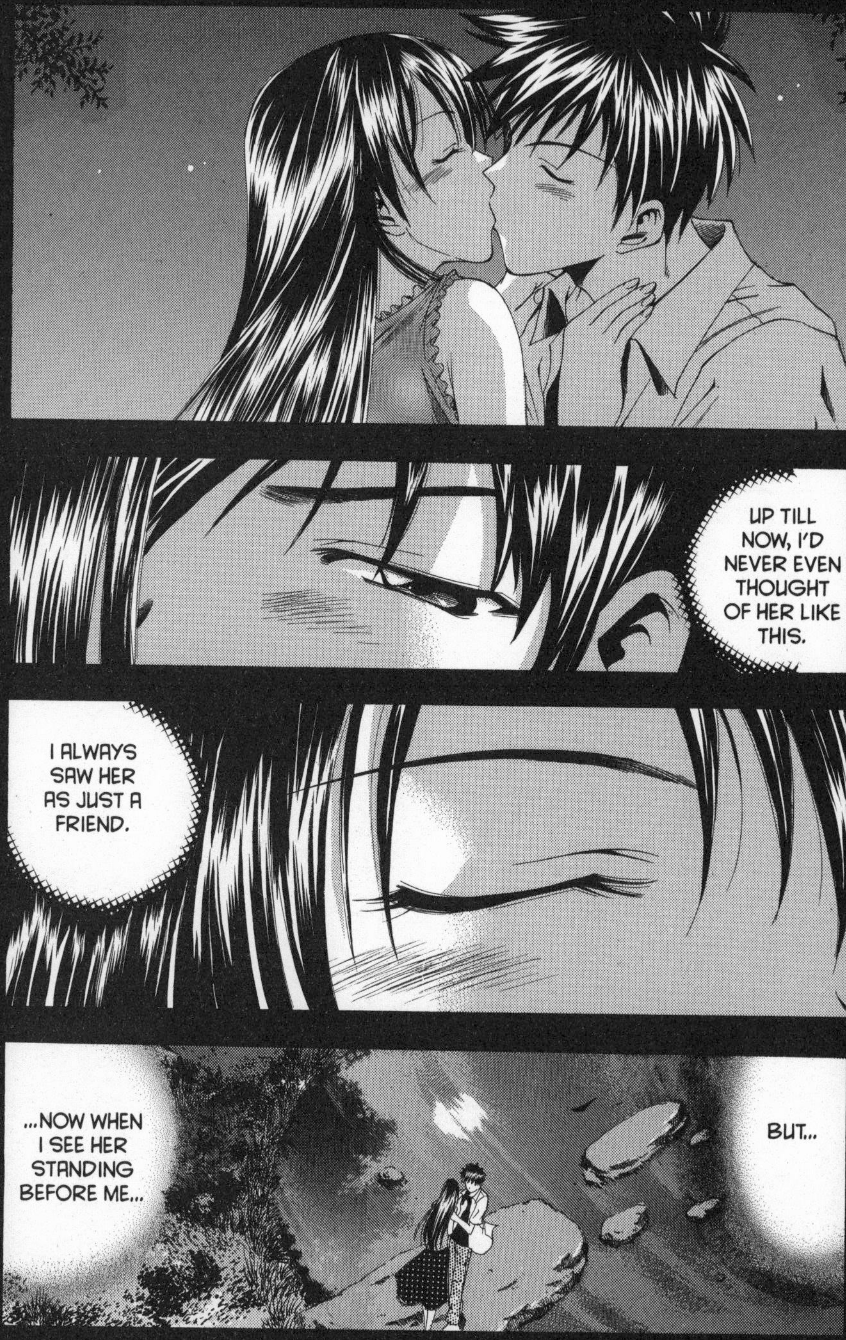
UP TILL NOW, I'D NEVER EVEN THOUGHT OF HER LIKE THIS.
I ALWAYS SAW HER AS JUST A FRIEND.
BUT...
...NOW WHEN I SEE HER STANDING BEFORE ME...

SHE LOOKS LIKE THE CUTEST GIRL...

...IN THE WHOLE WIDE WORLD.

SUZUKA

#36 EXPOSE

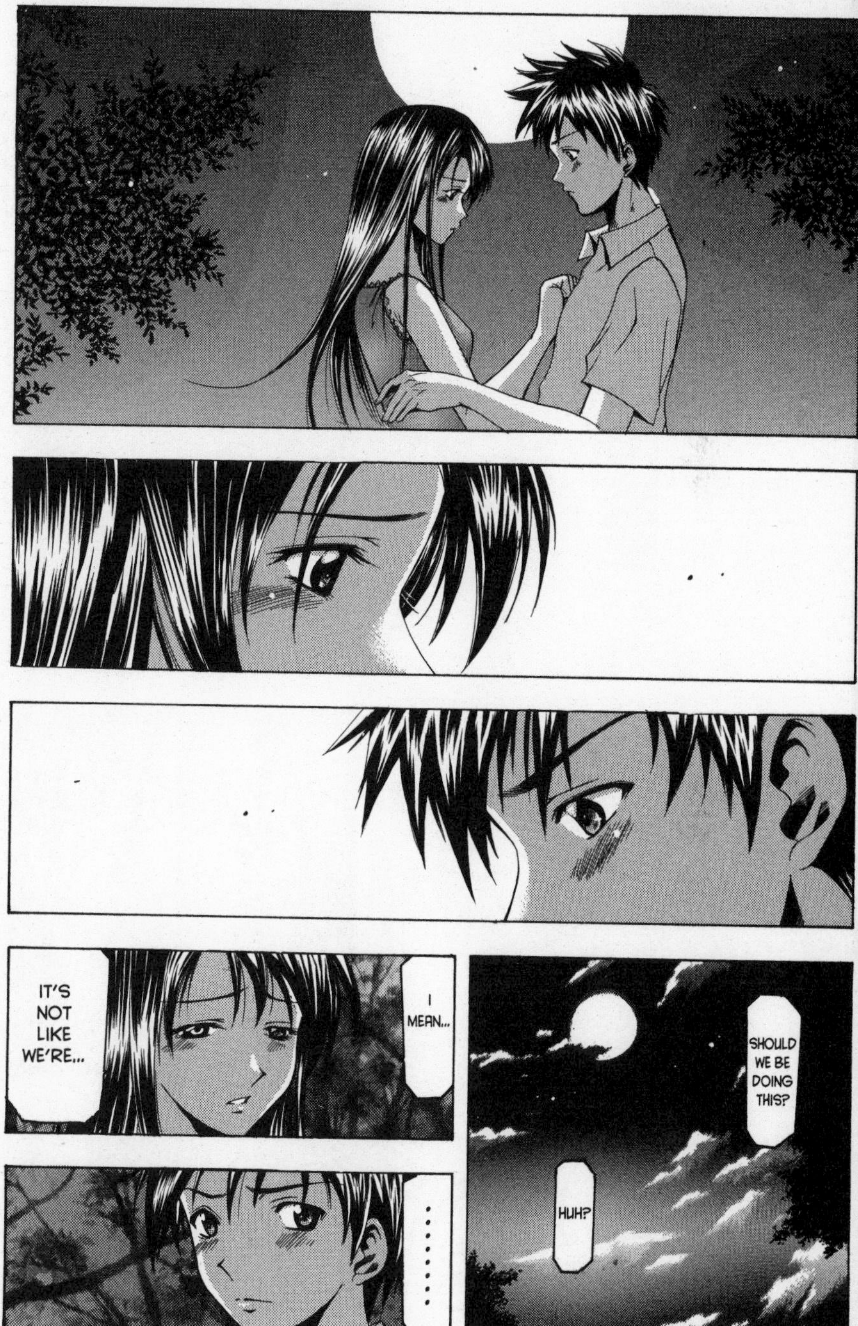
SHOULD WE BE DOING THIS?
HUH?
I MEAN...
IT'S NOT LIKE WE'RE...
....

WELL...

WHY DON'T WE START GOING OUT?

N-NO, NOT AT ALL.

UH... WAIT...DID THAT SOUND REALLY LAME? SORRY.

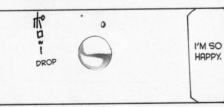

ポロッ!
DROP

I'M SO HAPPY.

EH?

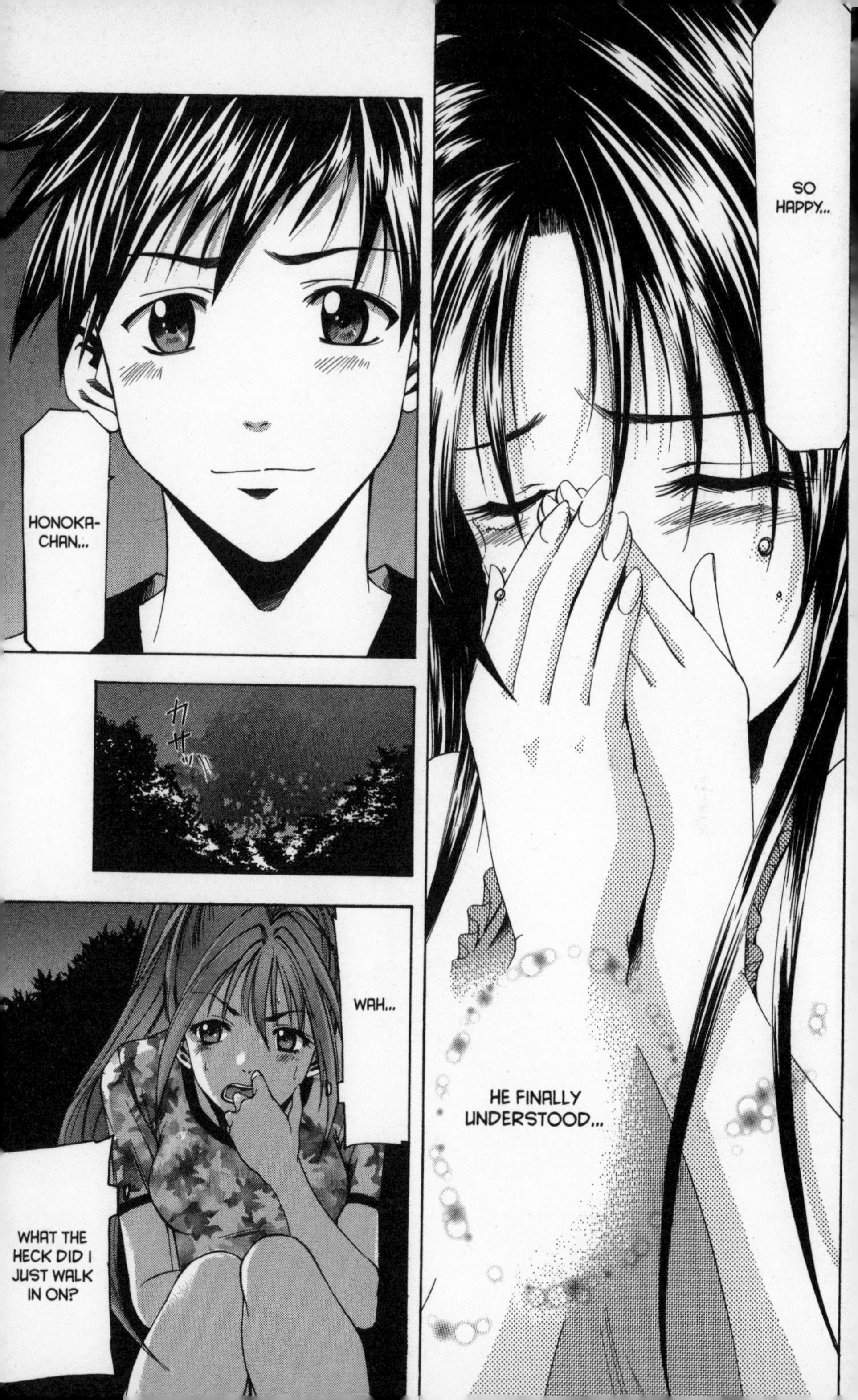
SO HAPPY...
HE FINALLY UNDERSTOOD...
HONOKA-CHAN...
カサッ
WAH...
WHAT THE HECK DID I JUST WALK IN ON?

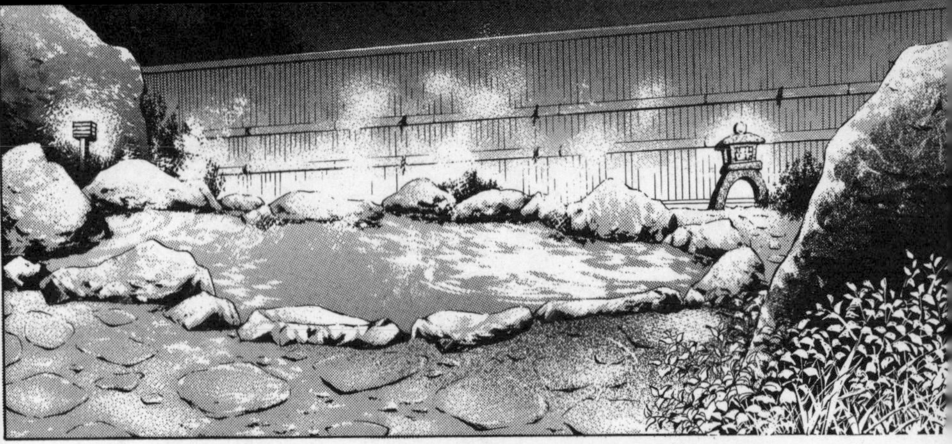
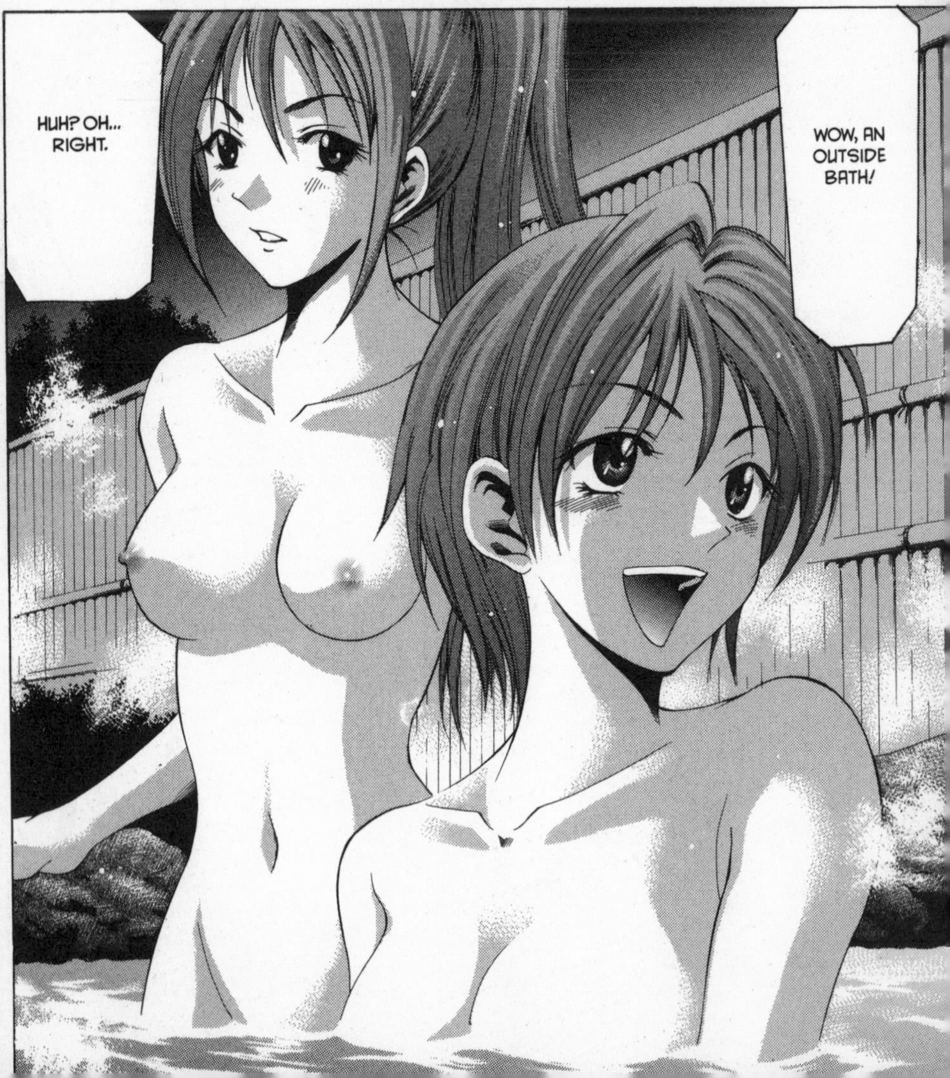
WOW, AN OUTSIDE BATH!
HUH? OH... RIGHT.

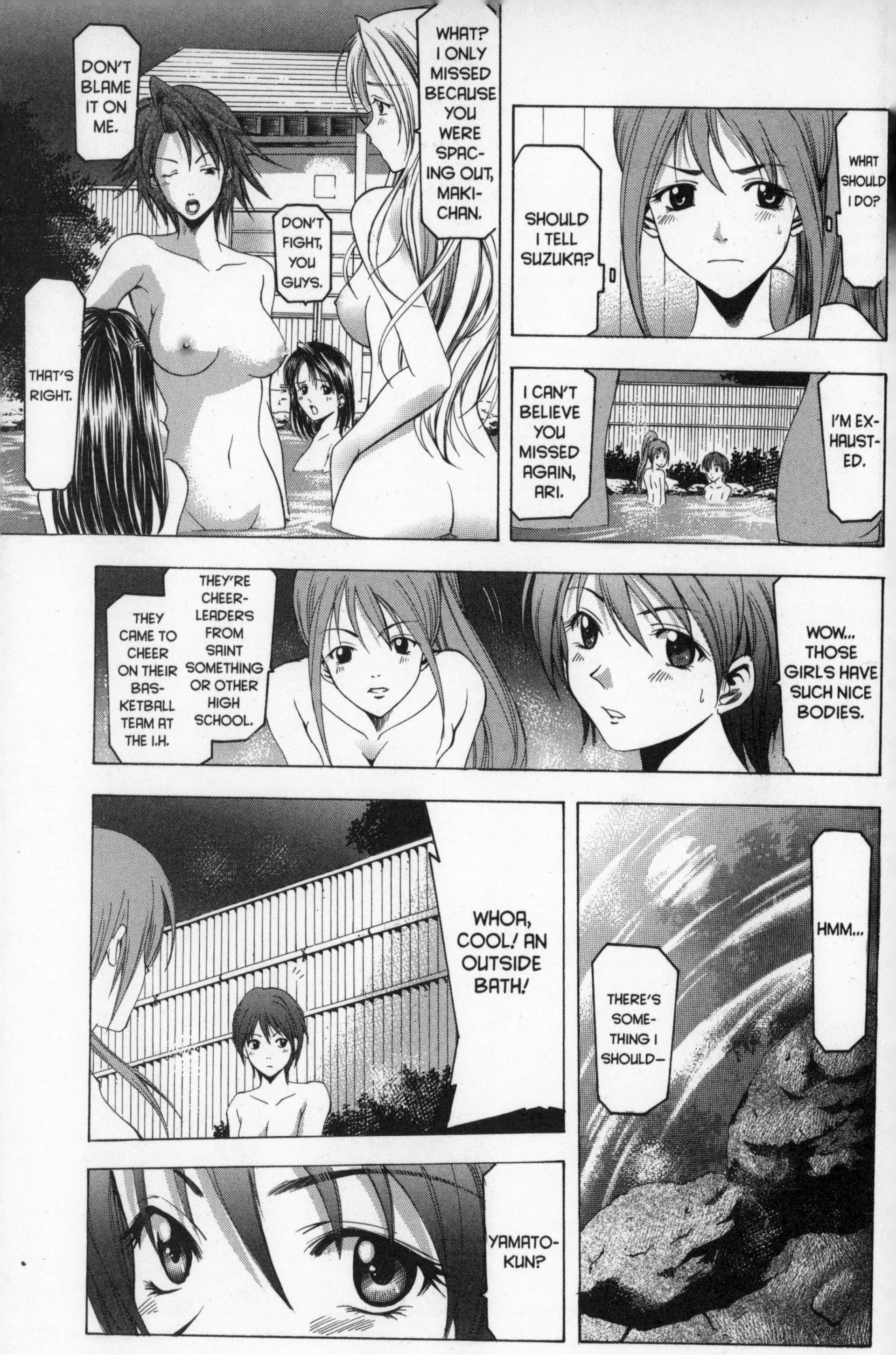
WHAT SHOULD I DO?
SHOULD I TELL SUZUKA?
I'M EXHAUSTED.
I CAN'T BELIEVE YOU MISSED AGAIN, ARI.
WHAT? I ONLY MISSED BECAUSE YOU WERE SPACING OUT, MAKI-CHAN.
DON'T BLAME IT ON ME.
DON'T FIGHT, YOU GUYS.
THAT'S RIGHT.
WOW... THOSE GIRLS HAVE SUCH NICE BODIES.
THEY'RE CHEERLEADERS FROM SAINT SOMETHING OR OTHER HIGH SCHOOL.
THEY CAME TO CHEER ON THEIR BASKETBALL TEAM AT THE I.H.
HMM...
THERE'S SOMETHING I SHOULD—
WHOA, COOL! AN OUTSIDE BATH!
YAMATO-KUN?

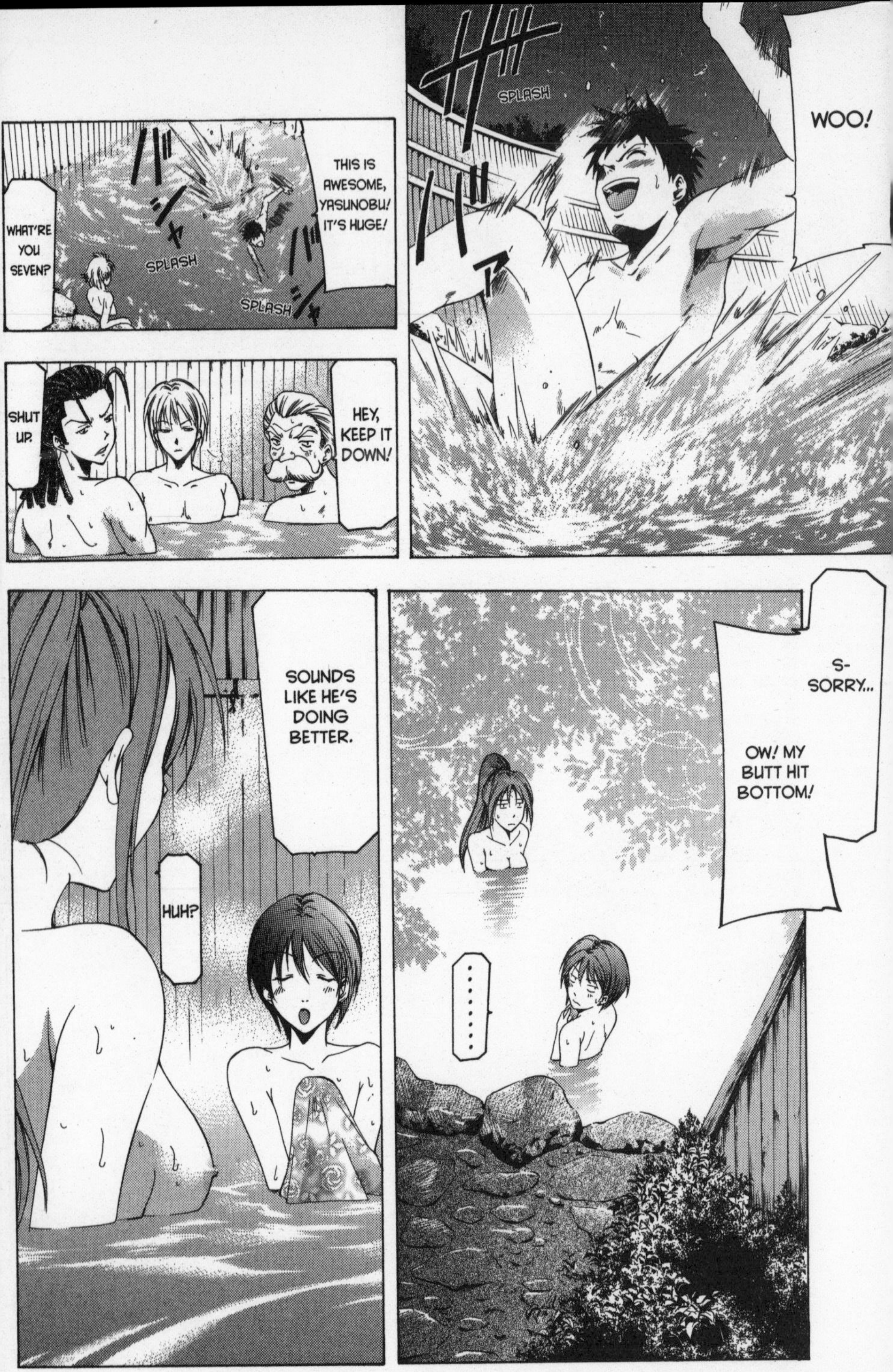
SPLASH
WOO!
THIS IS AWESOME, YASUNOBU! IT'S HUGE!
SPLASH
SPLASH
WHAT'RE YOU SEVEN?
HEY, KEEP IT DOWN!
SHUT UP.
S- SORRY...
OW! MY BUTT HIT BOTTOM!
......
SOUNDS LIKE HE'S DOING BETTER.
HUH?

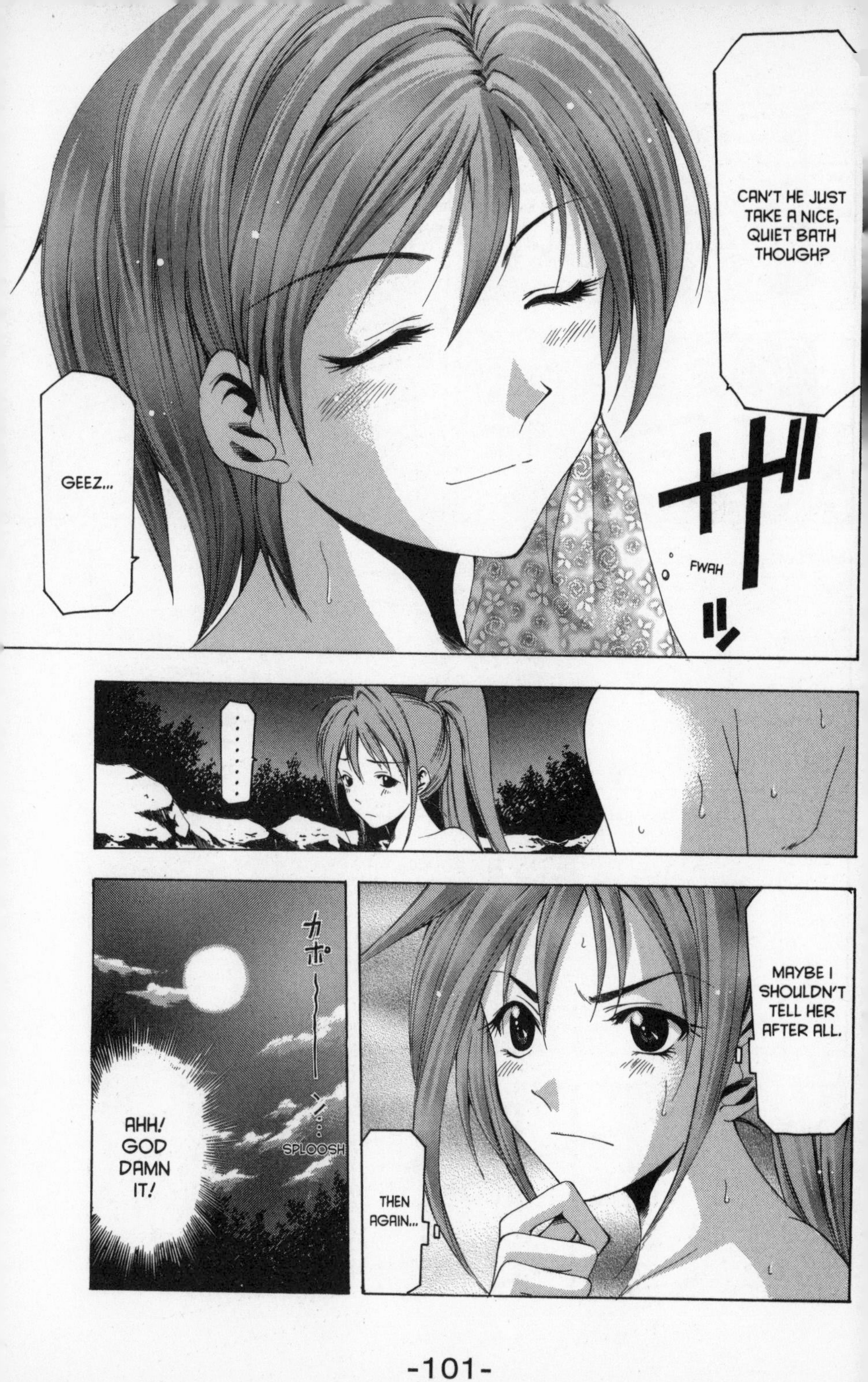
CAN'T HE JUST TAKE A NICE, QUIET BATH THOUGH?
ザッ
FWAH
GEEZ...
......
MAYBE I SHOULDN'T TELL HER AFTER ALL.
THEN AGAIN...
カポーーーン...
SPLOOSH
AHH! GOD DAMN IT!

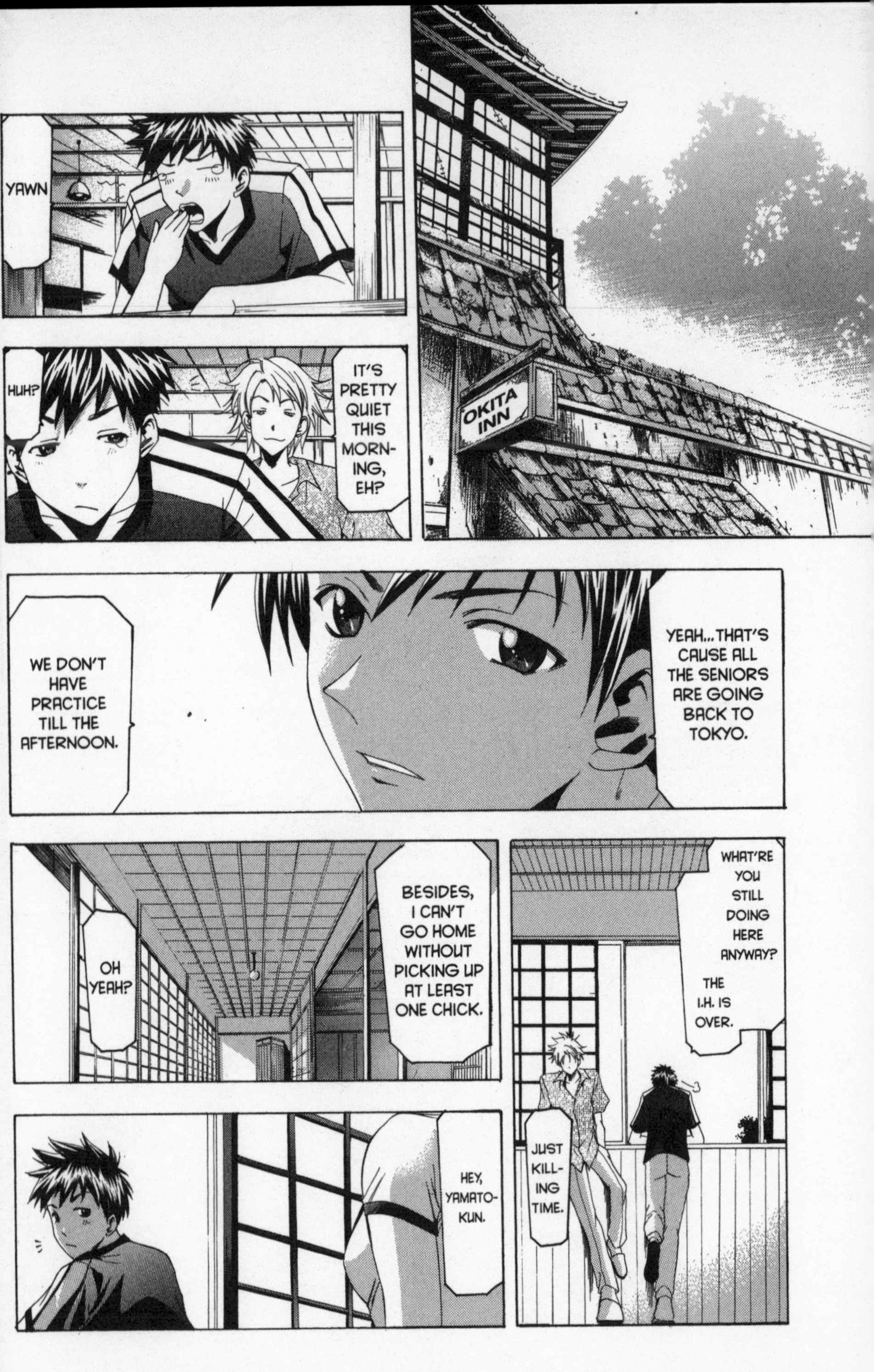
OKITA INN
YAWN
IT'S PRETTY QUIET THIS MORNING, EH?
HUH?
YEAH... THAT'S CAUSE ALL THE SENIORS ARE GOING BACK TO TOKYO.
WE DON'T HAVE PRACTICE TILL THE AFTERNOON.
WHAT'RE YOU STILL DOING HERE ANYWAY?
THE I.H. IS OVER.
JUST KILLING TIME.
BESIDES, I CAN'T GO HOME WITHOUT PICKING UP AT LEAST ONE CHICK.
OH YEAH?
HEY, YAMATO-KUN.

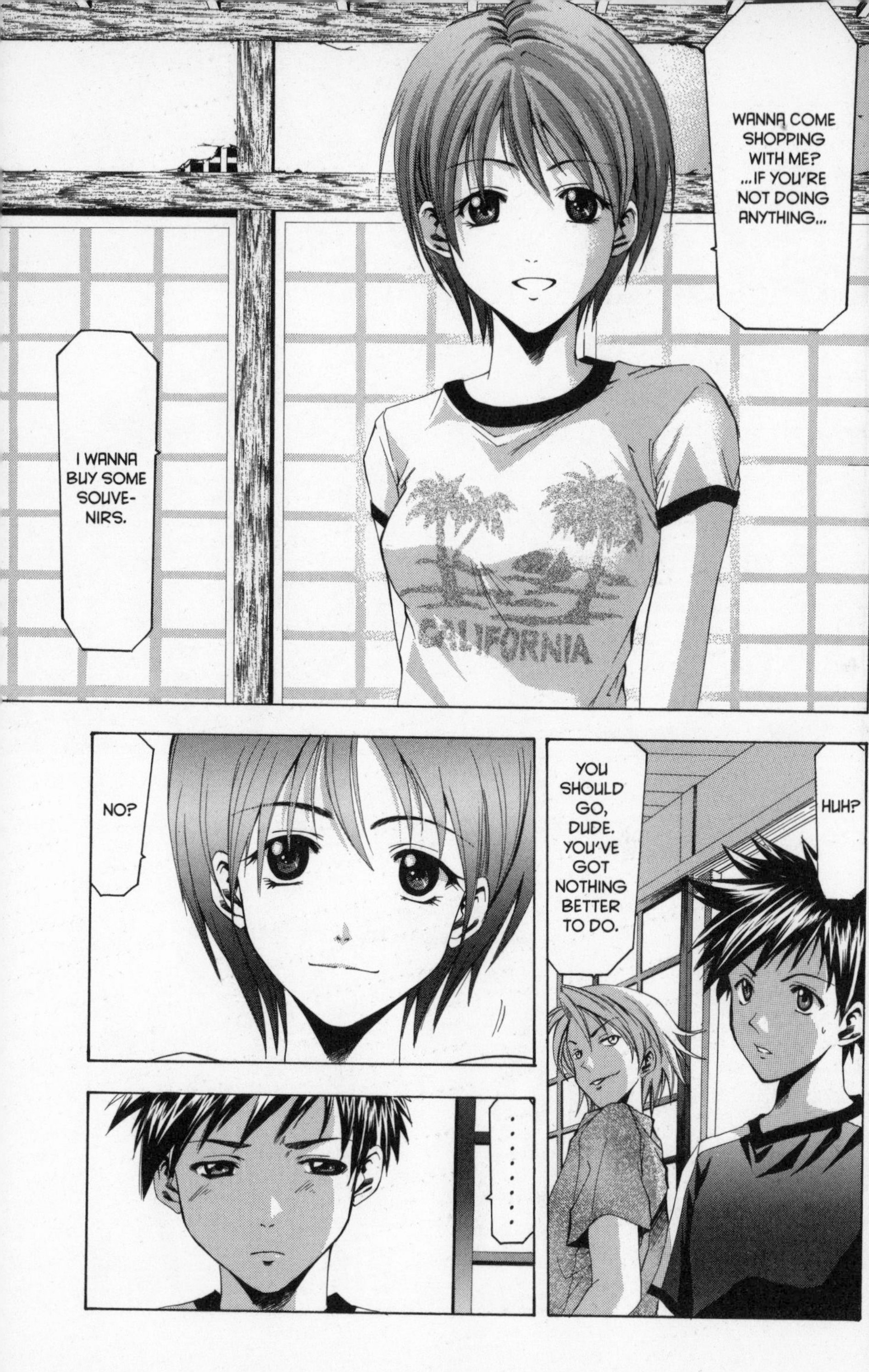
WANNA COME SHOPPING WITH ME? ...IF YOU'RE NOT DOING ANYTHING...
I WANNA BUY SOME SOUVE-NIRS.
HUH?
YOU SHOULD GO, DUDE. YOU'VE GOT NOTHING BETTER TO DO.
NO?
....

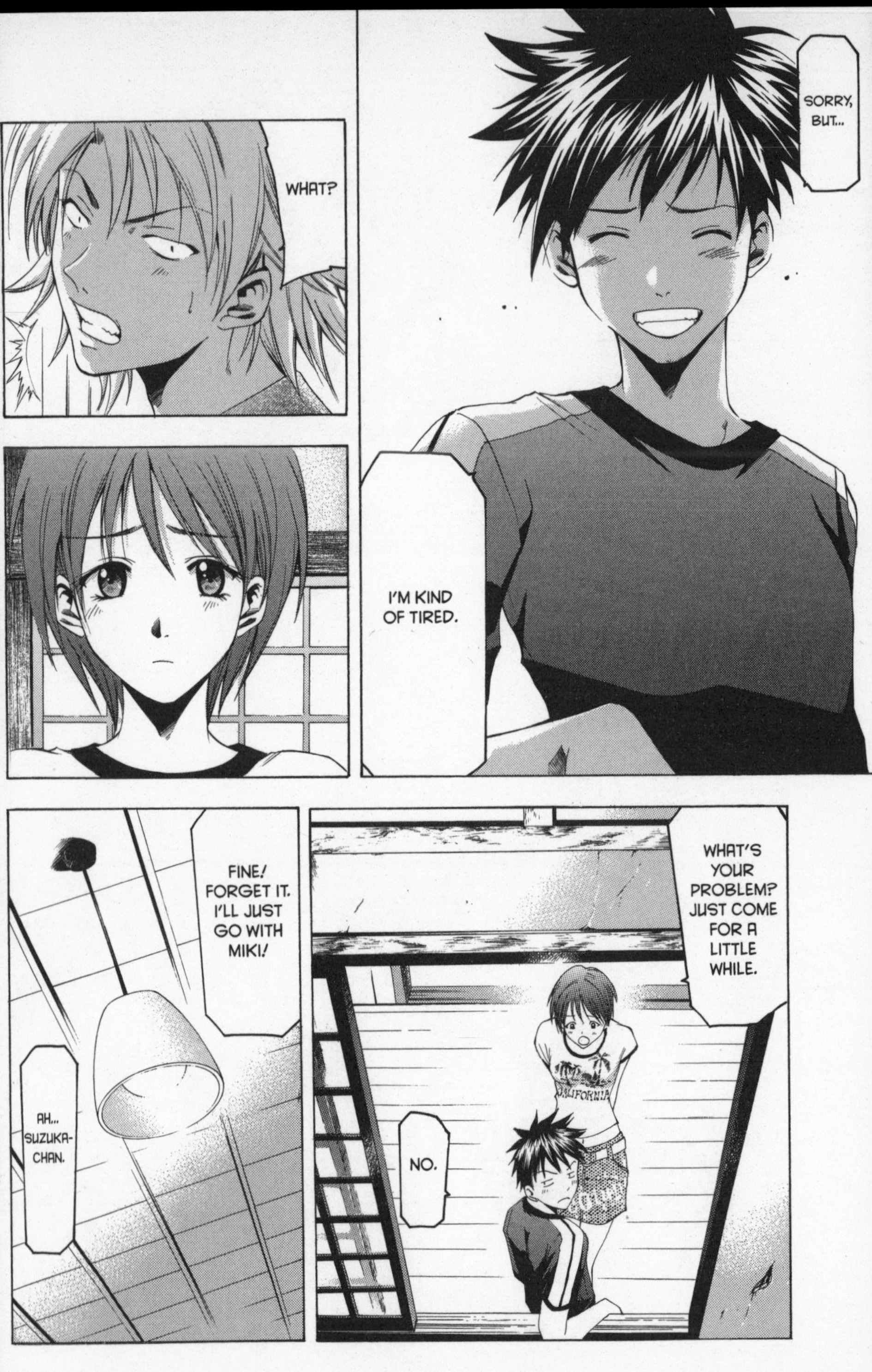
SORRY, BUT...
I'M KIND OF TIRED.
WHAT?
WHAT'S YOUR PROBLEM? JUST COME FOR A LITTLE WHILE.
NO.
CALIFORNIA
FINE! FORGET IT. I'LL JUST GO WITH MIKI!
AH... SUZUKA-CHAN.

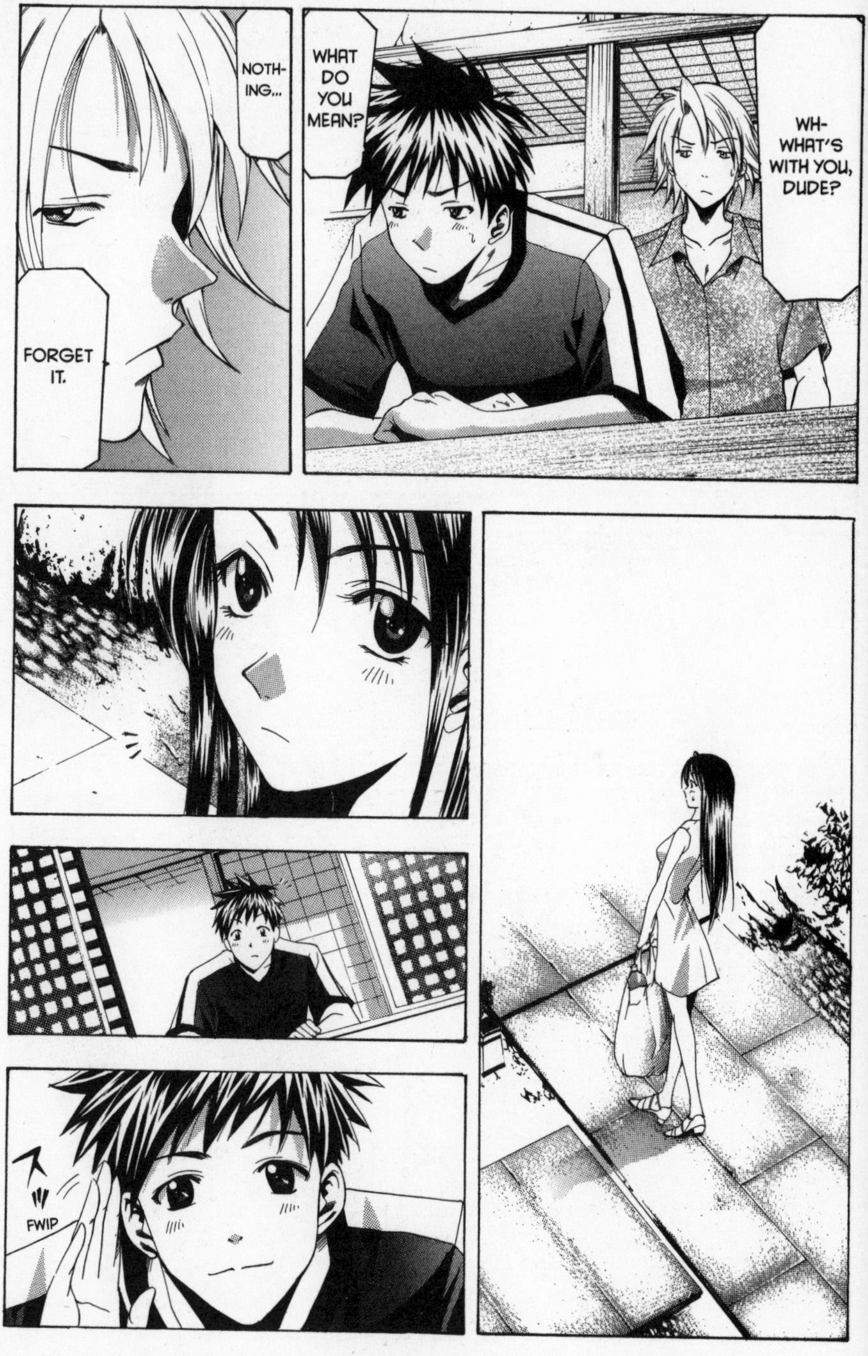
WH- WHAT'S WITH YOU, DUDE?
WHAT DO YOU MEAN?
NOTH- ING...
FORGET IT.
ス
FWIP

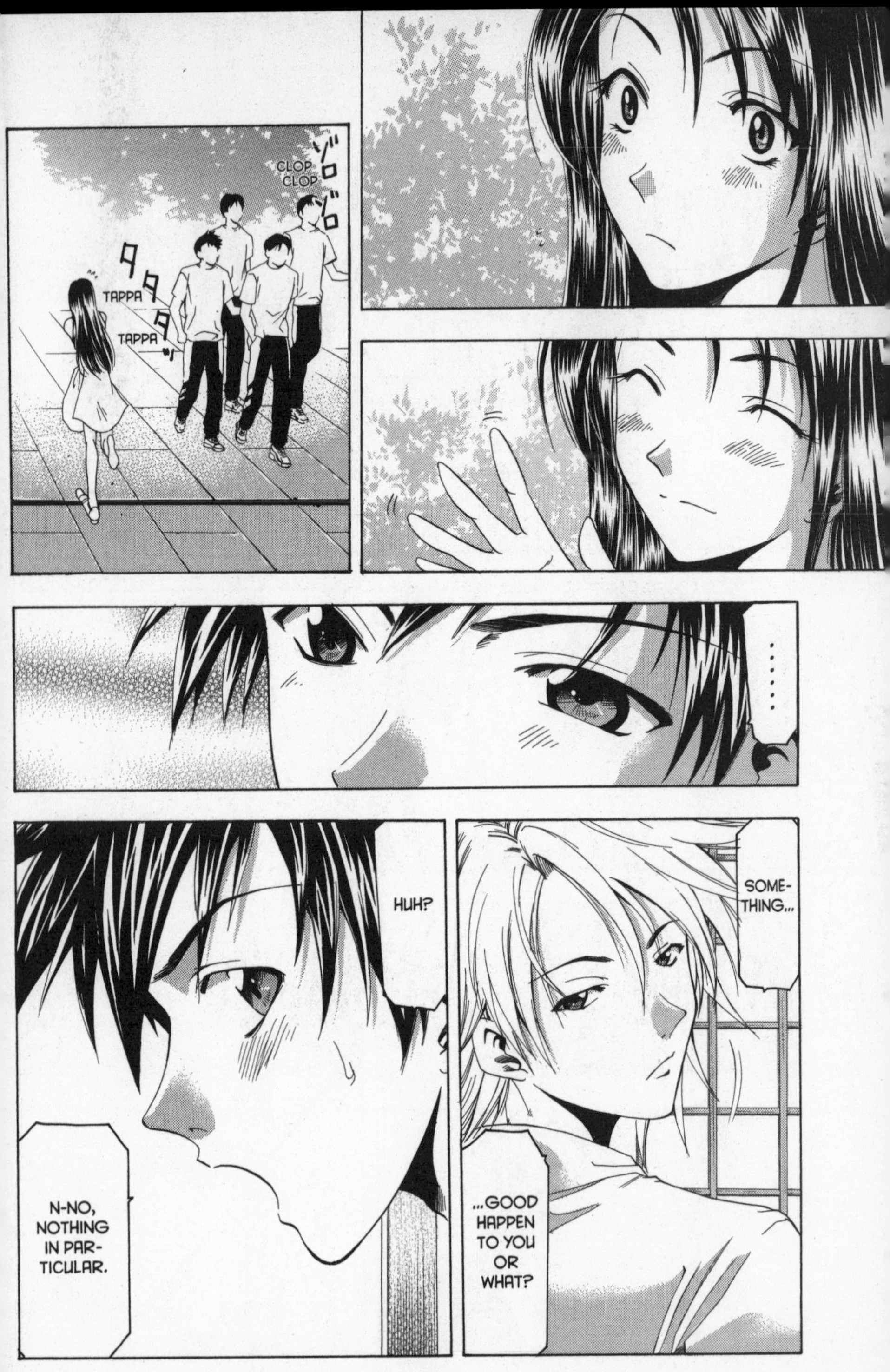
ゾロゾロ
CLOP CLOP
タタタ
TAPPA TAPPA
......
SOME-THING...
...GOOD HAPPEN TO YOU OR WHAT?
HUH?
N-NO, NOTHING IN PAR-TICULAR.

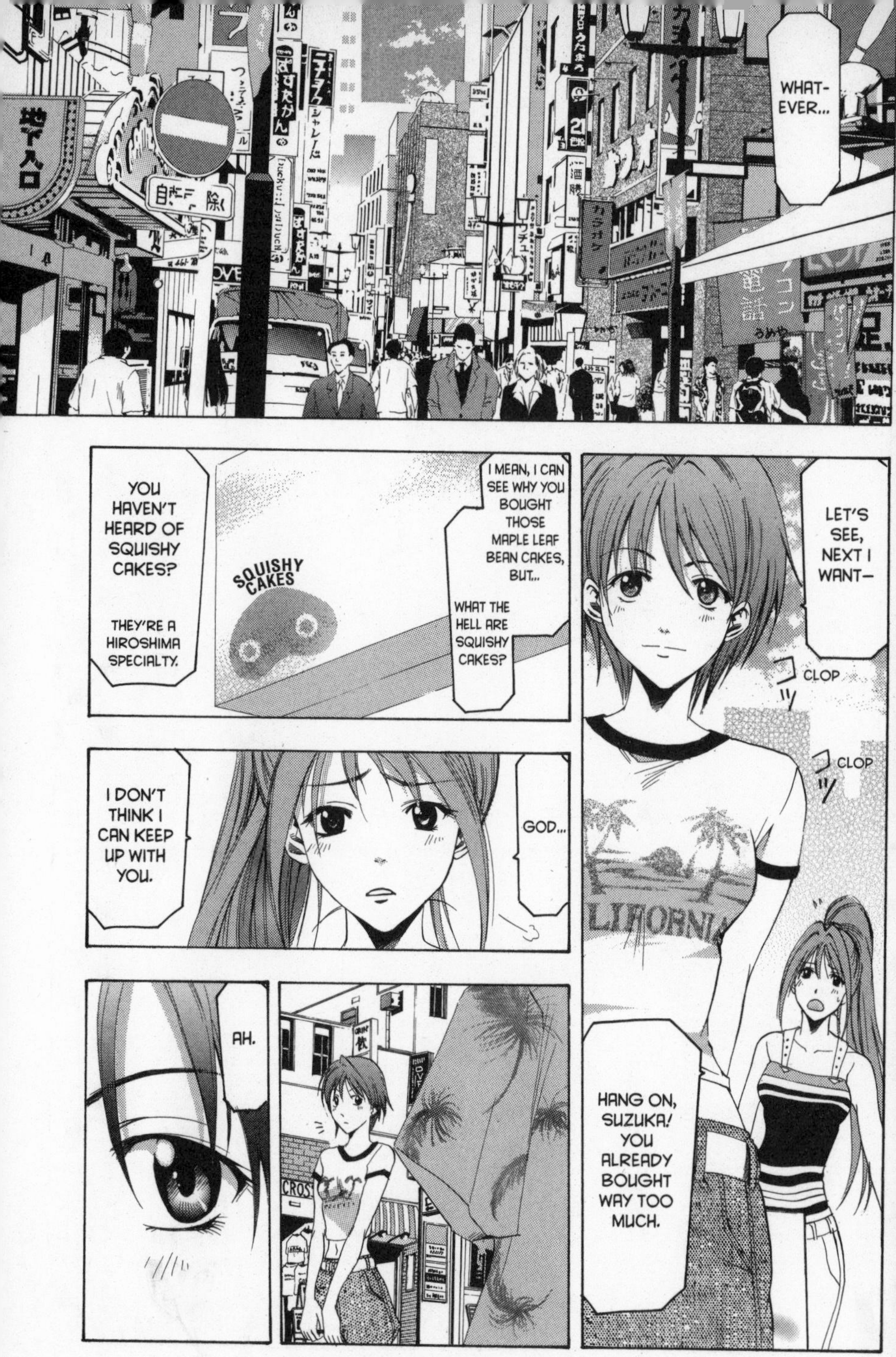
WHATEVER...
LET'S SEE, NEXT I WANT—
CLOP
CLOP
HANG ON, SUZUKA! YOU ALREADY BOUGHT WAY TOO MUCH.
I MEAN, I CAN SEE WHY YOU BOUGHT THOSE MAPLE LEAF BEAN CAKES, BUT...
WHAT THE HELL ARE SQUISHY CAKES?
SQUISHY CAKES
YOU HAVEN'T HEARD OF SQUISHY CAKES?
THEY'RE A HIROSHIMA SPECIALTY.
GOD...
I DON'T THINK I CAN KEEP UP WITH YOU.
AH.

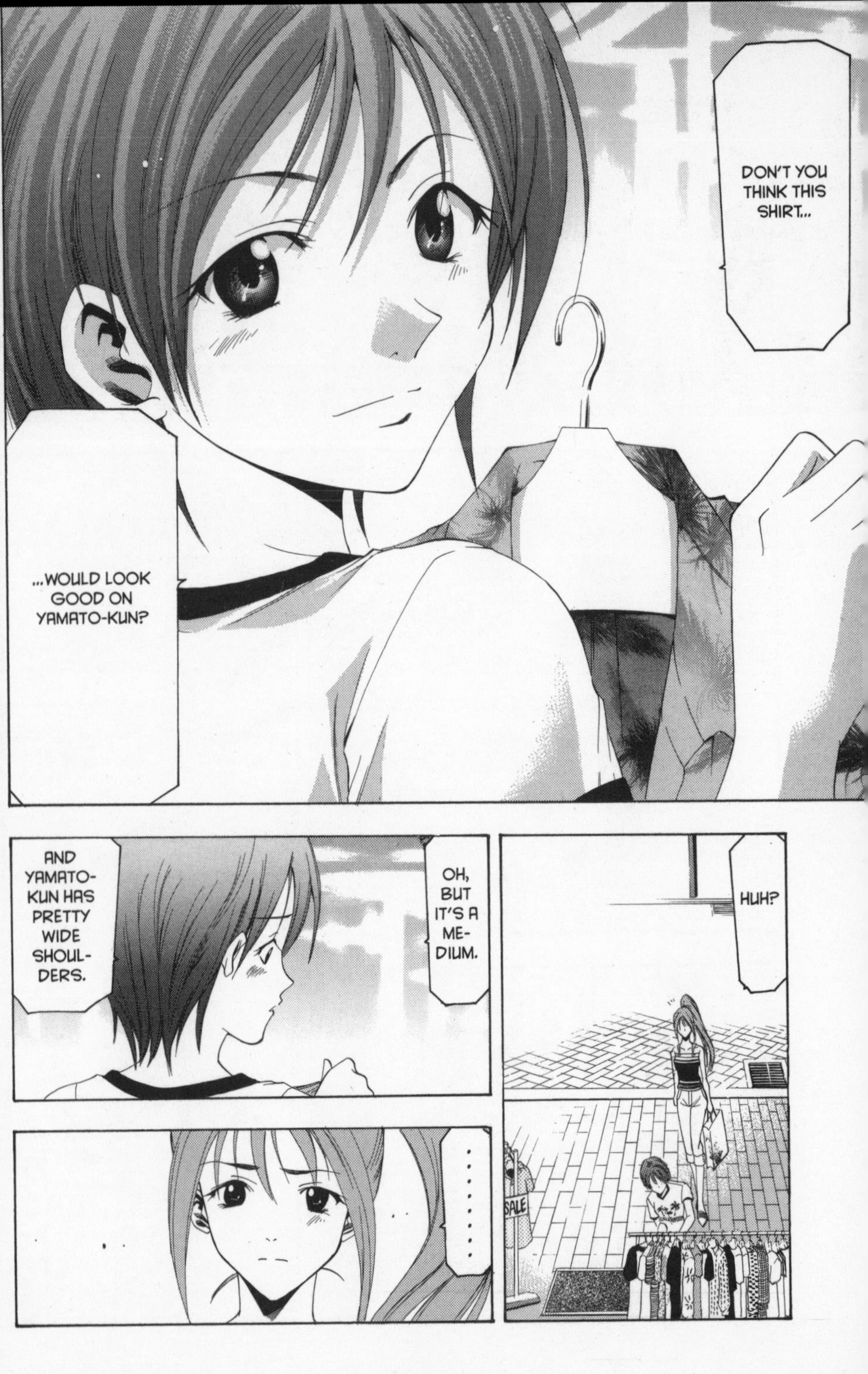
DON'T YOU THINK THIS SHIRT...
...WOULD LOOK GOOD ON YAMATO-KUN?
HUH?
SALE
OH, BUT IT'S A MEDIUM.
AND YAMATO-KUN HAS PRETTY WIDE SHOULDERS.
......

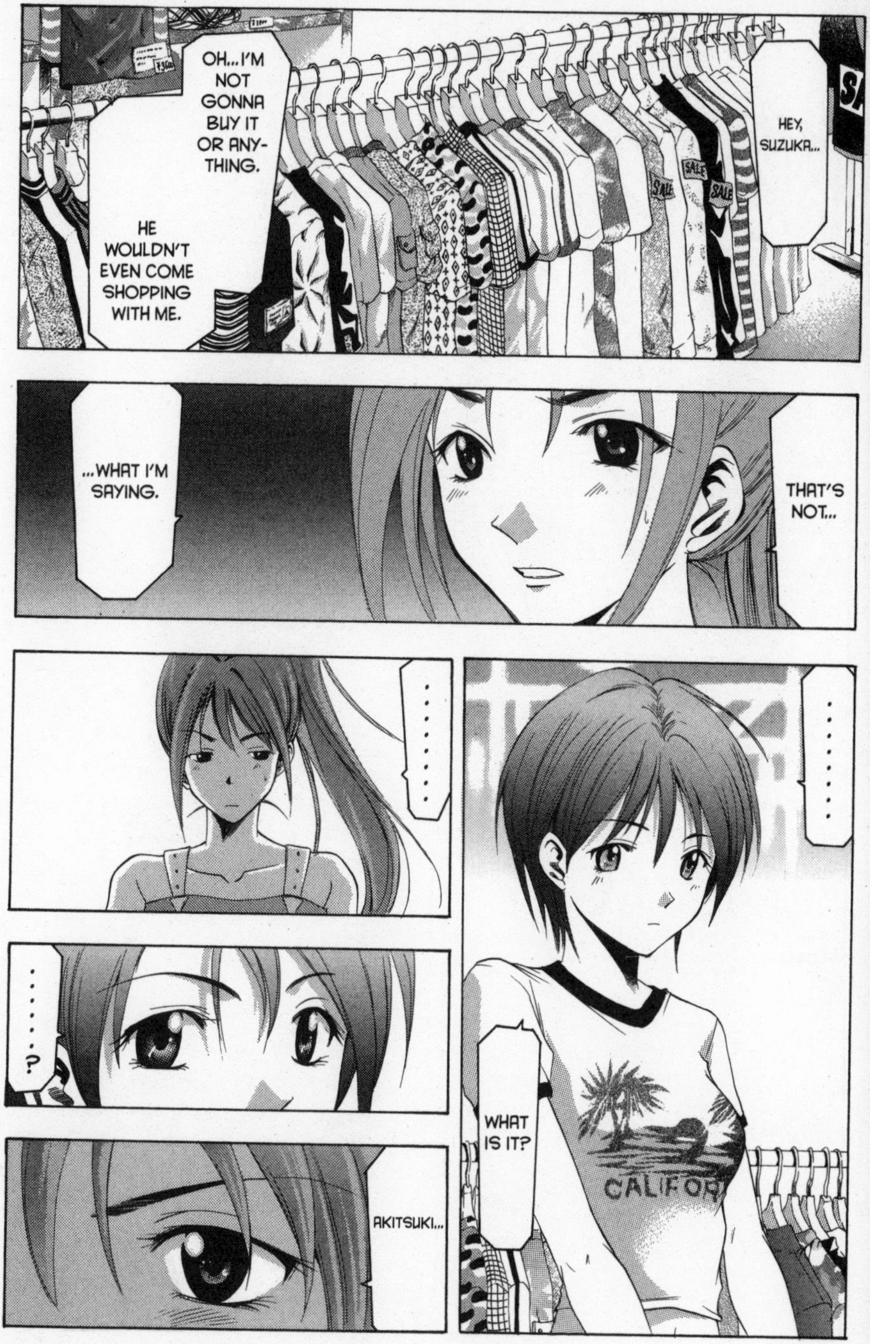
HEY, SUZUKA...
OH...I'M NOT GONNA BUY IT OR ANYTHING.
HE WOULDN'T EVEN COME SHOPPING WITH ME.
THAT'S NOT...
...WHAT I'M SAYING.
....
WHAT IS IT?
....
......?
AKITSUKI...

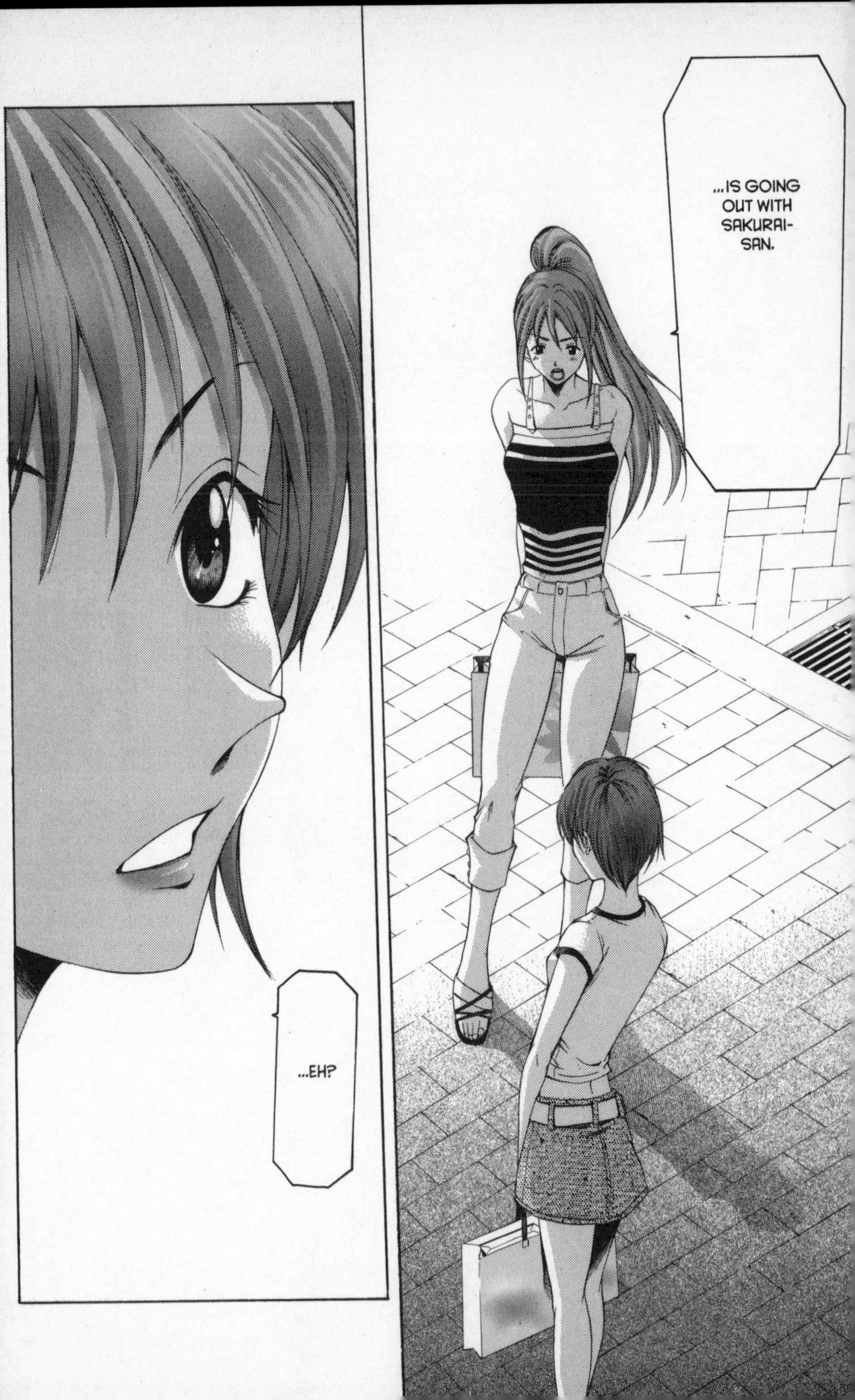
...IS GOING OUT WITH SAKURAI-SAN.
...EH?

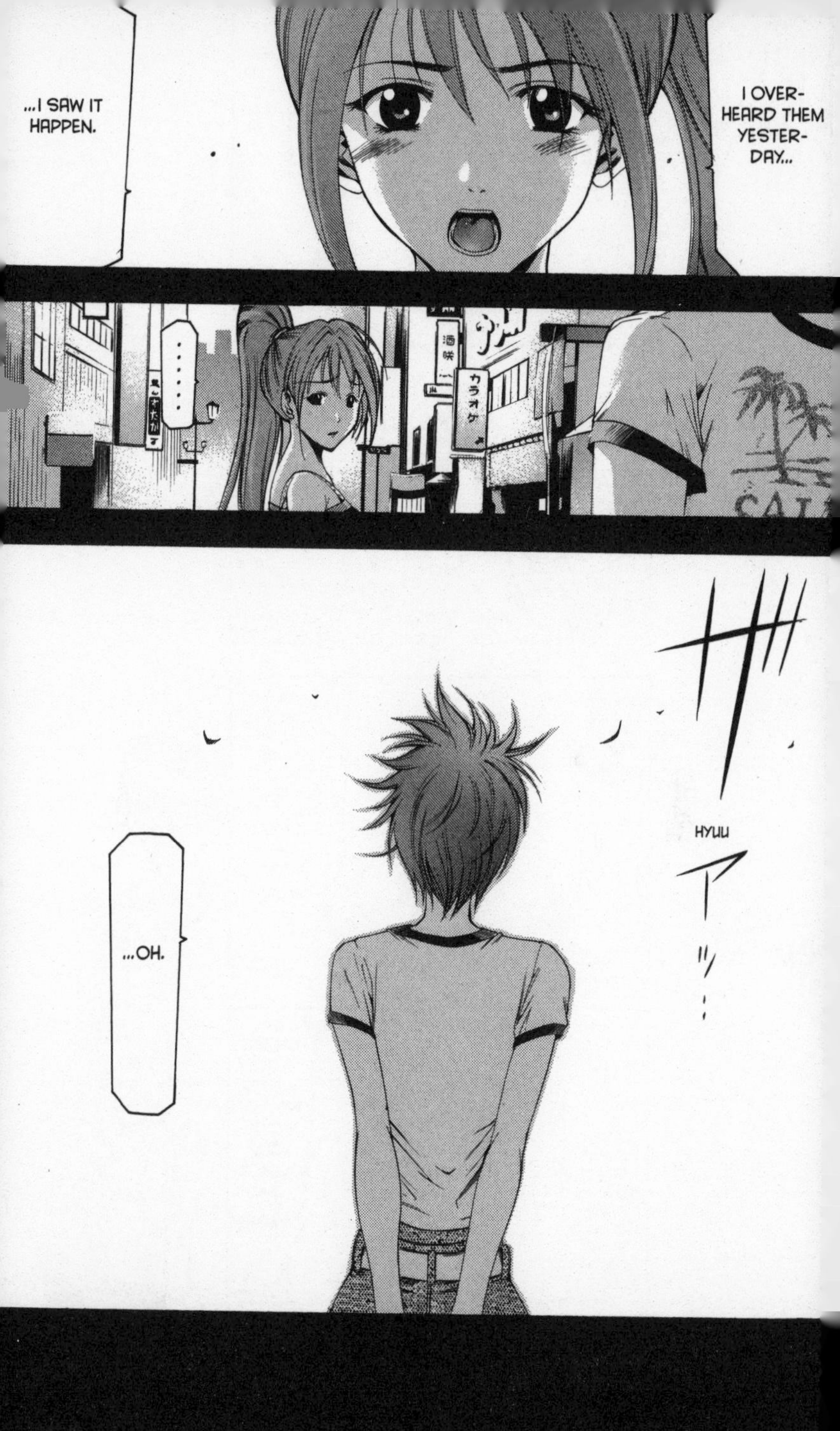
I OVER-HEARD THEM YESTER-DAY...
...I SAW IT HAPPEN.
....
HYUU
...OH.

SUZUKA
FOUR-PANEL THEATER
NUMBER TWENTY-ONE
MOTHER

WHEN-EVER MY MOM CALLS...
HELLO? IT'S MOM.
OH, I'M KIND OF BUSY RIGHT NOW. CAN I CALL YOU BACK LATER?
OH, SORRY, I'LL HANG UP.
OKAY, BYE.
OH, THAT'S RIGHT...DO YOU HAVE ENOUGH RICE? OUR NEW CROP JUST CAME IN. SHOULD I SEND YOU SOME?
NO, I'M OKAY.
OH, AND YOUR FATHER WENT ON A LITTLE TRIP YESTER-DAY.
......
THE REAL CONVER-SATION BEGINS AFTER SHE SAYS SHE'S GONNA HANG UP.
GRIP

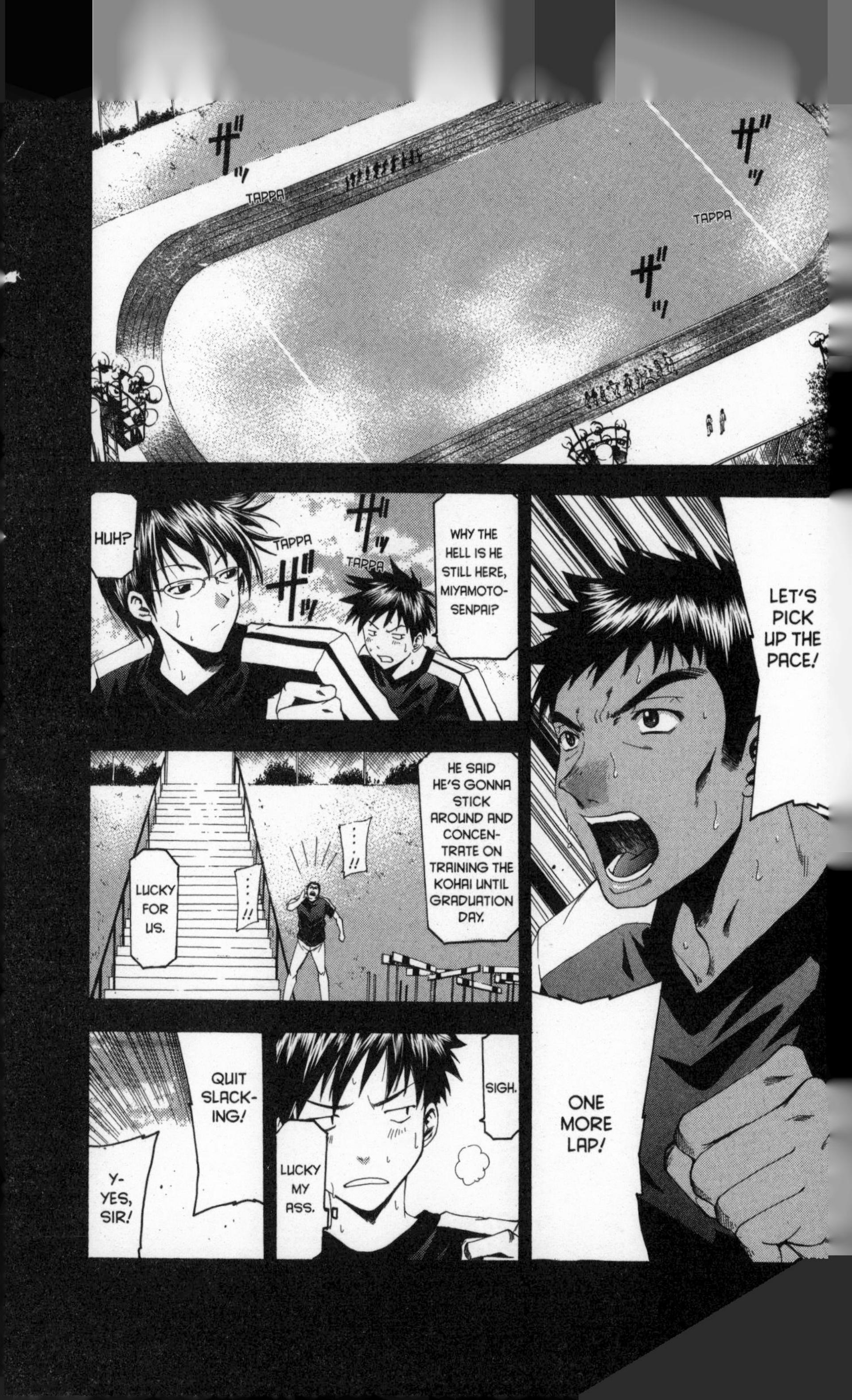
ザッ
TAPPA
ザッ
TAPPA
ザッ
LET'S PICK UP THE PACE!
ONE MORE LAP!
WHY THE HELL IS HE STILL HERE, MIYAMOTO-SENPAI?
ザッ
TAPPA
ザッ
TAPPA
HUH?
HE SAID HE'S GONNA STICK AROUND AND CONCENTRATE ON TRAINING THE KOHAI UNTIL GRADUATION DAY.
...!!
...!!
LUCKY FOR US.
SIGH.
LUCKY MY ASS.
QUIT SLACKING!
Y-YES, SIR!

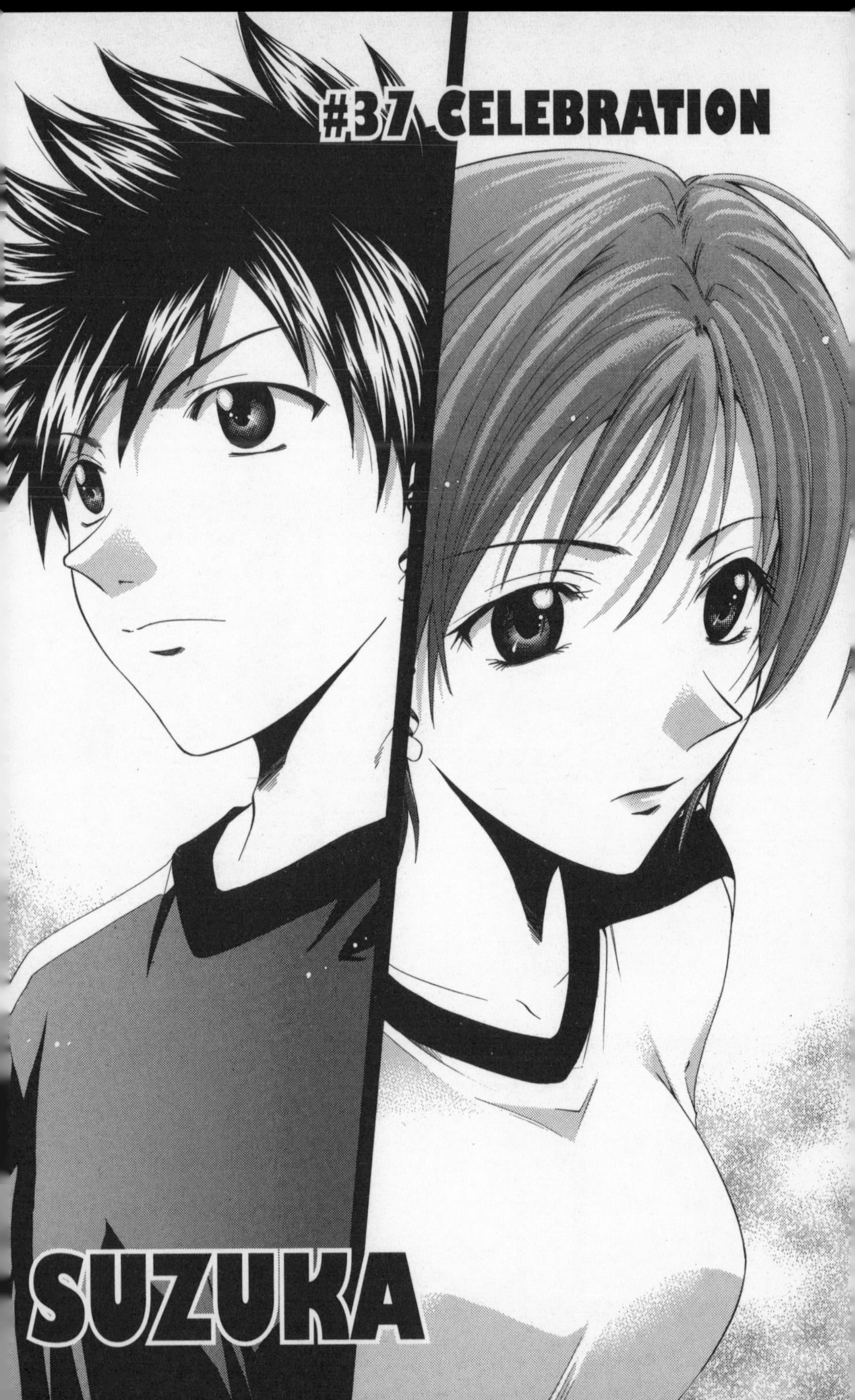
#37 CELEBRATION
SUZUKA

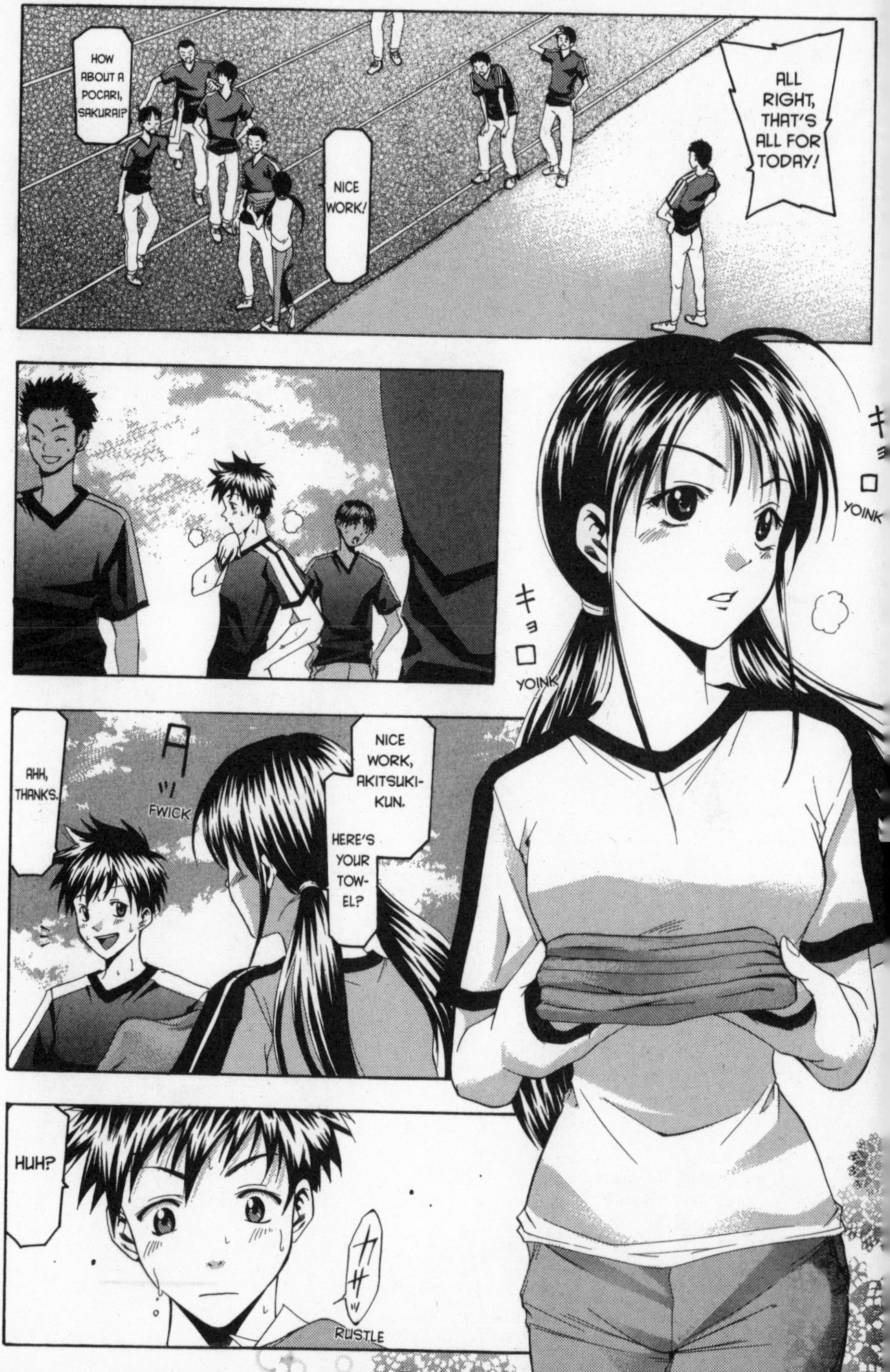

ALL RIGHT, THAT'S ALL FOR TODAY!
NICE WORK!
HOW ABOUT A POCARI, SAKURAI!?
キョロ
YOINK
キョロ
YOINK
NICE WORK, AKITSUKI-KUN.
HERE'S YOUR TOW-EL?
FWICK
AHH, THANKS.
RUSTLE
HUH?

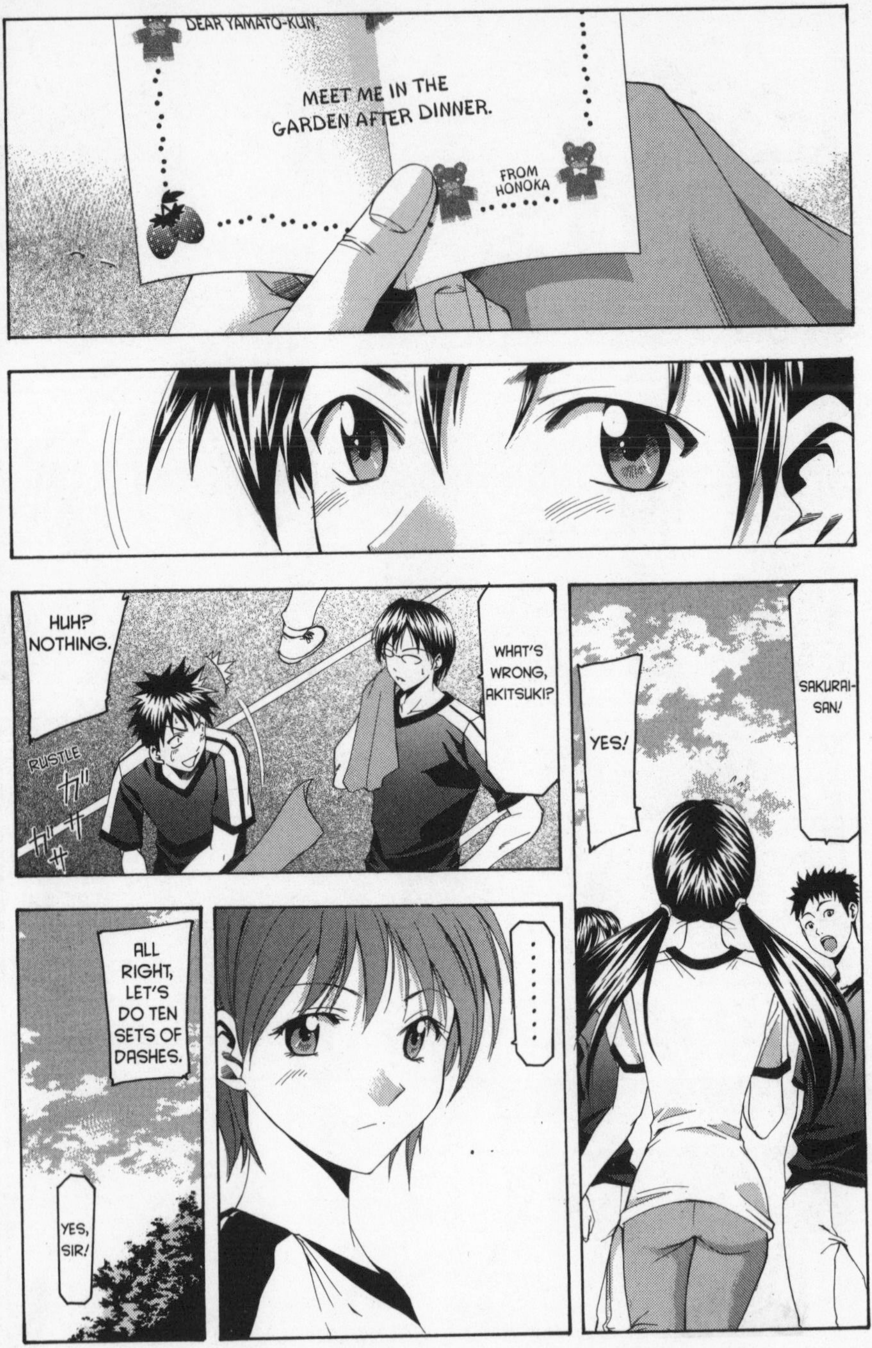
DEAR YAMATO-KUN,
MEET ME IN THE GARDEN AFTER DINNER.
FROM HONOKA
SAKURAI-SAN!
YES!
WHAT'S WRONG, AKITSUKI?
HUH? NOTHING.
RUSTLE
......
ALL RIGHT, LET'S DO TEN SETS OF DASHES.
YES, SIR!

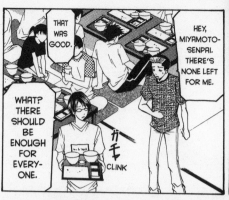

OKITA INN
HEY, MIYAMOTO-SENPAI. THERE'S NONE LEFT FOR ME.
THAT WAS GOOD.
WHAT? THERE SHOULD BE ENOUGH FOR EVERY-ONE.
CLINK
SPLASH
I'M SORRY, AKITSUKI-KUN. I SHOULDN'T HAVE CALLED YOU OUT HERE. YOU MUST BE TIRED AFTER THAT LONG PRACTICE.
NO.
I'M FINE.
I'M PRETTY USED TO IT NOW.
RE-ALLY?
YEAH.

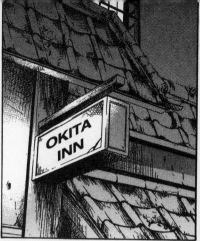

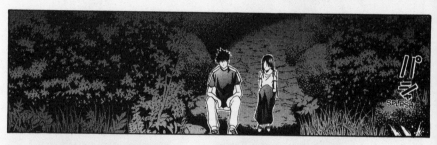

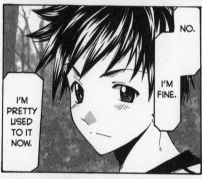

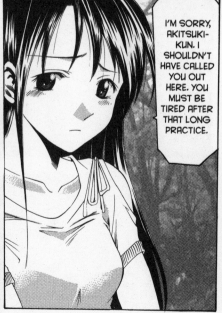

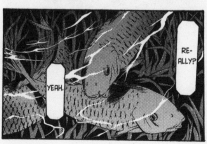

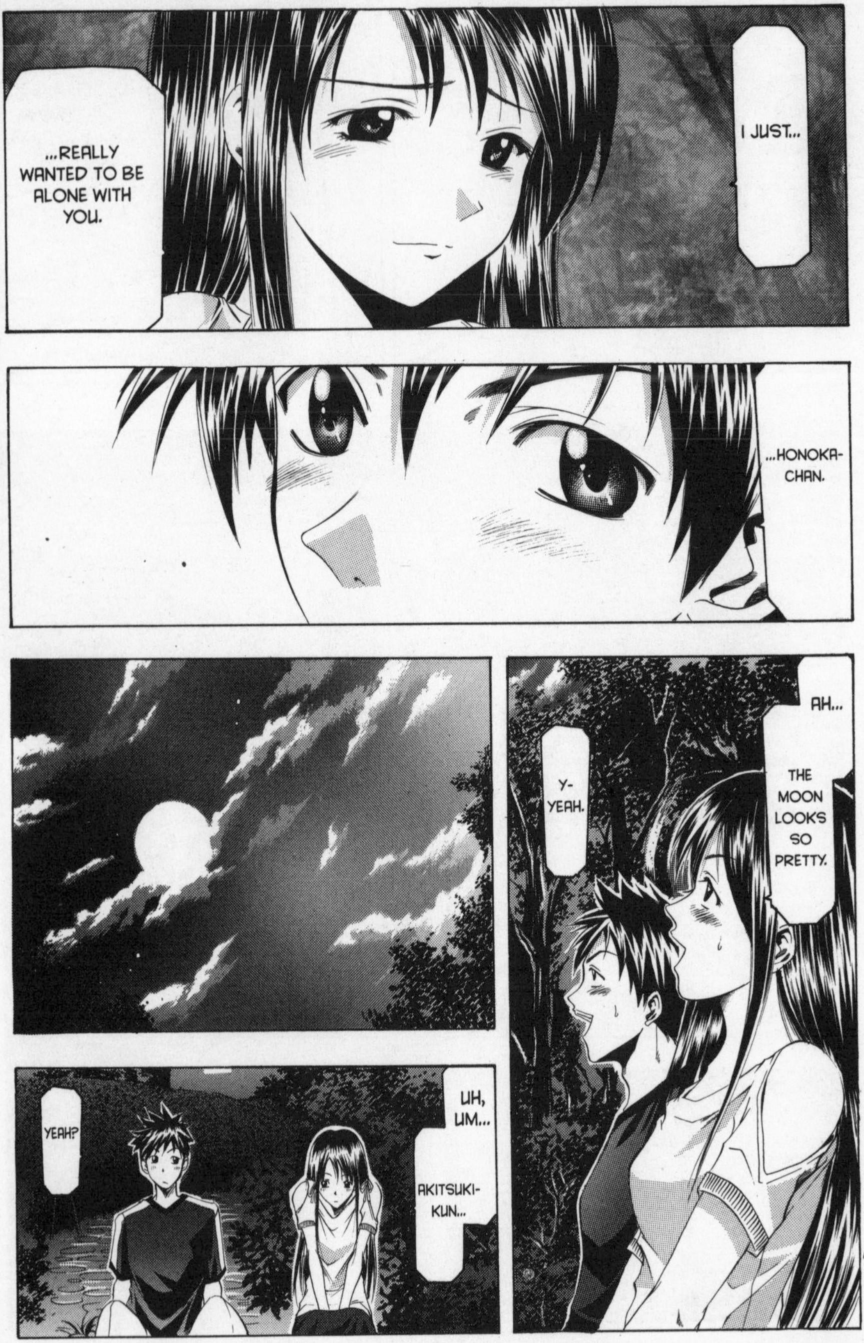
I JUST...
...REALLY WANTED TO BE ALONE WITH YOU.
...HONOKA-CHAN.
AH...
THE MOON LOOKS SO PRETTY.
Y-YEAH.
UH, UM...
AKITSUKI-KUN...
YEAH?

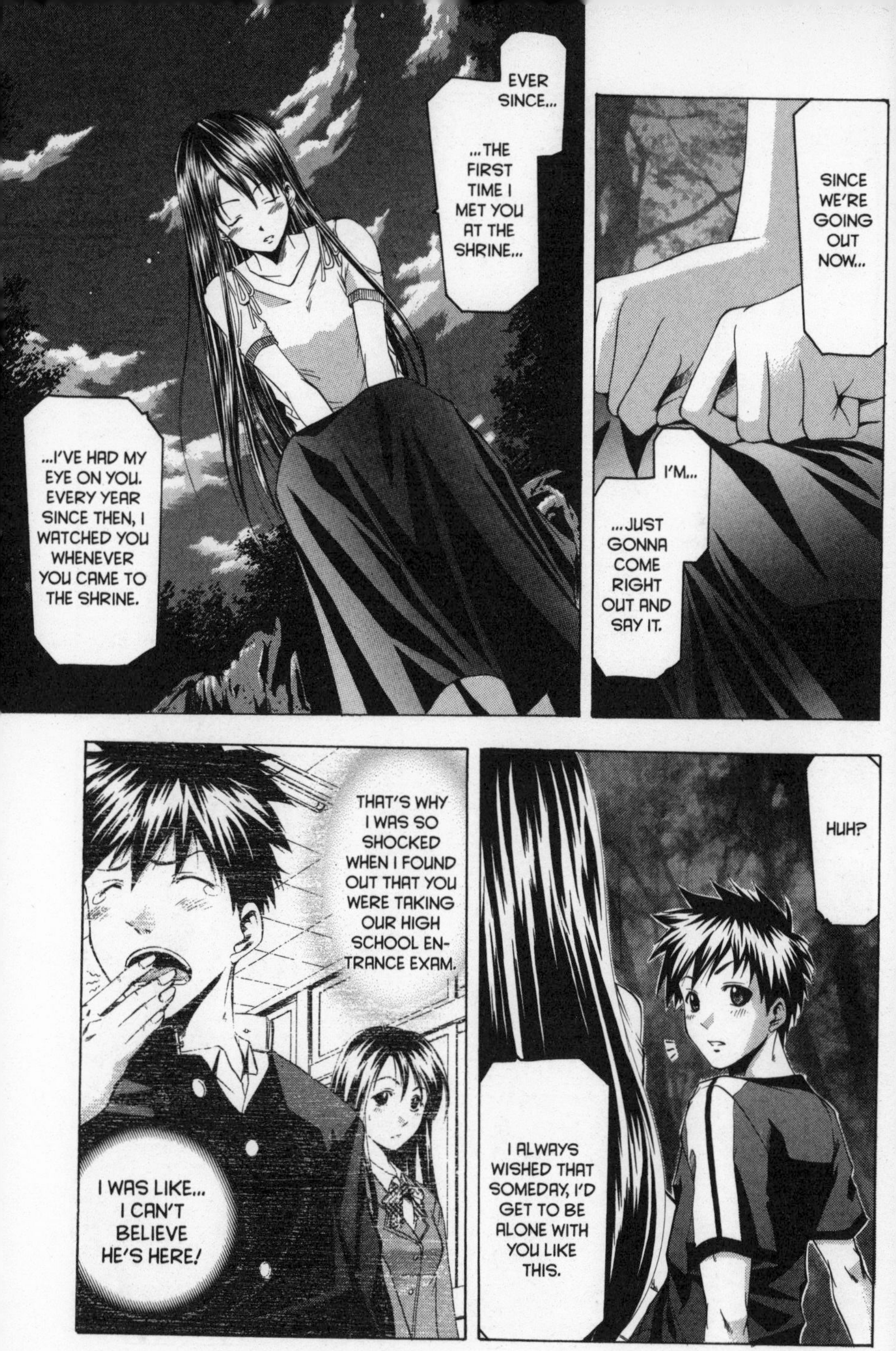
SINCE WE'RE GOING OUT NOW...
I'M...
...JUST GONNA COME RIGHT OUT AND SAY IT.
EVER SINCE...
...THE FIRST TIME I MET YOU AT THE SHRINE...
...I'VE HAD MY EYE ON YOU. EVERY YEAR SINCE THEN, I WATCHED YOU WHENEVER YOU CAME TO THE SHRINE.
HUH?
I ALWAYS WISHED THAT SOMEDAY, I'D GET TO BE ALONE WITH YOU LIKE THIS.
THAT'S WHY I WAS SO SHOCKED WHEN I FOUND OUT THAT YOU WERE TAKING OUR HIGH SCHOOL EN-TRANCE EXAM.
I WAS LIKE... I CAN'T BELIEVE HE'S HERE!

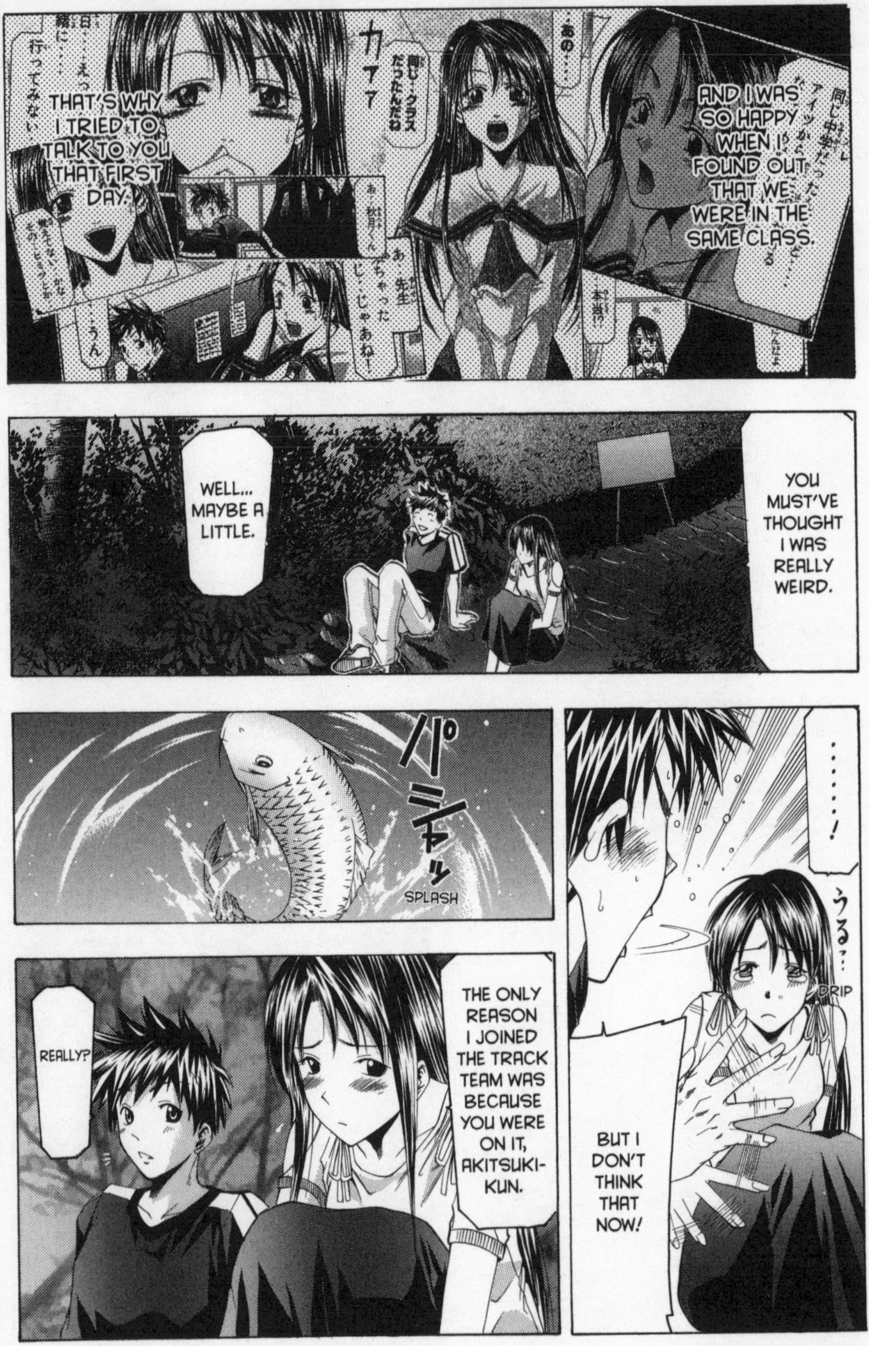
AND I WAS SO HAPPY WHEN I FOUND OUT THAT WE WERE IN THE SAME CLASS.
あの・・・
同じクラスだったんだね
カァァ
THAT'S WHY I TRIED TO TALK TO YOU THAT FIRST DAY.
YOU MUST'VE THOUGHT I WAS REALLY WEIRD.
WELL... MAYBE A LITTLE.
......!
うる…
DRIP
BUT I DON'T THINK THAT NOW!
パシャッ
SPLASH
THE ONLY REASON I JOINED THE TRACK TEAM WAS BECAUSE YOU WERE ON IT, AKITSUKI-KUN.
REALLY?

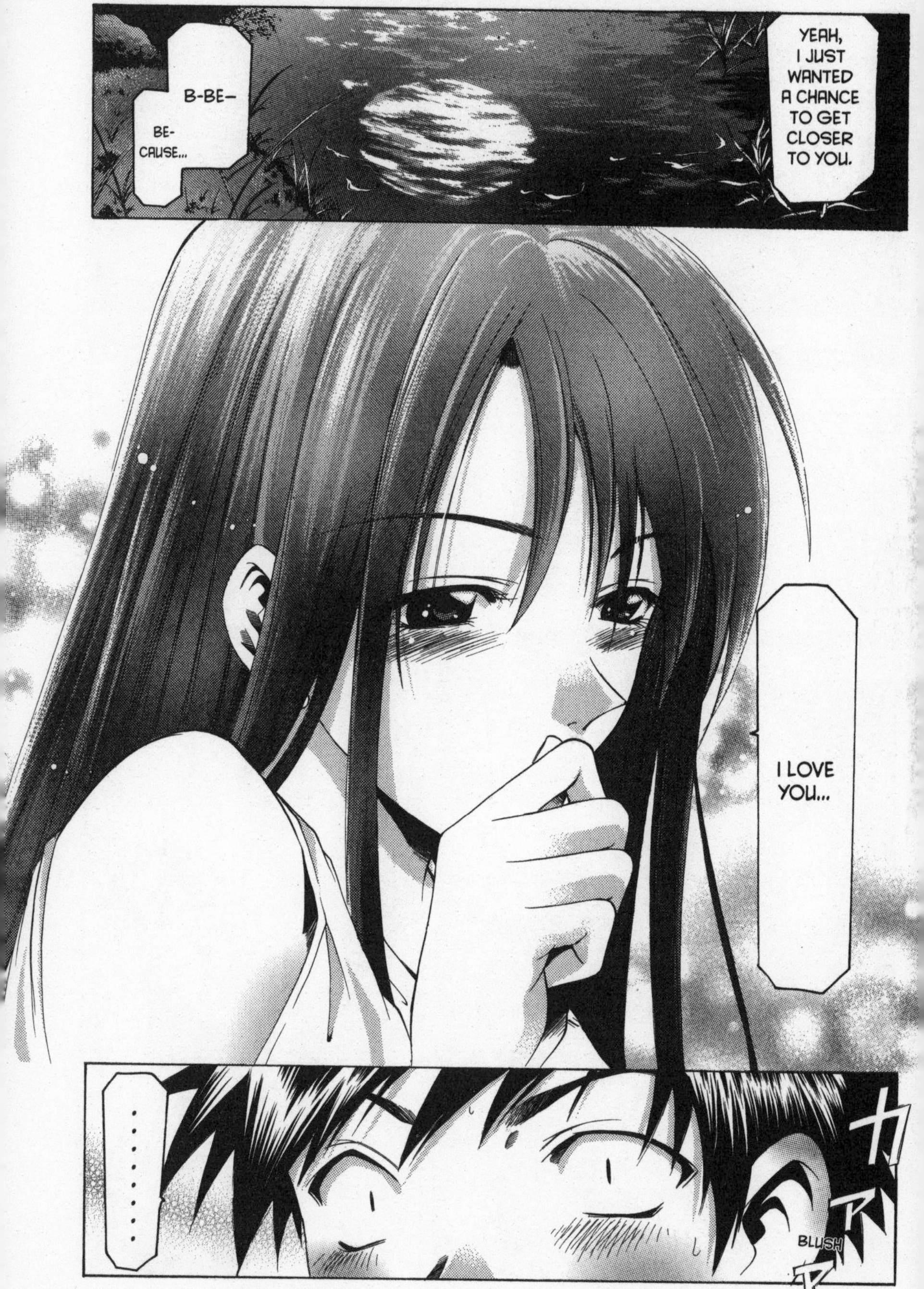
YEAH, I JUST WANTED A CHANCE TO GET CLOSER TO YOU.
B-BE— BE-CAUSE...
I LOVE YOU...
BLUSH
......

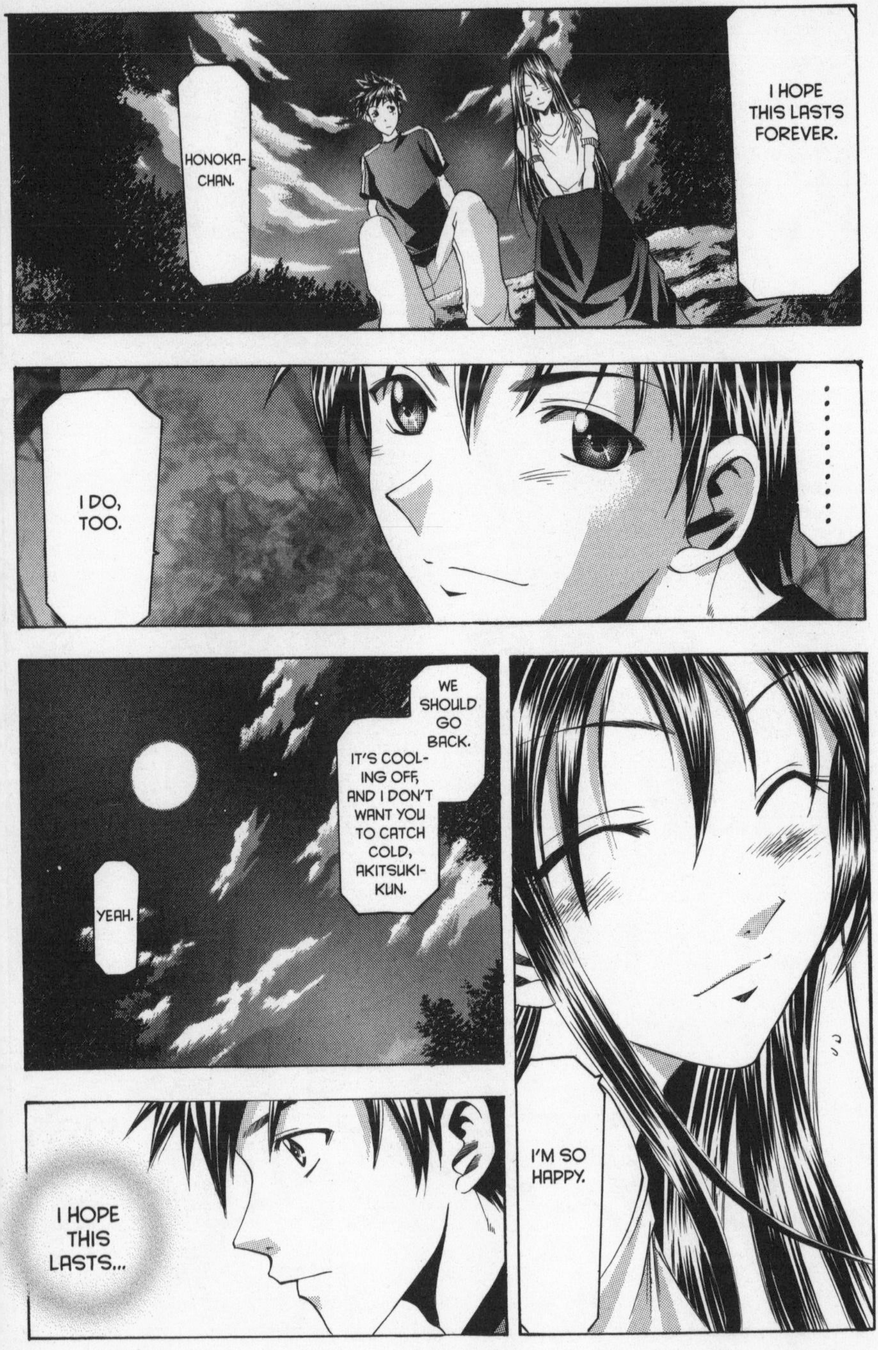
I HOPE THIS LASTS FOREVER.
HONOKA-CHAN.
......
I DO, TOO.
I'M SO HAPPY.
WE SHOULD GO BACK.
IT'S COOLING OFF, AND I DON'T WANT YOU TO CATCH COLD, AKITSUKI-KUN.
YEAH.
I HOPE THIS LASTS...

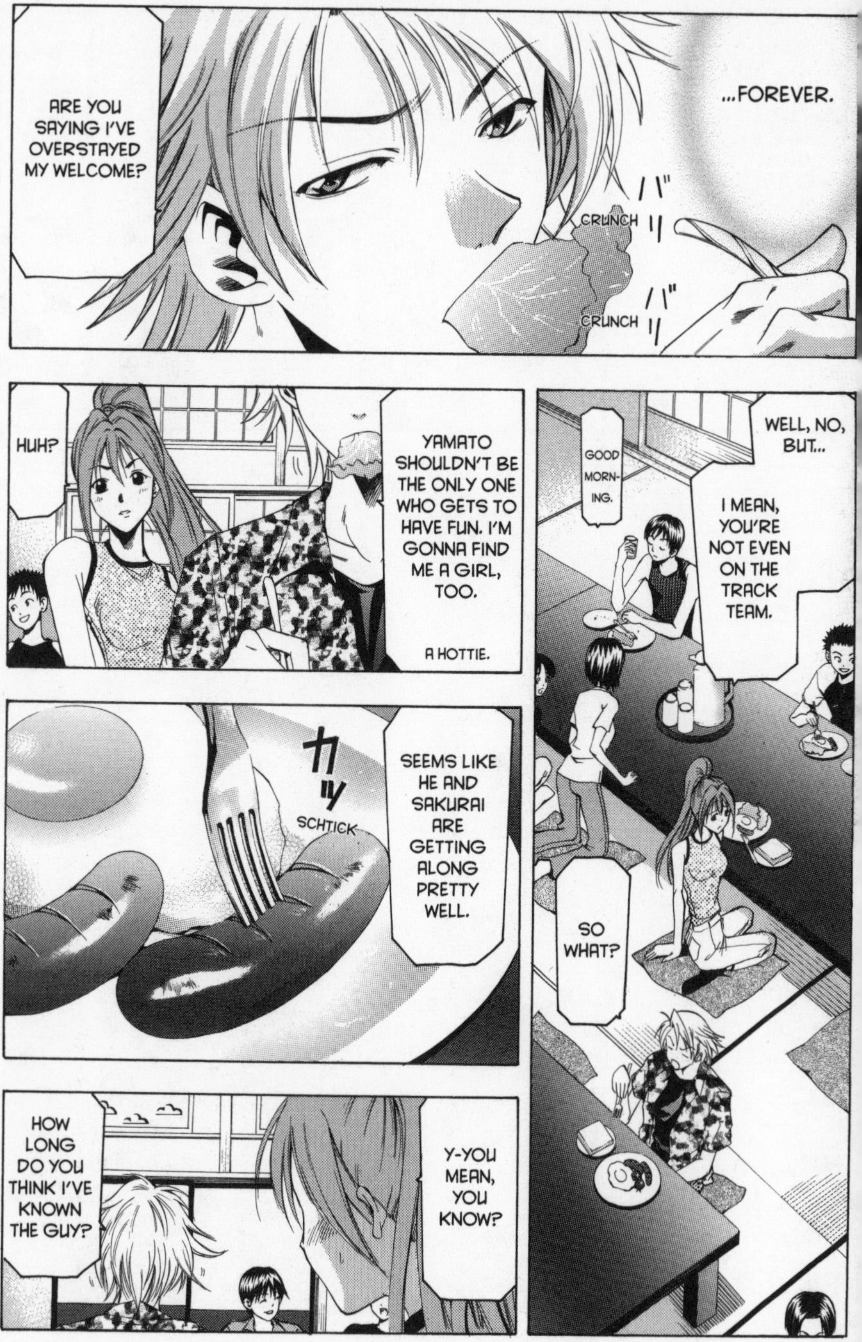
...FOREVER.
バリ
CRUNCH
バリ
CRUNCH
ARE YOU SAYING I'VE OVERSTAYED MY WELCOME?
WELL, NO, BUT...
I MEAN, YOU'RE NOT EVEN ON THE TRACK TEAM.
GOOD MORN-ING.
SO WHAT?
YAMATO SHOULDN'T BE THE ONLY ONE WHO GETS TO HAVE FUN. I'M GONNA FIND ME A GIRL, TOO.
A HOTTIE.
HUH?
SEEMS LIKE HE AND SAKURAI ARE GETTING ALONG PRETTY WELL.
カッ
SCHTICK
Y-YOU MEAN, YOU KNOW?
HOW LONG DO YOU THINK I'VE KNOWN THE GUY?

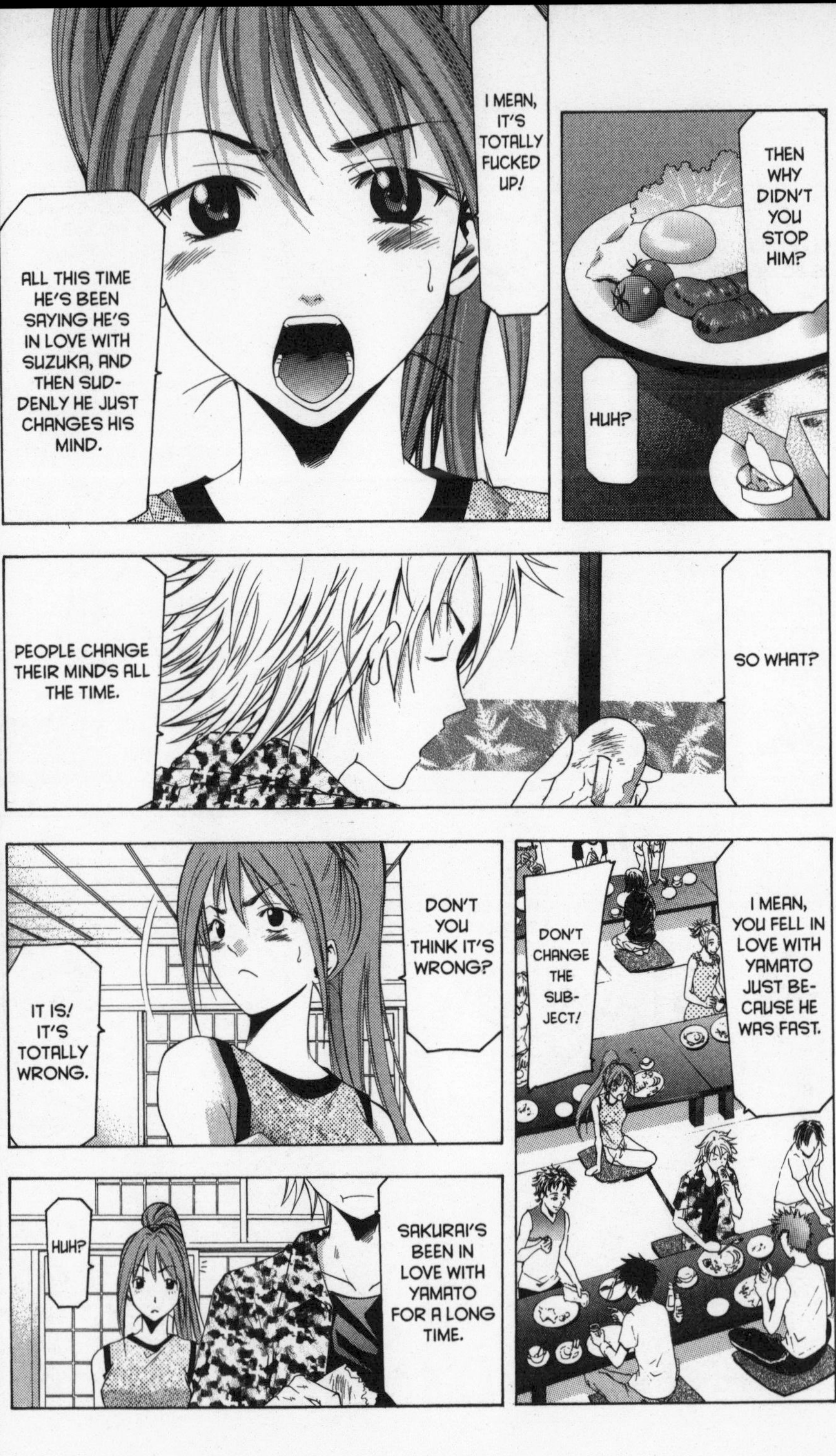
THEN WHY DIDN'T YOU STOP HIM?
HUH?
I MEAN, IT'S TOTALLY FUCKED UP!
ALL THIS TIME HE'S BEEN SAYING HE'S IN LOVE WITH SUZUKA, AND THEN SUD-DENLY HE JUST CHANGES HIS MIND.
SO WHAT?
PEOPLE CHANGE THEIR MINDS ALL THE TIME.
I MEAN, YOU FELL IN LOVE WITH YAMATO JUST BE-CAUSE HE WAS FAST.
DON'T CHANGE THE SUB-JECT!
DON'T YOU THINK IT'S WRONG?
IT IS! IT'S TOTALLY WRONG.
SAKURAI'S BEEN IN LOVE WITH YAMATO FOR A LONG TIME.
HUH?

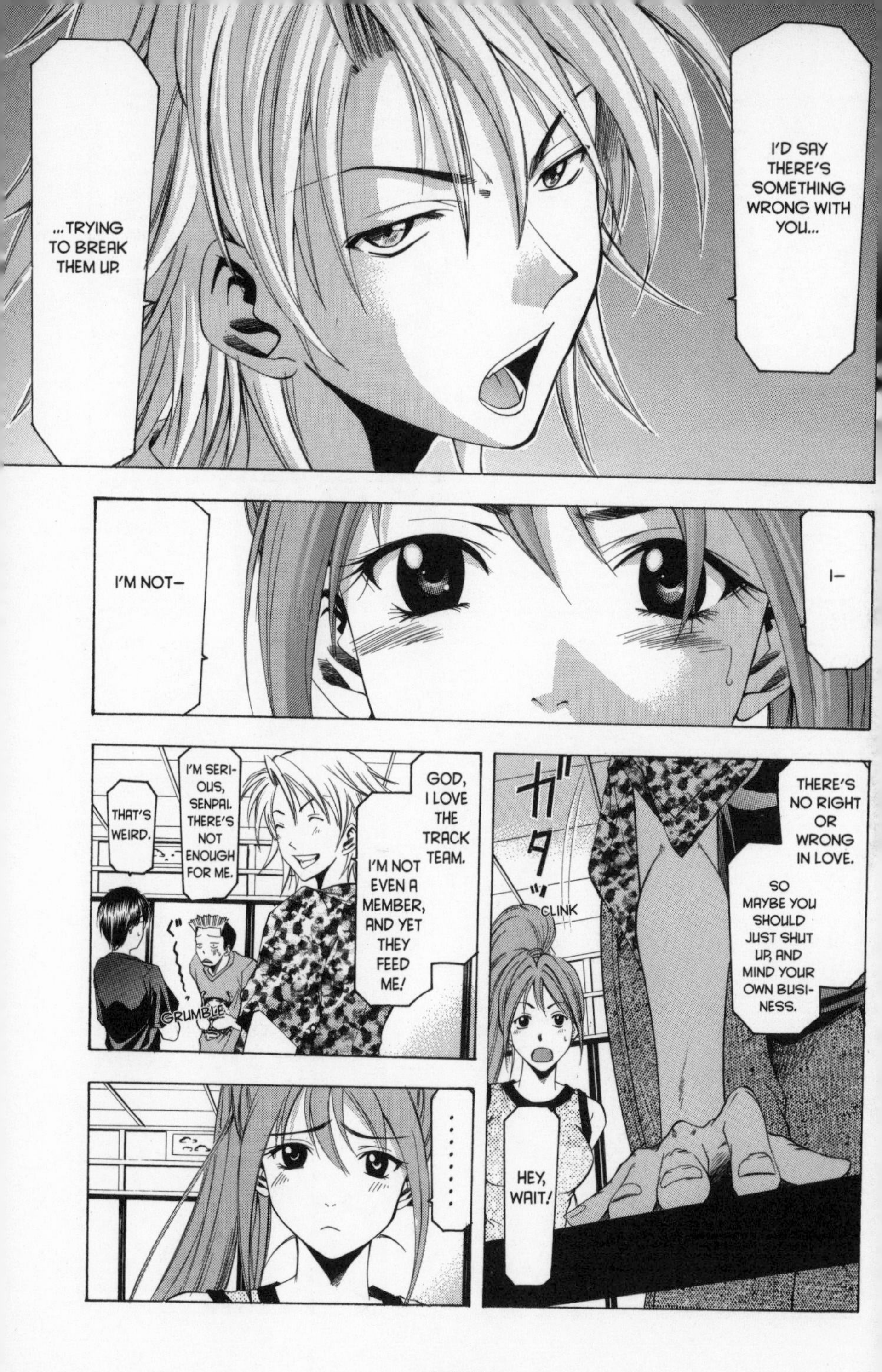
I'D SAY THERE'S SOMETHING WRONG WITH YOU...
...TRYING TO BREAK THEM UP.
I—
I'M NOT—
THERE'S NO RIGHT OR WRONG IN LOVE.
SO MAYBE YOU SHOULD JUST SHUT UP, AND MIND YOUR OWN BUSINESS.
ガタ
CLINK
HEY, WAIT!
GOD, I LOVE THE TRACK TEAM.
I'M NOT EVEN A MEMBER, AND YET THEY FEED ME!
I'M SERIOUS, SENPAI. THERE'S NOT ENOUGH FOR ME.
THAT'S WEIRD.
GRUMBLE
......

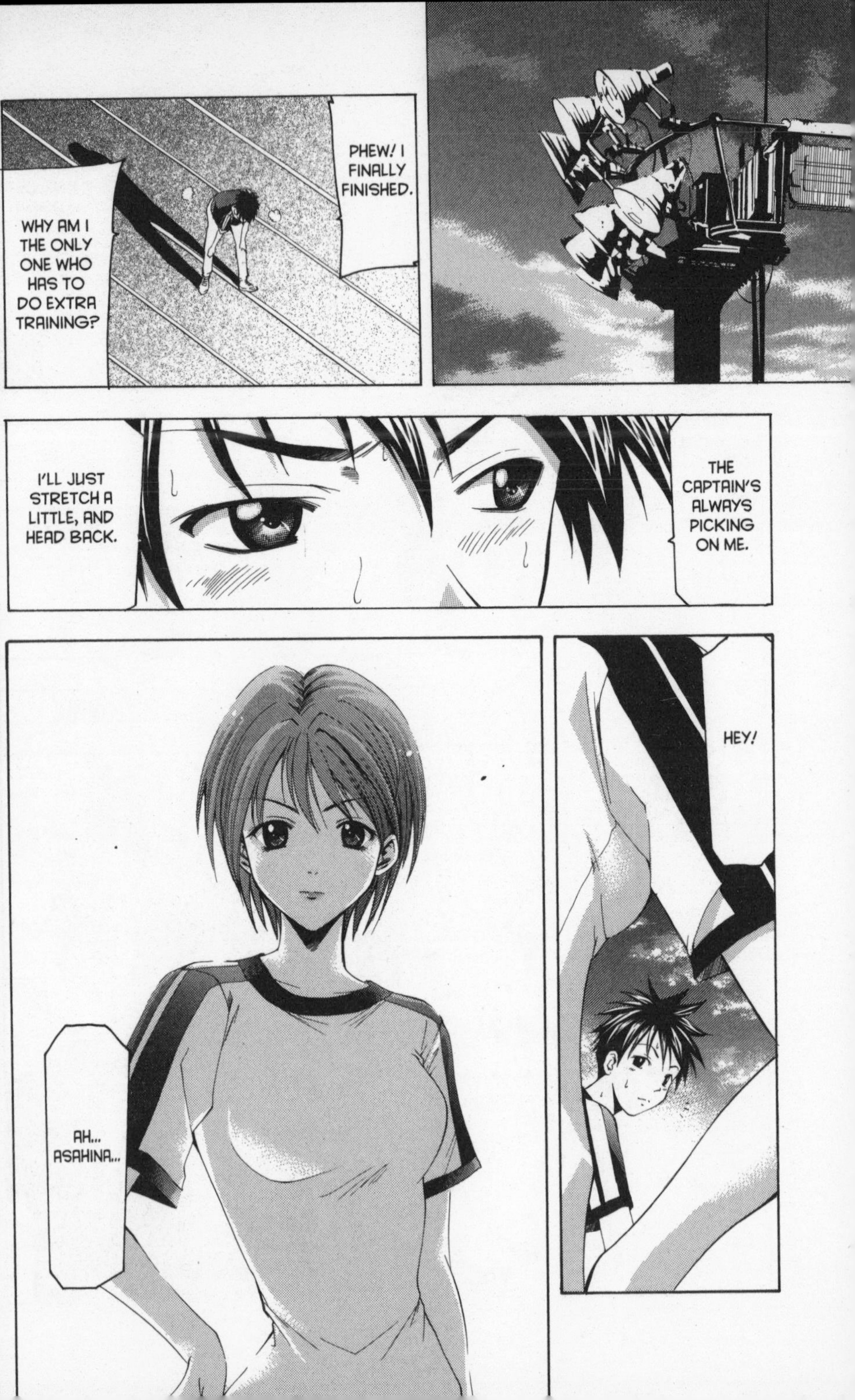
PHEW! I FINALLY FINISHED.
WHY AM I THE ONLY ONE WHO HAS TO DO EXTRA TRAINING?
THE CAPTAIN'S ALWAYS PICKING ON ME.
I'LL JUST STRETCH A LITTLE, AND HEAD BACK.
HEY!
AH... ASAHINA...

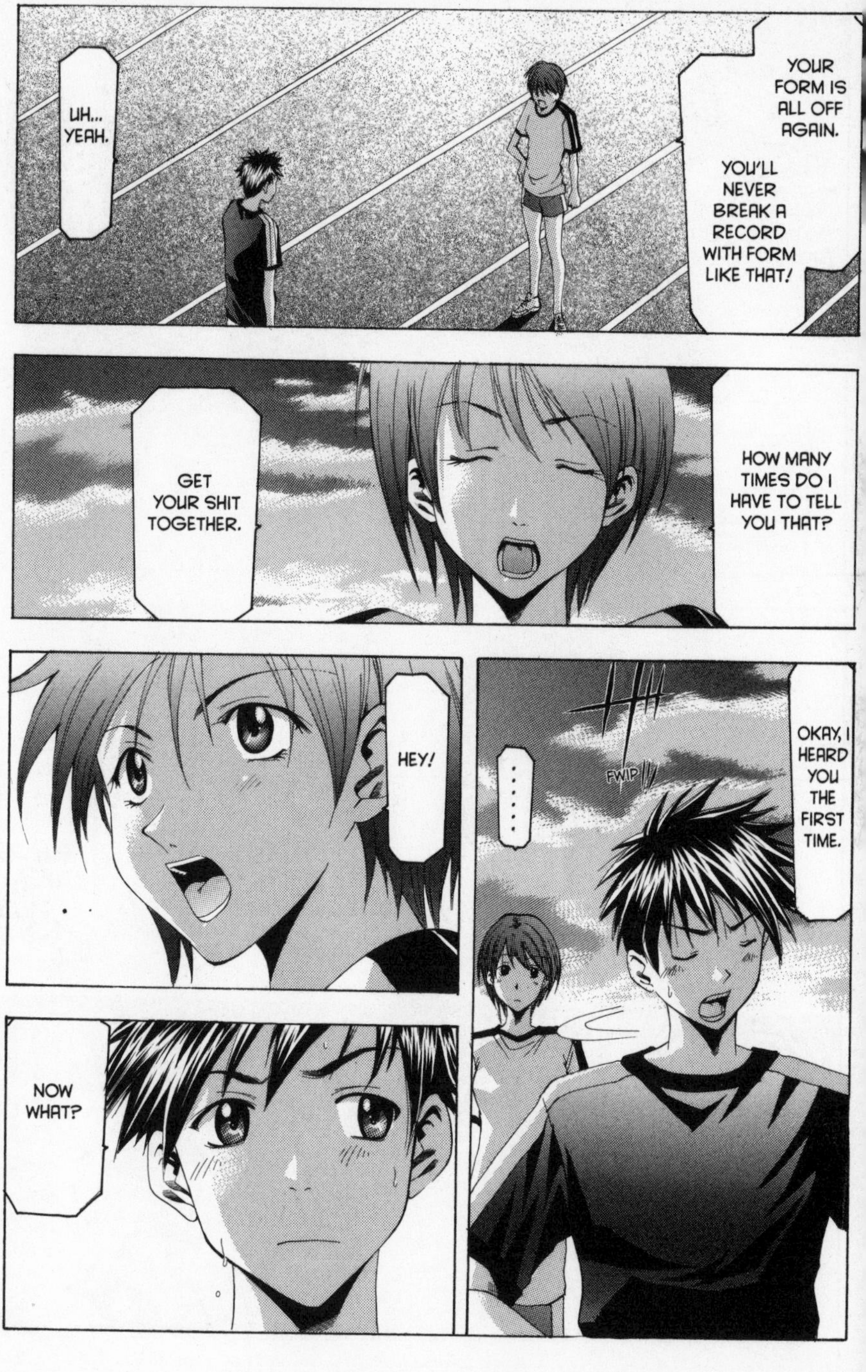
YOUR FORM IS ALL OFF AGAIN.
YOU'LL NEVER BREAK A RECORD WITH FORM LIKE THAT!
UH... YEAH.
HOW MANY TIMES DO I HAVE TO TELL YOU THAT?
GET YOUR SHIT TOGETHER.
OKAY, I HEARD YOU THE FIRST TIME.
FWIP
......
HEY!
NOW WHAT?

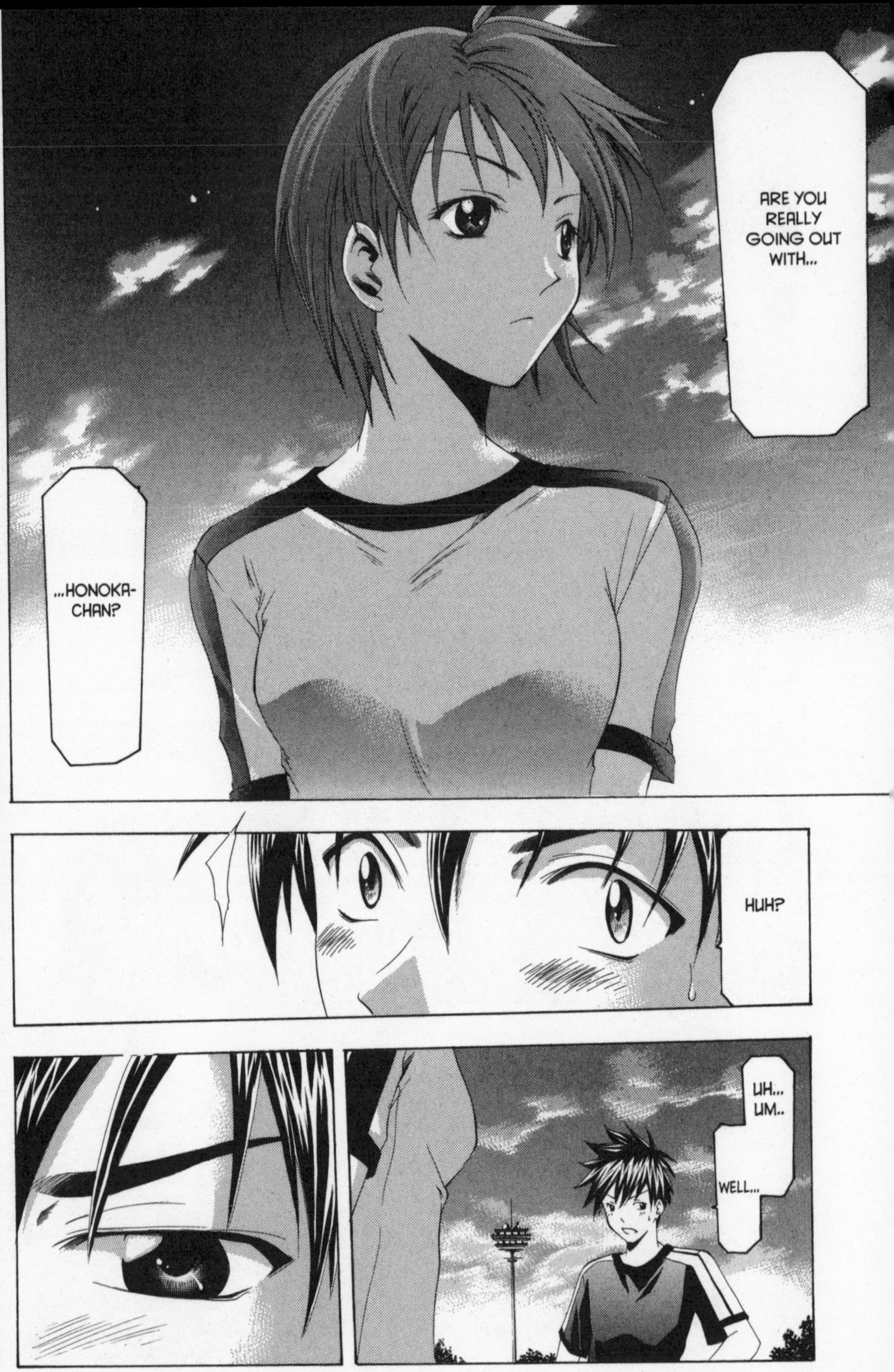
ARE YOU REALLY GOING OUT WITH...
...HONOKA-CHAN?
HUH?
UH... UM..
WELL...

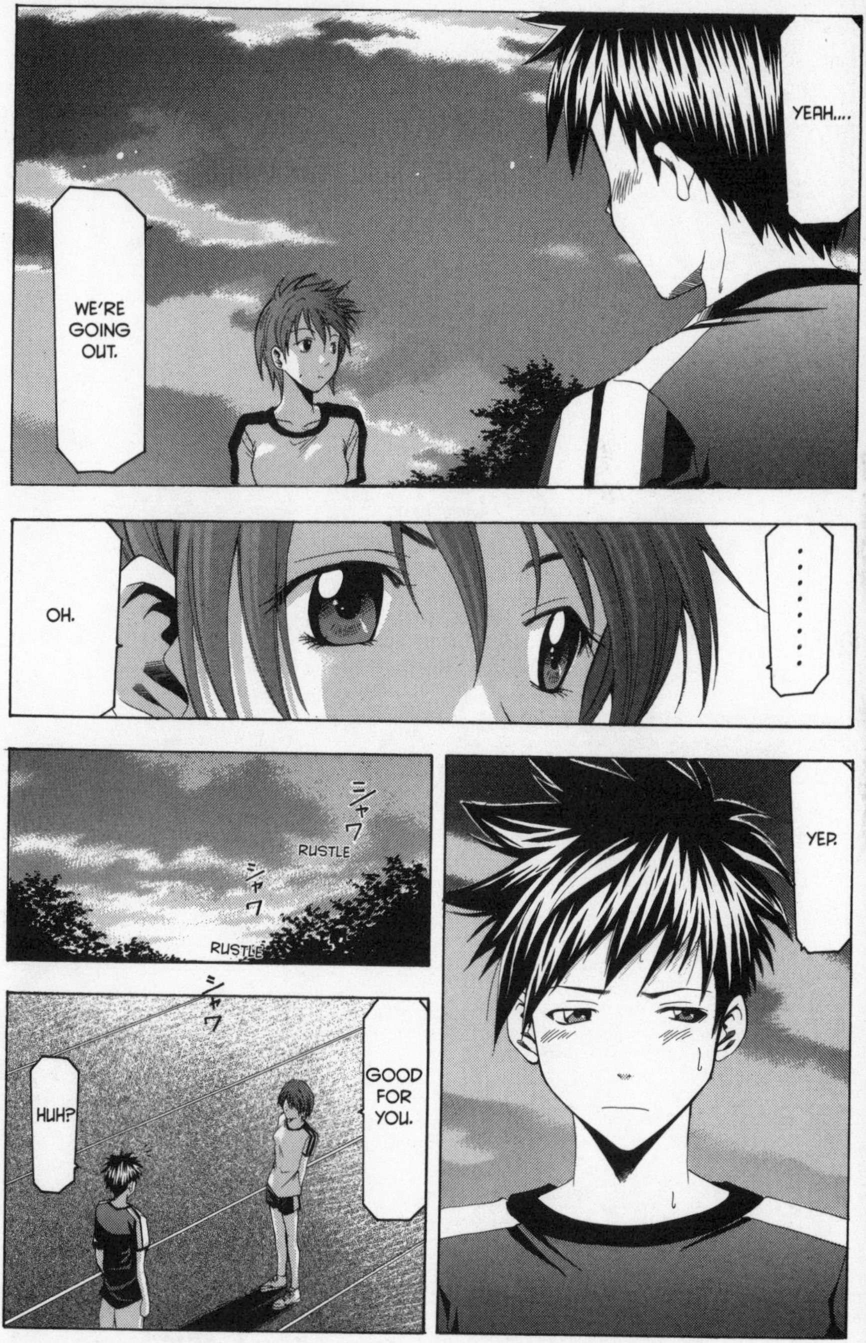
YEAH....
WE'RE GOING OUT.
....
OH.
YEP.
シャワ
RUSTLE
シャワ
RUSTLE
シャワ
GOOD FOR YOU.
HUH?

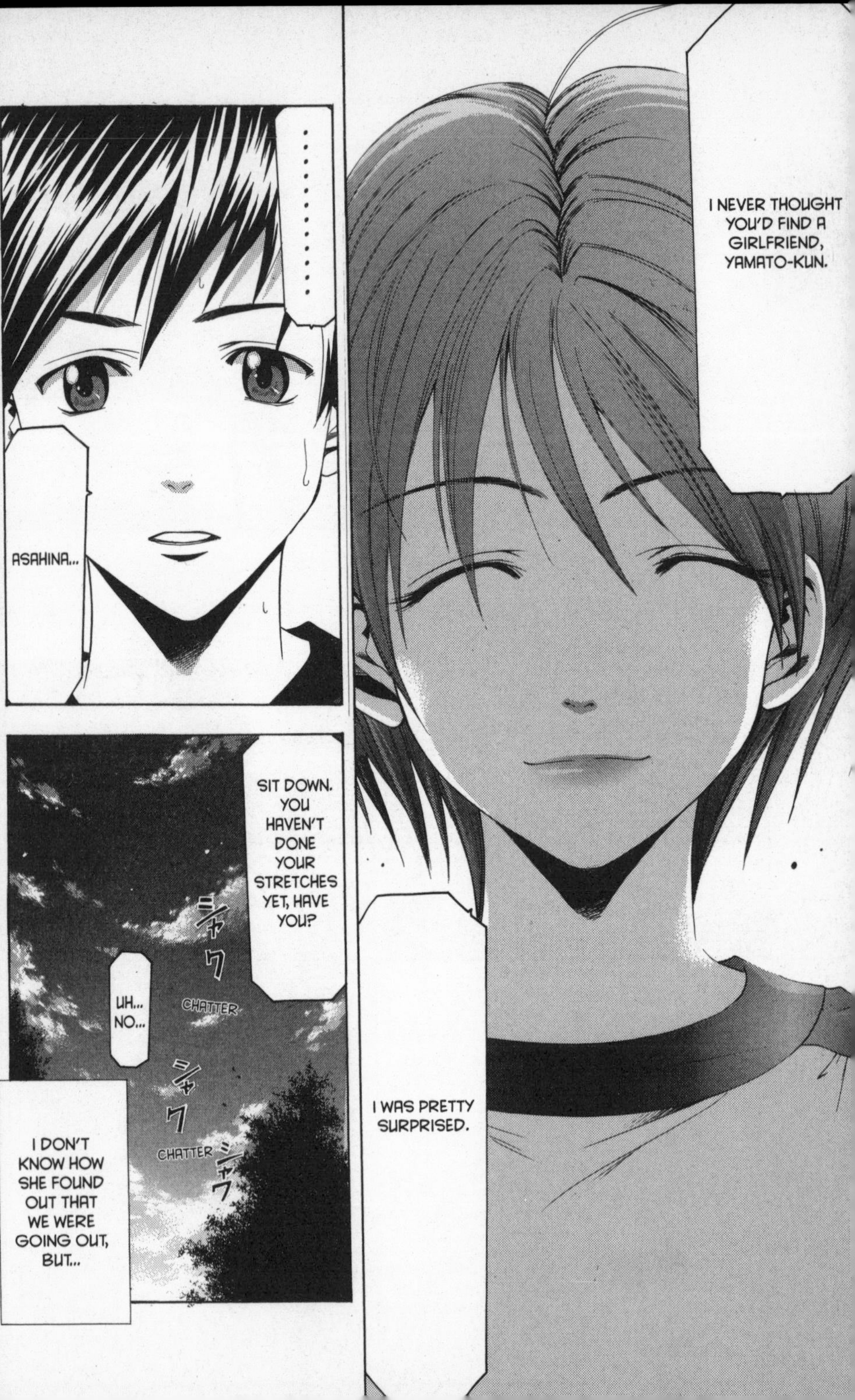

I NEVER THOUGHT YOU'D FIND A GIRLFRIEND, YAMATO-KUN.
I WAS PRETTY SURPRISED.
......
ASAHINA...
SIT DOWN. YOU HAVEN'T DONE YOUR STRETCHES YET, HAVE YOU?
シャク
CHATTER
UH... NO...
シャク
CHATTER シャク
I DON'T KNOW HOW SHE FOUND OUT THAT WE WERE GOING OUT, BUT...

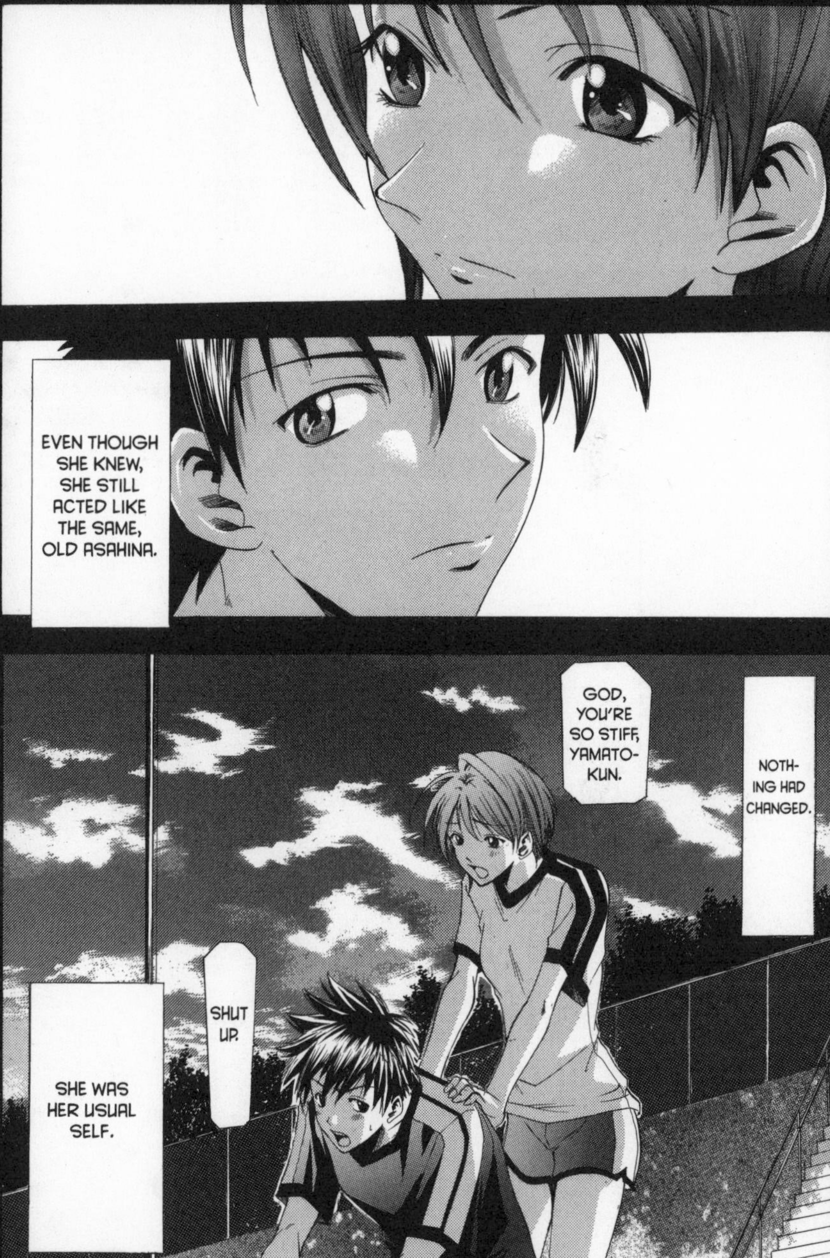
EVEN THOUGH SHE KNEW, SHE STILL ACTED LIKE THE SAME, OLD ASAHINA.
NOTHING HAD CHANGED.
GOD, YOU'RE SO STIFF, YAMATO-KUN.
SHUT UP.
SHE WAS HER USUAL SELF.

SUZUKA FOUR-PANEL THEATER NUMBER TWENTY-TWO

GOALS

FIVE YEARS AGO.
I'M GONNA WORK MY ASS OFF SO THAT SOMEDAY, MTA-SAN WILL BE MY CHIEF EDITOR.
THAT'S MY GOAL.
I WAS FULL OF PASSION AFTER GETTING MY FIRST SERIES.
HEY, I'LL BE YOUR EDITOR.
JUST DON'T GET CANCELLED BEFORE WE CAN WORK TOGETHER.
O-OKAY.
FAST FOR-WARD TO THE PRES-ENT.
HOW MUCH LONGER BEFORE YOU'LL BECOME MY CHIEF EDITOR, MTA-SAN?
AH, SORRY, BUT I CAN'T BE A CHIEF EDITOR. IT'S WAY TOO MUCH RESPONSI-BILITY FOR ME.
WELL, THERE GOES ONE OF MY LIFE'S GOALS.

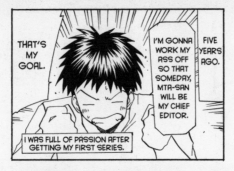

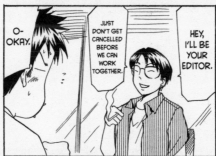

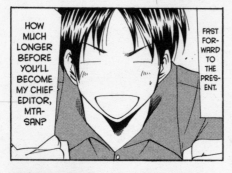

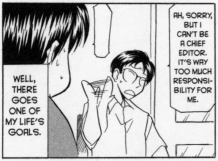

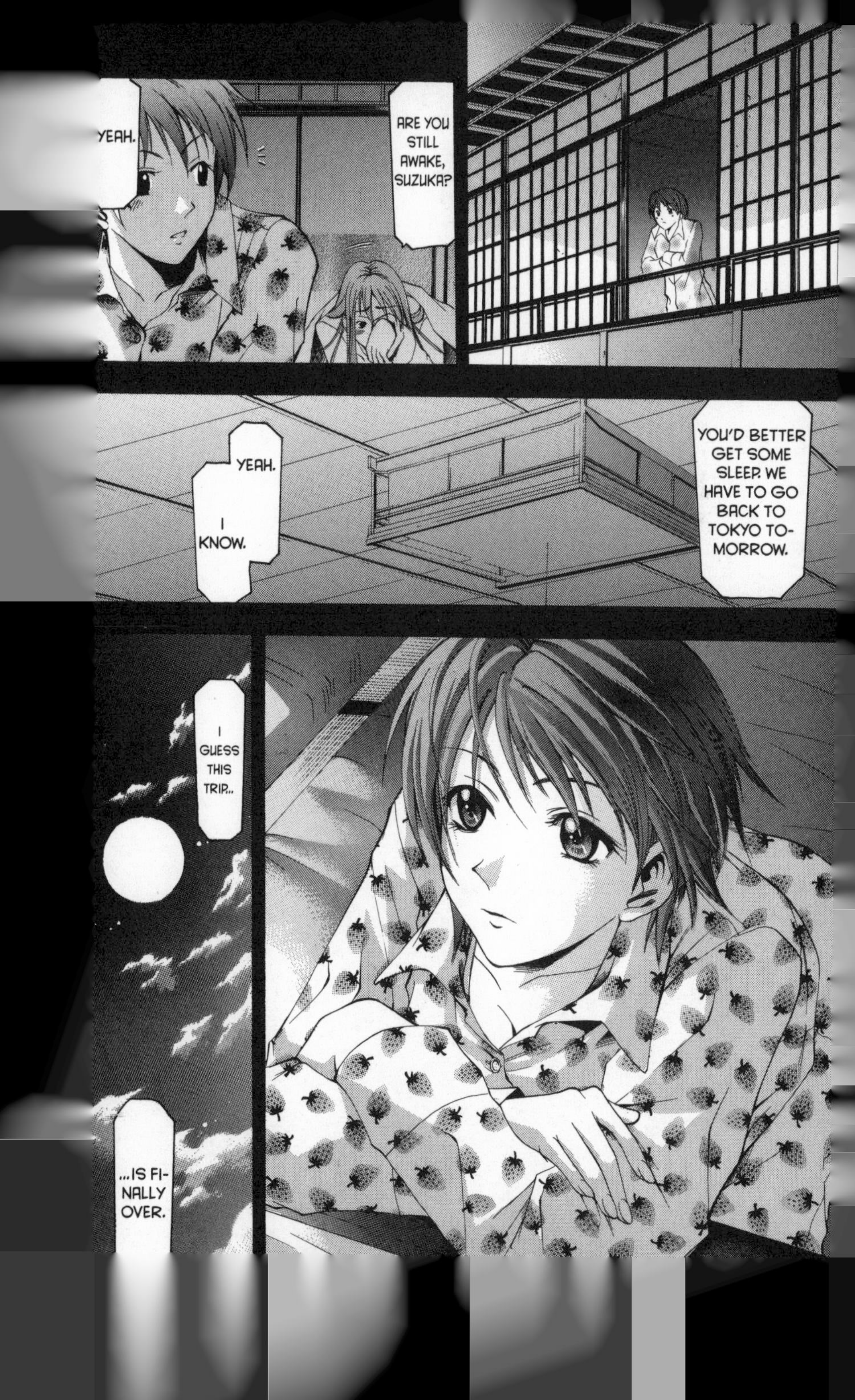
ARE YOU STILL AWAKE, SUZUKA?
YEAH.
YOU'D BETTER GET SOME SLEEP. WE HAVE TO GO BACK TO TOKYO TO-MORROW.
YEAH.
I KNOW.
I GUESS THIS TRIP...
...IS FI-NALLY OVER.

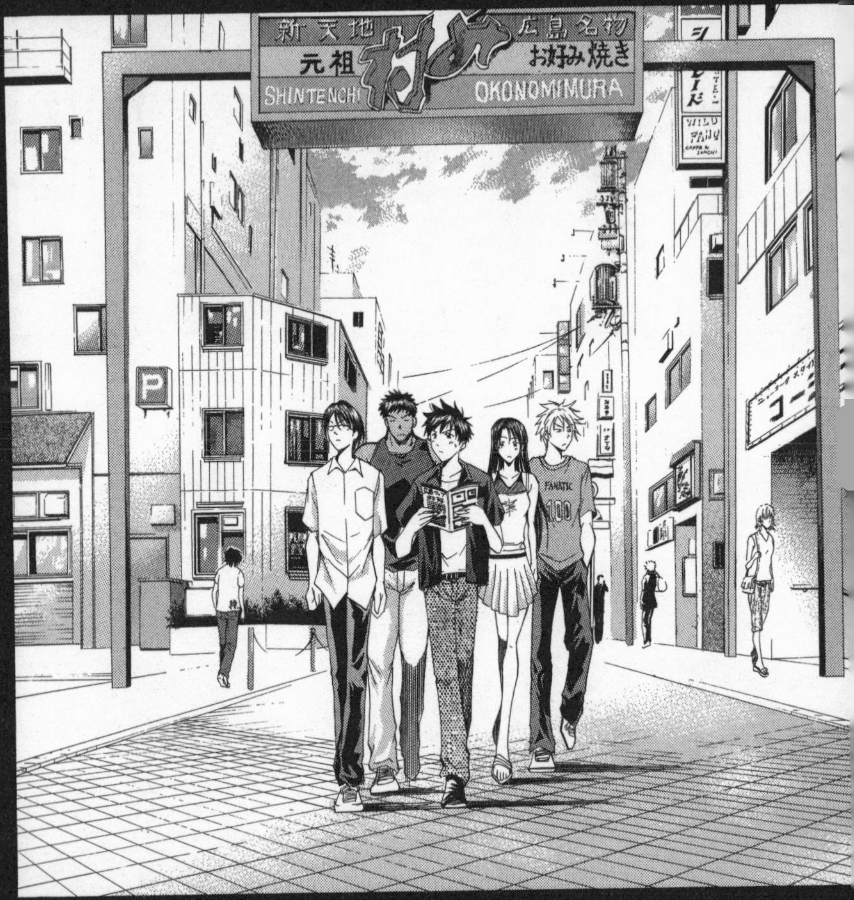
新天地
広島名物
元祖
お好み焼き
SHINTENCHI
OKONOMIMURA

SUZUKA

#38 LIGHTNING

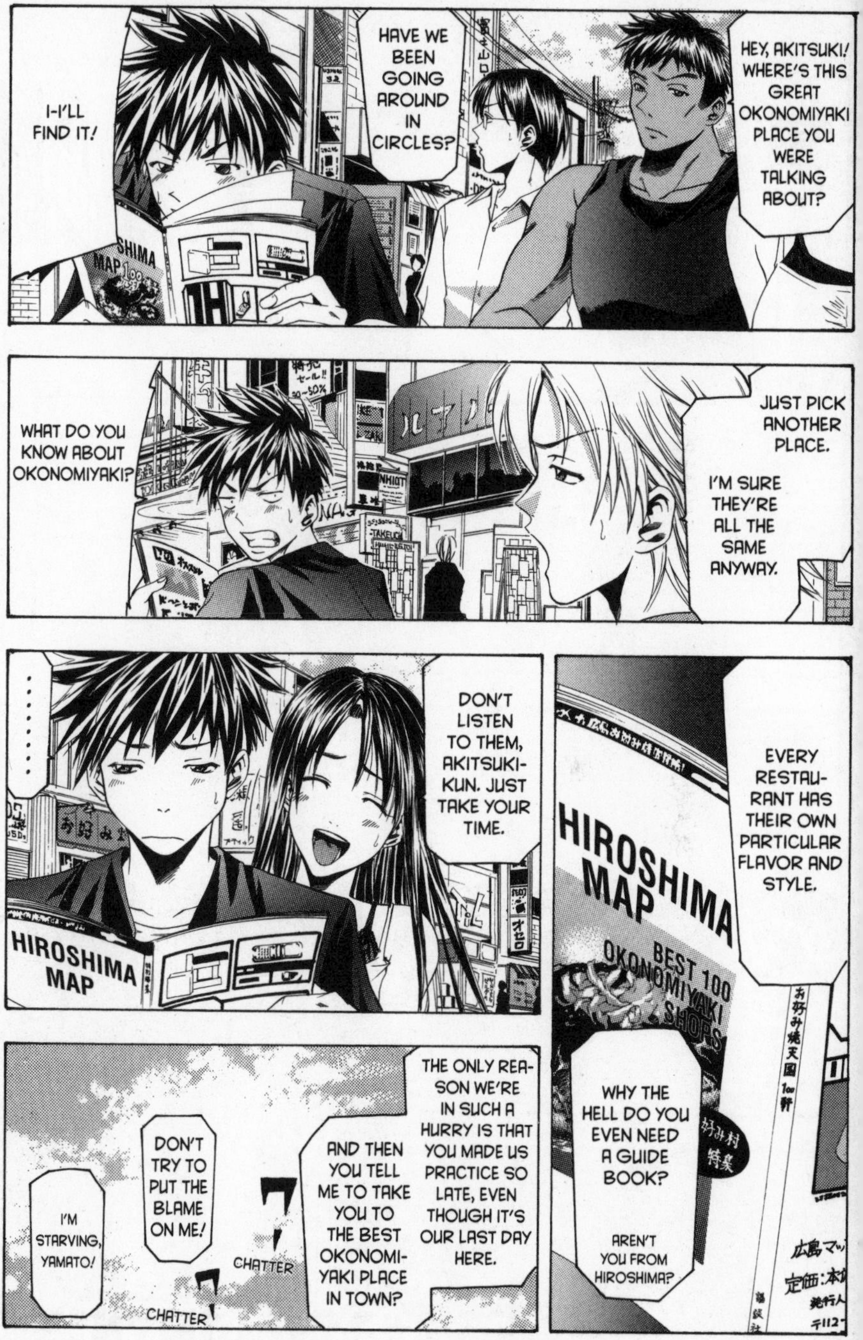
HEY, AKITSUKI! WHERE'S THIS GREAT OKONOMIYAKI PLACE YOU WERE TALKING ABOUT?
HAVE WE BEEN GOING AROUND IN CIRCLES?
I-I'LL FIND IT!
JUST PICK ANOTHER PLACE.
I'M SURE THEY'RE ALL THE SAME ANYWAY.
WHAT DO YOU KNOW ABOUT OKONOMIYAKI?
EVERY RESTAURANT HAS THEIR OWN PARTICULAR FLAVOR AND STYLE.
HIROSHIMA MAP
BEST 100 OKONOMIYAKI SHOPS
WHY THE HELL DO YOU EVEN NEED A GUIDE BOOK?
AREN'T YOU FROM HIROSHIMA?
DON'T LISTEN TO THEM, AKITSUKI-KUN. JUST TAKE YOUR TIME.
......
HIROSHIMA MAP
THE ONLY REASON WE'RE IN SUCH A HURRY IS THAT YOU MADE US PRACTICE SO LATE, EVEN THOUGH IT'S OUR LAST DAY HERE.
AND THEN YOU TELL ME TO TAKE YOU TO THE BEST OKONOMIYAKI PLACE IN TOWN?
CHATTER
DON'T TRY TO PUT THE BLAME ON ME!
CHATTER
I'M STARVING, YAMATO!

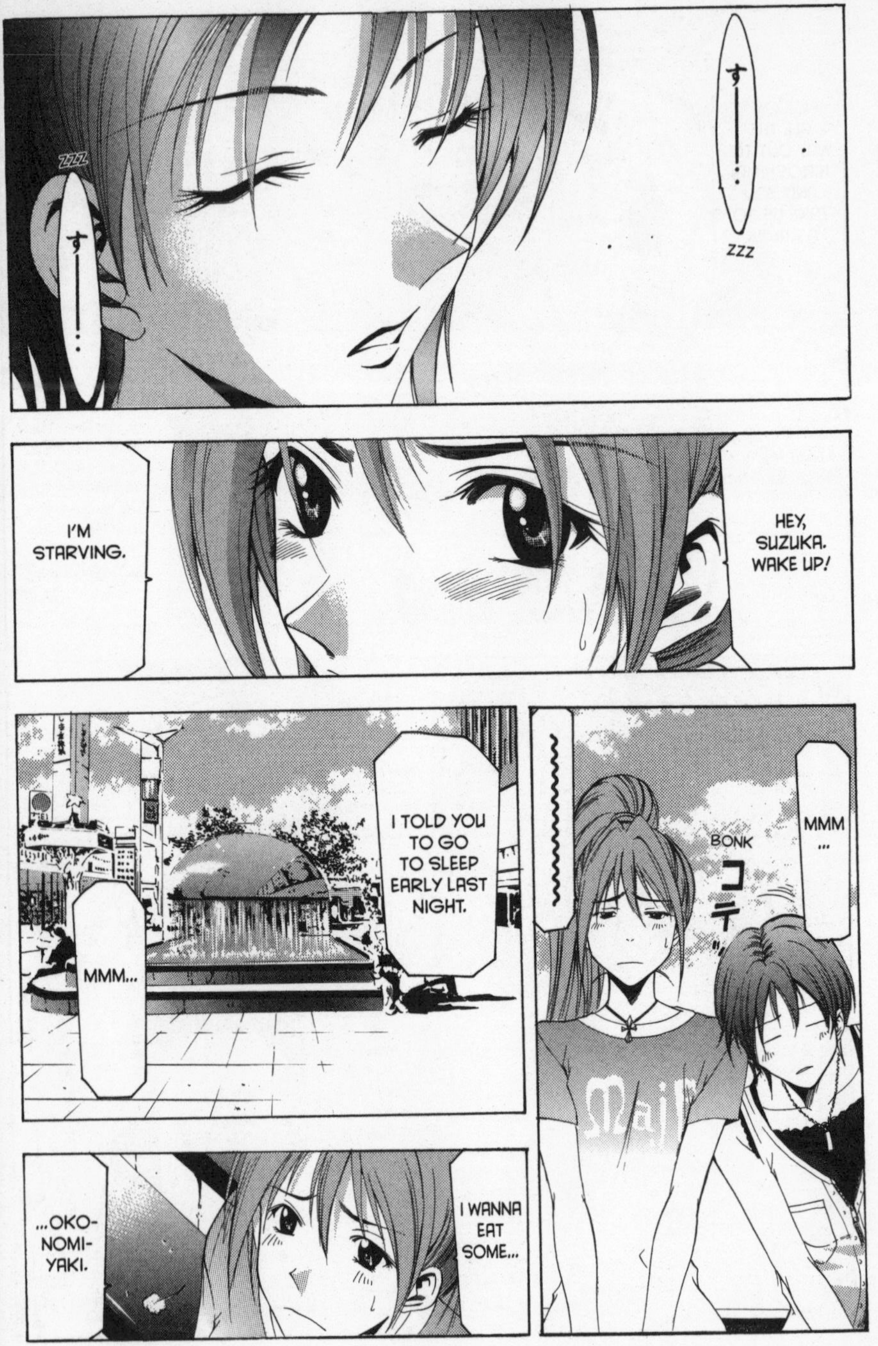
す――!!…
ZZZ
す――!!…
ZZZ
HEY, SUZUKA. WAKE UP!
I'M STARVING.
MMM ...
BONK
コテ
I TOLD YOU TO GO TO SLEEP EARLY LAST NIGHT.
MMM...
I WANNA EAT SOME...
...OKO-NOMI-YAKI.

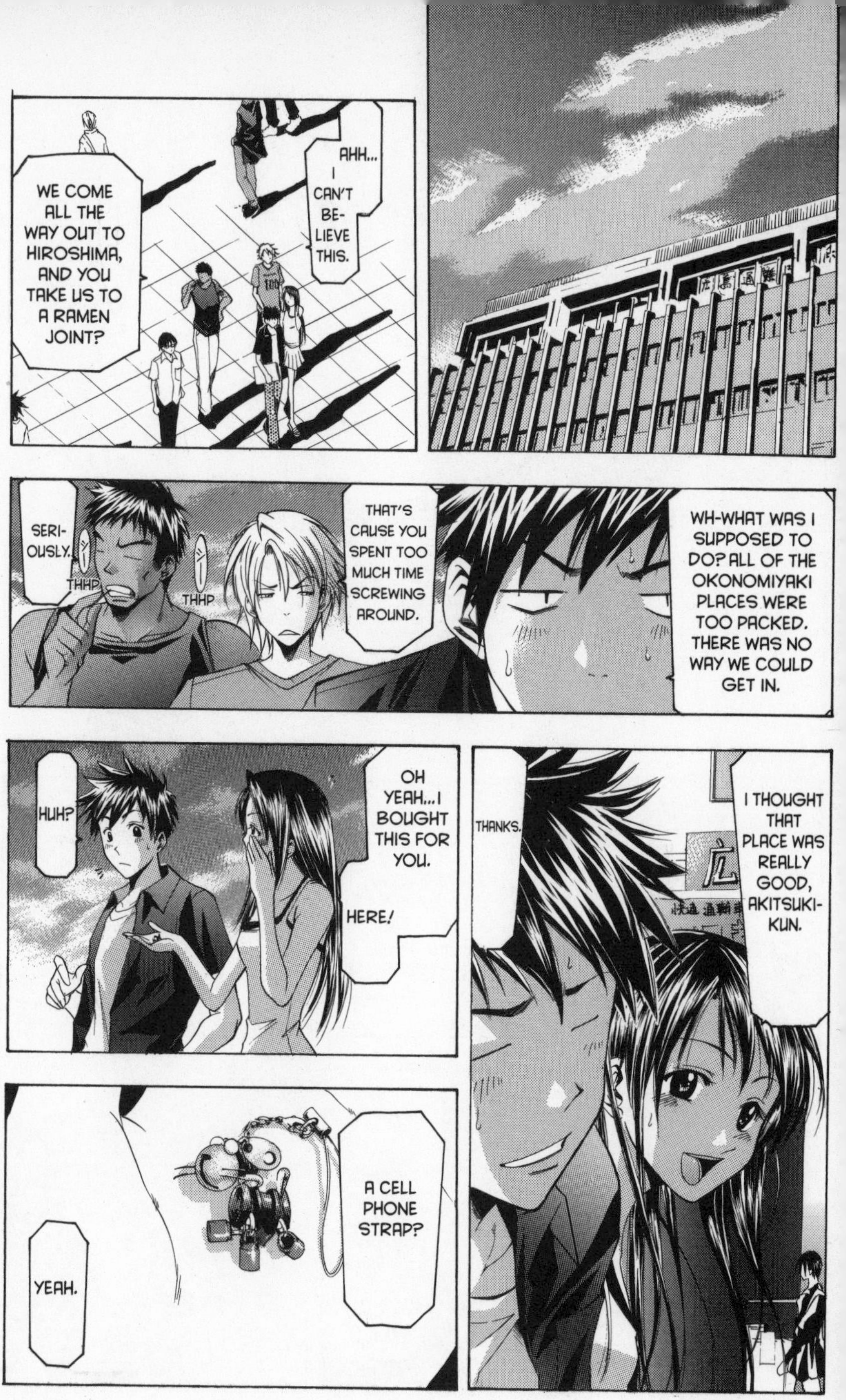
AHH... I CAN'T BE-LIEVE THIS.
WE COME ALL THE WAY OUT TO HIROSHIMA, AND YOU TAKE US TO A RAMEN JOINT?
WH-WHAT WAS I SUPPOSED TO DO? ALL OF THE OKONOMIYAKI PLACES WERE TOO PACKED. THERE WAS NO WAY WE COULD GET IN.
THAT'S CAUSE YOU SPENT TOO MUCH TIME SCREWING AROUND.
THHP
SERI-OUSLY.
THHP
I THOUGHT THAT PLACE WAS REALLY GOOD, AKITSUKI-KUN.
THANKS.
OH YEAH...I BOUGHT THIS FOR YOU.
HERE!
HUH?
A CELL PHONE STRAP?
YEAH.

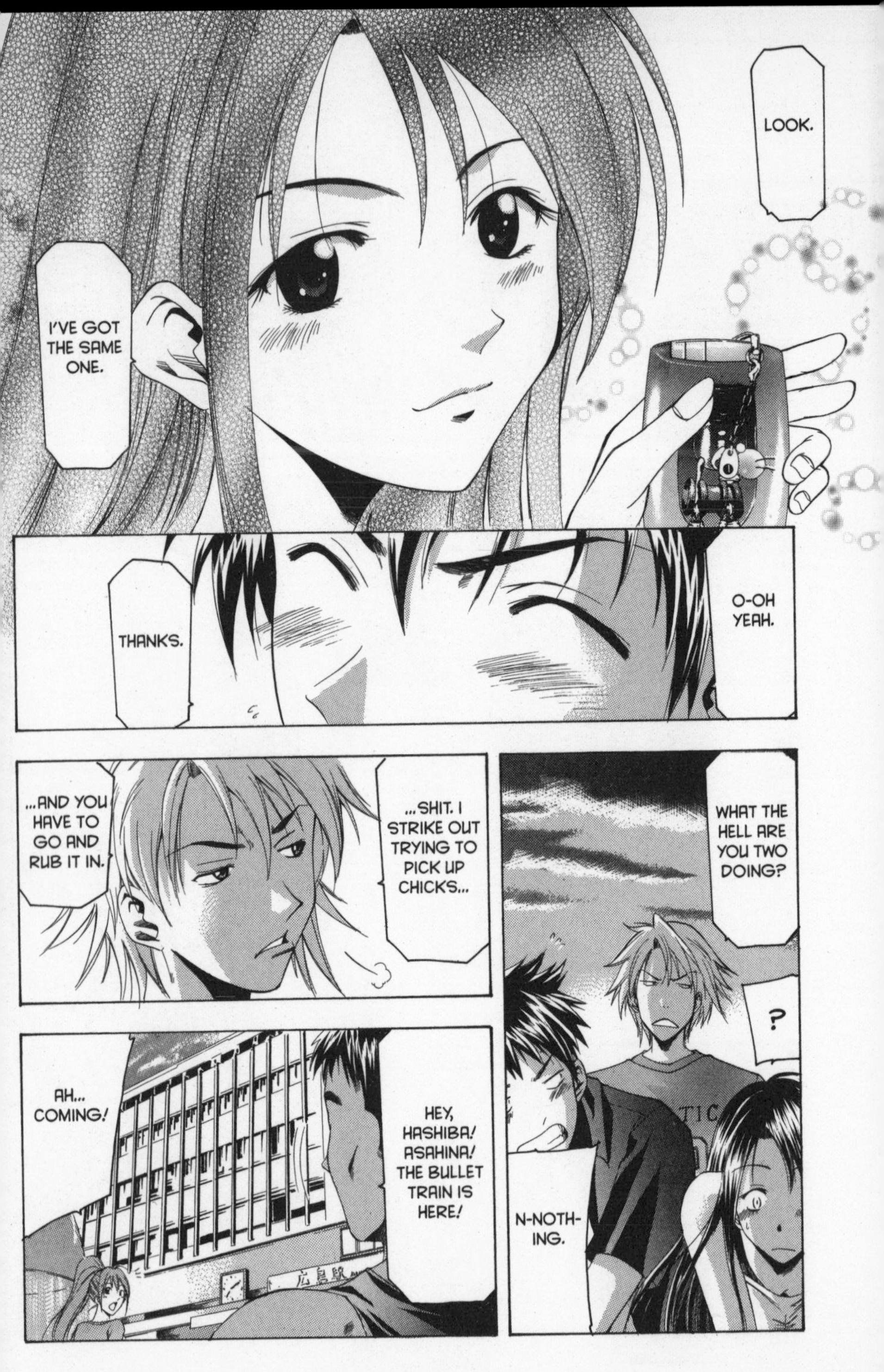
LOOK.
I'VE GOT THE SAME ONE.
O-OH YEAH.
THANKS.
WHAT THE HELL ARE YOU TWO DOING?
?
N-NOTHING.
...SHIT. I STRIKE OUT TRYING TO PICK UP CHICKS...
...AND YOU HAVE TO GO AND RUB IT IN.
HEY, HASHIBA! ASAHINA! THE BULLET TRAIN IS HERE!
AH... COMING!
広島駅

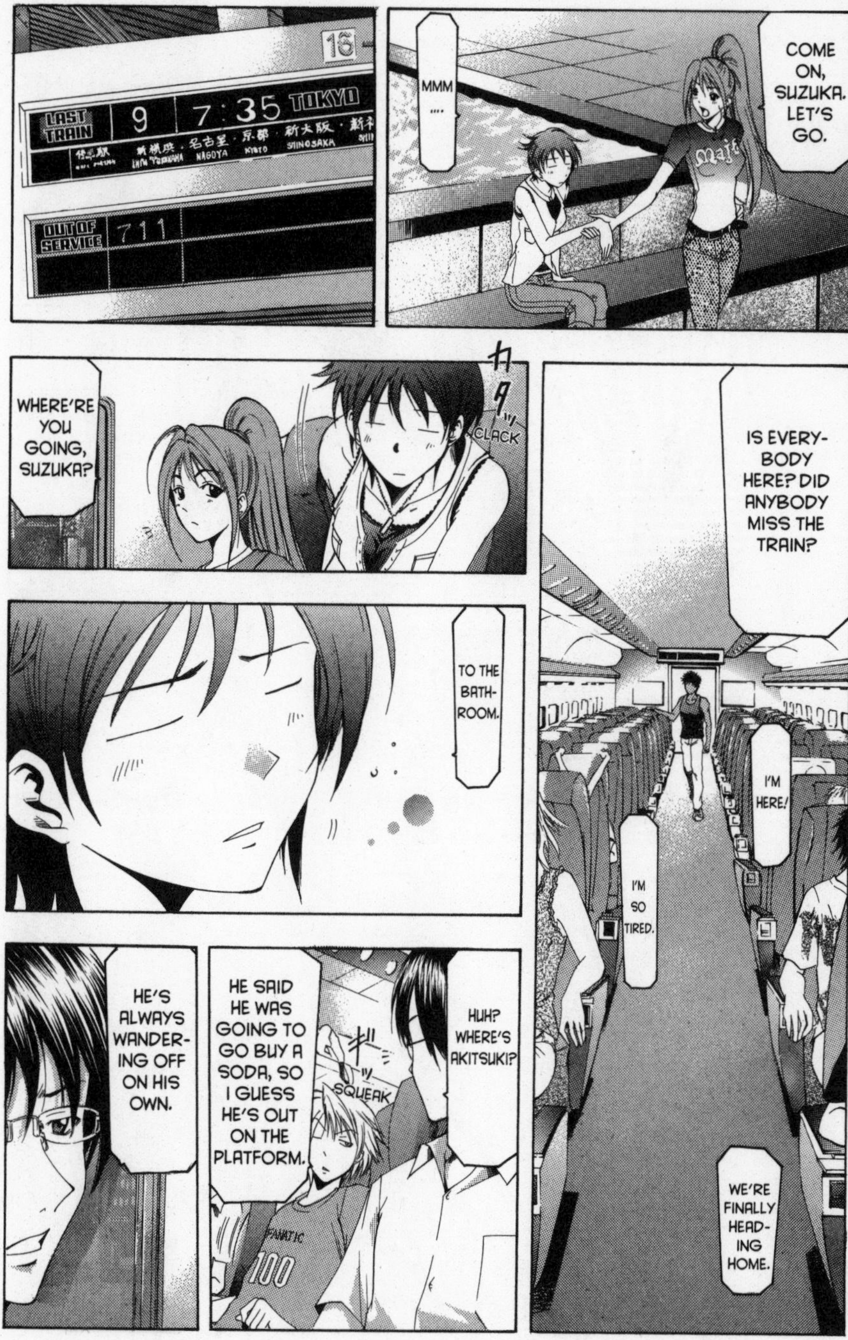
COME ON, SUZUKA. LET'S GO.
MMM ....
16
LAST TRAIN
9
7:35
TOKYO
名古屋 · 京都 · 新大阪
NAGOYA KYOTO SHINOSAKA
OUT OF SERVICE
711
IS EVERY-BODY HERE? DID ANYBODY MISS THE TRAIN?
I'M HERE!
I'M SO TIRED.
WE'RE FINALLY HEAD-ING HOME.
CLACK
WHERE'RE YOU GOING, SUZUKA?
TO THE BATH-ROOM.
HUH? WHERE'S AKITSUKI?
SQUEAK
HE SAID HE WAS GOING TO GO BUY A SODA, SO I GUESS HE'S OUT ON THE PLATFORM.
HE'S ALWAYS WANDER-ING OFF ON HIS OWN.

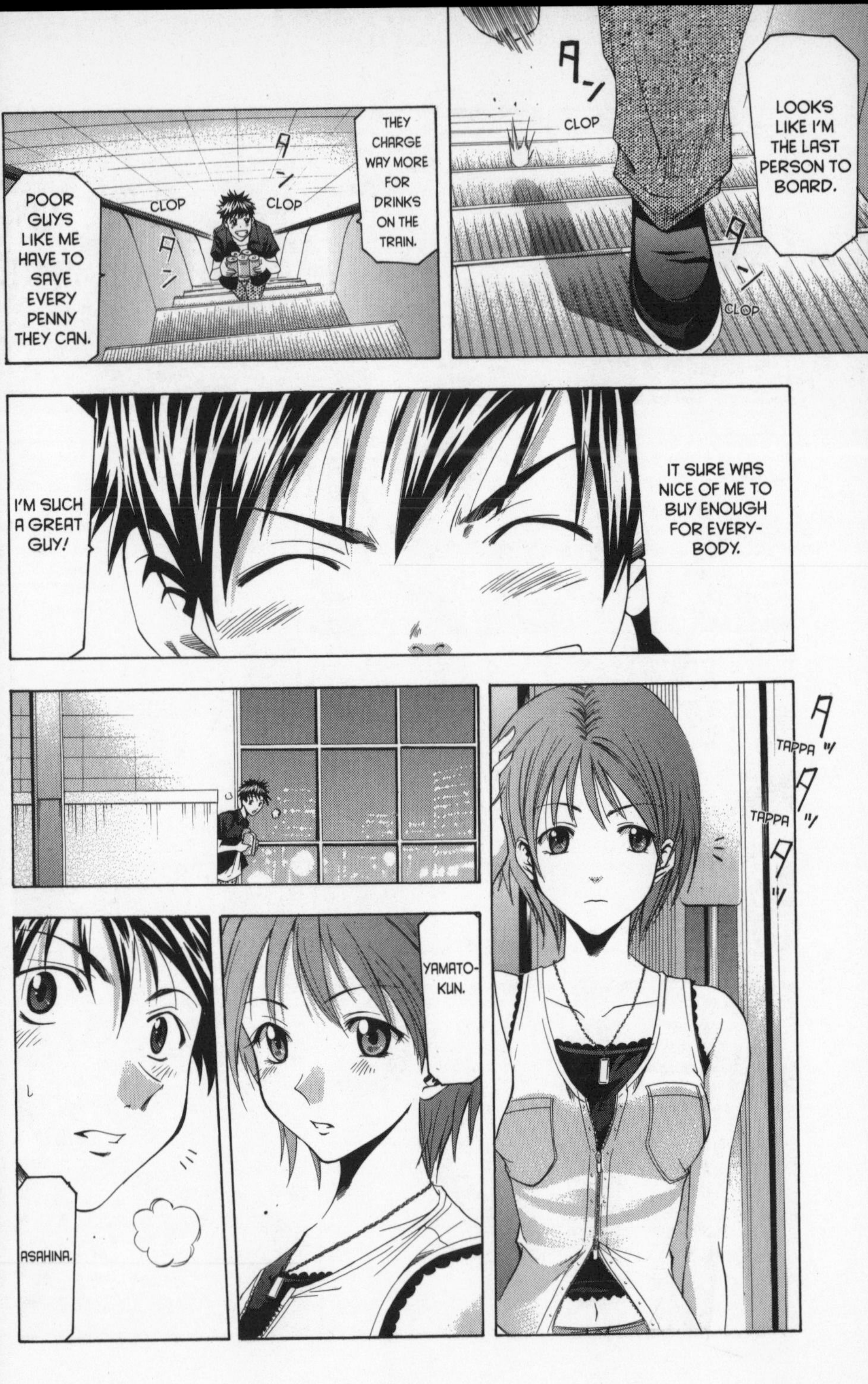
LOOKS LIKE I'M THE LAST PERSON TO BOARD.
CLOP
CLOP
THEY CHARGE WAY MORE FOR DRINKS ON THE TRAIN.
CLOP
CLOP
POOR GUYS LIKE ME HAVE TO SAVE EVERY PENNY THEY CAN.
IT SURE WAS NICE OF ME TO BUY ENOUGH FOR EVERY-BODY.
I'M SUCH A GREAT GUY!
TAPPA
TAPPA
YAMATO-KUN.
ASAHINA.

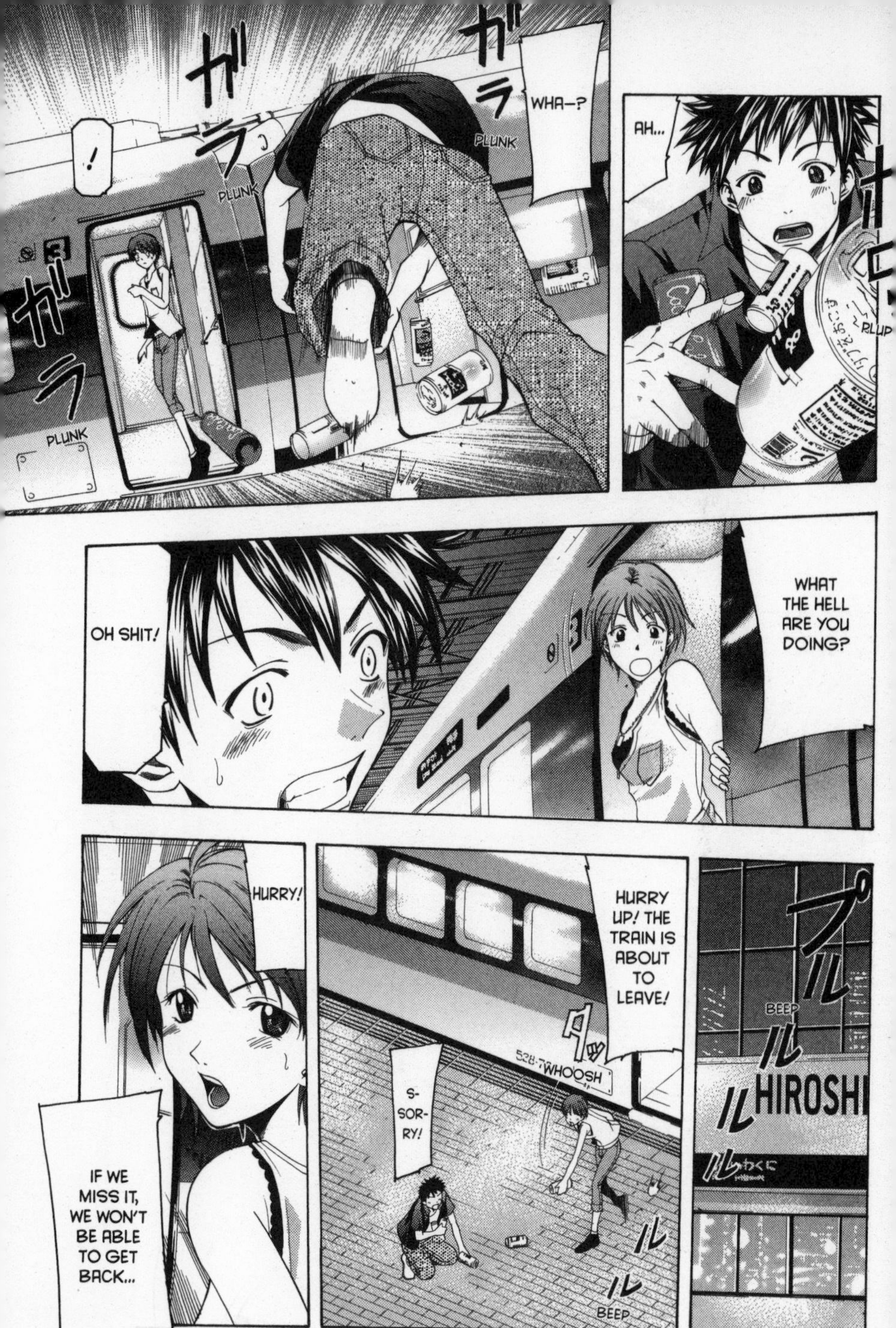
AH...
PLUP
WHA–?
PLUNK
!
PLUNK
PLUNK
WHAT THE HELL ARE YOU DOING?
OH SHIT!
BEEP
HIROSHI
HURRY UP! THE TRAIN IS ABOUT TO LEAVE!
WHOOSH
S-SOR-RY!
BEEP
HURRY!
IF WE MISS IT, WE WON'T BE ABLE TO GET BACK...

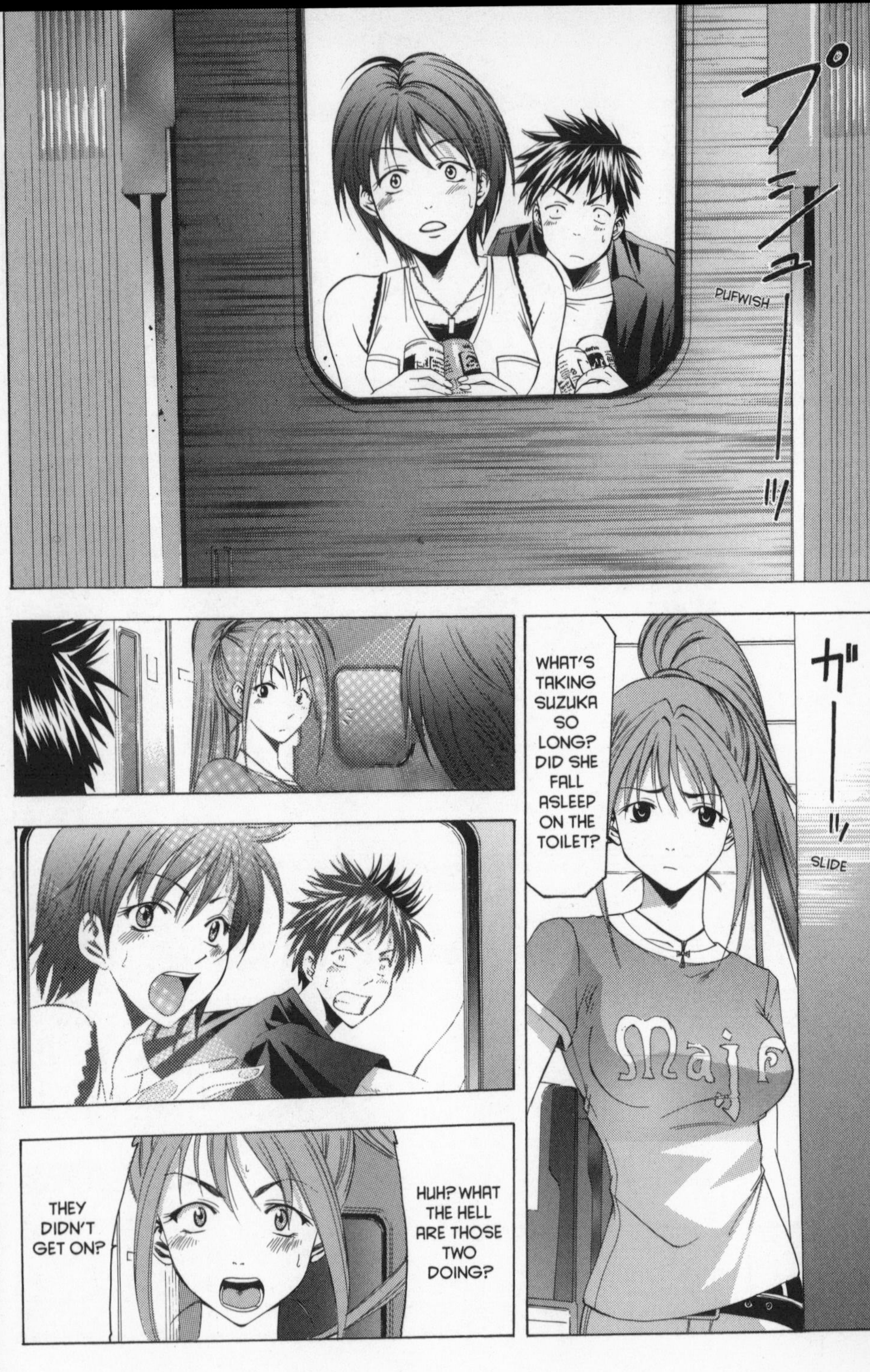
プシューッ
PUFWISH
ガーッ
SLIDE
WHAT'S TAKING SUZUKA SO LONG? DID SHE FALL ASLEEP ON THE TOILET?
HUH? WHAT THE HELL ARE THOSE TWO DOING?
THEY DIDN'T GET ON?

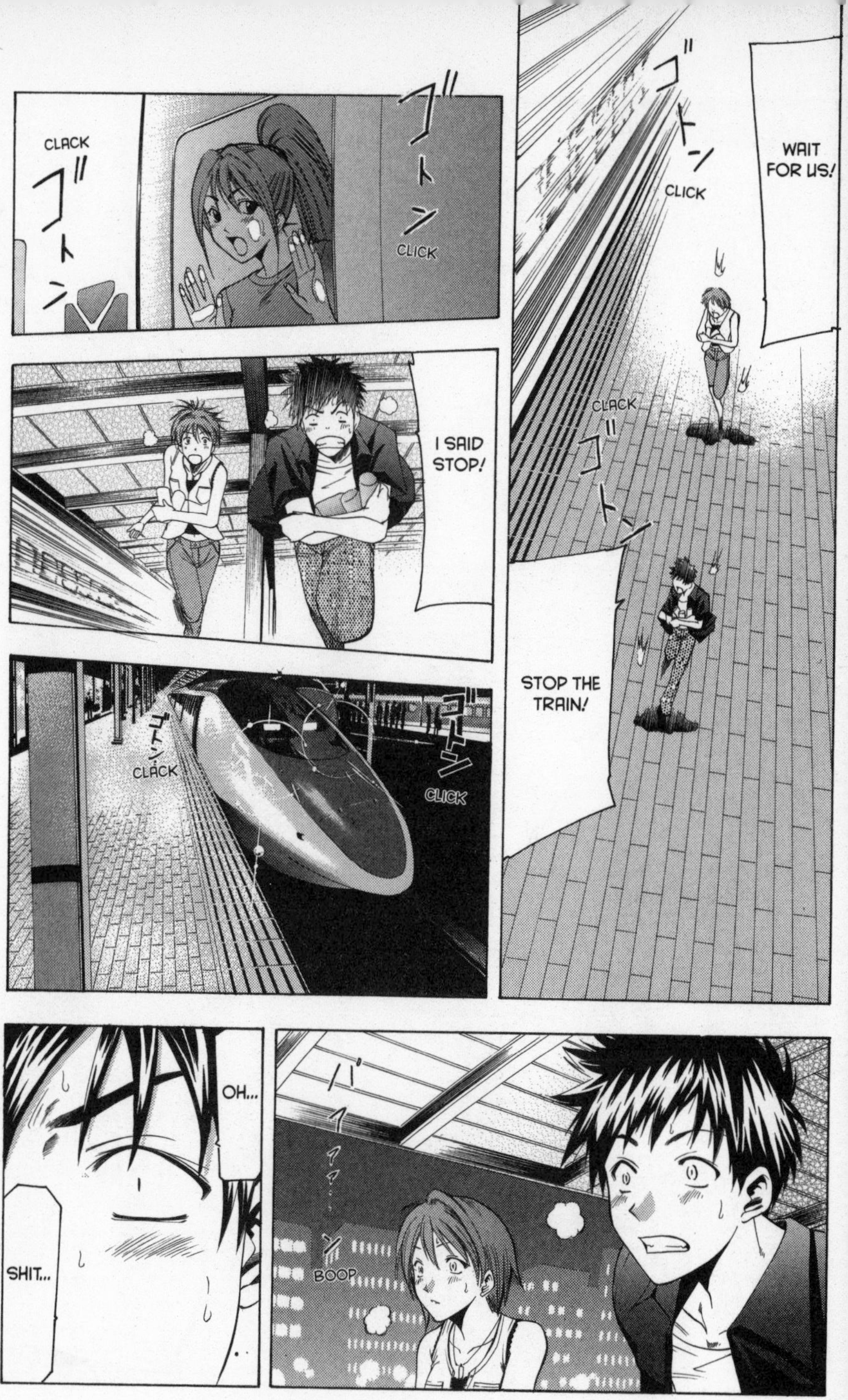

WAIT FOR US!
ゴトン
CLICK
CLACK
ゴトン
STOP THE TRAIN!
CLACK
ゴトン
ゴトン
CLICK
I SAID STOP!
ゴトン
CLACK
ゴトン
CLICK
BOOP
OH...
SHIT...

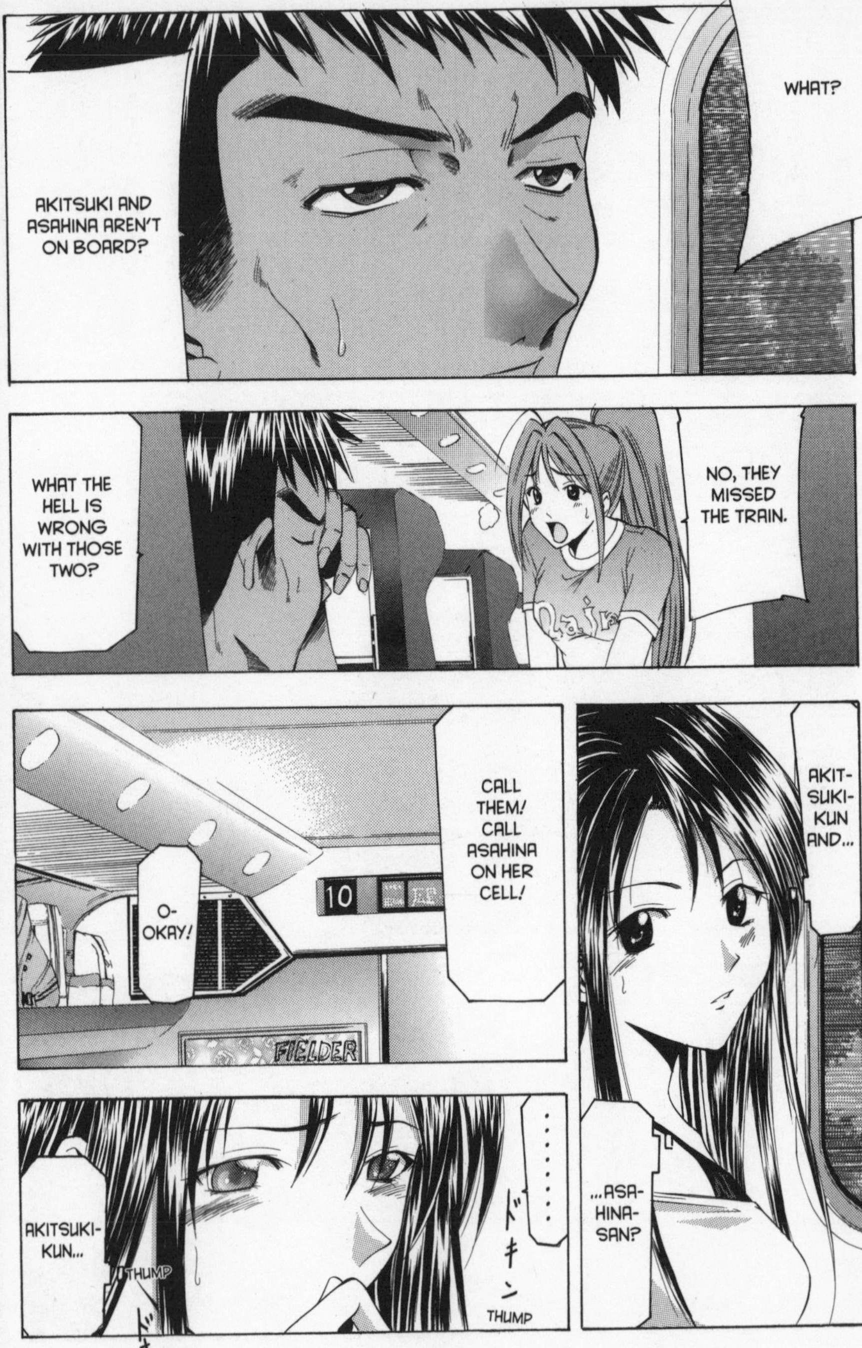
WHAT?
AKITSUKI AND ASAHINA AREN'T ON BOARD?
NO, THEY MISSED THE TRAIN.
WHAT THE HELL IS WRONG WITH THOSE TWO?
AKIT-SUKI-KUN AND...
...ASA-HINA-SAN?
CALL THEM! CALL ASAHINA ON HER CELL!
O-OKAY!
10
FIELDER
......
ドキン
THUMP
AKITSUKI-KUN...
THUMP
ドキン

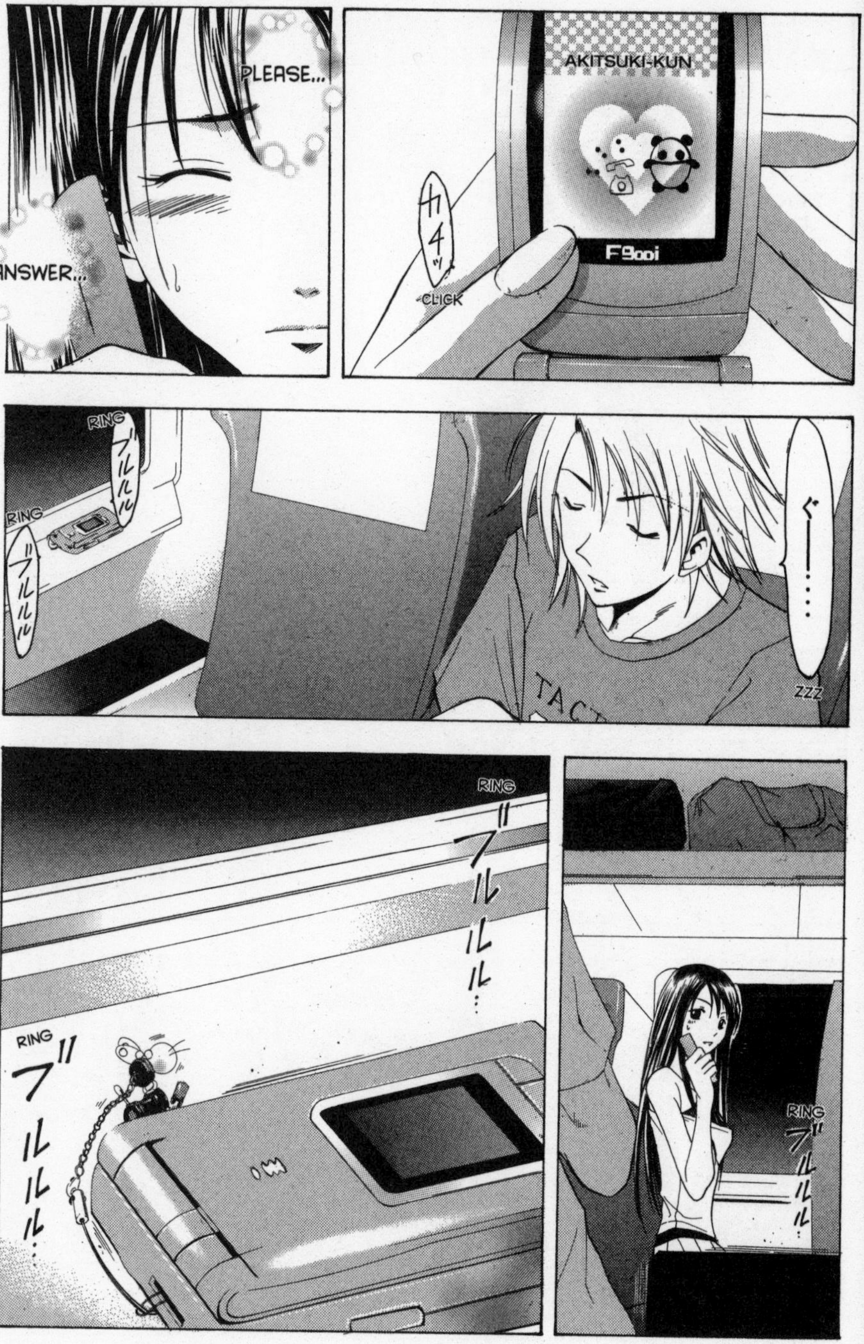
AKITSUKI-KUN
F900i
カチッ
CLICK
PLEASE...
ANSWER...
ぐー……
ZZZ
ブルルル
RING
ブルルル
RING
ブルルル…
RING
ブルルル…
RING
ブルルル…
RING

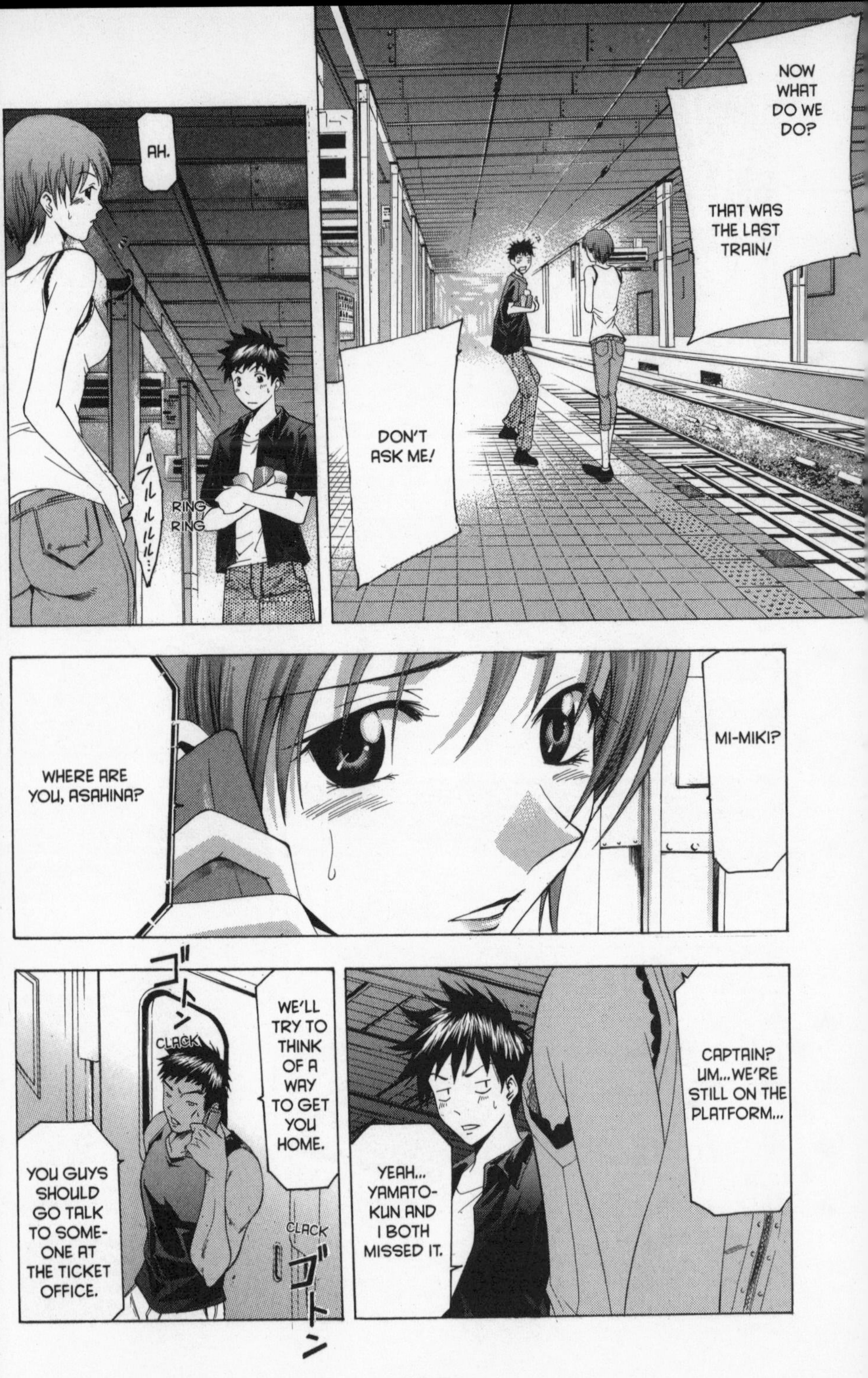
NOW WHAT DO WE DO?
THAT WAS THE LAST TRAIN!
DON'T ASK ME!
AH.
ブルルルル…
RING RING
MI-MIKI?
WHERE ARE YOU, ASAHINA?
CAPTAIN? UM...WE'RE STILL ON THE PLATFORM...
YEAH... YAMATO-KUN AND I BOTH MISSED IT.
ゴトン
CLACK
WE'LL TRY TO THINK OF A WAY TO GET YOU HOME.
YOU GUYS SHOULD GO TALK TO SOME-ONE AT THE TICKET OFFICE.
CLACK
ゴトン

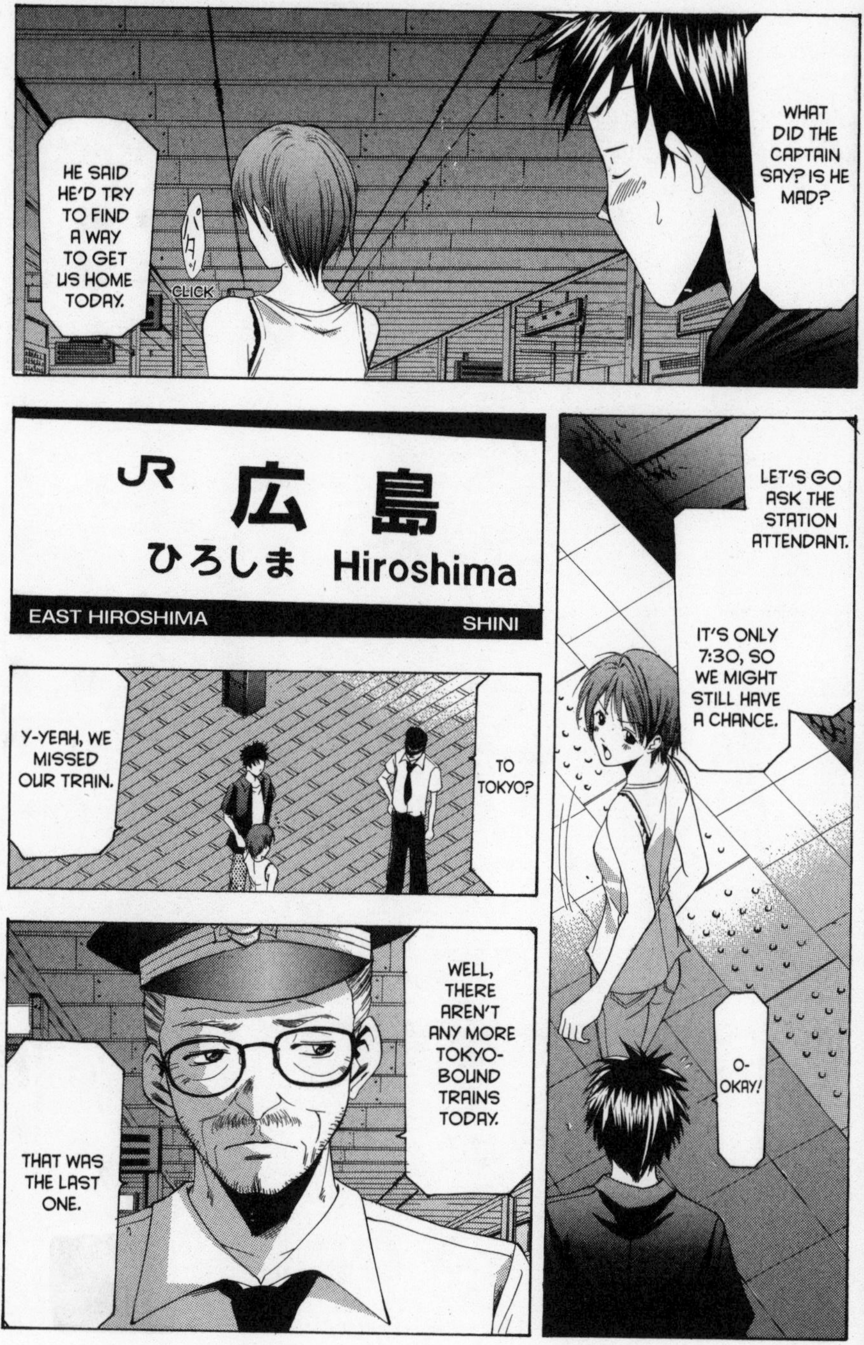
WHAT DID THE CAPTAIN SAY? IS HE MAD?
パタッ
CLICK
HE SAID HE'D TRY TO FIND A WAY TO GET US HOME TODAY.
LET'S GO ASK THE STATION ATTENDANT.
IT'S ONLY 7:30, SO WE MIGHT STILL HAVE A CHANCE.
O-OKAY!
JR 広島
ひろしま Hiroshima
EAST HIROSHIMA
SHINI
TO TOKYO?
Y-YEAH, WE MISSED OUR TRAIN.
WELL, THERE AREN'T ANY MORE TOKYO-BOUND TRAINS TODAY.
THAT WAS THE LAST ONE.

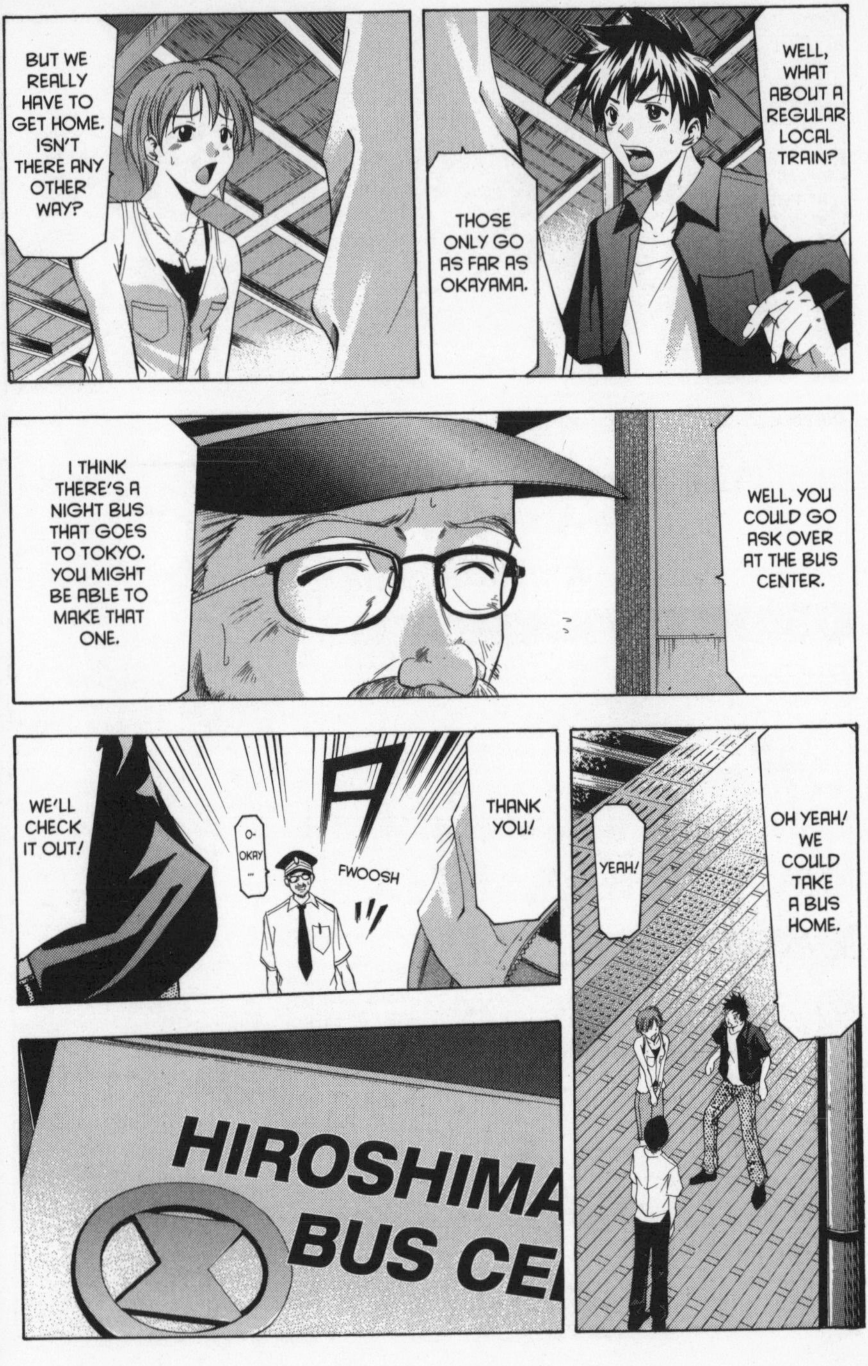
WELL, WHAT ABOUT A REGULAR LOCAL TRAIN?
THOSE ONLY GO AS FAR AS OKAYAMA.
BUT WE REALLY HAVE TO GET HOME. ISN'T THERE ANY OTHER WAY?
WELL, YOU COULD GO ASK OVER AT THE BUS CENTER.
I THINK THERE'S A NIGHT BUS THAT GOES TO TOKYO. YOU MIGHT BE ABLE TO MAKE THAT ONE.
OH YEAH! WE COULD TAKE A BUS HOME.
YEAH!
THANK YOU!
O-OKAY ...
FWOOSH
WE'LL CHECK IT OUT!
HIROSHIMA
BUS CE

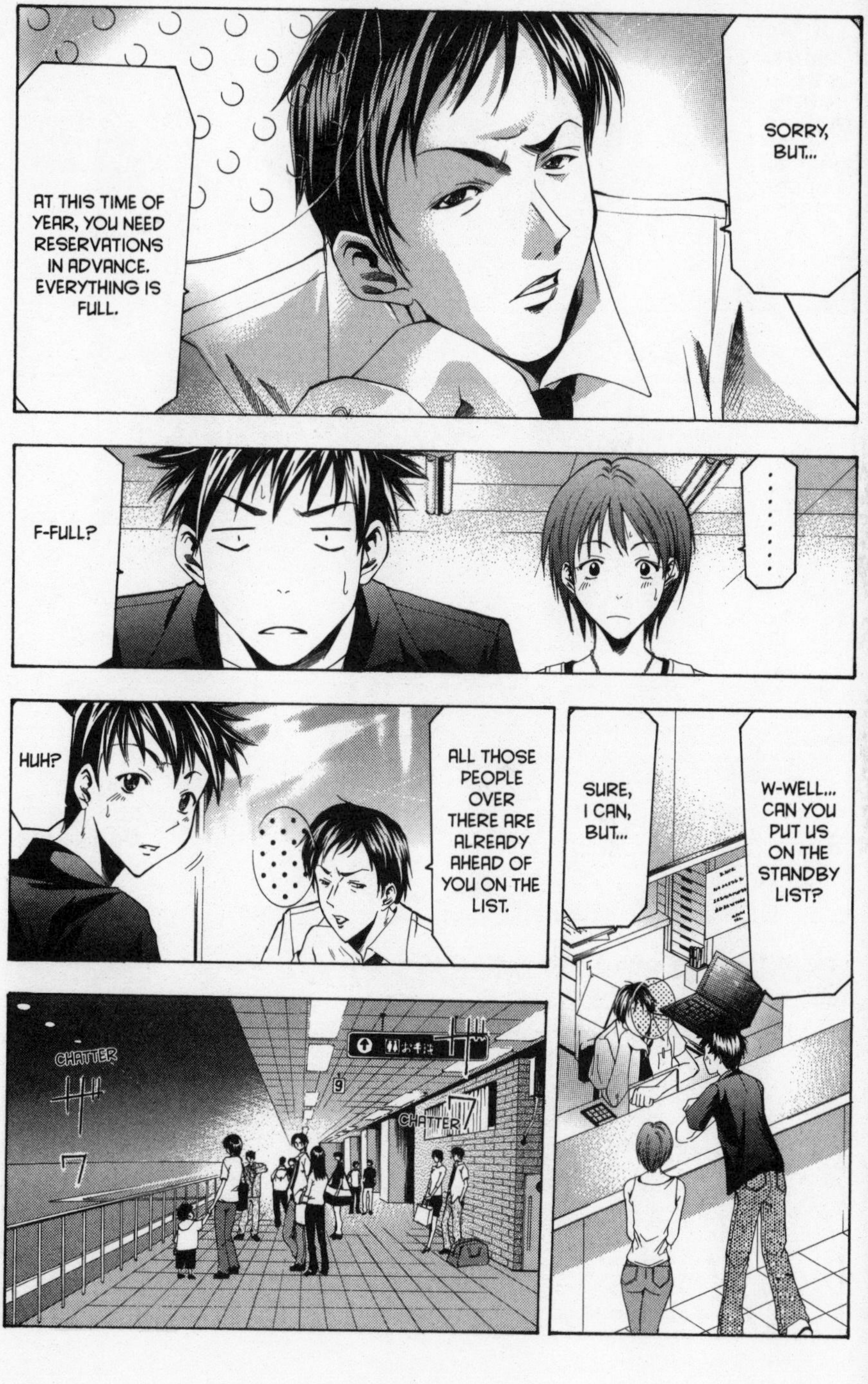
SORRY, BUT...
AT THIS TIME OF YEAR, YOU NEED RESERVATIONS IN ADVANCE. EVERYTHING IS FULL.
....
F-FULL?
W-WELL... CAN YOU PUT US ON THE STANDBY LIST?
SURE, I CAN, BUT...
ALL THOSE PEOPLE OVER THERE ARE ALREADY AHEAD OF YOU ON THE LIST.
HUH?
CHATTER
CHATTER

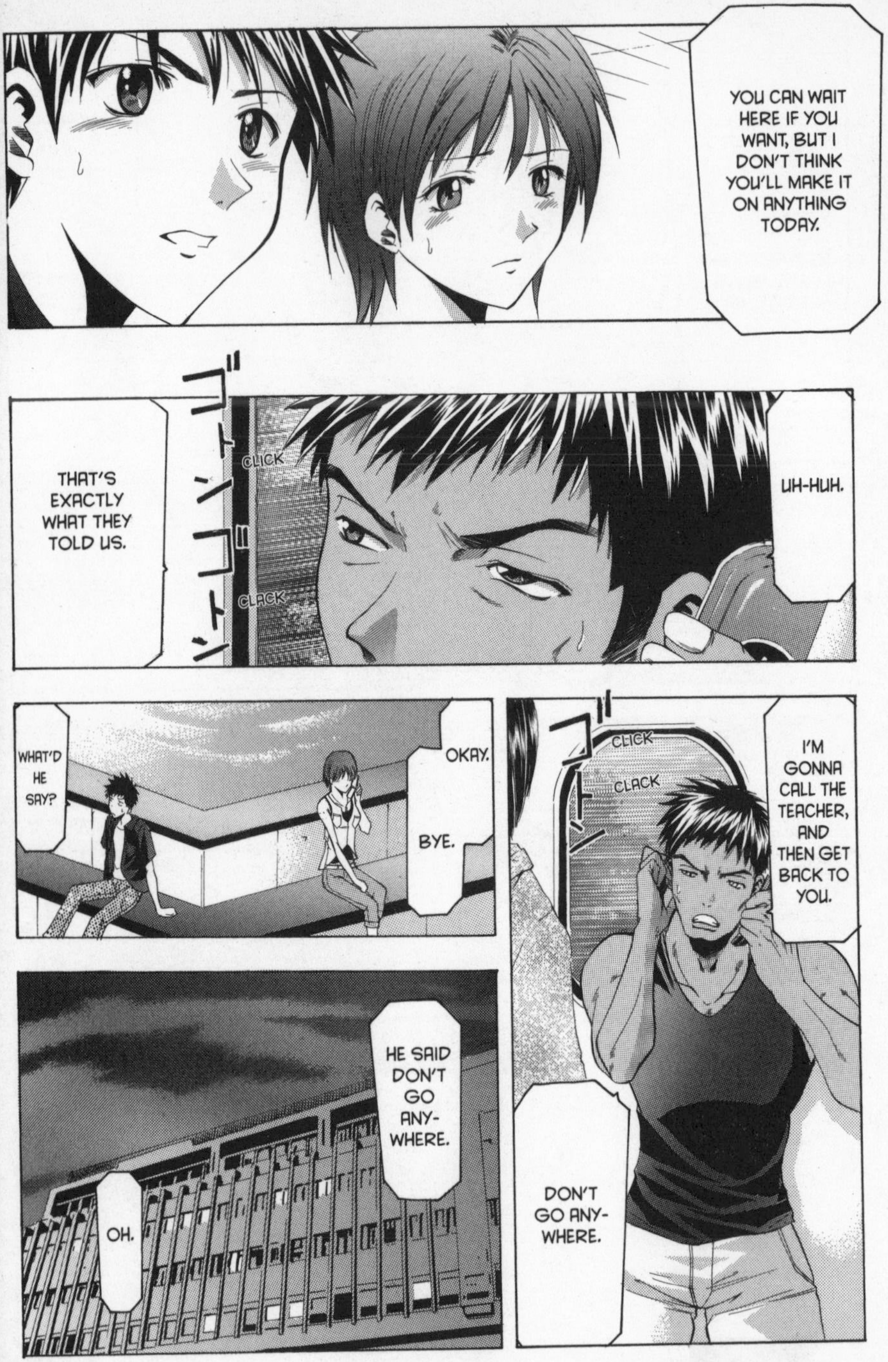
YOU CAN WAIT HERE IF YOU WANT, BUT I DON'T THINK YOU'LL MAKE IT ON ANYTHING TODAY.
UH-HUH.
ゴトンゴトン
CLICK
CLACK
THAT'S EXACTLY WHAT THEY TOLD US.
ゴト
CLICK
CLACK
I'M GONNA CALL THE TEACHER, AND THEN GET BACK TO YOU.
DON'T GO ANY-WHERE.
OKAY.
BYE.
WHAT'D HE SAY?
HE SAID DON'T GO ANY-WHERE.
OH.

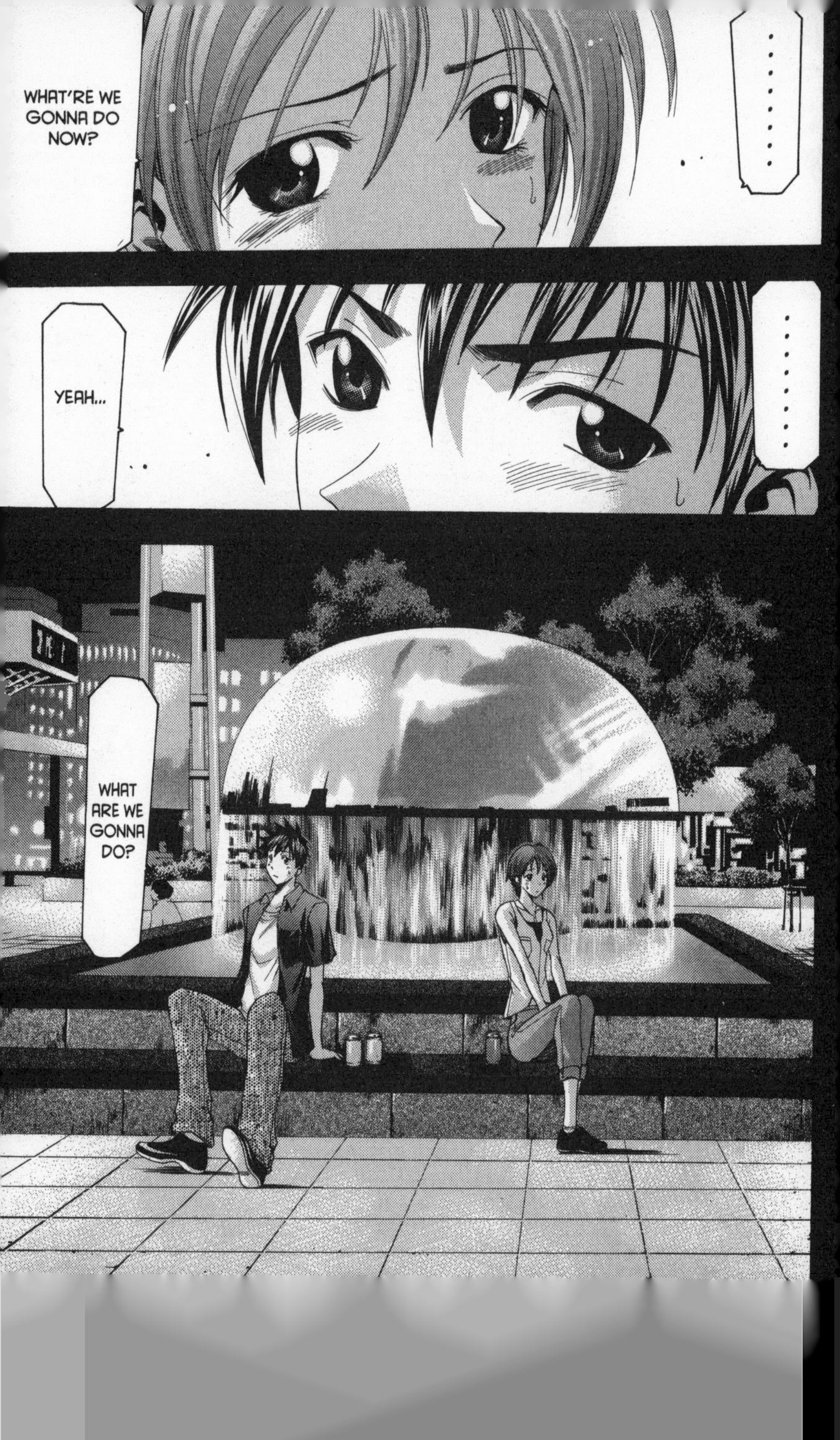
......
WHAT'RE WE GONNA DO NOW?
......
YEAH...
WHAT ARE WE GONNA DO?

SUZUKA FOUR-PANEL THEATER NUMBER TWENTY-THREE

CRIMINAL TRAITS

TV
THE SLASH AND RUN KILLER IS STILL ON THE LOOSE. HERE IS A DESCRIPTION OF THE SUSPECT.
SCRIBBLE
SCRIBBLE
A SLASH AND RUN KILLER...
MY ASSISTANTS.
HE'S IN HIS LATE TWENTIES TO EARLY THIRTIES...
...WITH A THIN BUILD...
SCRIBBLE
SCRIBBLE
HMM...
HE'S ABOUT 5'10" OR 5' 11", AND WAS LAST SEEN...
...WEARING A BLACK T-SHIRT.
SHIVER
....
THE SUSPECT IS SAID TO HAVE A PALE COMPLEXION.
STARE
NO! NO!
IT WAS A PERFECT DESCRIPTION OF ME.

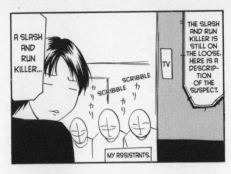

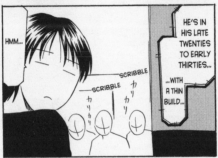

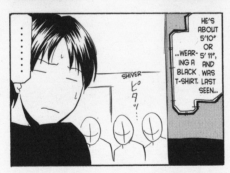

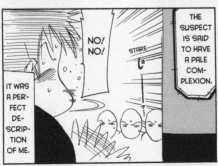

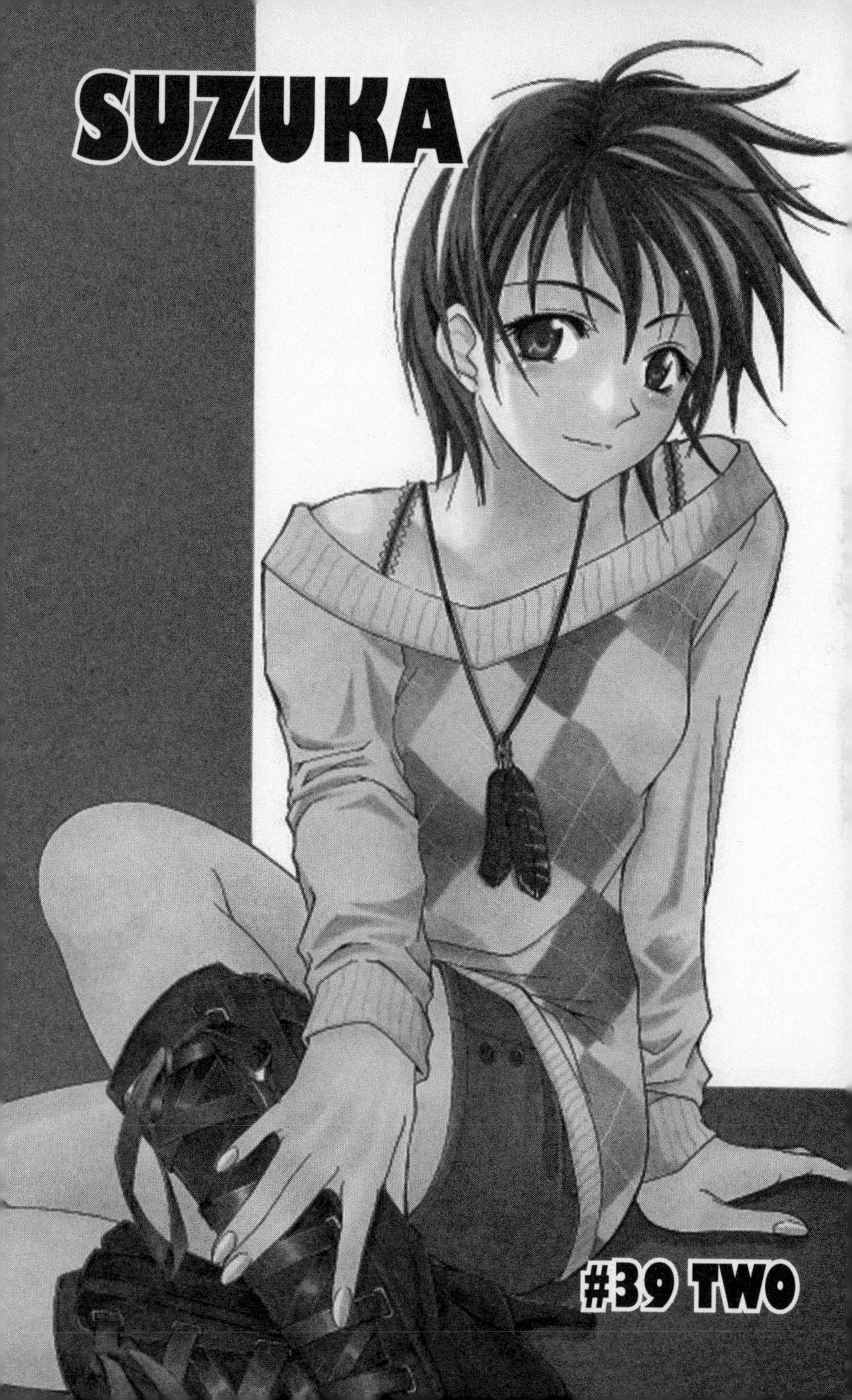
SUZUKA
#39 TWO

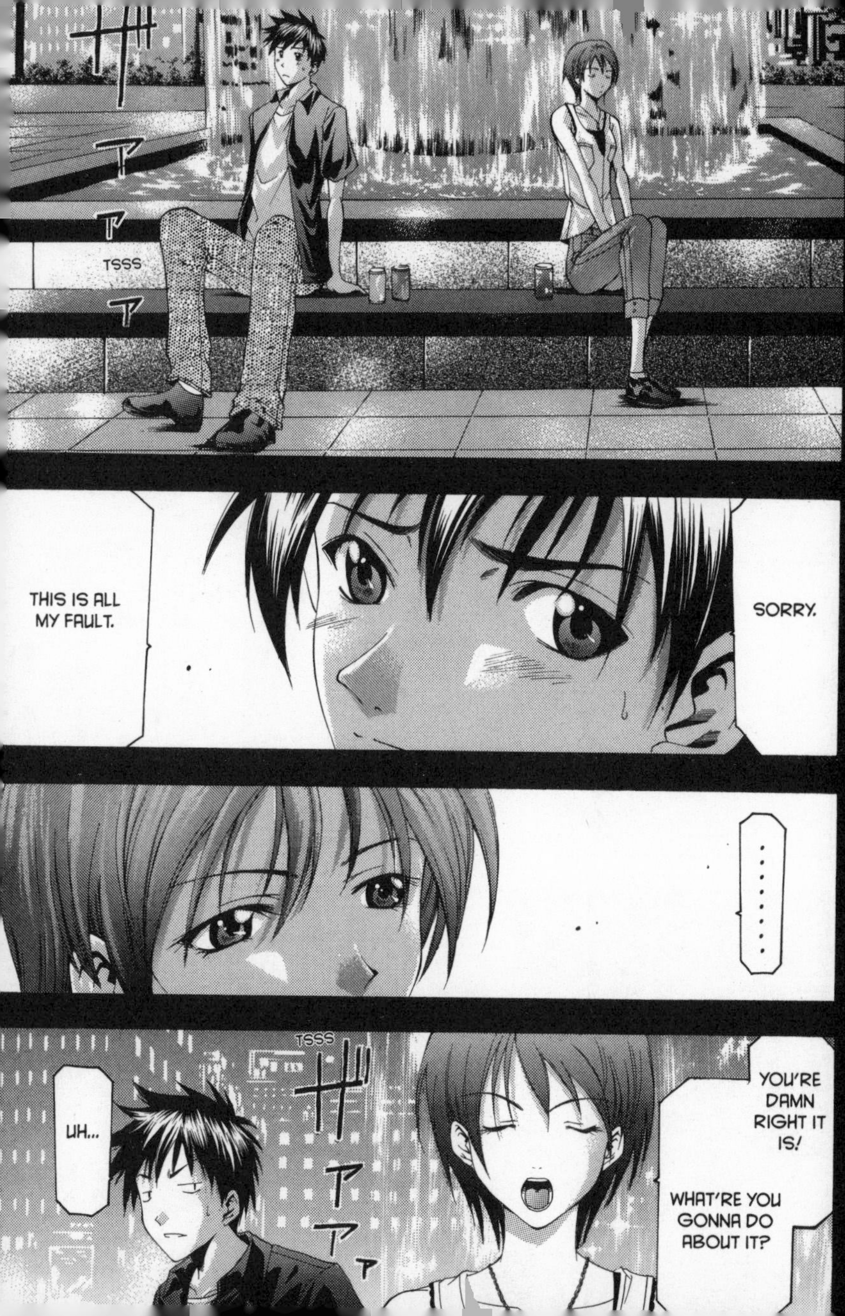
TSSS
SORRY.
THIS IS ALL MY FAULT.
......
YOU'RE DAMN RIGHT IT IS!
WHAT'RE YOU GONNA DO ABOUT IT?
TSSS
UH...

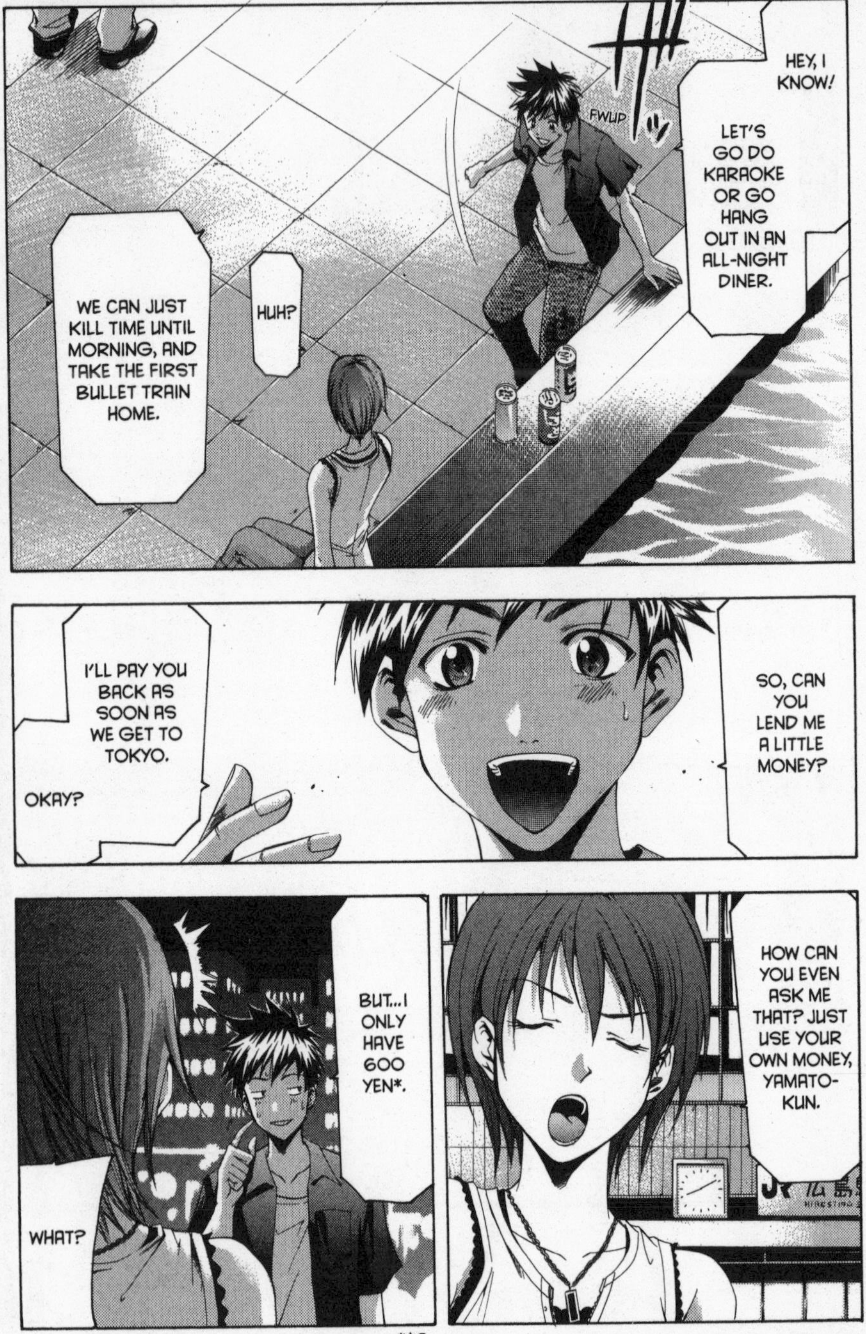
HEY, I KNOW!
FWUP
LET'S GO DO KARAOKE OR GO HANG OUT IN AN ALL-NIGHT DINER.
HUH?
WE CAN JUST KILL TIME UNTIL MORNING, AND TAKE THE FIRST BULLET TRAIN HOME.
SO, CAN YOU LEND ME A LITTLE MONEY?
I'LL PAY YOU BACK AS SOON AS WE GET TO TOKYO.
OKAY?
HOW CAN YOU EVEN ASK ME THAT? JUST USE YOUR OWN MONEY, YAMATO-KUN.
BUT...I ONLY HAVE 600 YEN*.
WHAT?

*$6

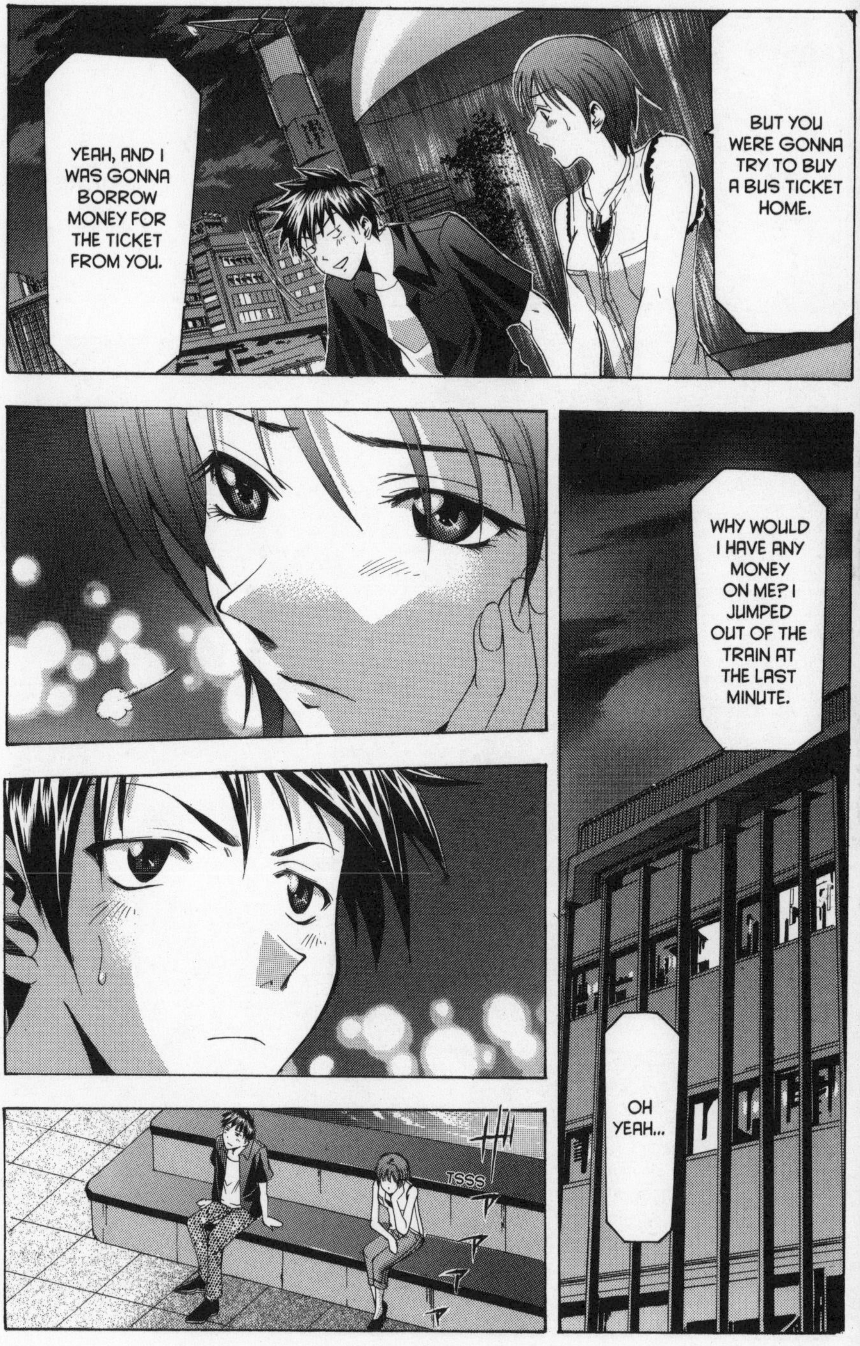
BUT YOU WERE GONNA TRY TO BUY A BUS TICKET HOME.
YEAH, AND I WAS GONNA BORROW MONEY FOR THE TICKET FROM YOU.
WHY WOULD I HAVE ANY MONEY ON ME? I JUMPED OUT OF THE TRAIN AT THE LAST MINUTE.
OH YEAH...
TSSS

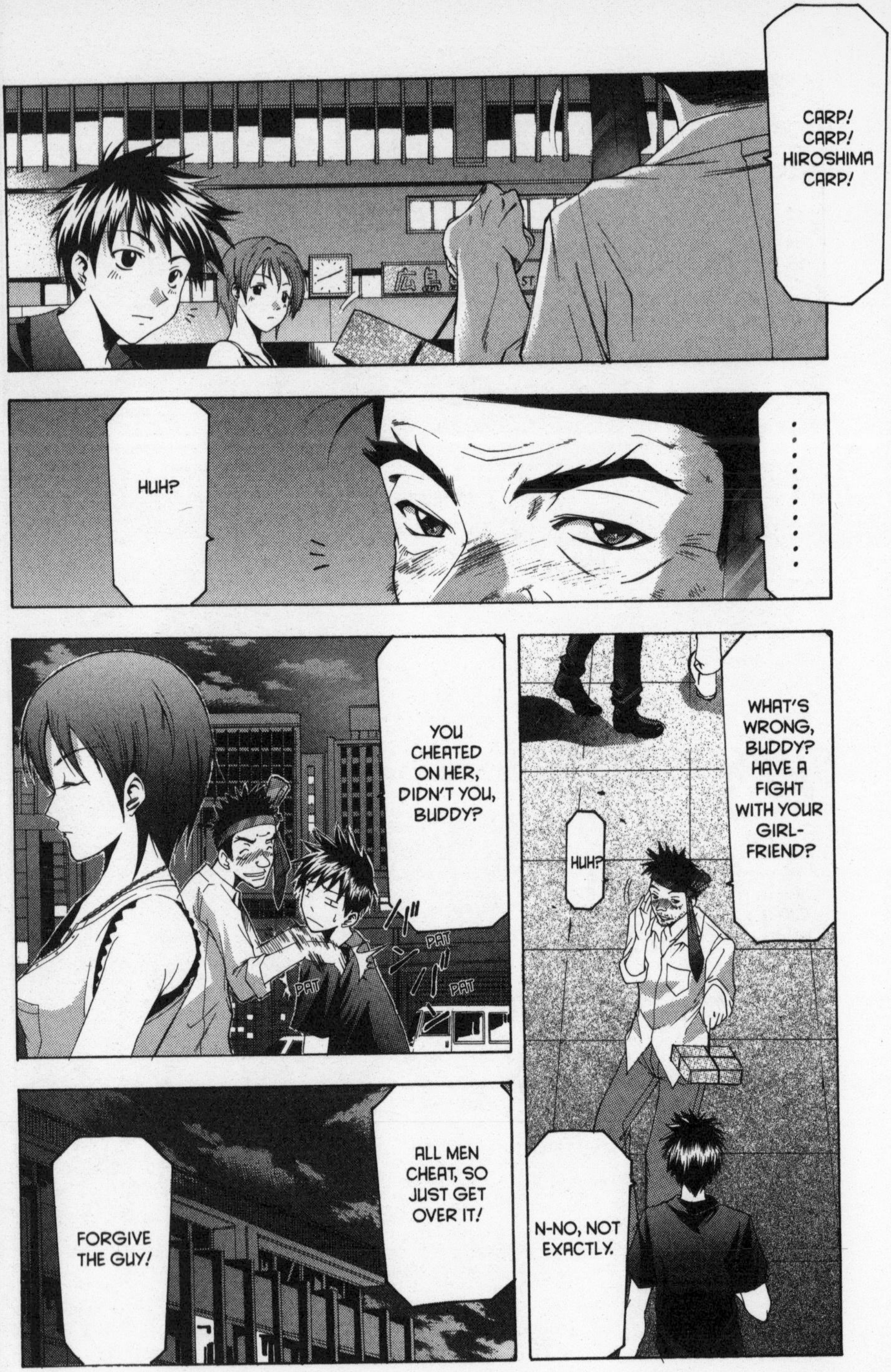
CARP! CARP! HIROSHIMA CARP!
広島
....
HUH?
WHAT'S WRONG, BUDDY? HAVE A FIGHT WITH YOUR GIRL-FRIEND?
HUH?
N-NO, NOT EXACTLY.
YOU CHEATED ON HER, DIDN'T YOU, BUDDY?
PAT
PAT
PAT
ALL MEN CHEAT, SO JUST GET OVER IT!
FORGIVE THE GUY!

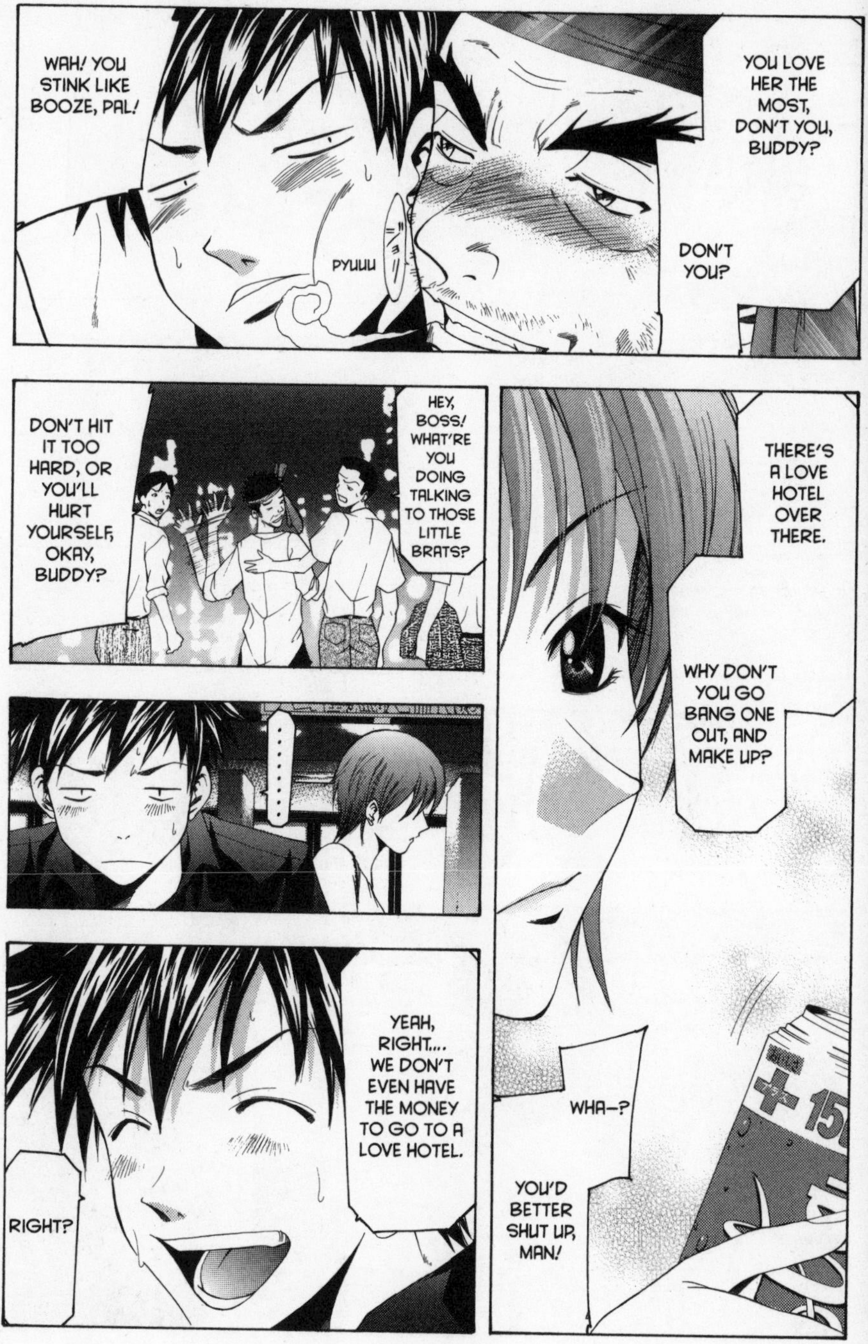
YOU LOVE HER THE MOST, DON'T YOU, BUDDY?
DON'T YOU?
WAH! YOU STINK LIKE BOOZE, PAL!
PYUUU
THERE'S A LOVE HOTEL OVER THERE.
WHY DON'T YOU GO BANG ONE OUT, AND MAKE UP?
WHA-?
YOU'D BETTER SHUT UP, MAN!
HEY, BOSS! WHAT'RE YOU DOING TALKING TO THOSE LITTLE BRATS?
DON'T HIT IT TOO HARD, OR YOU'LL HURT YOURSELF, OKAY, BUDDY?
....
YEAH, RIGHT.... WE DON'T EVEN HAVE THE MONEY TO GO TO A LOVE HOTEL.
RIGHT?

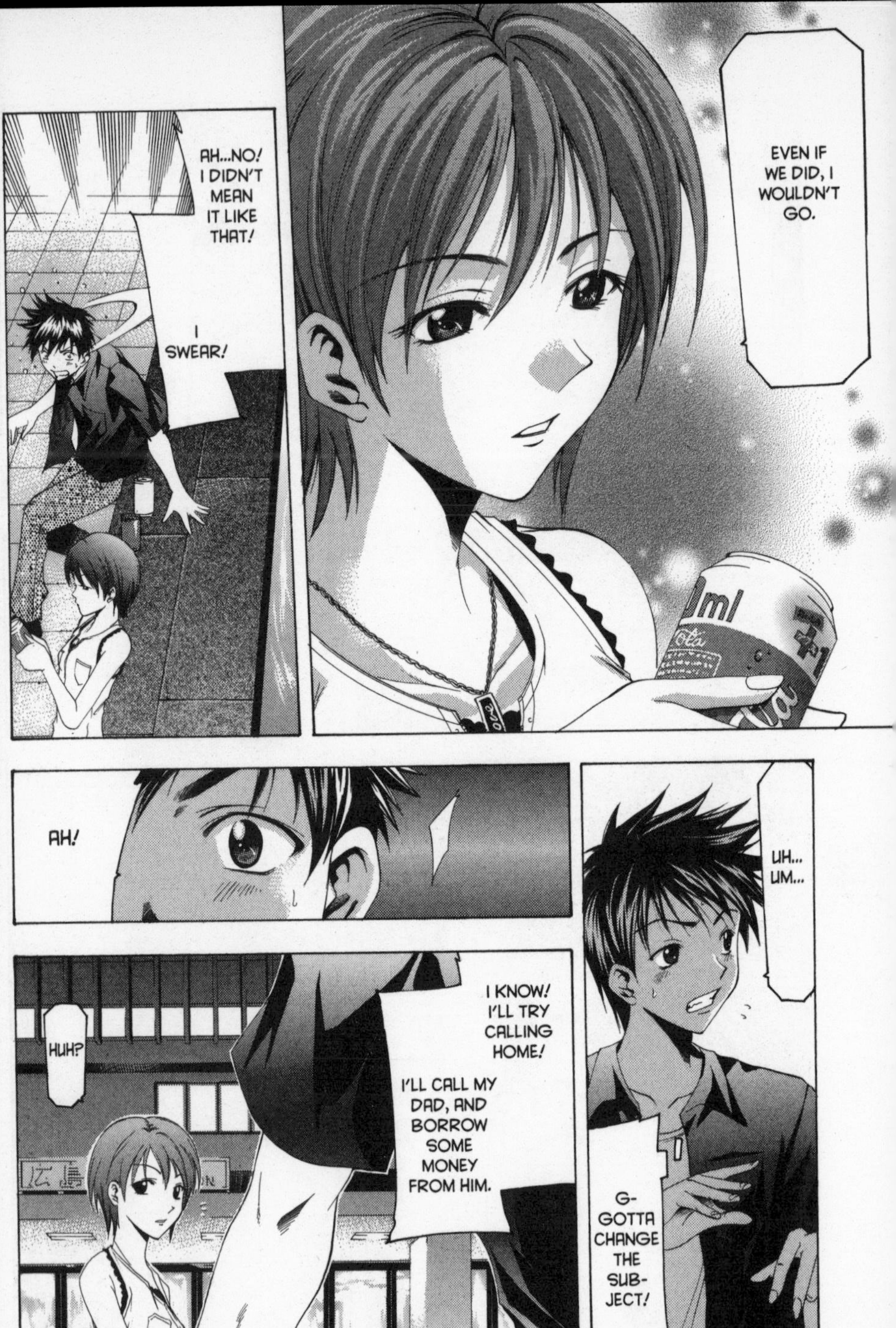
EVEN IF WE DID, I WOULDN'T GO.
AH...NO! I DIDN'T MEAN IT LIKE THAT!
I SWEAR!
UH... UM...
G-GOTTA CHANGE THE SUB-JECT!
AH!
I KNOW! I'LL TRY CALLING HOME!
I'LL CALL MY DAD, AND BORROW SOME MONEY FROM HIM.
HUH?
広島

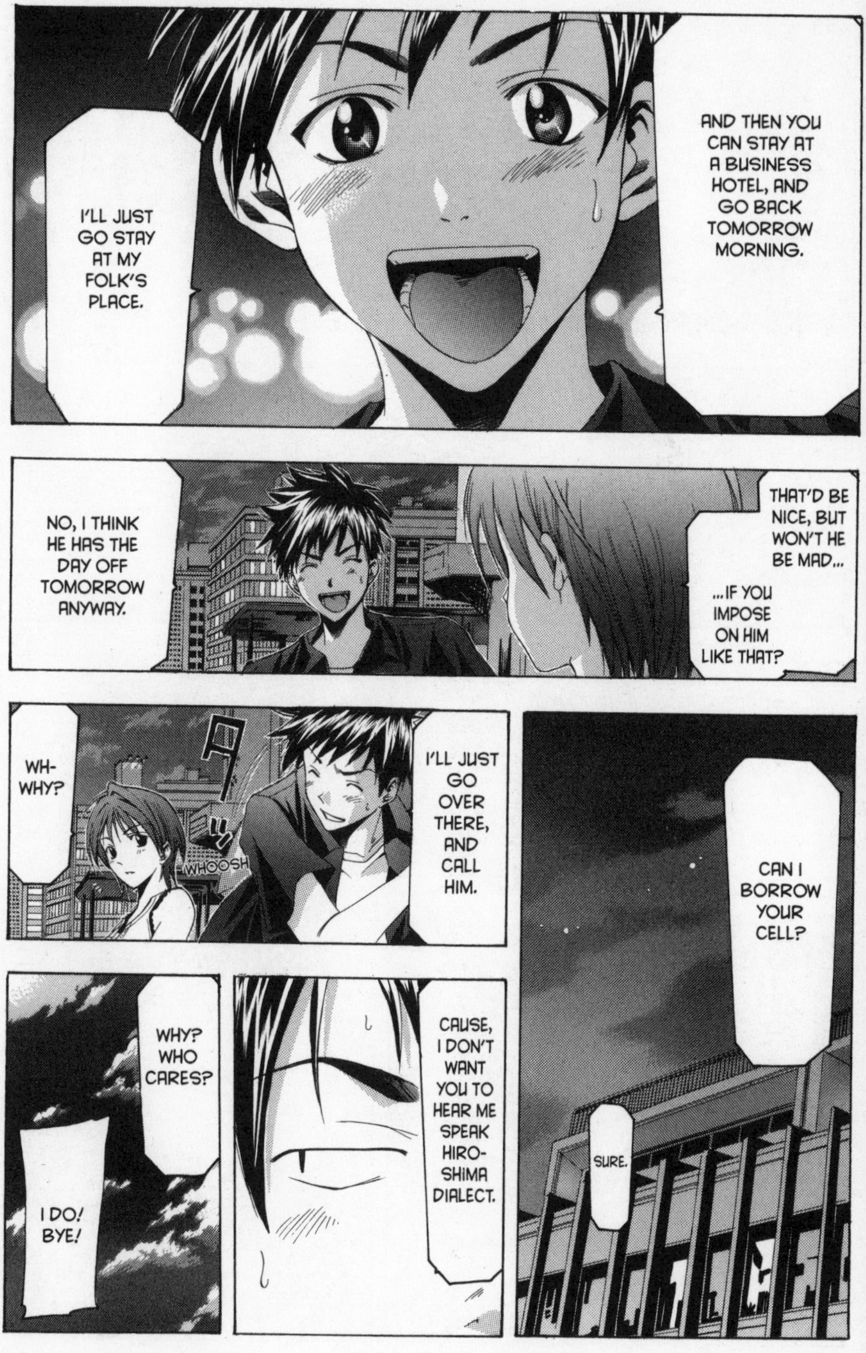
AND THEN YOU CAN STAY AT A BUSINESS HOTEL, AND GO BACK TOMORROW MORNING.
I'LL JUST GO STAY AT MY FOLK'S PLACE.
THAT'D BE NICE, BUT WON'T HE BE MAD...
...IF YOU IMPOSE ON HIM LIKE THAT?
NO, I THINK HE HAS THE DAY OFF TOMORROW ANYWAY.
CAN I BORROW YOUR CELL?
SURE.
I'LL JUST GO OVER THERE, AND CALL HIM.
WHOOSH
WH-WHY?
CAUSE, I DON'T WANT YOU TO HEAR ME SPEAK HIRO-SHIMA DIALECT.
WHY? WHO CARES?
I DO! BYE!

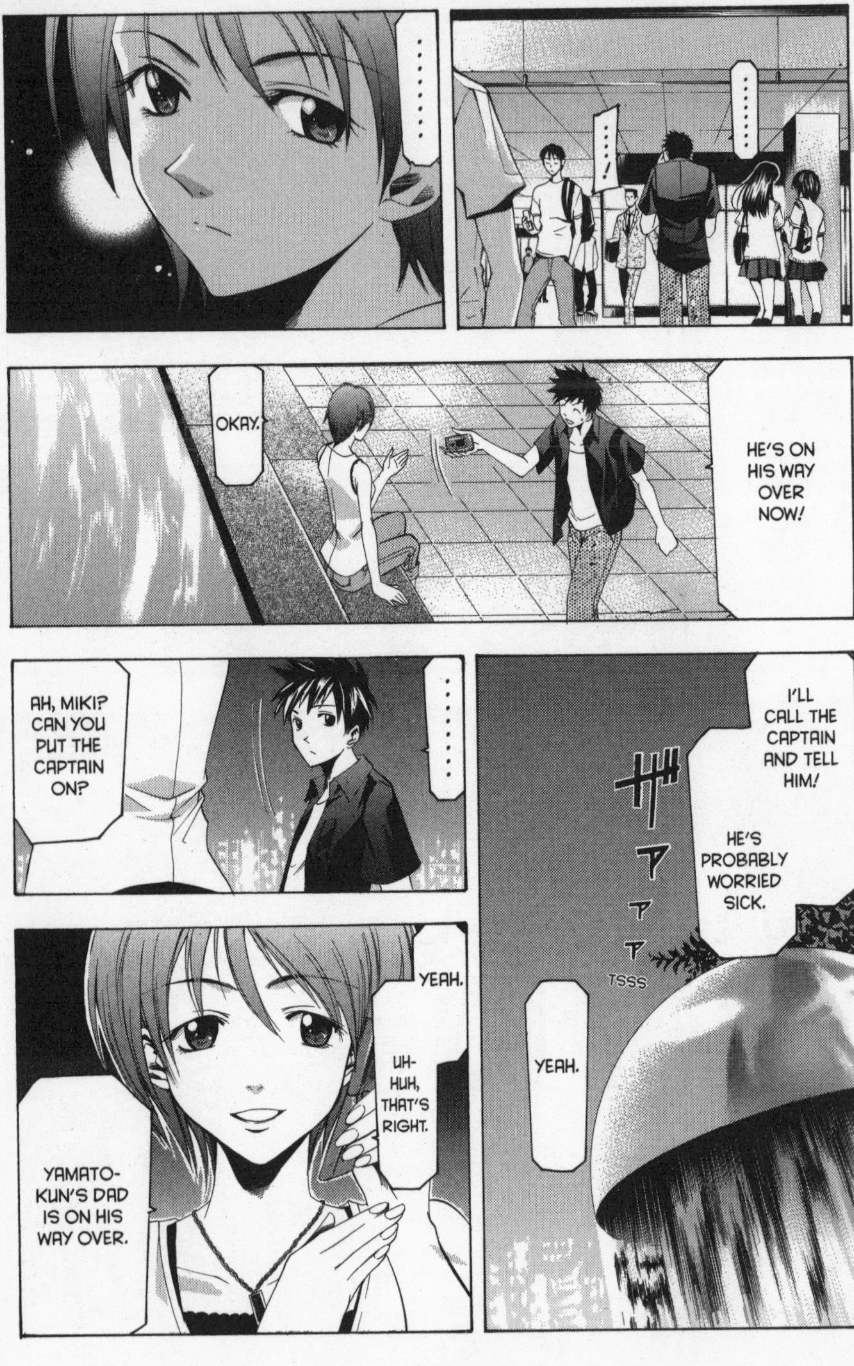

......
....!
......
HE'S ON HIS WAY OVER NOW!
OKAY.
I'LL CALL THE CAPTAIN AND TELL HIM!
HE'S PROBABLY WORRIED SICK.
TSSS
YEAH.
......
AH, MIKI? CAN YOU PUT THE CAPTAIN ON?
YEAH.
UH-HUH, THAT'S RIGHT.
YAMATO-KUN'S DAD IS ON HIS WAY OVER.

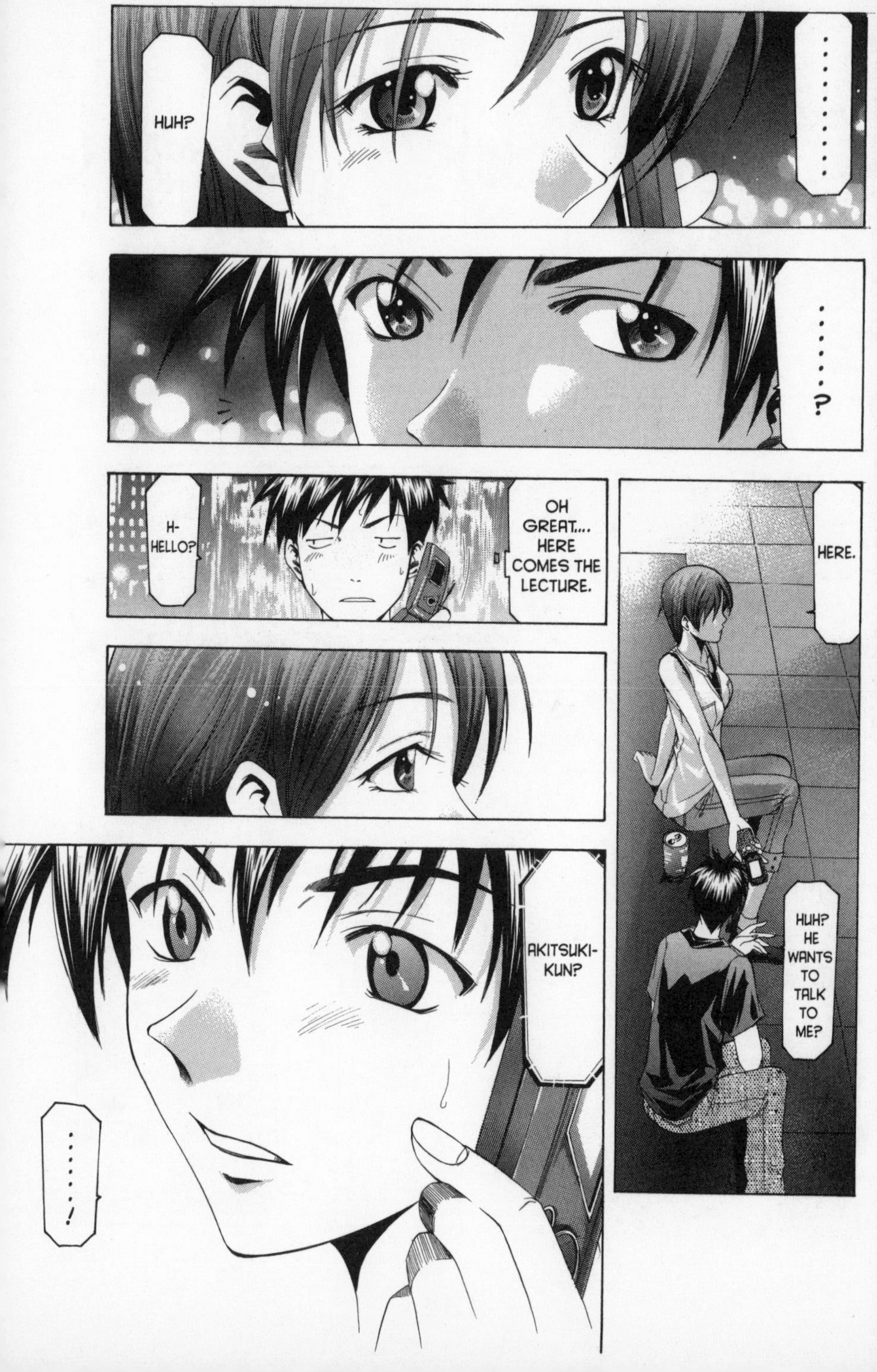
....
HUH?
......?
HERE.
HUH? HE WANTS TO TALK TO ME?
OH GREAT.... HERE COMES THE LECTURE.
H- HELLO?
AKITSUKI-KUN?
......!

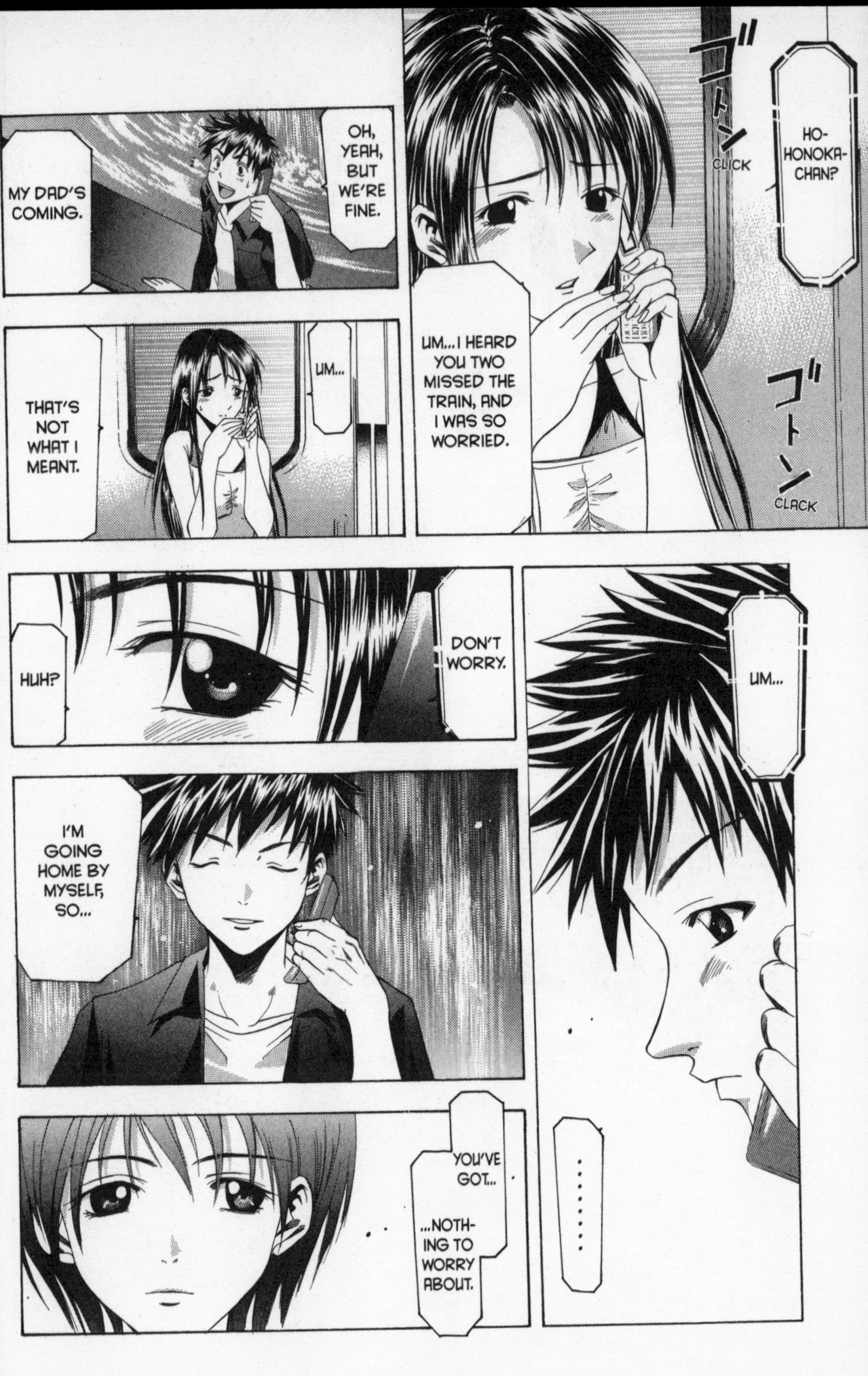
HO-HONOKA-CHAN?
ゴトン
CLICK
UM...I HEARD YOU TWO MISSED THE TRAIN, AND I WAS SO WORRIED.
ゴトン
CLACK
OH, YEAH, BUT WE'RE FINE.
MY DAD'S COMING.
UM...
THAT'S NOT WHAT I MEANT.
UM...
....
DON'T WORRY.
HUH?
I'M GOING HOME BY MYSELF, SO...
YOU'VE GOT...
...NOTHING TO WORRY ABOUT.

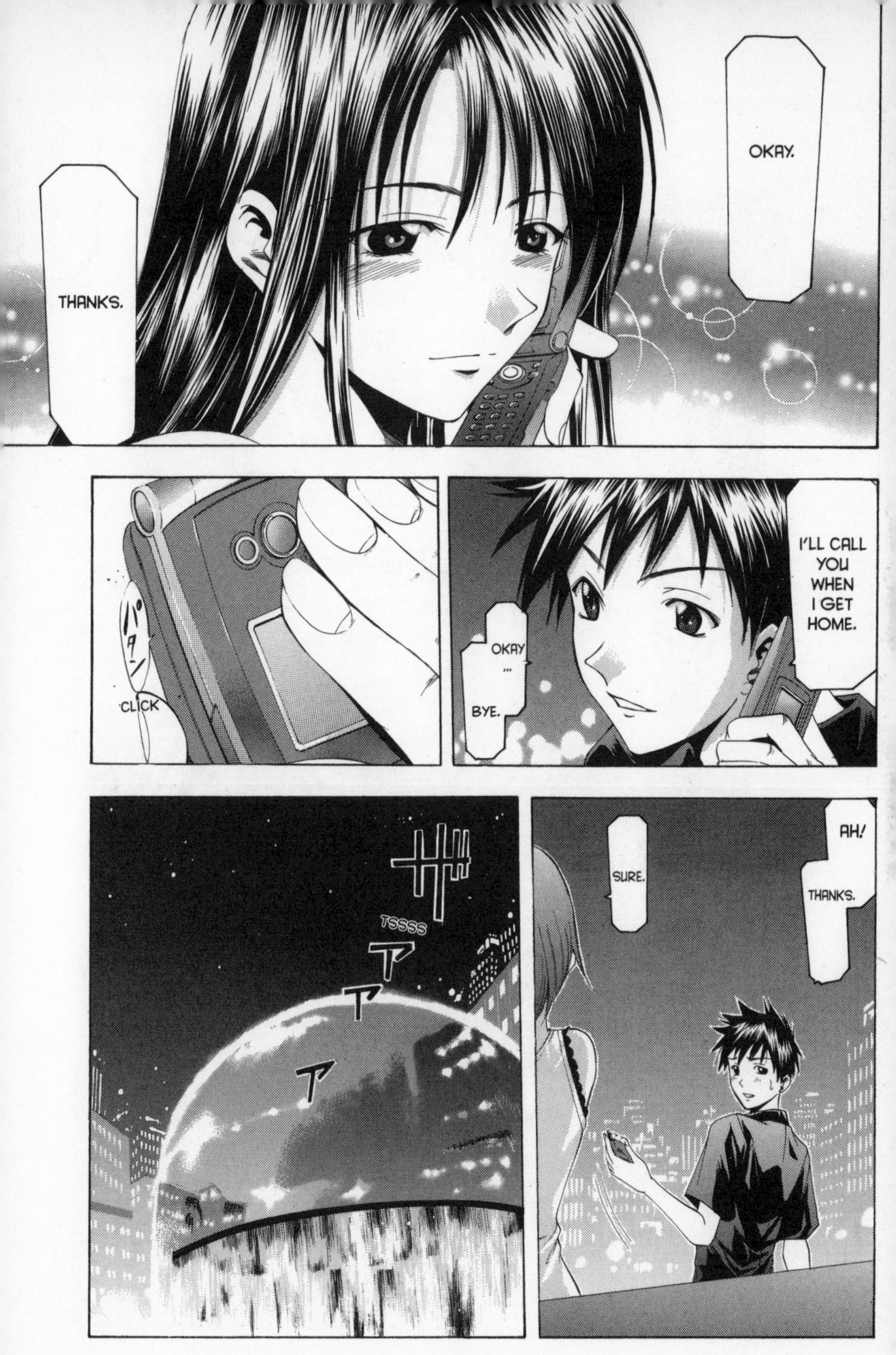
OKAY.
THANKS.
I'LL CALL YOU WHEN I GET HOME.
OKAY ... BYE.
パタン
CLICK
AH! THANKS.
SURE.
TSSSS

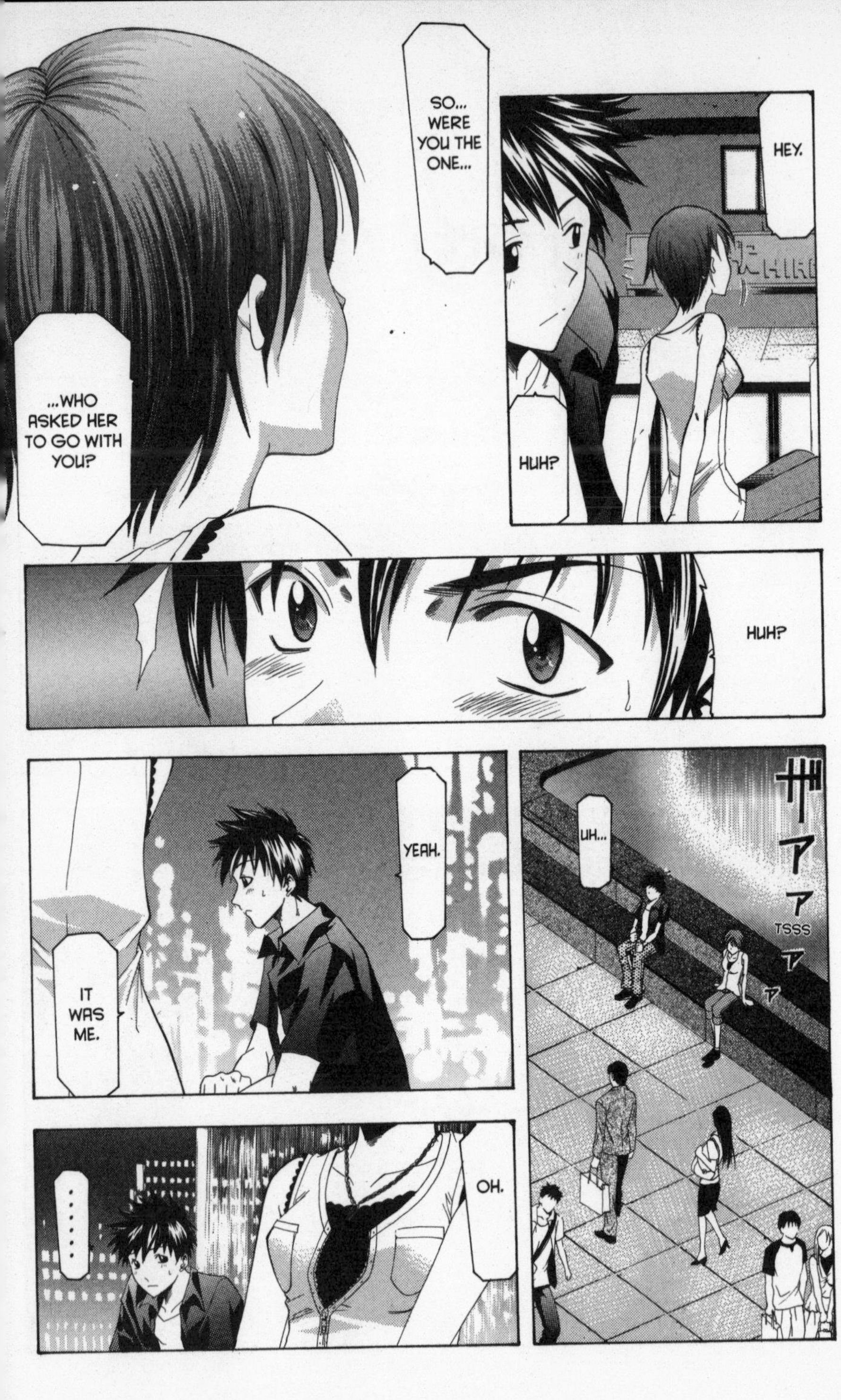
HEY.
HUH?
SO... WERE YOU THE ONE...
...WHO ASKED HER TO GO WITH YOU?
HUH?
UH...
ザァァァ
TSSS
YEAH.
IT WAS ME.
OH.
......

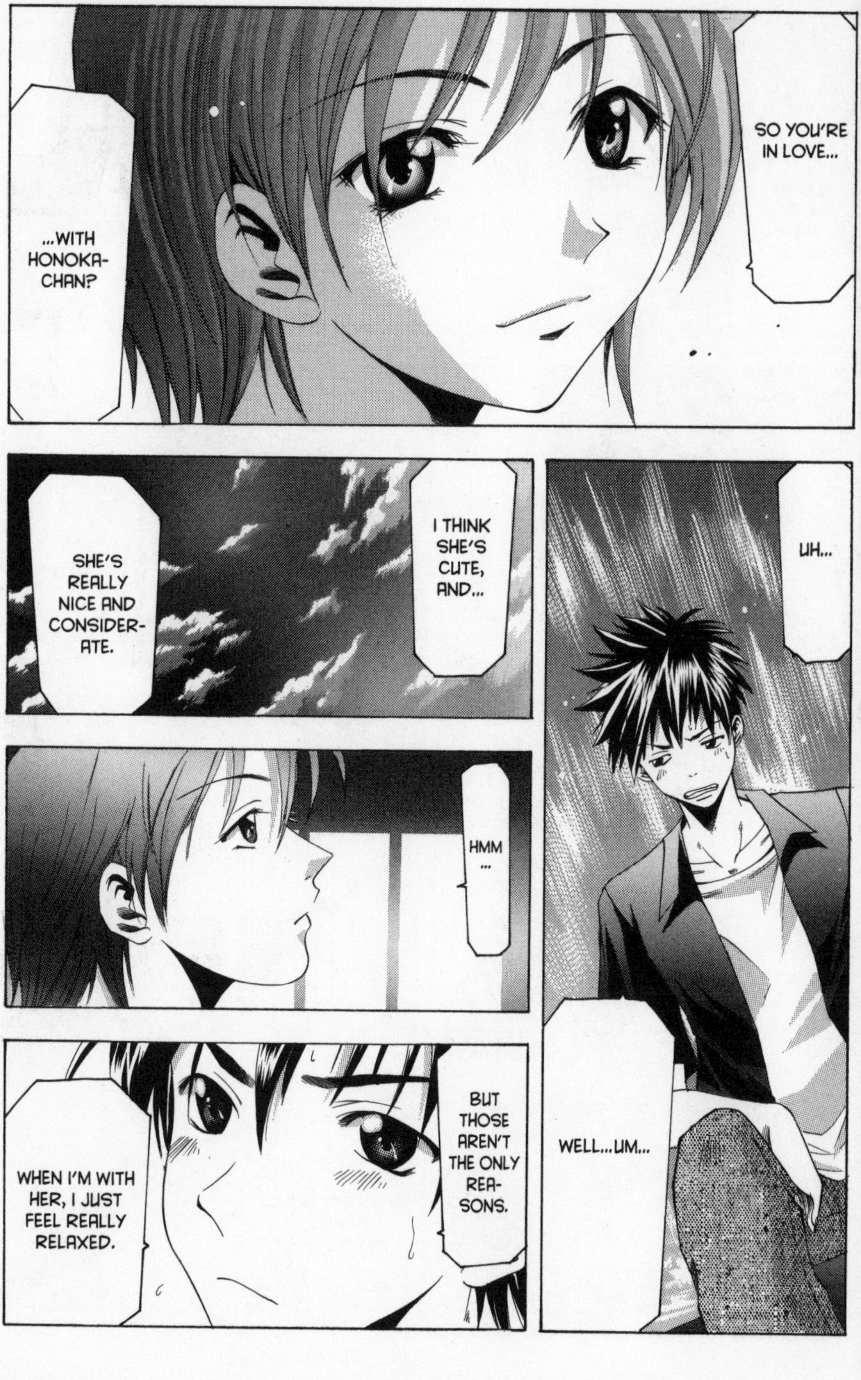
SO YOU'RE IN LOVE...
...WITH HONOKA-CHAN?
UH...
WELL...UM...
I THINK SHE'S CUTE, AND...
SHE'S REALLY NICE AND CONSIDER-ATE.
HMM...
BUT THOSE AREN'T THE ONLY REA-SONS.
WHEN I'M WITH HER, I JUST FEEL REALLY RELAXED.

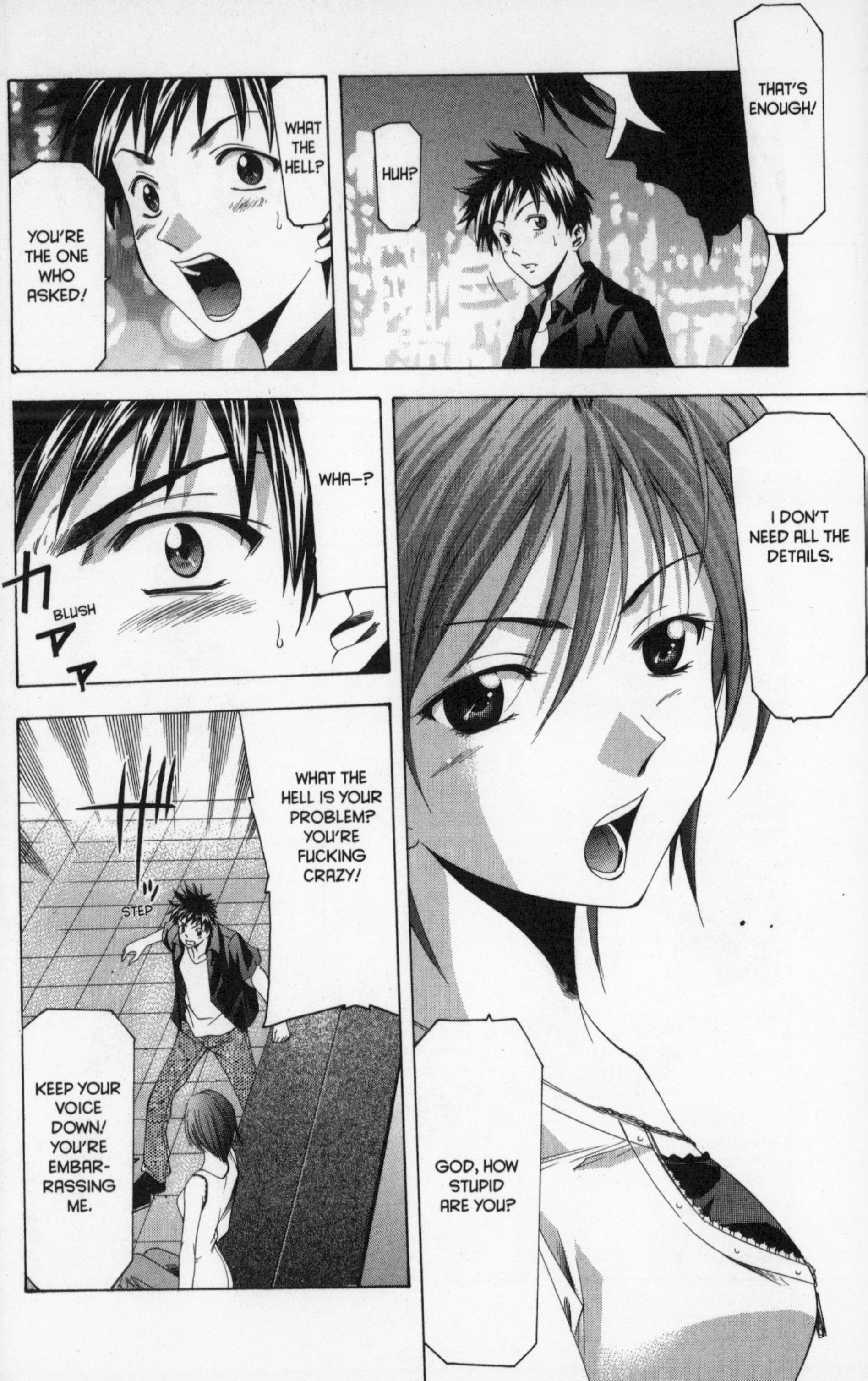
THAT'S ENOUGH!
HUH?
WHAT THE HELL?
YOU'RE THE ONE WHO ASKED!
I DON'T NEED ALL THE DETAILS.
GOD, HOW STUPID ARE YOU?
WHA–?
BLUSH
WHAT THE HELL IS YOUR PROBLEM? YOU'RE FUCKING CRAZY!
STEP
KEEP YOUR VOICE DOWN! YOU'RE EMBARRASSING ME.

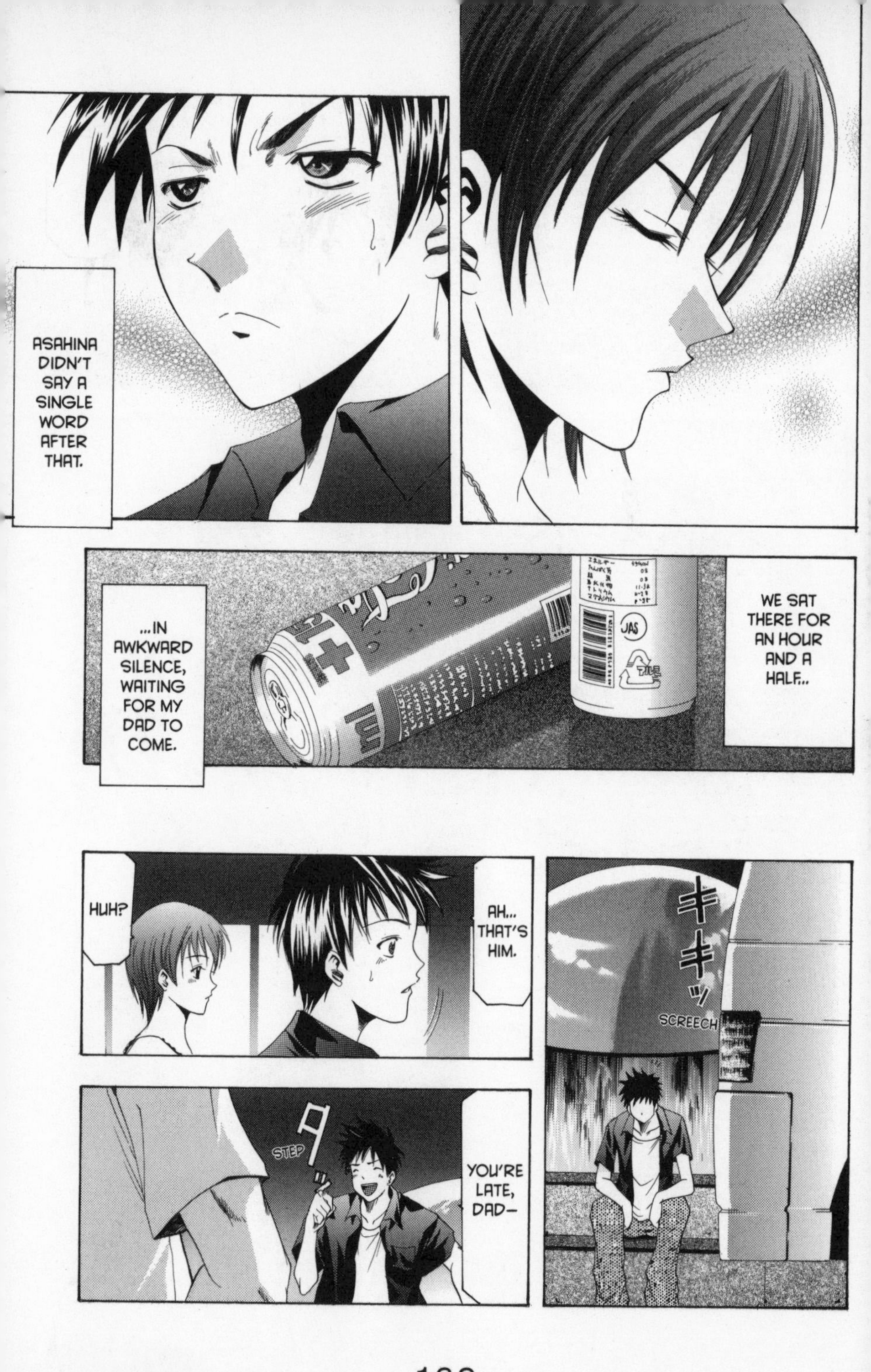
ASAHINA DIDN'T SAY A SINGLE WORD AFTER THAT.
WE SAT THERE FOR AN HOUR AND A HALF...
...IN AWKWARD SILENCE, WAITING FOR MY DAD TO COME.
キキッ
SCREECH
AH... THAT'S HIM.
HUH?
YOU'RE LATE, DAD—
タ
STEP

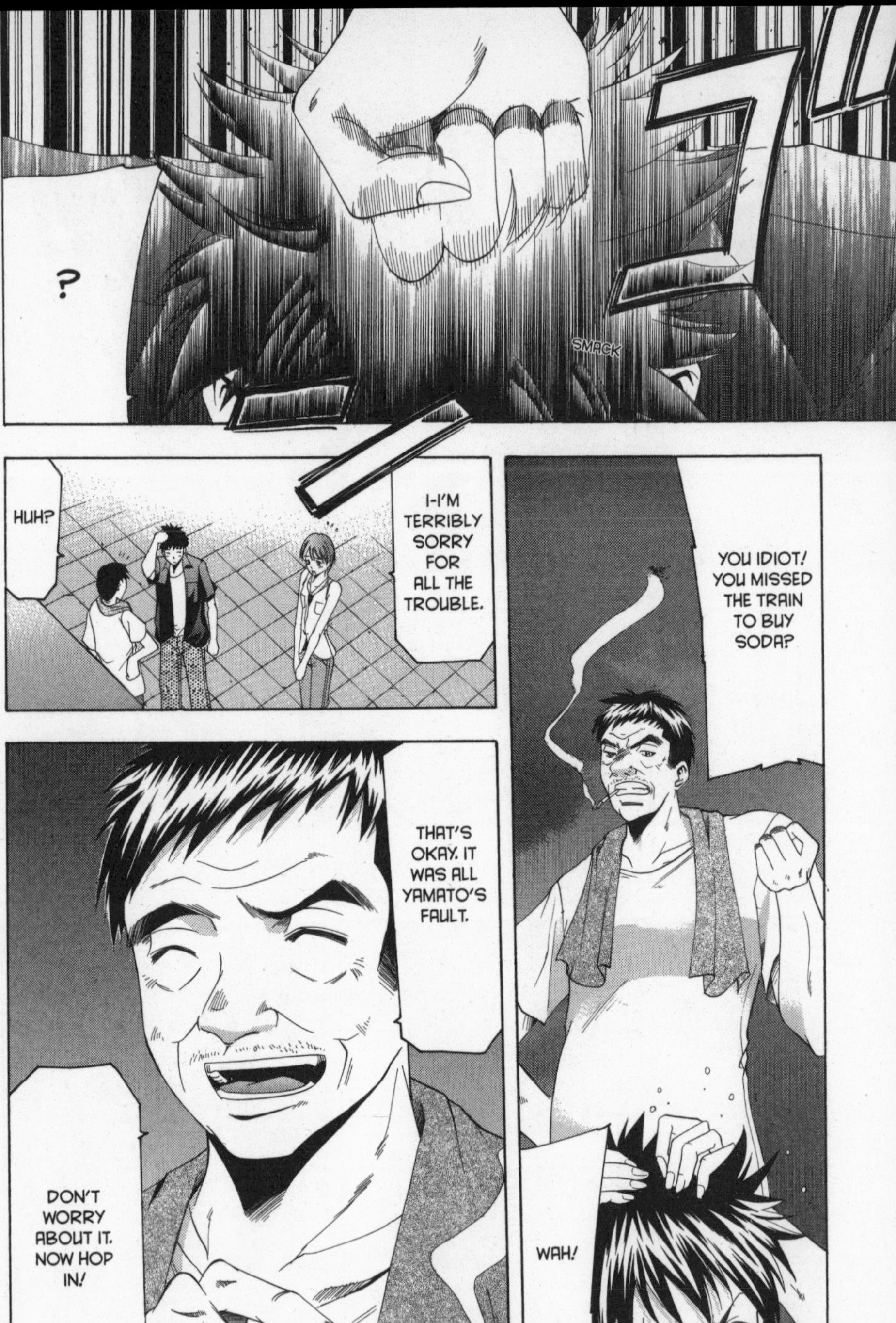
SMACK
?
YOU IDIOT! YOU MISSED THE TRAIN TO BUY SODA?
WAH!
I-I'M TERRIBLY SORRY FOR ALL THE TROUBLE.
HUH?
THAT'S OKAY. IT WAS ALL YAMATO'S FAULT.
DON'T WORRY ABOUT IT. NOW HOP IN!

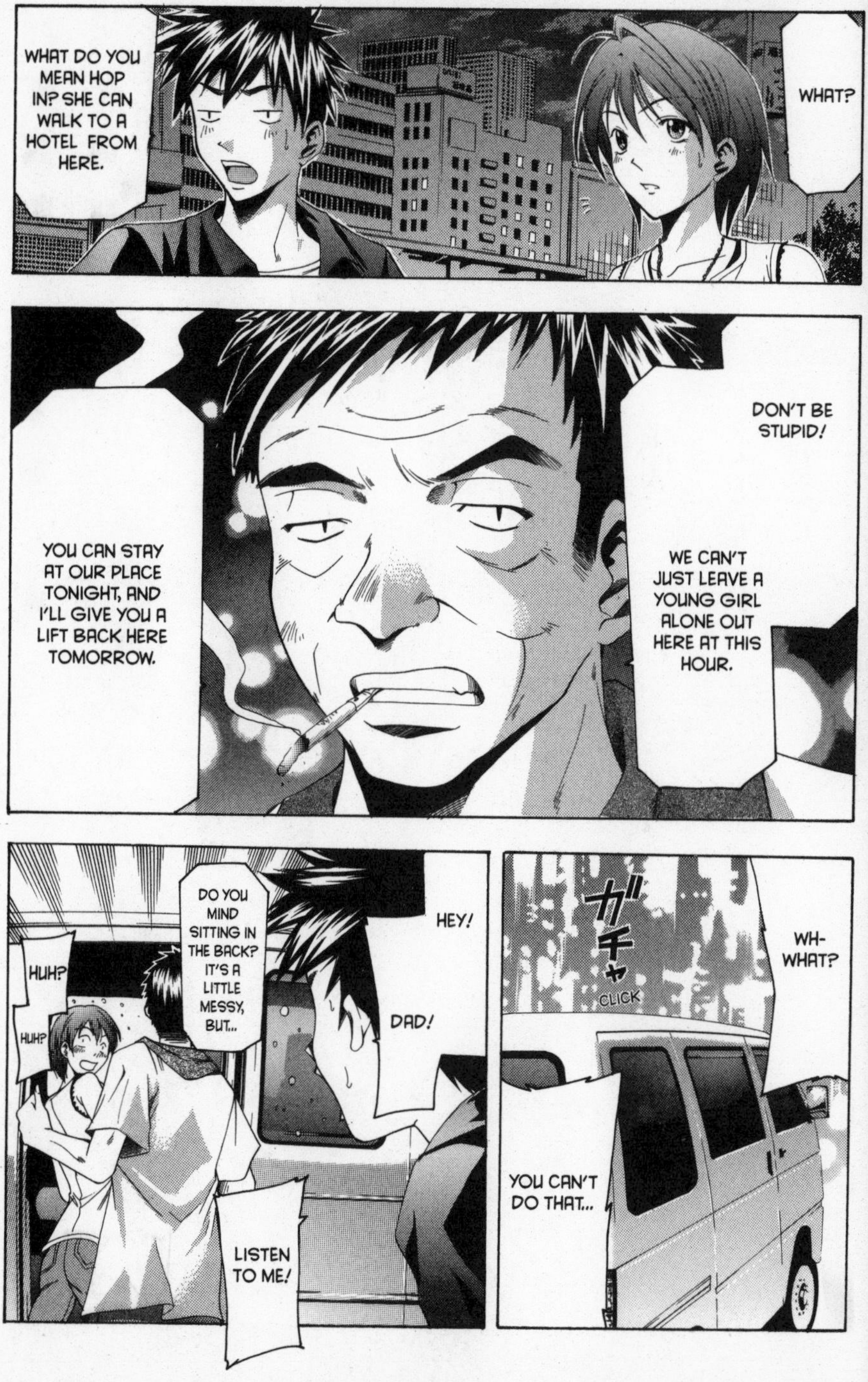
WHAT?
WHAT DO YOU MEAN HOP IN? SHE CAN WALK TO A HOTEL FROM HERE.
DON'T BE STUPID!
WE CAN'T JUST LEAVE A YOUNG GIRL ALONE OUT HERE AT THIS HOUR.
YOU CAN STAY AT OUR PLACE TONIGHT, AND I'LL GIVE YOU A LIFT BACK HERE TOMORROW.
WH- WHAT?
ガチャ
CLICK
YOU CAN'T DO THAT...
HEY!
DAD!
DO YOU MIND SITTING IN THE BACK? IT'S A LITTLE MESSY, BUT...
HUH?
HUH?
LISTEN TO ME!

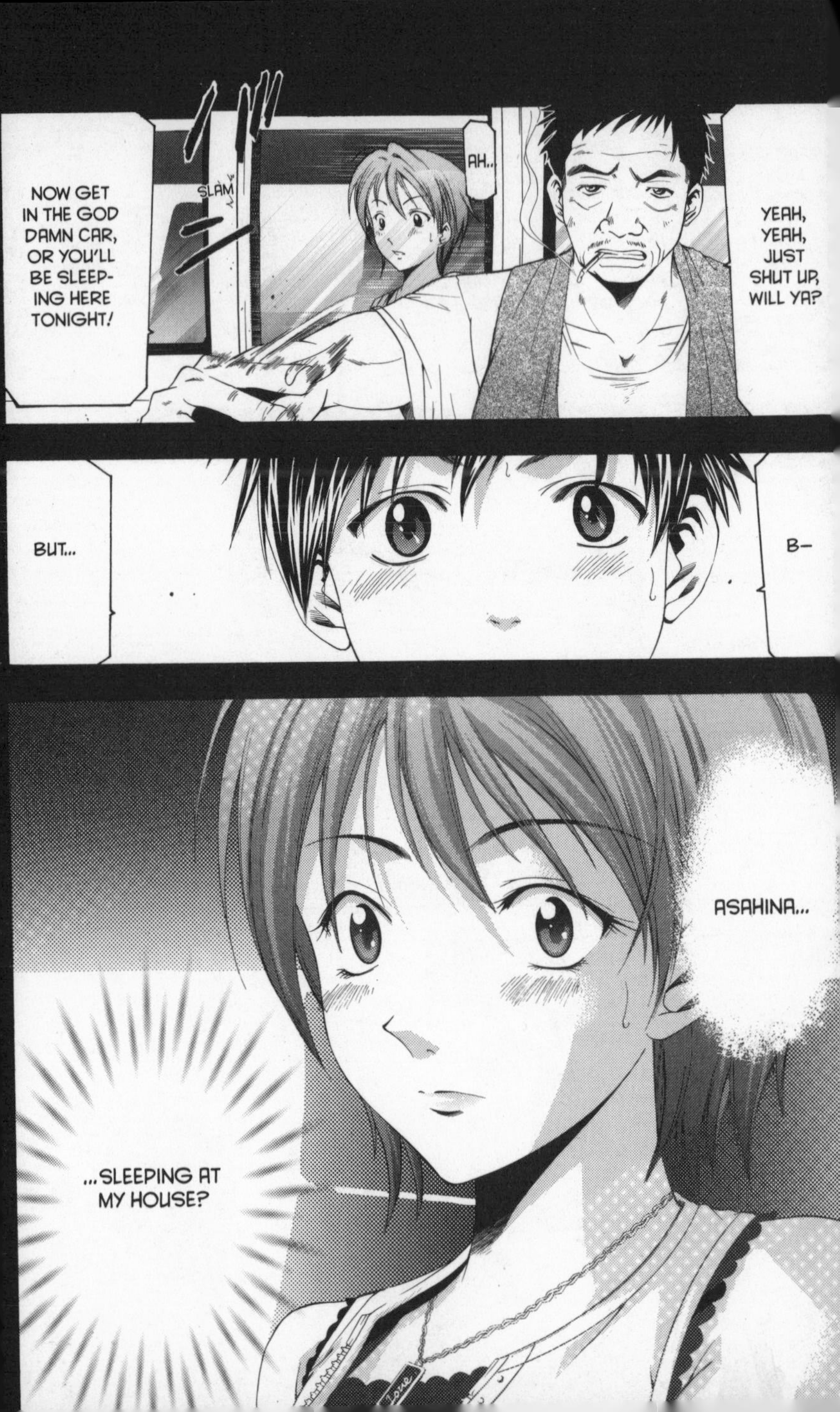
YEAH, YEAH, JUST SHUT UP, WILL YA?
AH...
SLAM
NOW GET IN THE GOD DAMN CAR, OR YOU'LL BE SLEEP-ING HERE TONIGHT!
B–
BUT...
ASAHINA...
...SLEEPING AT MY HOUSE?

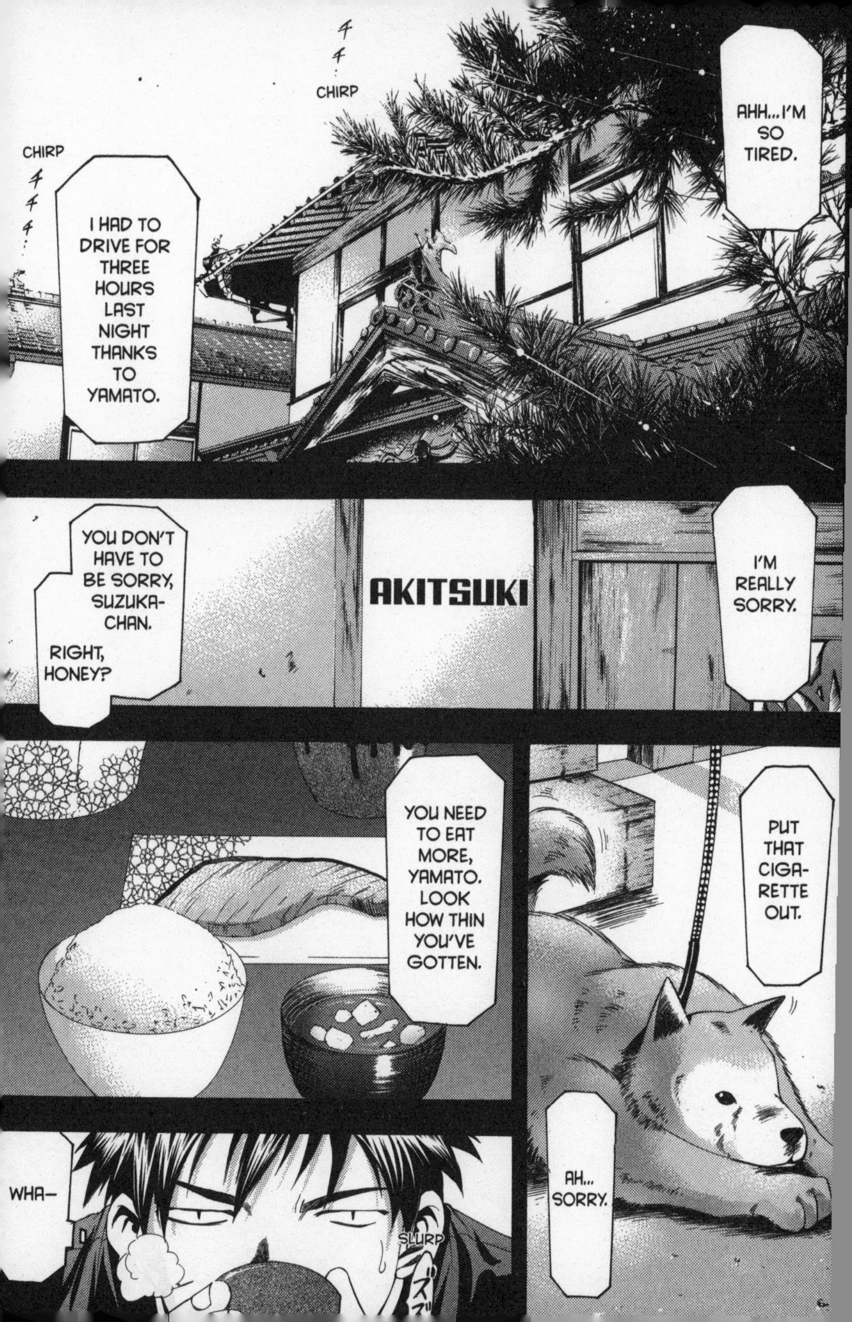
AHH...I'M SO TIRED.
CHIRP
CHIRP
I HAD TO DRIVE FOR THREE HOURS LAST NIGHT THANKS TO YAMATO.
I'M REALLY SORRY.
AKITSUKI
YOU DON'T HAVE TO BE SORRY, SUZUKA-CHAN.
RIGHT, HONEY?
PUT THAT CIGA-RETTE OUT.
AH... SORRY.
YOU NEED TO EAT MORE, YAMATO. LOOK HOW THIN YOU'VE GOTTEN.
SLURP
WHA-

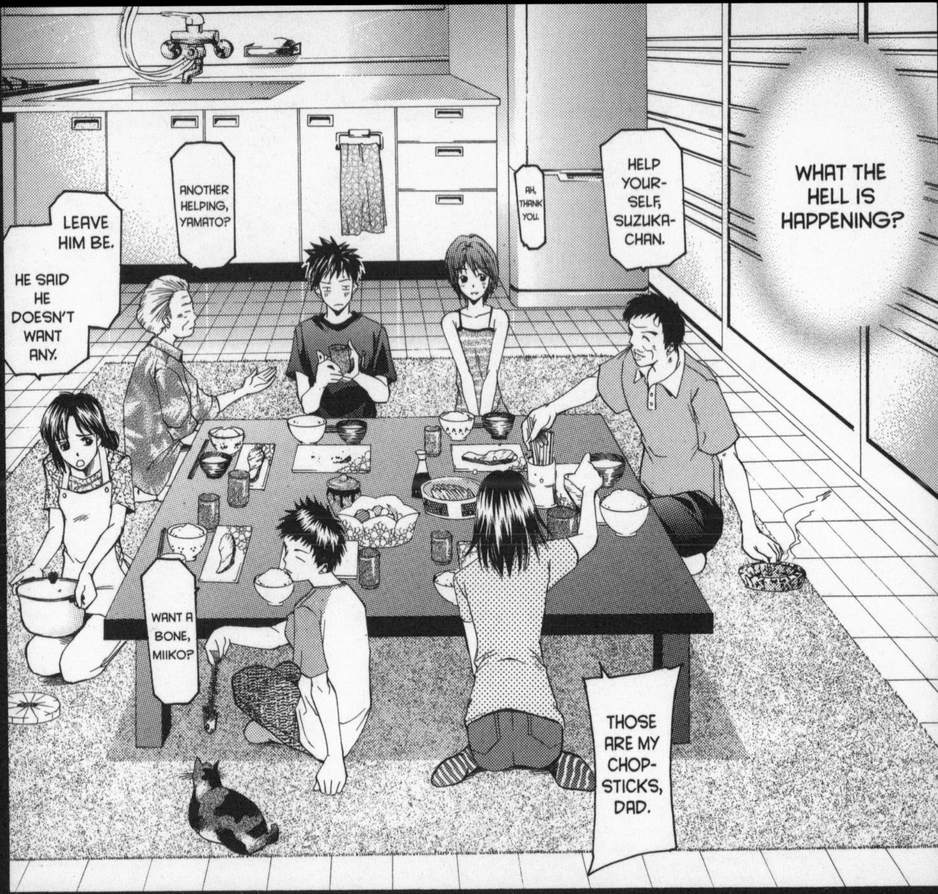
WHAT THE HELL IS HAPPENING?
HELP YOUR-SELF, SUZUKA-CHAN.
AH, THANK YOU.
ANOTHER HELPING, YAMATO?
LEAVE HIM BE.
HE SAID HE DOESN'T WANT ANY.
THOSE ARE MY CHOP-STICKS, DAD.
WANT A BONE, MIIKO?

SUZUKA

#40 HOME

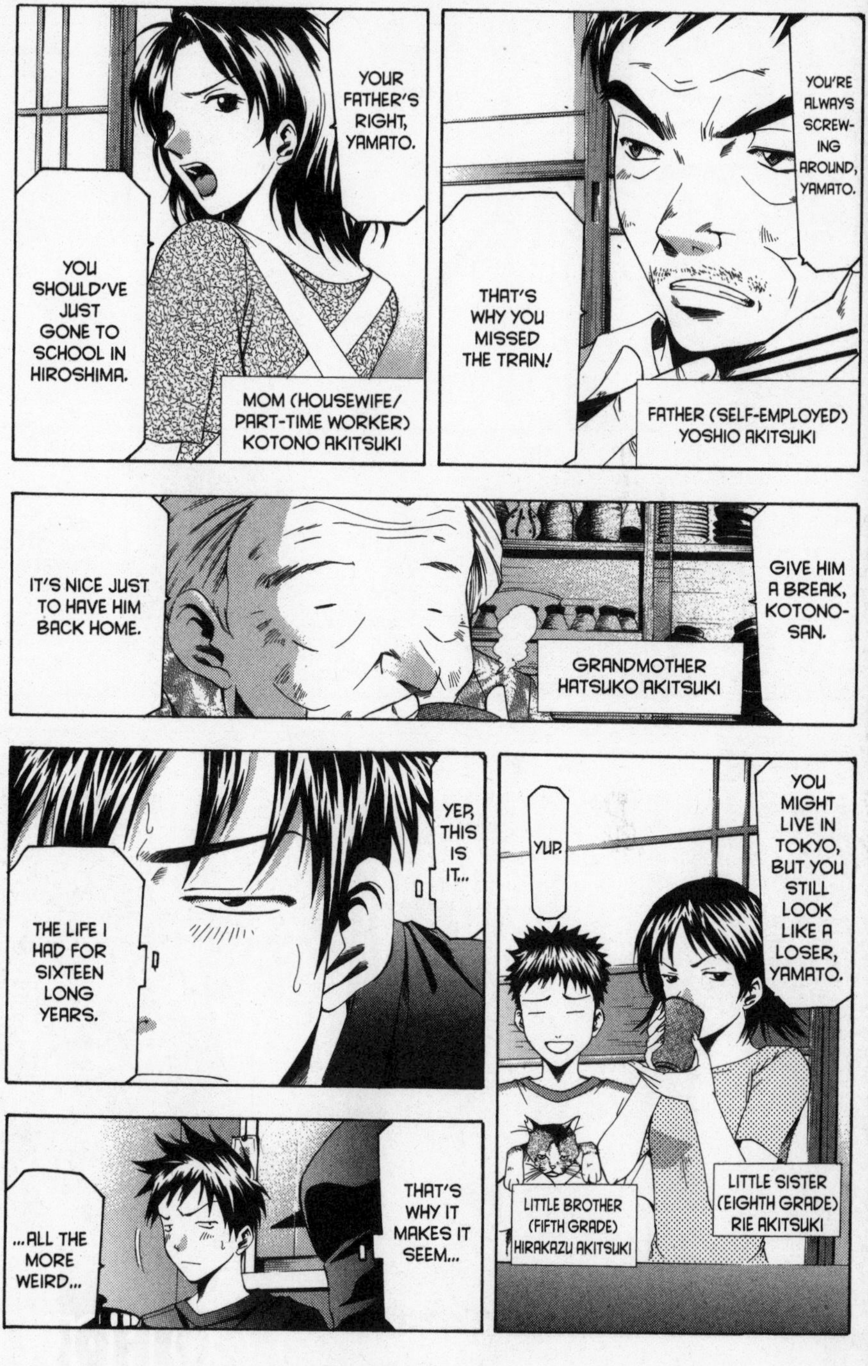
YOU'RE ALWAYS SCREWING AROUND, YAMATO.
THAT'S WHY YOU MISSED THE TRAIN!
FATHER (SELF-EMPLOYED) YOSHIO AKITSUKI
YOUR FATHER'S RIGHT, YAMATO.
YOU SHOULD'VE JUST GONE TO SCHOOL IN HIROSHIMA.
MOM (HOUSEWIFE/ PART-TIME WORKER) KOTONO AKITSUKI
GIVE HIM A BREAK, KOTONO-SAN.
GRANDMOTHER HATSUKO AKITSUKI
IT'S NICE JUST TO HAVE HIM BACK HOME.
YOU MIGHT LIVE IN TOKYO, BUT YOU STILL LOOK LIKE A LOSER, YAMATO.
YUP.
LITTLE SISTER (EIGHTH GRADE) RIE AKITSUKI
LITTLE BROTHER (FIFTH GRADE) HIRAKAZU AKITSUKI
YEP, THIS IS IT...
THE LIFE I HAD FOR SIXTEEN LONG YEARS.
THAT'S WHY IT MAKES IT SEEM...
...ALL THE MORE WEIRD...

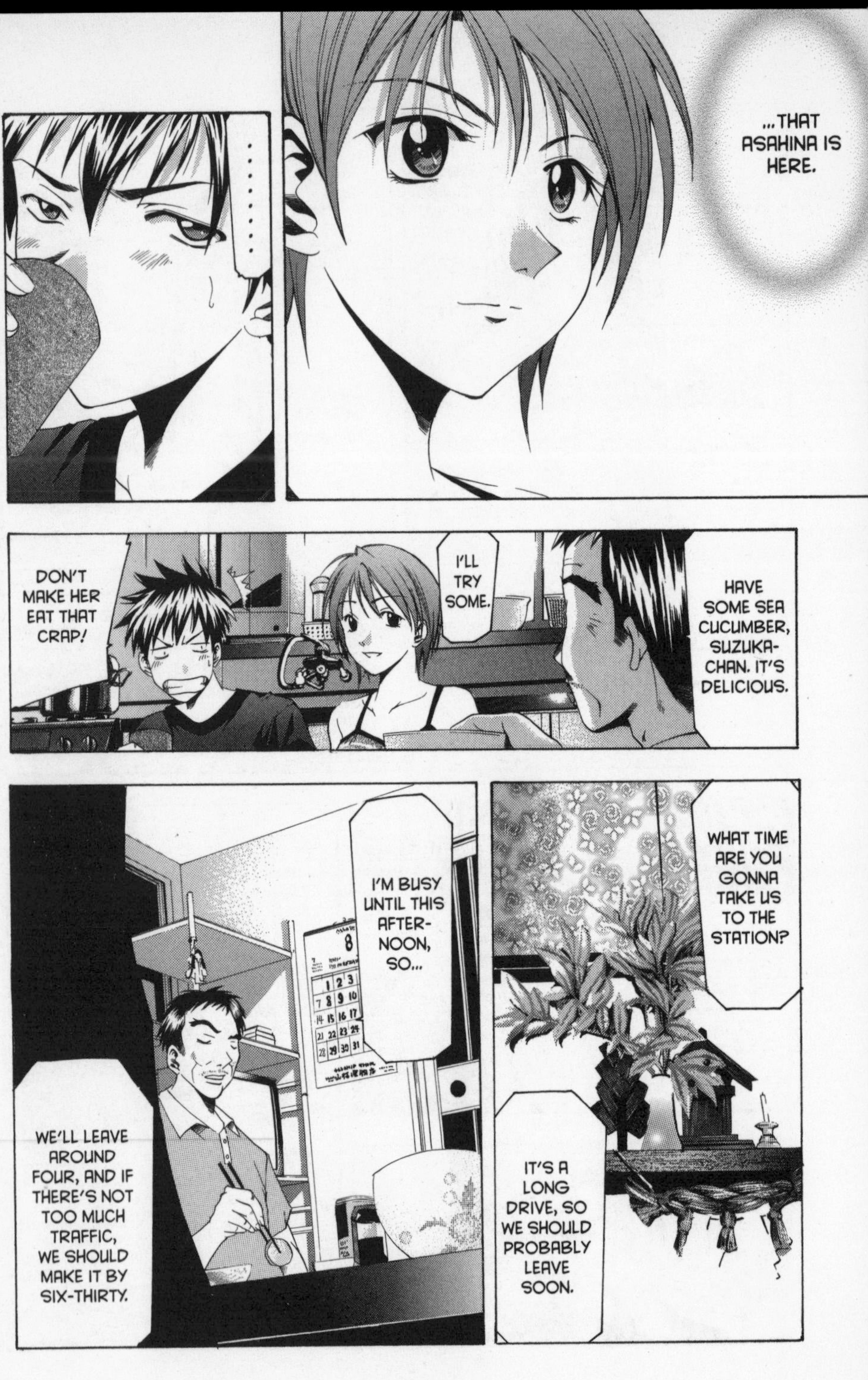
...THAT ASAHINA IS HERE.
......
HAVE SOME SEA CUCUMBER, SUZUKA-CHAN. IT'S DELICIOUS.
I'LL TRY SOME.
DON'T MAKE HER EAT THAT CRAP!
WHAT TIME ARE YOU GONNA TAKE US TO THE STATION?
IT'S A LONG DRIVE, SO WE SHOULD PROBABLY LEAVE SOON.
I'M BUSY UNTIL THIS AFTER-NOON, SO...
WE'LL LEAVE AROUND FOUR, AND IF THERE'S NOT TOO MUCH TRAFFIC, WE SHOULD MAKE IT BY SIX-THIRTY.

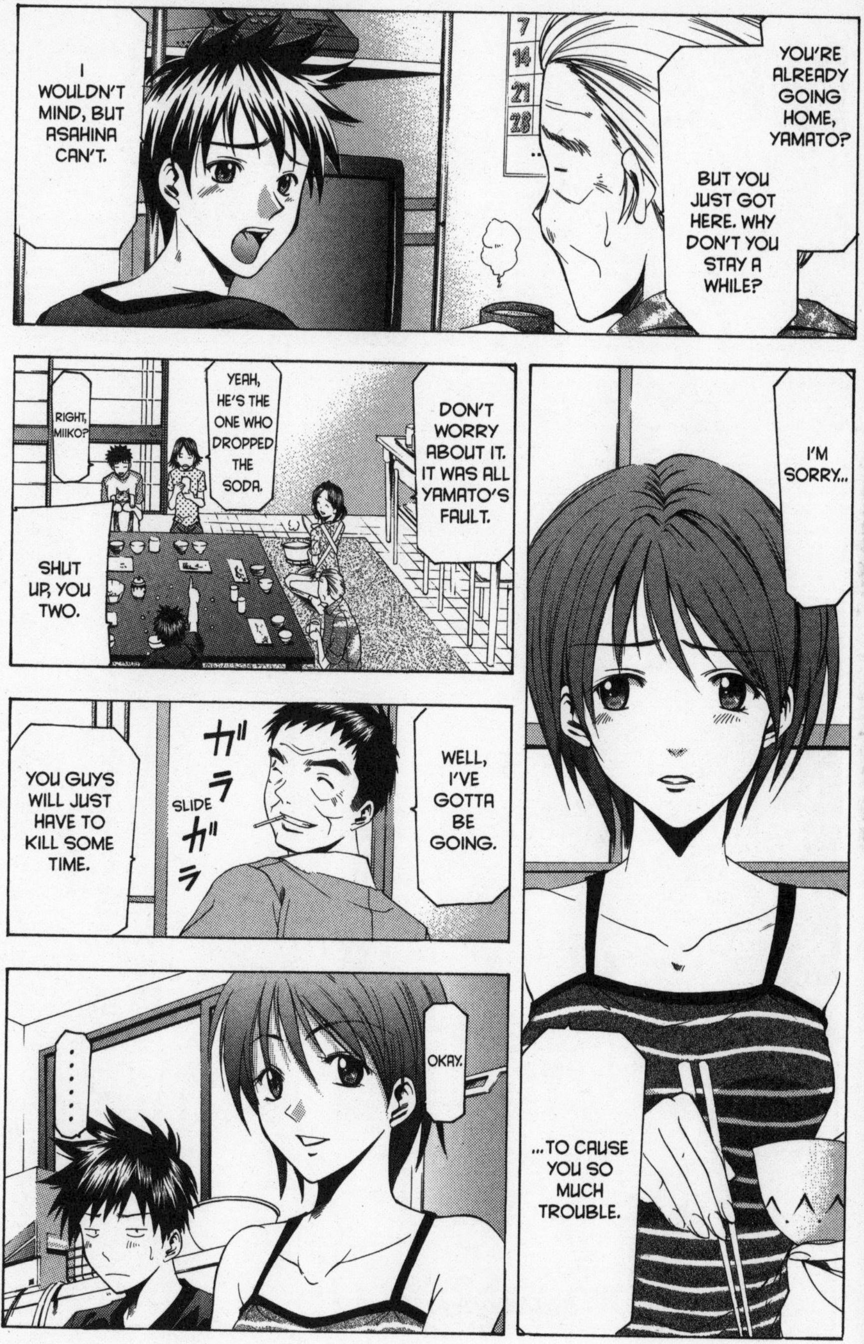
YOU'RE ALREADY GOING HOME, YAMATO?
BUT YOU JUST GOT HERE. WHY DON'T YOU STAY A WHILE?
...
I WOULDN'T MIND, BUT ASAHINA CAN'T.
I'M SORRY...
...TO CAUSE YOU SO MUCH TROUBLE.
DON'T WORRY ABOUT IT. IT WAS ALL YAMATO'S FAULT.
YEAH, HE'S THE ONE WHO DROPPED THE SODA.
RIGHT, MIIKO?
SHUT UP, YOU TWO.
WELL, I'VE GOTTA BE GOING.
ガラガラ
SLIDE
YOU GUYS WILL JUST HAVE TO KILL SOME TIME.
OKAY.
......

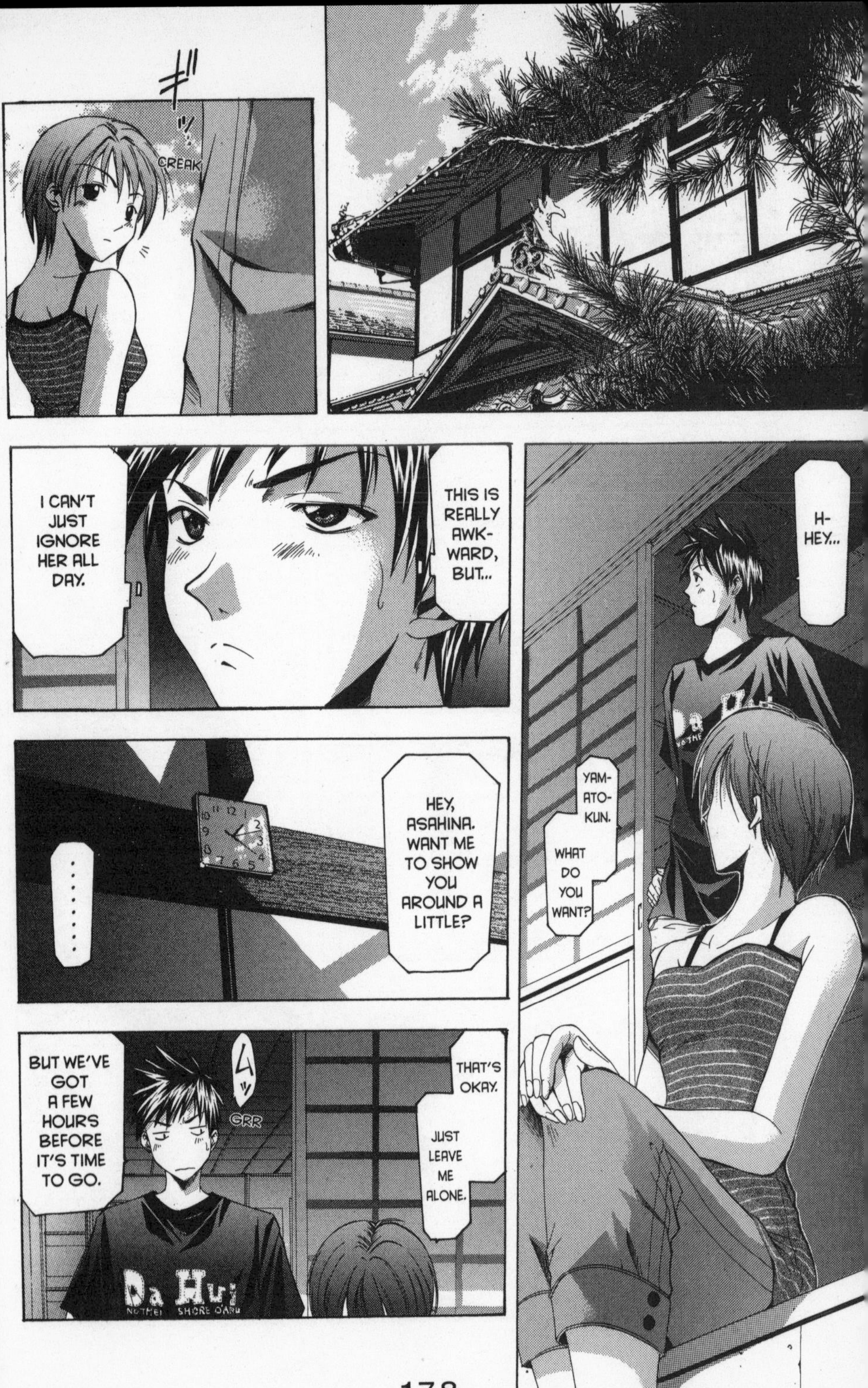
ギッ
CREAK
H-HEY...
YAM-ATO-KUN.
WHAT DO YOU WANT?
THIS IS REALLY AWK-WARD, BUT...
I CAN'T JUST IGNORE HER ALL DAY.
HEY, ASAHINA. WANT ME TO SHOW YOU AROUND A LITTLE?
....
THAT'S OKAY.
JUST LEAVE ME ALONE.
ムッ
GRR
BUT WE'VE GOT A FEW HOURS BEFORE IT'S TIME TO GO.

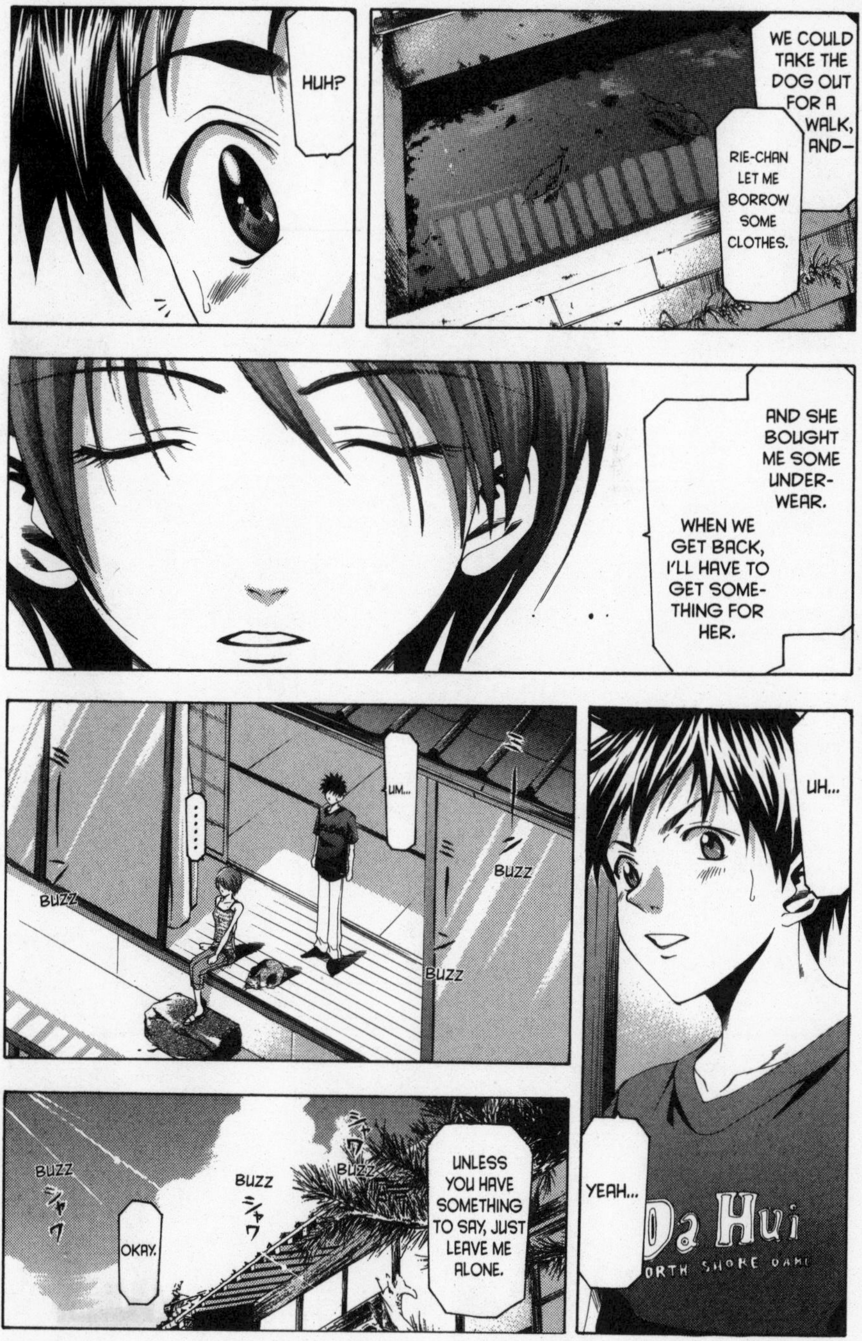
WE COULD TAKE THE DOG OUT FOR A WALK, AND—
RIE-CHAN LET ME BORROW SOME CLOTHES.
HUH?
AND SHE BOUGHT ME SOME UNDERWEAR.
WHEN WE GET BACK, I'LL HAVE TO GET SOMETHING FOR HER.
UH...
YEAH...
Da Hui
UM...
......
BUZZ
BUZZ
BUZZ
シャワ
BUZZ
UNLESS YOU HAVE SOMETHING TO SAY, JUST LEAVE ME ALONE.
BUZZ
シャワ
OKAY.
BUZZ
シャワ

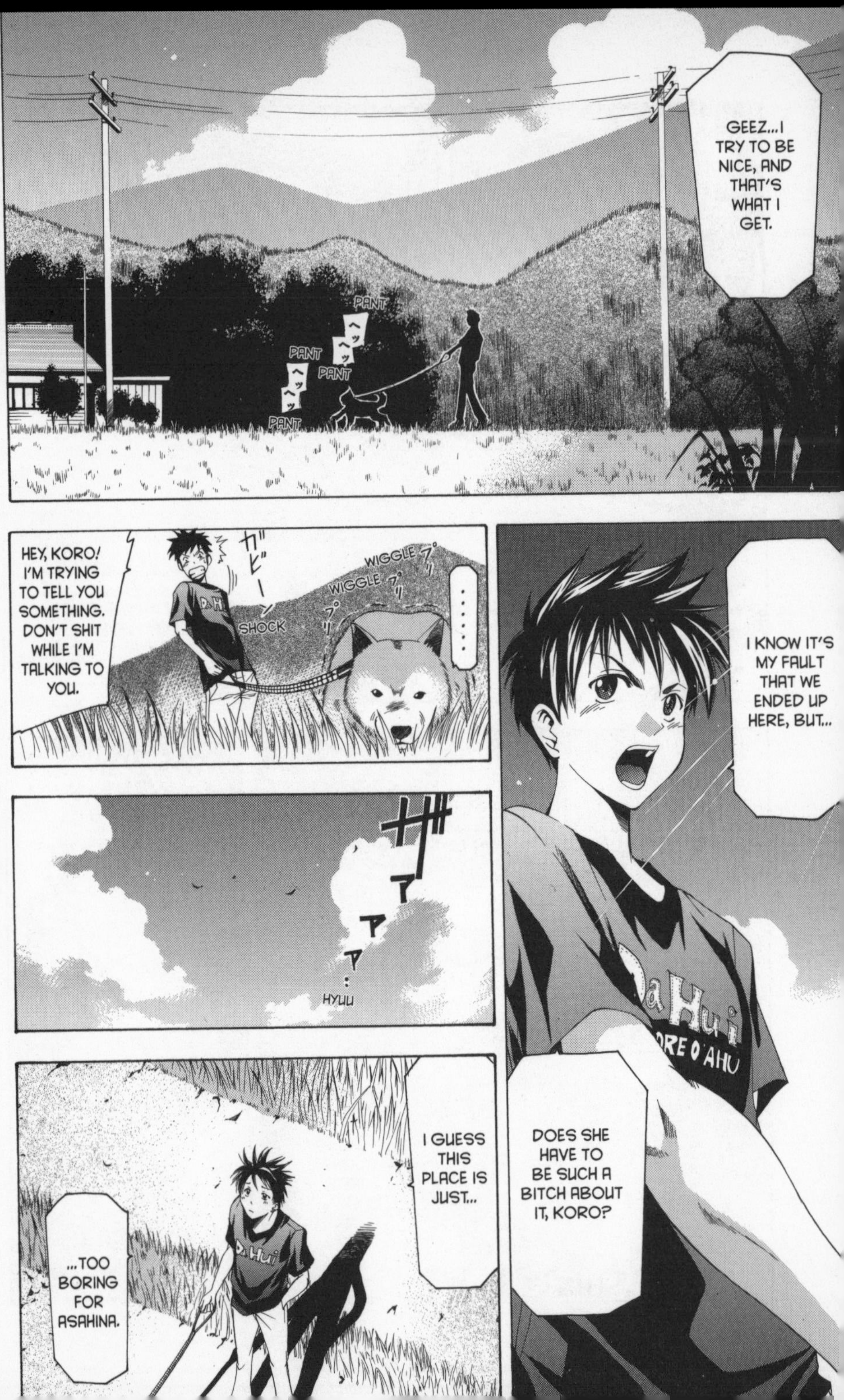
GEEZ...I TRY TO BE NICE, AND THAT'S WHAT I GET.
PANT
ヘッ
ヘッ
PANT
PANT
ヘッ
ヘッ
PANT
I KNOW IT'S MY FAULT THAT WE ENDED UP HERE, BUT...
DOES SHE HAVE TO BE SUCH A BITCH ABOUT IT, KORO?
......
プリ
WIGGLE
プリ
WIGGLE
プリ
ガビーン
SHOCK
HEY, KORO! I'M TRYING TO TELL YOU SOMETHING. DON'T SHIT WHILE I'M TALKING TO YOU.
ザァァァ...
HYUU
I GUESS THIS PLACE IS JUST...
...TOO BORING FOR ASAHINA.

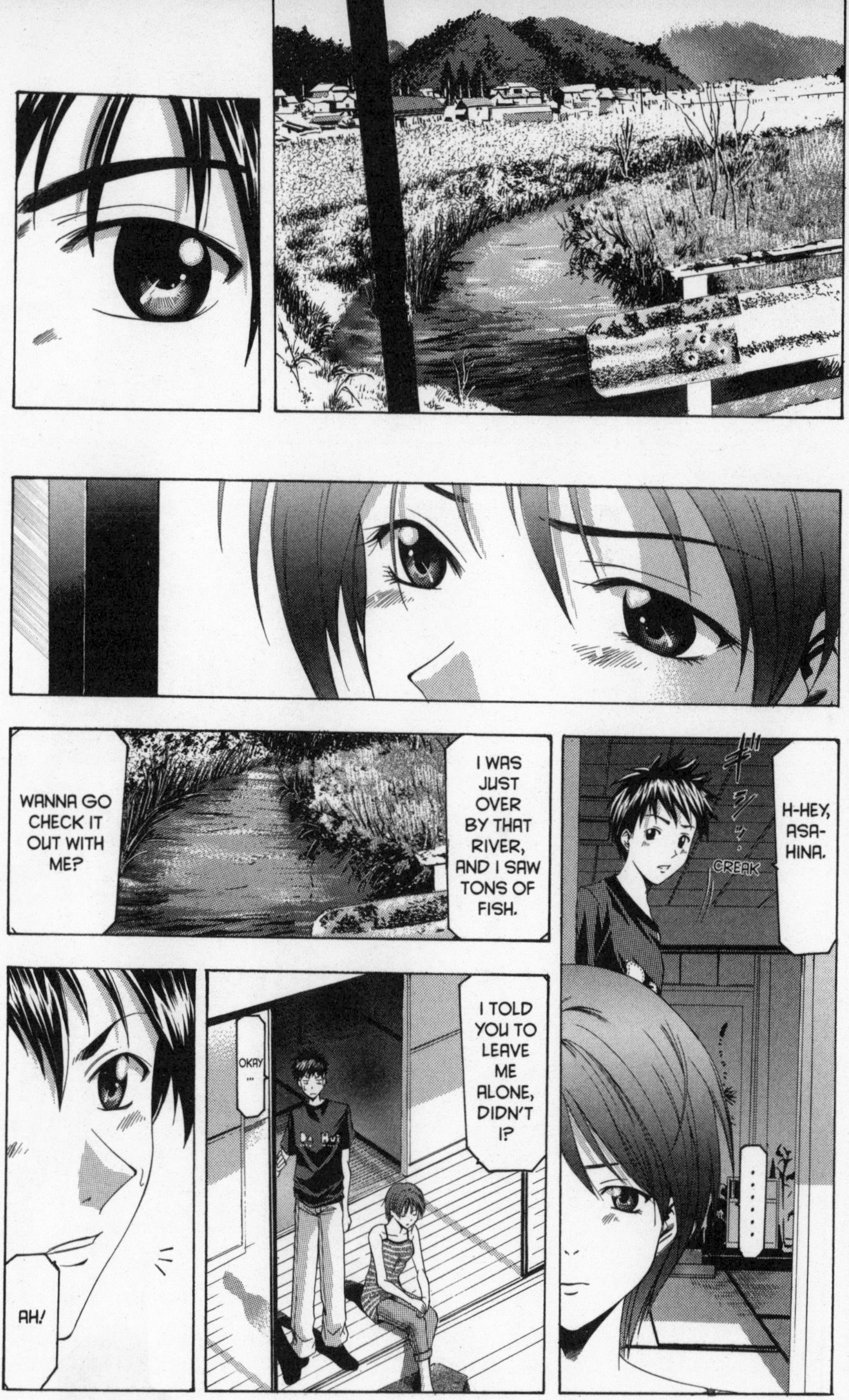
H-HEY, ASA-HINA.
CREAK
I WAS JUST OVER BY THAT RIVER, AND I SAW TONS OF FISH.
WANNA GO CHECK IT OUT WITH ME?
......
I TOLD YOU TO LEAVE ME ALONE, DIDN'T I?
OKAY ...
AH!

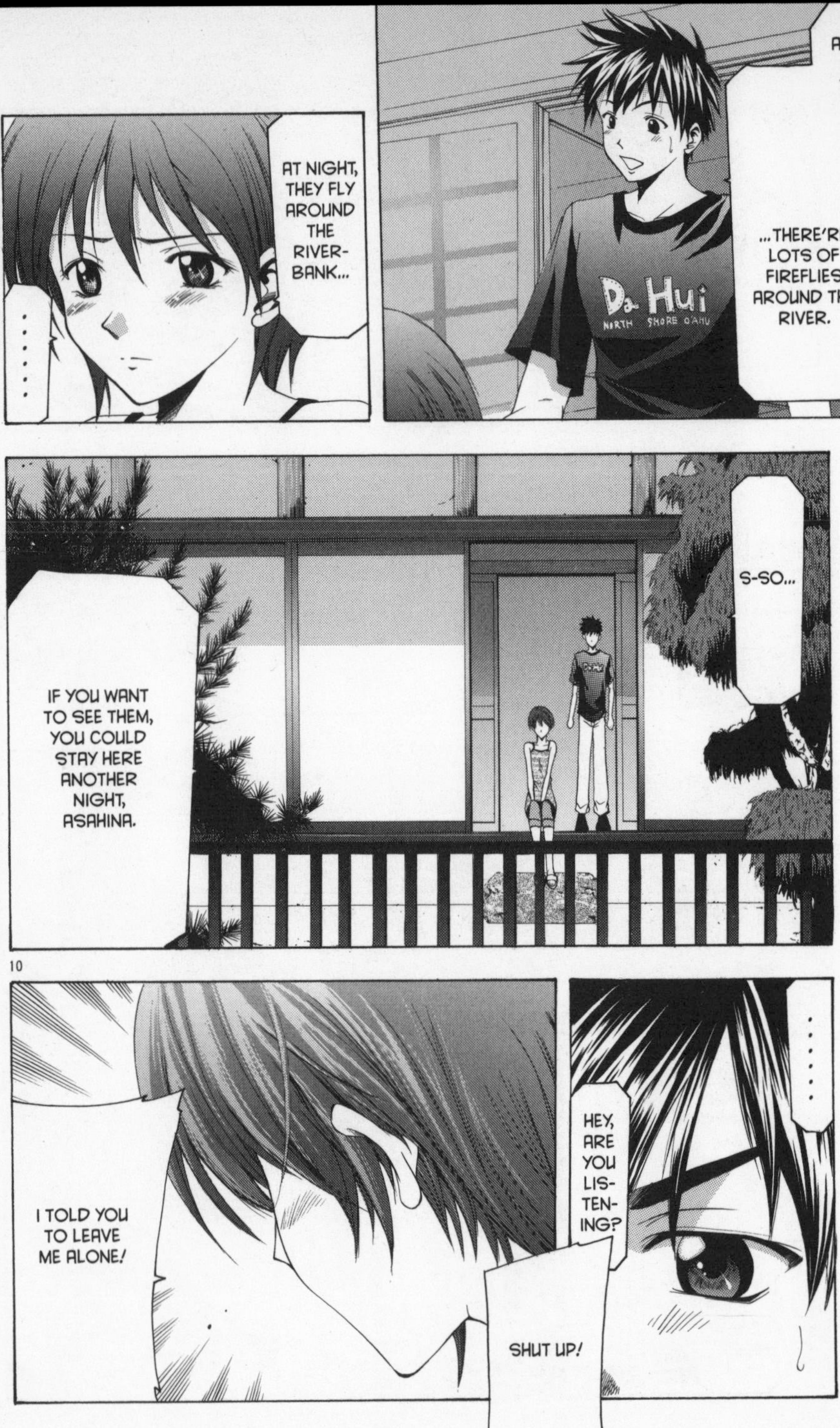
ACTUALL AT THIS TIME OF YEAR...
...THERE'RE LOTS OF FIREFLIES AROUND THE RIVER.
AT NIGHT, THEY FLY AROUND THE RIVER-BANK...
......
S-SO...
IF YOU WANT TO SEE THEM, YOU COULD STAY HERE ANOTHER NIGHT, ASAHINA.
......
HEY, ARE YOU LIS-TEN-ING?
SHUT UP!
I TOLD YOU TO LEAVE ME ALONE!
10

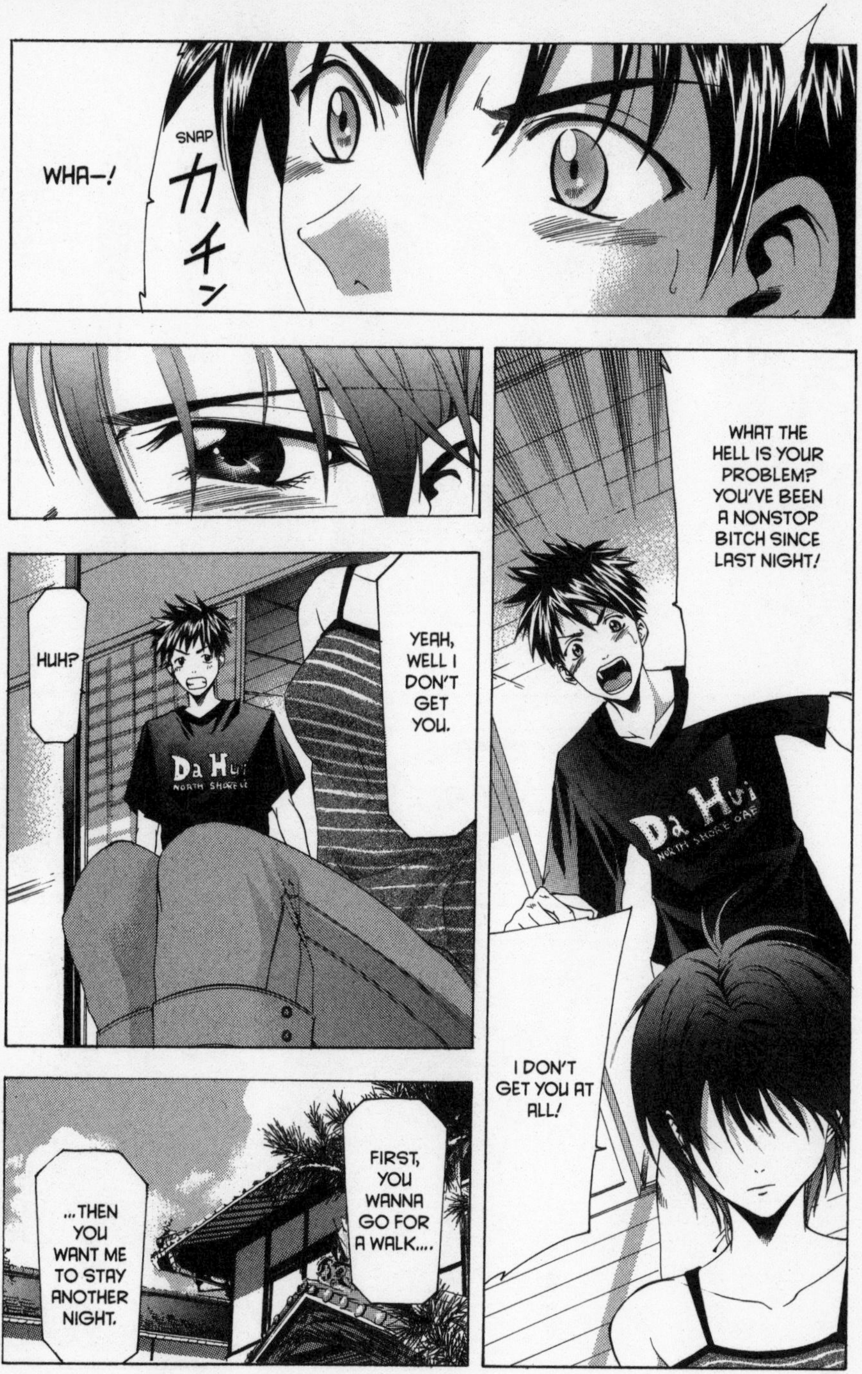
SNAP
カチン
WHA–!
WHAT THE HELL IS YOUR PROBLEM? YOU'VE BEEN A NONSTOP BITCH SINCE LAST NIGHT!
I DON'T GET YOU AT ALL!
YEAH, WELL I DON'T GET YOU.
HUH?
FIRST, YOU WANNA GO FOR A WALK....
...THEN YOU WANT ME TO STAY ANOTHER NIGHT.

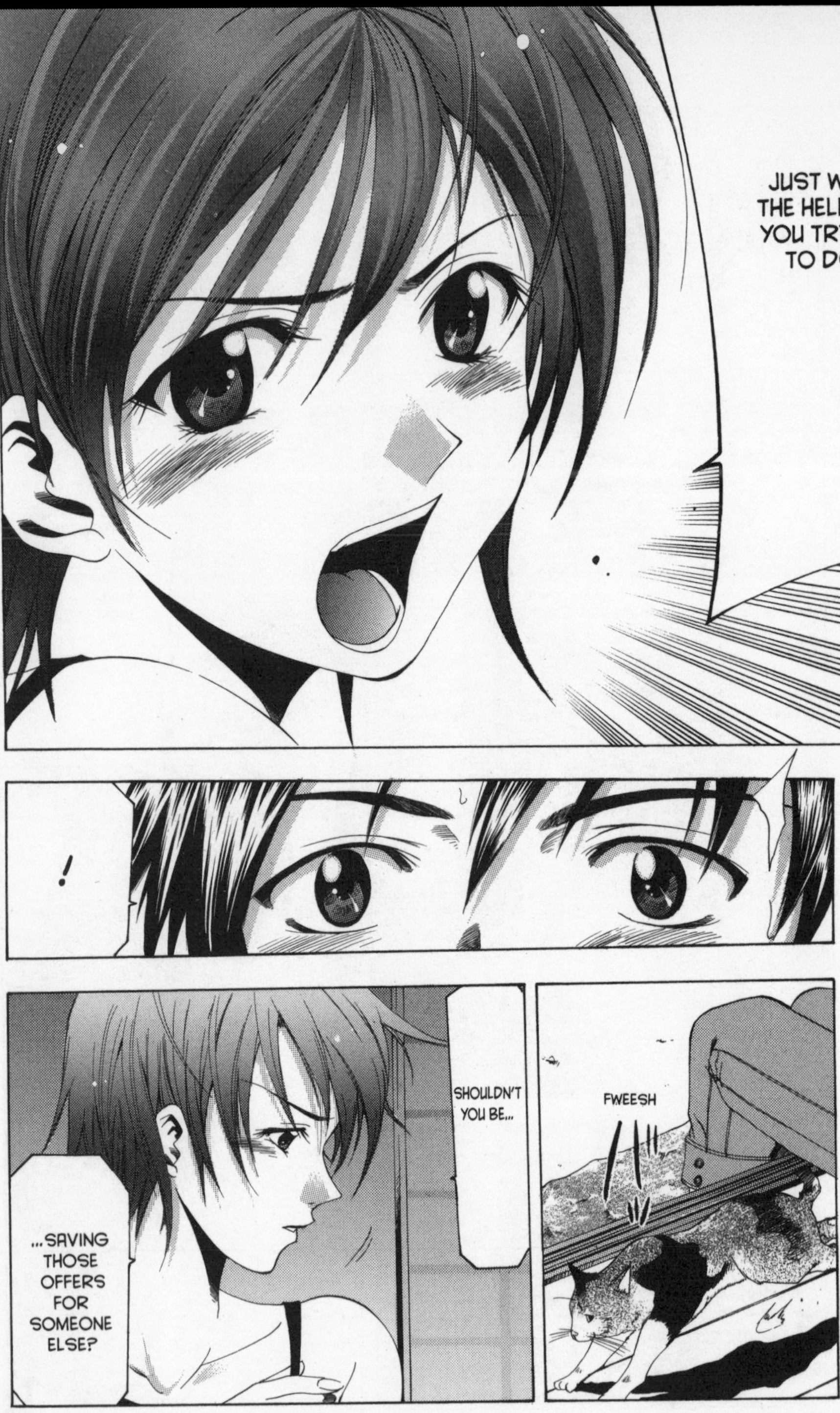
JUST WHAT THE HELL ARE YOU TRYING TO DO?
!
FWEESH
SHOULDN'T YOU BE...
...SAVING THOSE OFFERS FOR SOMEONE ELSE?

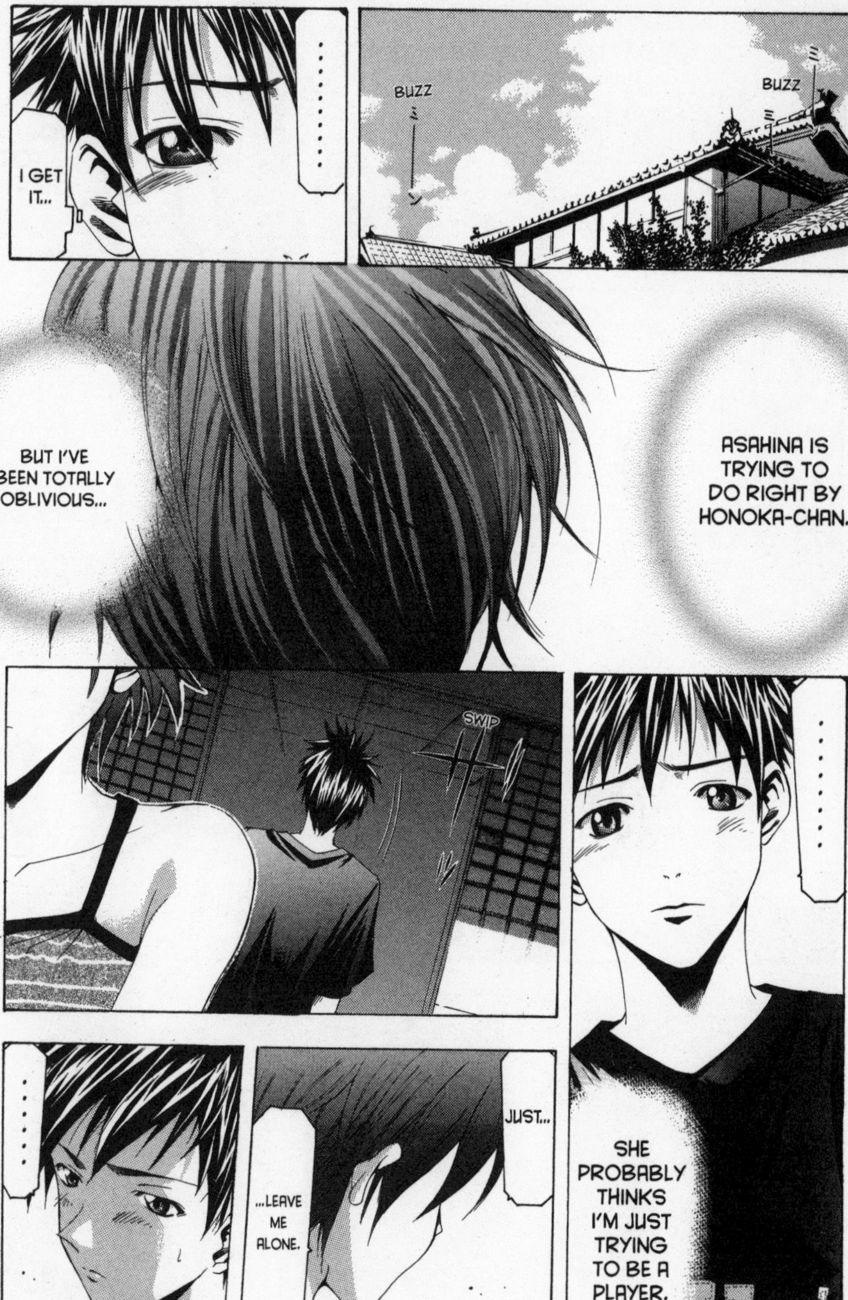
BUZZ
BUZZ
……
I GET IT...
ASAHINA IS TRYING TO DO RIGHT BY HONOKA-CHAN.
BUT I'VE BEEN TOTALLY OBLIVIOUS...
……
SHE PROBABLY THINKS I'M JUST TRYING TO BE A PLAYER.
SWIP
JUST...
...LEAVE ME ALONE.
……

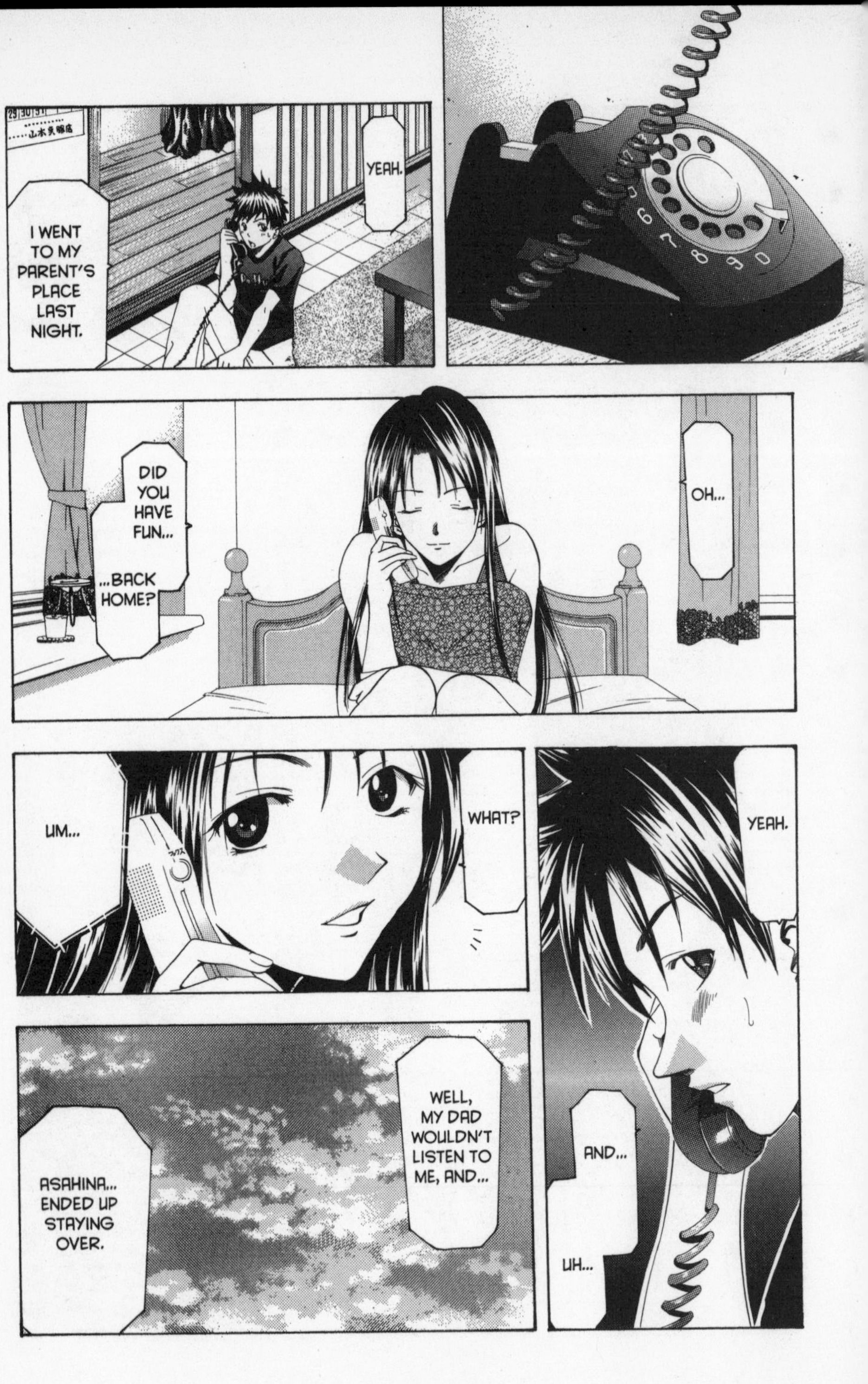
YEAH.
I WENT TO MY PARENT'S PLACE LAST NIGHT.
OH...
DID YOU HAVE FUN...
...BACK HOME?
YEAH.
AND...
UH...
WHAT?
UM...
WELL, MY DAD WOULDN'T LISTEN TO ME, AND...
ASAHINA... ENDED UP STAYING OVER.

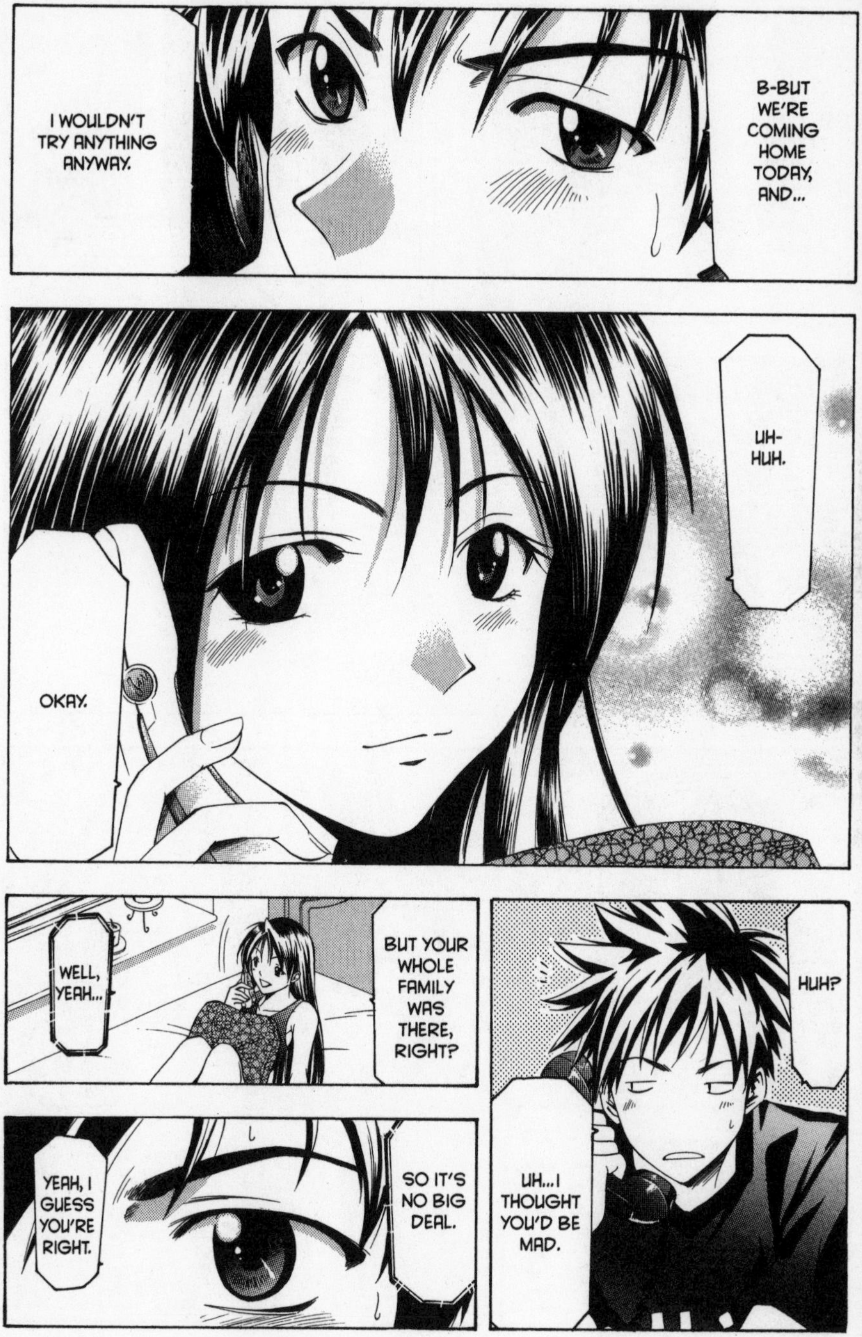
B-BUT WE'RE COMING HOME TODAY, AND...
I WOULDN'T TRY ANYTHING ANYWAY.
UH-HUH.
OKAY.
HUH?
UH...I THOUGHT YOU'D BE MAD.
BUT YOUR WHOLE FAMILY WAS THERE, RIGHT?
WELL, YEAH...
SO IT'S NO BIG DEAL.
YEAH, I GUESS YOU'RE RIGHT.

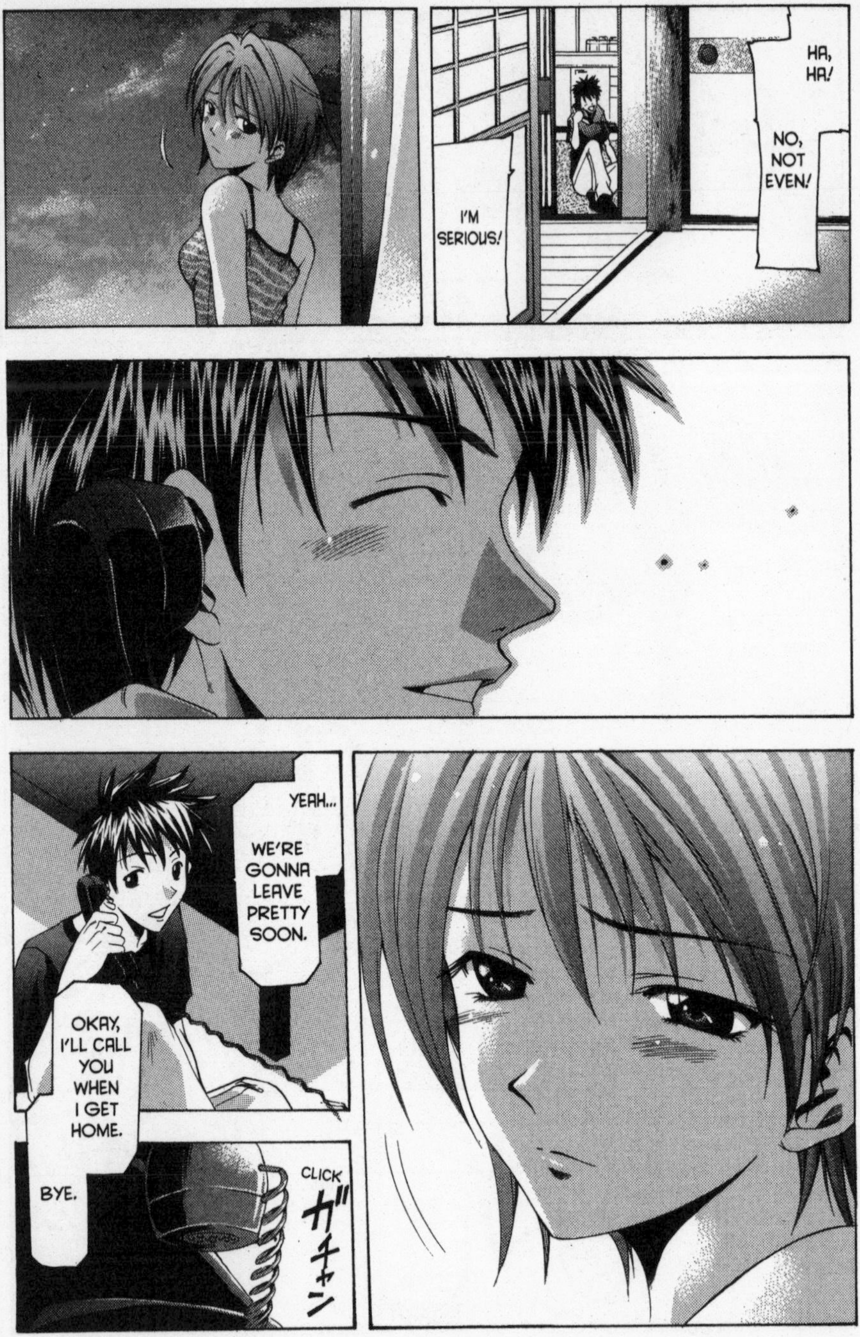
HA, HA!
NO, NOT EVEN!
I'M SERIOUS!
YEAH...
WE'RE GONNA LEAVE PRETTY SOON.
OKAY, I'LL CALL YOU WHEN I GET HOME.
CLICK
ガチャン
BYE.

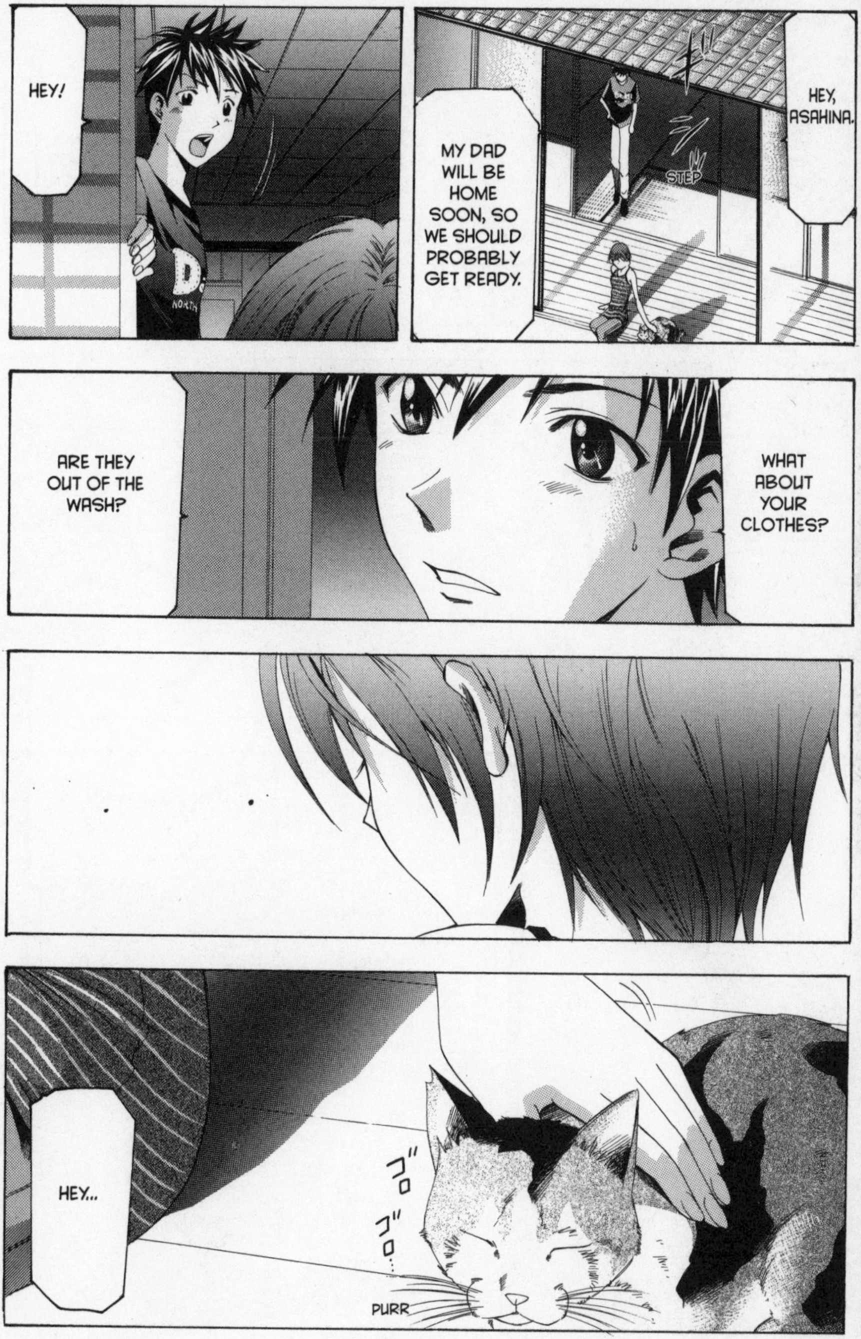
HEY, ASAHINA.
MY DAD WILL BE HOME SOON, SO WE SHOULD PROBABLY GET READY.
STEP
HEY!
WHAT ABOUT YOUR CLOTHES?
ARE THEY OUT OF THE WASH?
ゴロゴロ…
HEY...
PURR

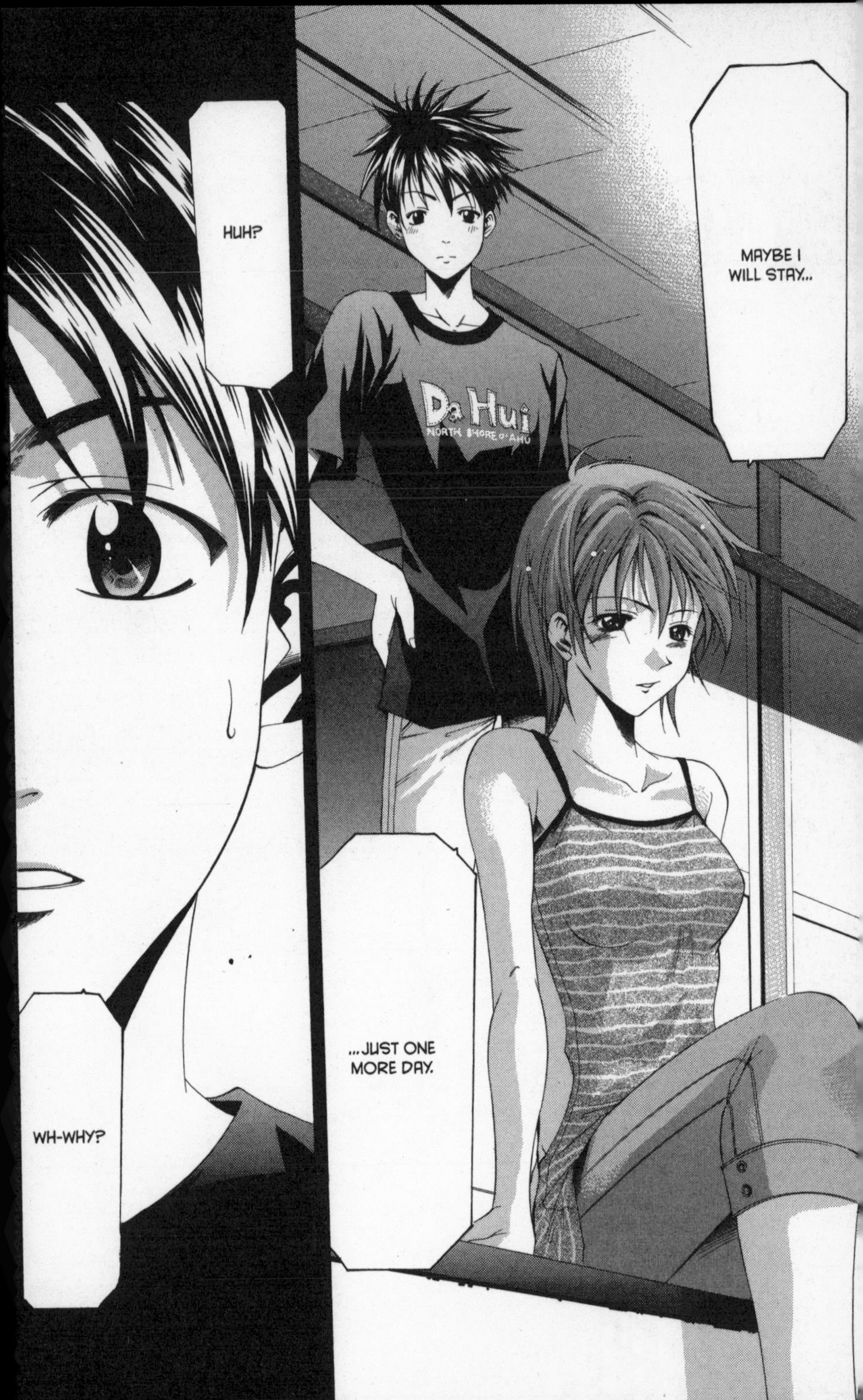
MAYBE I WILL STAY...
Da Hui
NORTH SHORE O'AHU
...JUST ONE MORE DAY.
HUH?
WH-WHY?

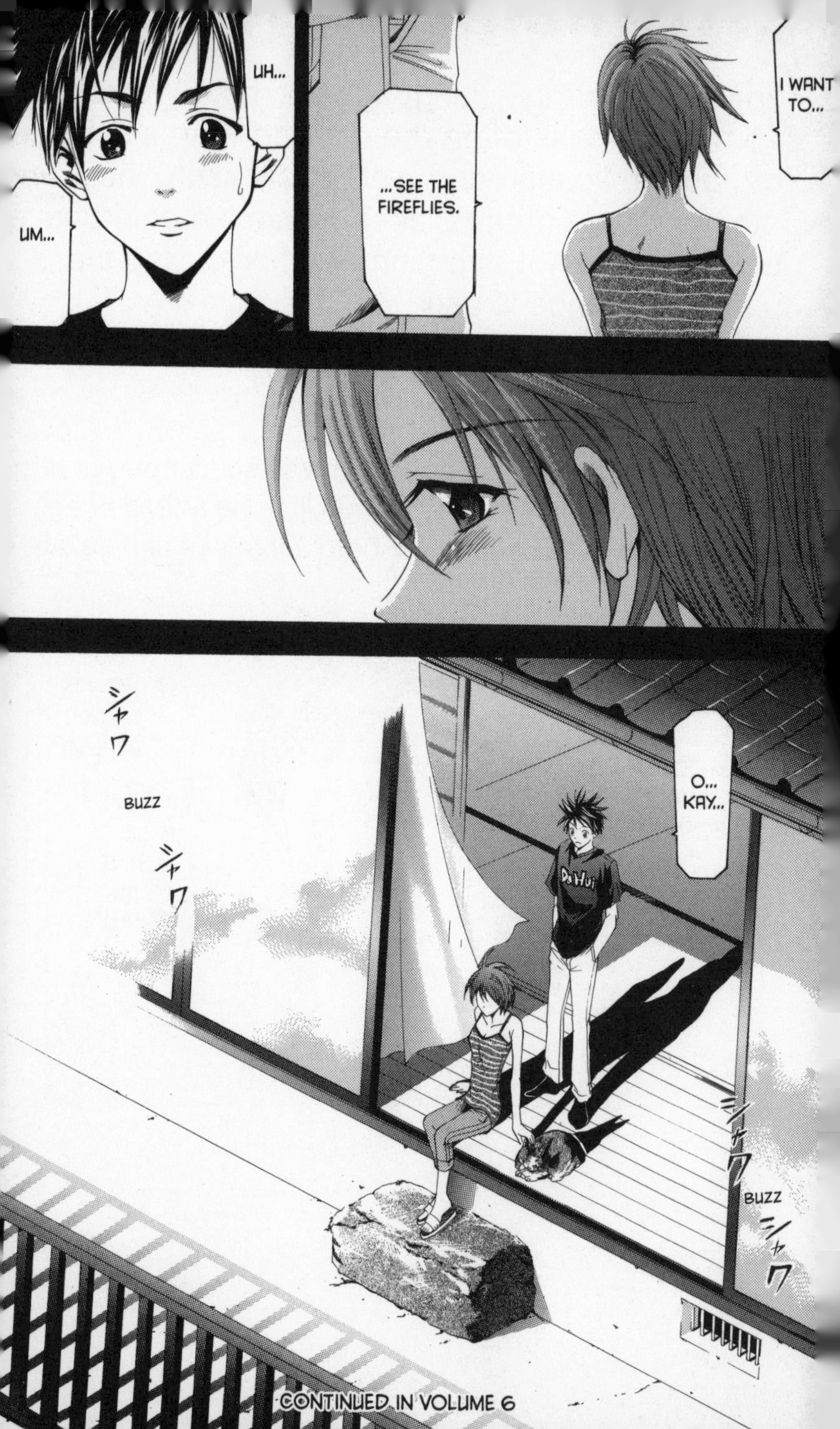
I WANT TO...
...SEE THE FIREFLIES.
UH...
UM...
O... KAY...
シャワ
BUZZ
シャワ
シャワ
BUZZ
シャワ
CONTINUED IN VOLUME 6

Translation Notes

Japanese is a tricky language for most Westerners, and translation is often more an art than a science. For your edification and reading pleasure, here are notes on some of the places where we could have gone in a different direction or where a Japanese cultural reference is used.

Nakata, page 72

Hidetoshi Nakata is a famous Japanese soccer player who recently shocked the soccer world when he retired at age twenty-nine. He has played for both Japanese and Italian teams.

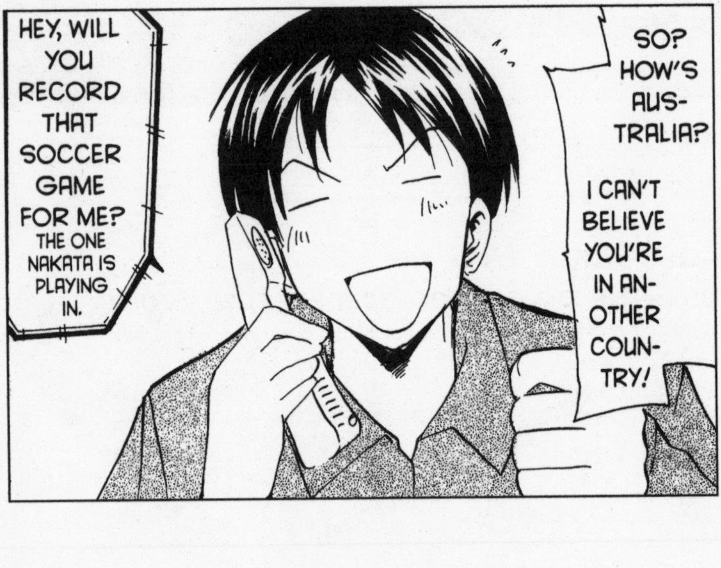
SO? HOW'S AUS-TRALIA?
I CAN'T BELIEVE YOU'RE IN AN-OTHER COUN-TRY!
HEY, WILL YOU RECORD THAT SOCCER GAME FOR ME? THE ONE NAKATA IS PLAYING IN.

An outside bath!, page 99

Japanese inns often have communal baths. The baths are generally separated into male and female sections by a bamboo fence or other structure.

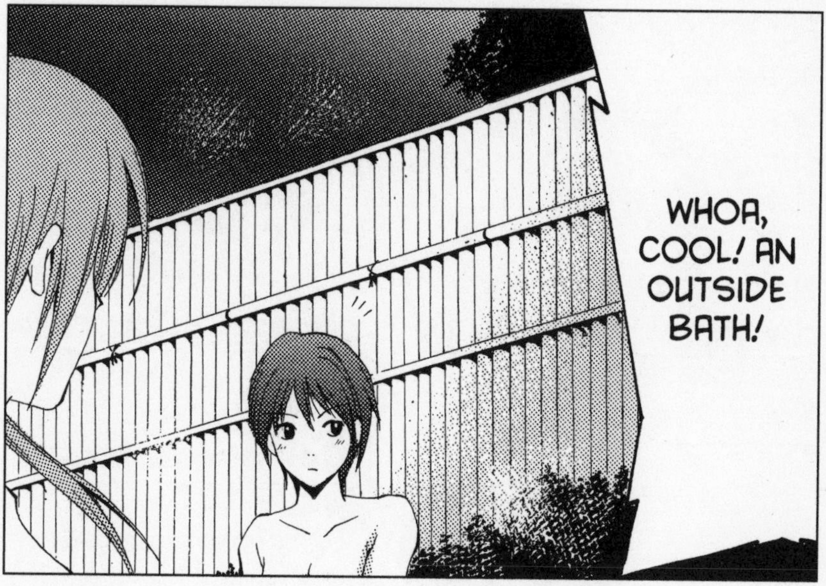
WHOA, COOL! AN OUTSIDE BATH!

Pocari, page 115

Pocari Sweat is a popular Japanese sports drink.

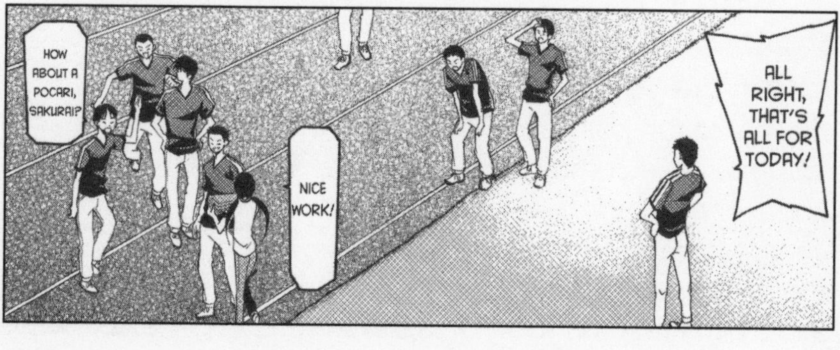
ALL RIGHT, THAT'S ALL FOR TODAY!
NICE WORK!
HOW ABOUT A POCARI, SAKURAI?

Okonomiyaki, page 135

Hiroshima is famous for *okonomiyaki*—a Japanese-style pancake. It's made of batter and a mixture of meat, vegetables, and egg. Hiroshima-style *okonomiyaki* generally includes noodles as well.

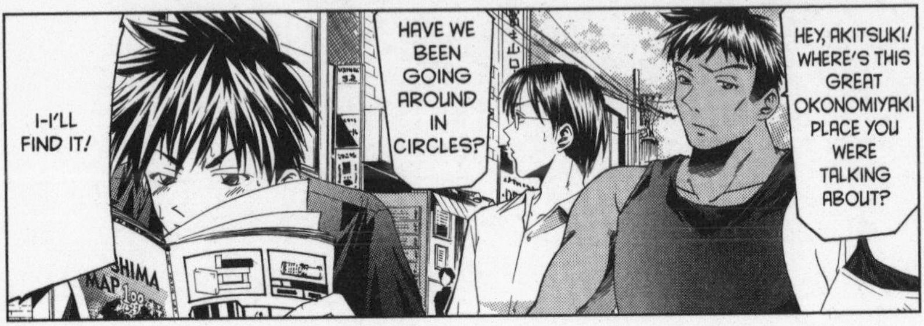
HEY, AKITSUKI! WHERE'S THIS GREAT OKONOMIYAKI PLACE YOU WERE TALKING ABOUT?
HAVE WE BEEN GOING AROUND IN CIRCLES?
I-I'LL FIND IT!
SHIMA MAP

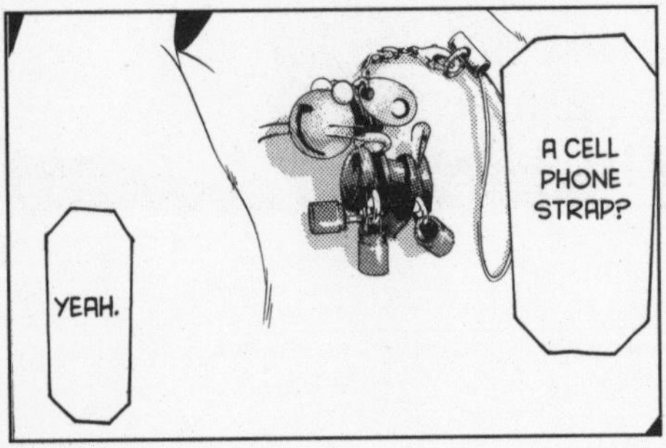
A CELL PHONE STRAP?
YEAH.

Cell phone strap, page 137

Cell phone straps are little straps, often with cute characters tied onto them, that people attach to their cell phones.

Slash and run killer, page 152

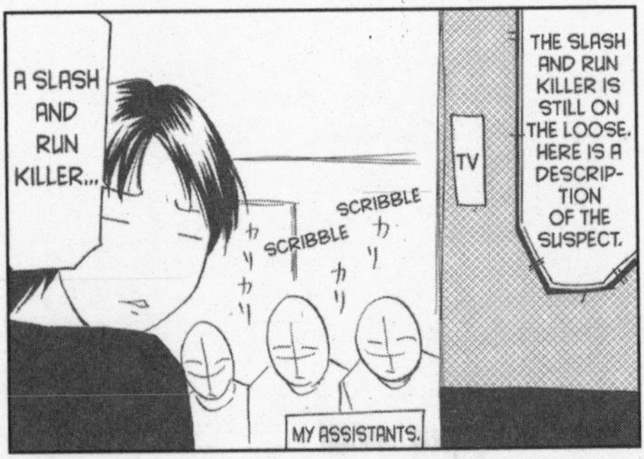
THE SLASH AND RUN KILLER IS STILL ON THE LOOSE. HERE IS A DESCRIPTION OF THE SUSPECT.
TV
A SLASH AND RUN KILLER...
SCRIBBLE
カリ
SCRIBBLE
カリ
カリ
カリ
MY ASSISTANTS.

Slash and run killings, or *toorima,* are a common crime phenomenon in Japan. In a slash and run, the perpetrator picks out a random target on the street, casually passes by, stabs them, and then flees the scene.

Hiroshima Carp, page 158

The Hiroshima Carp are a baseball team. This inebriated fellow is singing the Carp's theme song.

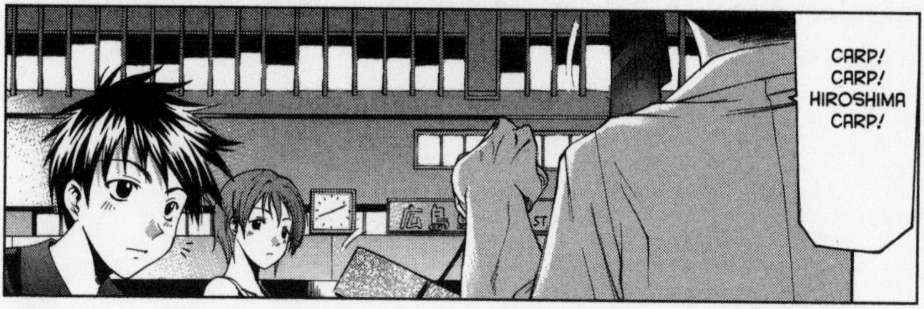
CARP! CARP! HIROSHIMA CARP!

Love hotel, page 159

Love hotels are specifically designed for couples seeking privacy. They can be rented by the night or, during the daytime, by the hour.

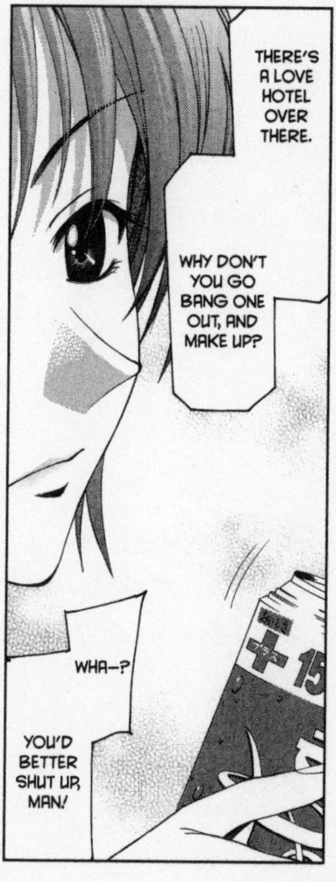
THERE'S A LOVE HOTEL OVER THERE.
WHY DON'T YOU GO BANG ONE OUT, AND MAKE UP?
WHA-?
YOU'D BETTER SHUT UP, MAN!

Preview of Volume 6

We're pleased to present you with a preview of *Suzuka,* Volume 6.
This volume will be available on November 27, 2007.

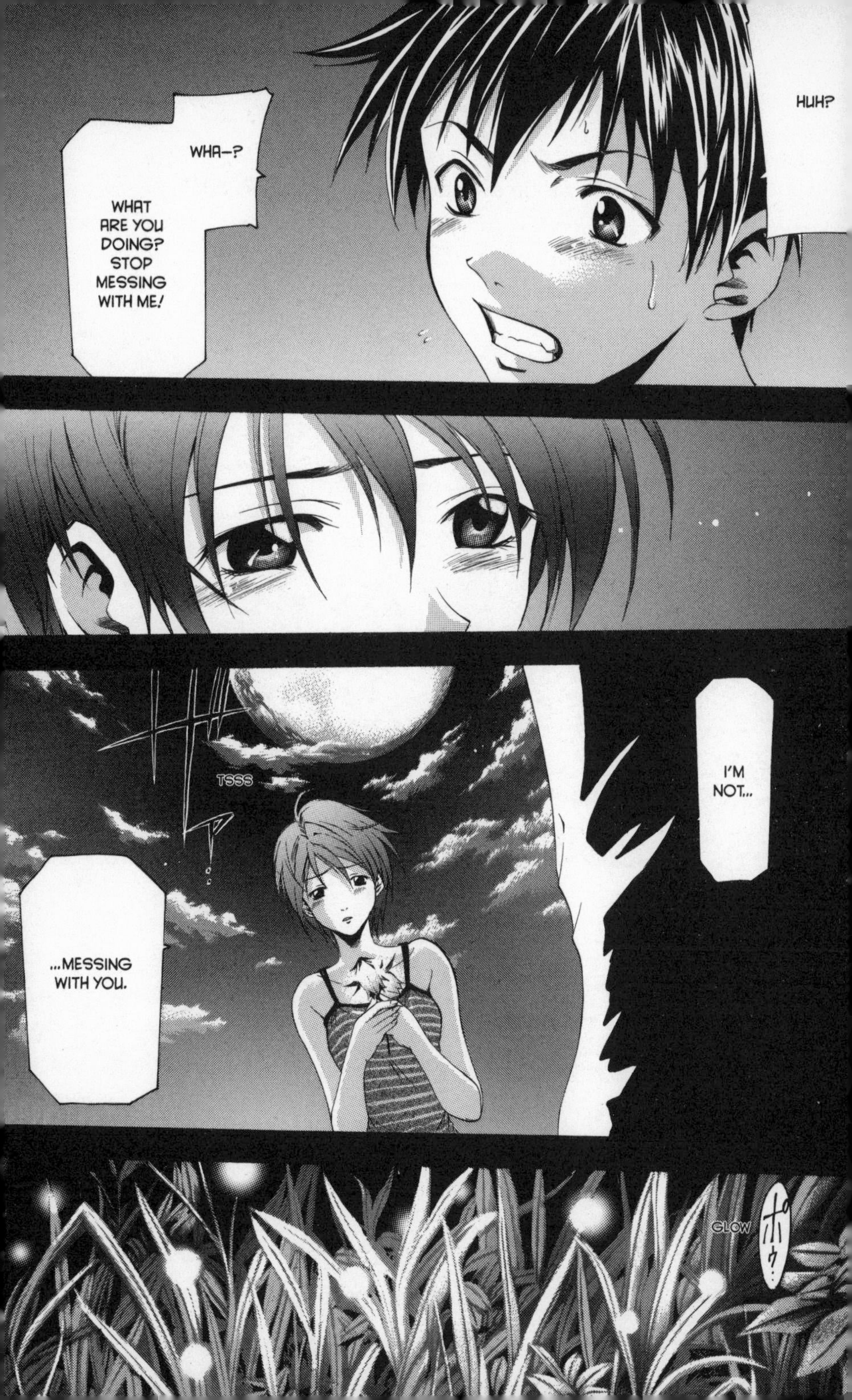
HUH?
WHA–?
WHAT ARE YOU DOING? STOP MESSING WITH ME!
I'M NOT...
TSSS
...MESSING WITH YOU.
ポゥ…
GLOW

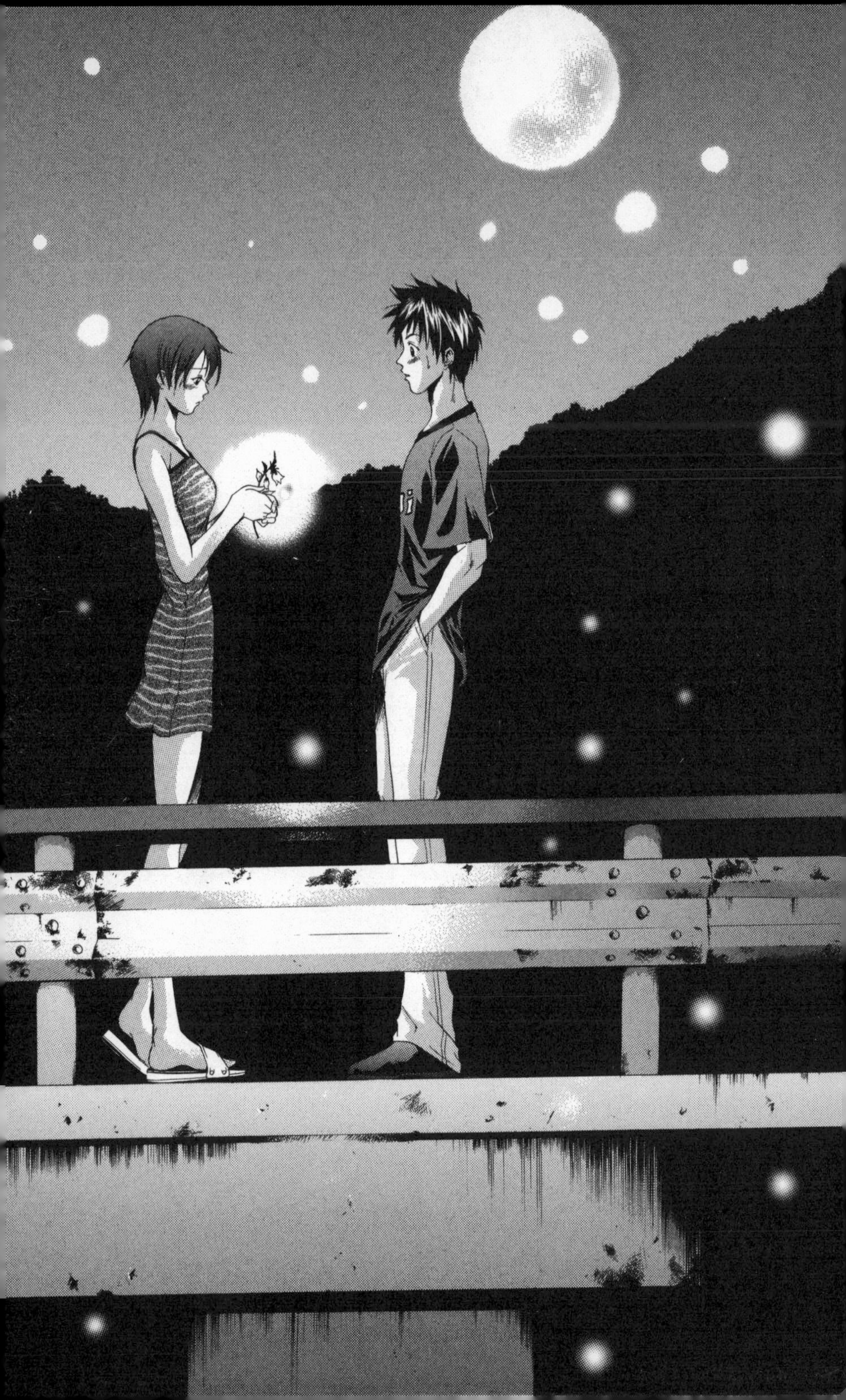

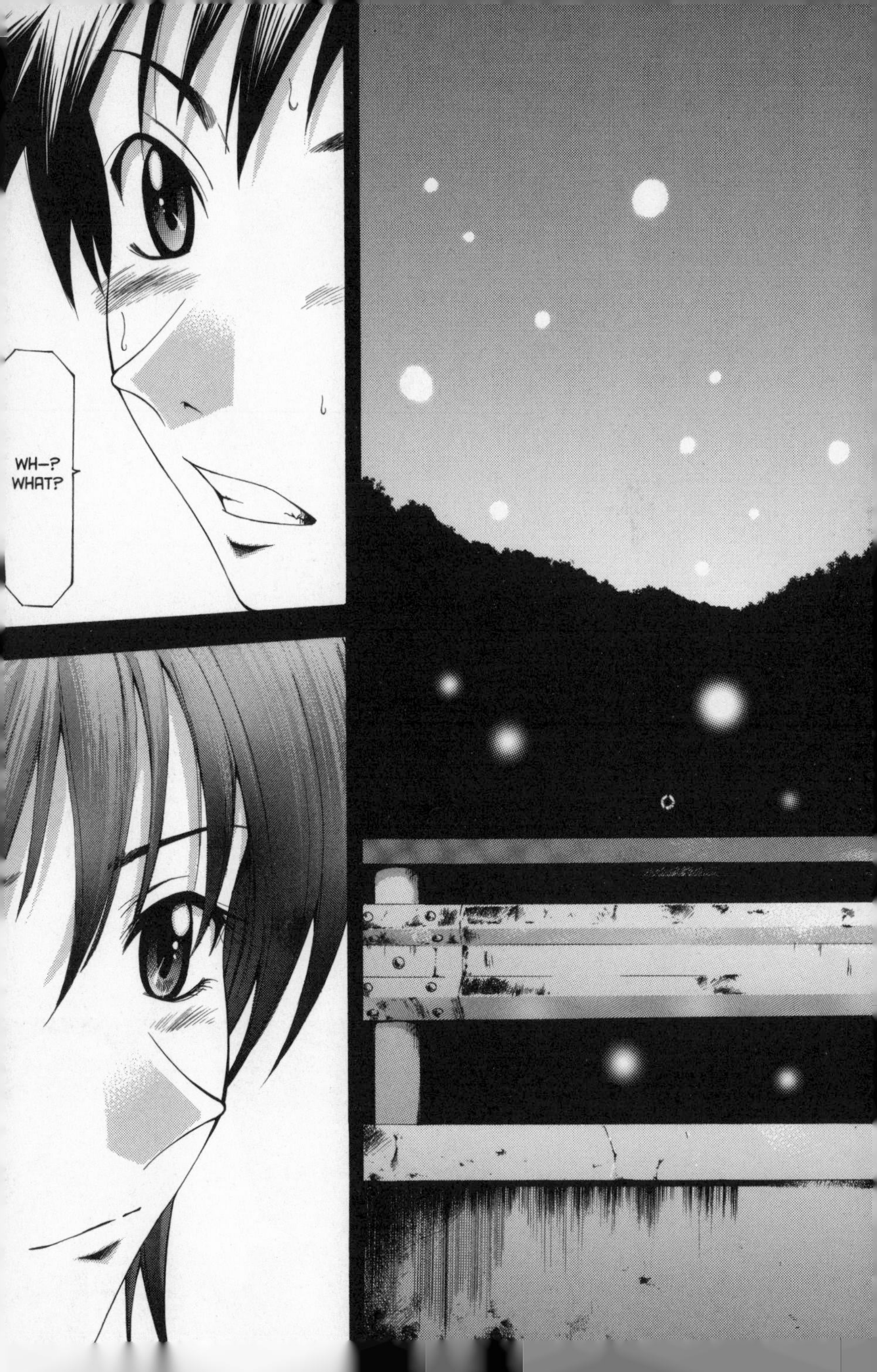
WH-? WHAT?

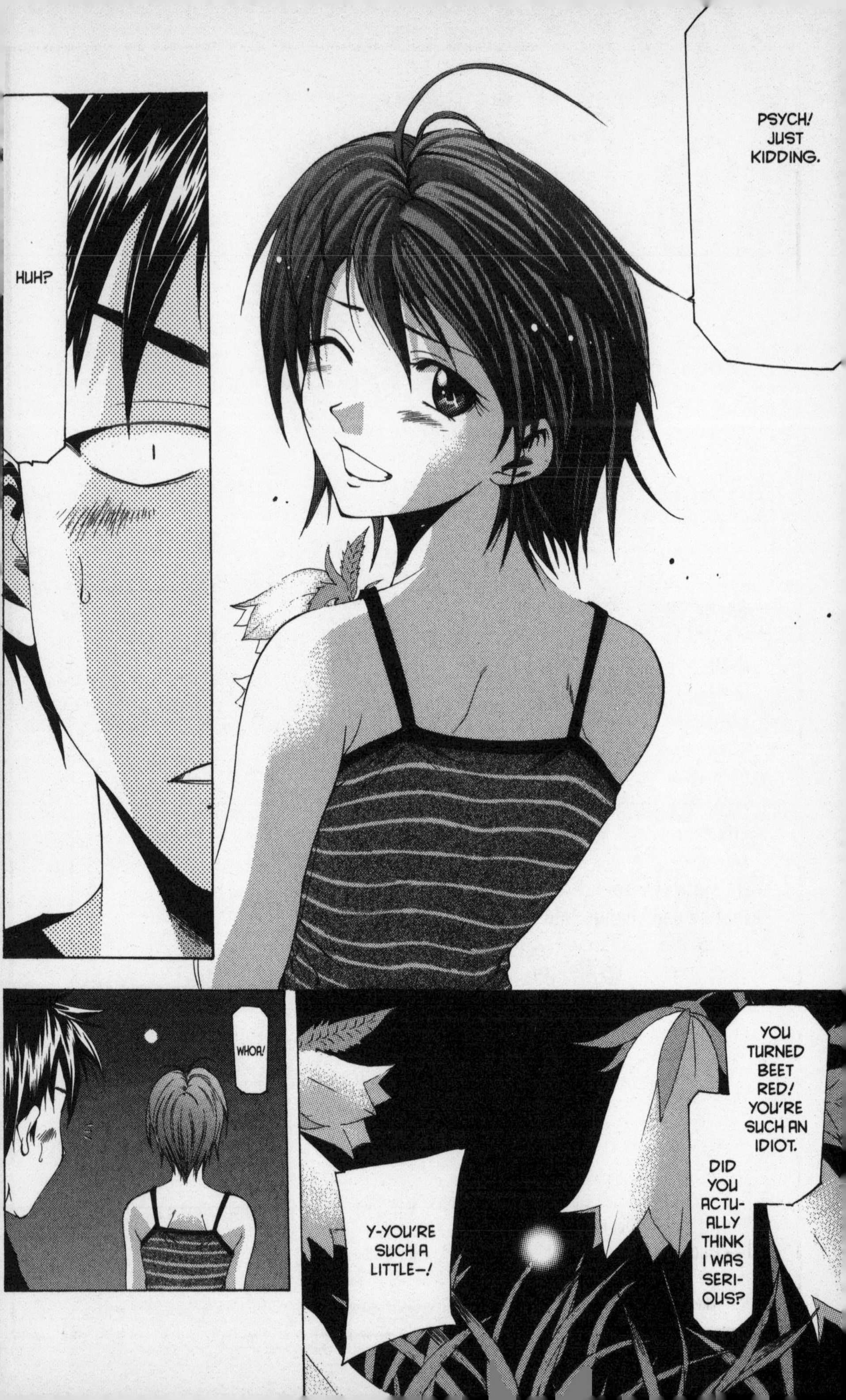
PSYCH! JUST KIDDING.
HUH?
YOU TURNED BEET RED! YOU'RE SUCH AN IDIOT.
DID YOU ACTUALLY THINK I WAS SERIOUS?
Y-YOU'RE SUCH A LITTLE—!
WHOA!

HIROYUKI TAMAKOSHI

JUST ONE OF THE GIRLS

A whole new Gacha Gacha story line begins! Akira Hatsushiba is just your typical, average high school kid . . . until a glitch in a Gacha Gacha video game changes his life forever. Now, every time Akira sneezes, his entire body undergoes a gender-bending switcheroo! That's right, Akira is always just an *achoo* away from getting in touch with his feminine side. But it's not all bad. Akira has had a crush on Yurika Sakuraba ever since he first laid eyes on her. He's always been too shy, but now that he can change into a girl, Akira finally has a chance to get close to Yurika. Being a girl certainly has its advantages!

Special extras in each volume! Read them all!

VISIT WWW.DELREYMANGA.COM TO:
- Read sample pages
- View release date calendars for upcoming volumes
- Sign up for Del Rey's free manga e-newsletter
- Find out the latest about new Del Rey Manga series

RATING   M AGES 18+

 **DEL REY MANGA**

The Otaku's Choice

TOMARE! [STOP!]

You are going the wrong way!

Manga is a completely different type of reading experience.

To start at the *beginning*, go to the *end!*

That's right! Authentic manga is read the traditional Japanese way—from right to left, exactly the *opposite* of how American books are read. It's easy to follow: Just go to the other end of the book, and read each page—and each panel—from right side to left side, starting at the top right. Now you're experiencing manga as it was meant to be.